# INTERCESSIONS
# ❖ FOR MASS ❖

Mary Grace Melcher, OCD

## LITURGICAL PRESS
### Collegeville, Minnesota

www.litpress.org

*Nihil Obstat:* Reverend Robert Harren, *Censor deputatus.*
*Imprimatur:* ✠ Most Reverend John F. Kinney, J.C.D., D.D., Bishop of St. Cloud, Minnesota, October 12, 2012.

Cover design by Ann Blattner. *Holy Mother Church* icon by Deacon Charles Rohrbacher. Used with permission.

Library of Congress Control Number: 2013930546

ISBN 978-0-8146-3481-3
ISBN 978-0-8146-3482-0 (ebook)

# CONTENTS

## PROPER OF TIME
### SUNDAYS, SOLEMNITIES, FEASTS

CONTENTS

## ❧ WEEKDAYS ❧

## ❧ ORDINARY TIME ❧

# PROPER OF SAINTS

# PROPER OF TIME

## SUNDAYS, SOLEMNITIES, FEASTS
# YEAR A

## SEASON OF ADVENT

### 1st Sunday of Advent

*Isa 2:1-5, Ps 122, Rom 13:11-14,*
*Matt 24:37-44*

For the whole church, summoned again to wake from sleep, to throw off the works of darkness and to put on the armor of light, that we may respond joyously to this message

That the Lord's house may be established on the highest peak, and all nations stream toward Him for instruction and counsel

That we may stay awake, ready and watching for the coming of our Lord and Master, that His arrival may not be a disruption of our lives, but the goal of all our desires

For the grace to keep our souls in silence and vigilance, alert to the many small arrivals of the Lord that come through events and circumstances, and through those we love

For those whose Advent is full of pain, illness, loneliness, hunger, and poverty, that we may be willing to reach out to them and assist them in their every need

For our faithful departed, who have set foot within the gates of the heavenly Jerusalem, that they may enjoy everlasting peace

### 2nd Sunday of Advent

*Isa 11:1-10, Ps 72, Rom 15:4-9,*
*Matt 3:1-12*

That the spirit of the Lord may rest upon all who are entrusted with authority in the church, giving them wisdom, counsel, and strength

That God may raise up sovereigns in every nation who will judge the poor with justice, and decide aright for the oppressed and afflicted

That in keeping with Christ Jesus, we may learn to think in harmony with one another, welcoming one another for the glory of God

That John the Baptist, the thundering preacher of Advent repentance, may cry out again in the desert of our secular world, compelling us to make straight the way of the Lord

That the God of endurance and encouragement may lift up and console those who are weighed down with poverty, disease, or grief, especially those who have asked for our prayers

That Jesus, who has baptized us with the Holy Spirit and with fire, may take our faithful departed like chosen wheat into His barn, to be safe in heaven forever

### 3rd Sunday in Advent

*Isa 35:1-6a, 10, Ps 146, Jas 5:7-10,*
*Matt 11:2-11*

That our holy shepherds in the church
may prolong in our midst the role of John
the Baptist, preparing the way of the Lord
in our hearts by their preaching and the
witness of their lives

For the prophets of our own day, especially
those who suffer for their stance on justice
and morality, that they may have the faith
in Jesus which will see them through their
time of trial

For the grace of patience in our relations
with ourselves, with one another, and with
our God; for the gift of graceful waiting
during the slow process of growth and
progress

That we may enlarge our expectations of
God, who promises more joy and glory
than we know how to imagine, and that
our faith may create the space God looks
for to fill with His blessing

That Jesus, who gave sight to the blind and
cured lepers and made the deaf hear, may
also hear us when we intercede for those
who are most in need of healing and mercy

That our faithful departed may be among
God's ransomed ones who enter Zion
singing and crowned with everlasting joy

### 4th Sunday in Advent

*Isa 7:10-14, Ps 24, Rom 1:1-7,*
*Matt 1:18-24*

For our holy shepherds, that like St. Joseph
they may be righteous and ready to do
all that the Lord commands them, thus
sheltering and protecting the church

For all the nations, that they may be
brought into the obedience of faith in God
and the justice of His holy laws

That we may not weary God through
resistance and unbelief, but like Mary
and Joseph bring Him submissive hearts
and trusting spirits, ready to rejoice in the
wonders He wishes to work for us

That Mary's flame of virginal love and
purity may illuminate and stand guard
over our Advent prayers and preparations
for the coming of her divine Son

For all who suffer, those who are lonely and
hungry, homeless and abandoned, that
our love may comfort them and they may
receive a blessing of grace from the Lord

That Jesus, established as Son of God in
power through His resurrection from death,
may purify our faithful departed and bring
them to His heavenly home

## SEASON OF CHRISTMAS

### Nativity of the Lord, at the Vigil
*Isa 62:1-5, Ps 89, Acts 13:16-17, 22-25, Matt 1:18-25*

For the church, God's chosen people, His virgin bride, that her rejoicing may be in her bridegroom, who took flesh in Jesus and came to dwell among us

That God's covenant of love may stand firm with all nations as they again seek to know His justice, obey His laws, and experience His peace

That we may imitate St. Joseph's faith and obedience, as He quietly left behind His own doubts and took Mary into His home, giving Jesus His name and the shelter of protecting love

That we may greet the birth of our divine Savior with the humility of John the Baptist, and herald His new coming into our lives with reverent joy

For those who are forsaken and desolate, that they may be called by a new name, and become a glorious crown in the hand of the Lord as He fills them with His joy

For all who have completed their course, who have passed beyond the gates of death, that they may be celebrating this Christmas in the exultation of the heavenly kingdom

### Nativity of the Lord, Mass at Midnight
*Isa 9:1-6, Ps 96, Titus 2:11-14, Luke 2:1-14*

For the whole church, celebrating the birth of Jesus with abundant love and great rejoicing, that all darkness may be illuminated by the great light she now presents to the world

For peace, that in the mastery of the child that is born to us, every unjust yoke may be smashed, every tool of war destroyed, and the deliberations of world leaders be ruled by the Prince of Peace

For the grace of hospitality, that we may see Jesus in the least of His brothers and sisters, and especially that no expectant mother be refused the comfort and shelter she needs to bear her child

That Mary, our mother, may show her Divine Child to everyone that comes in wonder to the manger, and lay Him to rest in our hearts as we approach this Eucharist

For those who keep a lonely watch in the night, those who have no one to care for them, that with the shepherds they may also know of angels who will bring them tidings of great joy in the name of Jesus

For our dear ones who have died, that they may see the final appearance of their blessed hope, the glory of the great God and of Jesus our Savior, in the clear light of heaven

## Christmas Mass at Dawn

*Isa 62:11-12, Ps 97, Titus 3:4-7,*
*Luke 2:15-20*

For the shepherds of the church, our bishops and priests, that as they lead us today in glorifying and praising God for the birth of the Savior, they themselves may be renewed in His joy

For the governments and leaders of the world, that the message of the angels may be realized in every effort they make to avoid armed conflict and promote peace

For all who are in pain in body, mind, emotions, or spirit, that this holy day may be a blessing of peace and light on their journey

That Jesus, who in His birth as one of us has made every human joy His own, may be at the heart of our family festivities, our gift giving, and every lovely custom we keep in His honor

That Mary, our Mother, may show her divine child to every wondering heart that approaches the manger, and lay Him to rest in each of us as we approach this Eucharist

For our beloved dead, that they may be celebrating this Christmas amid the joys and splendors of heaven

## Nativity of the Lord, Mass during the day

*Isa 52:7-10, Ps 98, Heb 1:1-6,*
*John 1:1-18*

For the church on this great feast of Christmas, that her whole soul may be consumed in praise as she sings to the Lord with melodious song for His great mercy in giving us our Savior

That God may be king among the nations, so that the feet of those who bring glad tidings may be beautiful upon the mountains as they bear good news and announce peace

That as the Lord comforts His people and redeems Jerusalem, we too may bring comfort and joy in the name of Jesus to all those whose lives we touch

That with the angels of God we may gladly worship the firstborn Son who has come into the world, and spread the good news of His redemption

For all who are still in the darkness of loneliness, depression, illness, or grief, that the great light who is Jesus may enlighten them and they may know the joy of our love in His name

For our dear ones who have died, that they may be soon brought into heaven, where Jesus has His seat at the right hand of the Majesty on high

## Holy Family

*general intentions*

For our Holy Father, head of the family that is the Body of Christ, that He may be held in honor within the church

For peace in our families, forgiveness of grievances, harmony of roles, and that our children may be safe and loved within the home, so that our nation and every nation may be built up in peace

That our families may be protected from the special dangers of our age: from abortion and euthanasia, from the inroads of materialism and violence; that faith and prayer and mutual love may keep them together in the Lord

For families in exile, for families that have lost their children, for families of the unemployed and the poor, that the Holy Family, which experienced all these situations, may be their comfort and hope

For the gift of vocations, that the Christian life of our families may flower in young lives consecrated to the Lord, whose ministry will serve in turn to strengthen the families of the future

For our loved ones who have died, for our elders who have gone before us, that they may rest in peace and help their beloved families with their prayers

## Blessed Virgin Mary, the Mother of God

*Num 6:22-27, Ps 67, Gal 4:4-7,
Luke 2:16-21*

For the whole church, that God's wisdom may strike root among us in the person of Jesus, making us a glorious people, the portion of the Lord, and the company of His holy ones

That God, who sends forth His command to the earth, may enable world leaders to keep His word, so that He may grant peace in our borders

For all of us as we celebrate this Christmas season, that the eyes of our hearts may be enlightened, and we may know what is the hope that belongs to our call in Christ Jesus

That the Word who was made flesh may give all those who believe in His name power to become children of God, shedding His light in the world by their lives of faith and good works

For all who are abandoned and forgotten in their need and suffering, that our prayer and our love may encircle them with joy and new beginnings of life

For our faithful departed ones, that God may bless them in Christ with every spiritual blessing in His heavenly home, giving them eternal rest and peace

## Second Sunday after Christmas, Years ABC

*Sir 24:1-2, 8-12, Ps 147, Eph 1:3-6, 15-18, John 1:1-18*

For the whole church, that God's wisdom may strike root among us in the person of Jesus, making us a glorious people, the portion of the Lord, and the company of His holy ones

That God, who sends forth His command to the earth, may enable world leaders to keep His word, so that He may grant peace in our borders

For all of us as we celebrate this Christmas season, that the eyes of our hearts may be enlightened, and we may know what is the hope that belongs to our call in Christ Jesus

That the Word who was made flesh may give all those who believe in His name power to become children of God, shedding His light in the world by their lives of faith and good works

For all who are abandoned and forgotten in their need and suffering, that our prayer and our love may encircle them with joy and new beginnings of life

For our faithful departed ones, that God may bless them in Christ with every spiritual blessing in His heavenly home, giving them eternal rest and peace

## The Epiphany of the Lord, Vigil

*general intentions*

For our leaders and teachers in the church, that they may be the first to worship at the manger and present their gifts of mind and heart to the Lord

That the Christmas grace of peace may radiate out into the whole world, exercising its gentle influence on the hearts of world leaders and turning their thoughts to the poor and the lowly

For all of us, represented by the foreigners who brought their adoration and their gifts to Jesus, that we may do all we can to spread the Good News and bring the whole world to His manger

That the faith and persevering search of the magi may inspire us during the dark times of our journey, when only the light of a great star leads us on through the night

For all who are suffering and poor and abandoned during this joyful season, that in memory of the Holy Family sheltered in a stable, we may reach out to them in love

For our loved ones who have gone before us marked with the sign of faith, that they may now see their Savior, unveiled in all His glory in heaven

## Epiphany

*Isa 60:1-6, Ps 72, Eph 3:2-3, 5-6,*
*Matt 2:1-12*

For the church, gathered as never before from all nations, that her holiness may shine out as a guiding star to bring to Jesus those who are still in the great darkness

For world leaders, that God may endow them with His judgment, so that they may govern His afflicted ones with justice and respect for the human dignity of each person

That wise men of every country and every religious background may come to understand the truth that Jesus alone is God made flesh and the Savior of the world, and place their gifts gratefully at His feet

That we who live in power and safety like Jerusalem of old may not miss the star rising over our heads, leading those with eyes to see down to humble Bethlehem with its hidden King

For all who travel a dark path through sickness, poverty, oppression, and every form of misery, that they may be overjoyed to find a star of guidance leading them to the mercy of the Lord

For our beloved departed ones, that they may come to rest in the radiant presence of the Savior whom they sought in the shadows of this passing world

## Baptism of the Lord

*Isa 42:1-4, 6-7, Ps 29, Acts 10:34-38,*
*Matt 3:13-17*

For our Holy Father, our bishops and priests, that they may be servants whom the Lord upholds and upon whom He puts His Spirit

For the victory of justice in every nation; that the Lord may raise up leaders who will work for life and for sound moral values in our world

That we may have a deeper appreciation of the great grace of our own baptism, and that we may become sons and daughters in whom the Father is well pleased

That Jesus may anoint us with power through the Holy Spirit to go about doing good in His name

For those who are suffering and tempted to lose heart— the bruised reeds and smoldering wicks of our day— that they may not be broken or quenched by the indifference of others, but helped and consoled

For our faithful departed ones, that in Jesus they may be brought out of confinement and darkness into the full light of heaven's joy and glory

## SEASON OF LENT

### 1st Sunday of Lent

*Gen 2:7-9, 3:1-7, Ps 51, Rom 5:12-19, Matt 4:1-11*

For our holy shepherds in the church, that by their example of obedience and fidelity many may be made righteous in the sight of God

For the kingdoms of the world in their magnificence and for their rulers, that they may come under the Lordship of Jesus and worship the true God

That all Catholics may enter this holy season of repentance and grace by partaking of the sacrament of penance and reconciliation

For all who are in a season of temptation, that with the strength of the Lord they may resist the insidious suggestions of the Evil One and emerge from the trial stronger and more free

For the sick, the poor and the marginalized, the imprisoned and the addicted, that our loving prayer and effective action during this Lenten season may relieve them

For our faithful departed ones, that after their time of testing and trial in the body they may know the ministry of the angels in heaven

### 2nd Sunday in Lent

*Gen 12:1-4a, Ps 33, 2 Tim 1:8b-10, Matt 17:1-9*

For the church, through whom all the communities of the earth have found blessing, that like Abraham she may be ready and willing to follow the Lord's bidding wherever He leads

That the Lord who loves justice and righteousness may be the strength and guiding light of world leaders, so that all people may walk in the ways of life and peace

That Jesus, who was transfigured before His disciples to strengthen them for His coming passion, may shine within our souls to help us in the trials of our faith journey

That we may acknowledge Jesus as the Father's beloved Son, in whom He is well pleased, and that we may listen to Him profoundly, learning everything from His example

For all who have asked our prayers in a time of sickness or any kind of suffering, that the Lord's mercy may be upon them as we place all our trust in Him on their behalf

For our faithful departed ones, that Jesus, who destroyed death and brought life and immortality to light, may now bring them into His heavenly kingdom forever

## 3rd Sunday of Lent

*Exod 17:3-7, Ps 95, Rom 5:1-2, 5-8,
John 4:5-42*

For our leaders in the church, who must respond to the demands of the people, that God may stand with them as He did with Moses, providing the waters of life in the church through their ministry

That the peoples of the earth may not test and tempt God with immorality and injustice, but listen to His voice and respond with reverence and obedience

That we may give Jesus the cool water of our faith and our love, and that we may understand the gift of God, knowing that Jesus is the One who gives us the living water of everlasting life

That our catechumens may be true worshipers who adore the Father in Spirit and in truth and who have no other spiritual food than to do the will of the One who has chosen them

That Jesus, who gently led the Samaritan woman to salvation, may reach out to all the sick and sinful souls who need to come home to His love during this holy season

For our faithful departed ones, that they who were justified by faith may now be at peace with God in heaven through our Lord Jesus Christ

## 4th Sunday of Lent

*1 Sam 16:6-13, Ps 23, Eph 5:8-14,
John 9:1-41*

For our holy leaders in the church, that like Samuel they may have the grace of discernment to read into our hearts, and the commission to pour out God's anointing in the assembly

That the grace of forgiveness may be active in nations where sin has caused deep wounds, healing and restoring by divine power the peace that man cannot of himself create

For those preparing for baptism, that like the man born blind, they may now be able to see the truth and believe in Jesus who gives them their spiritual sight

That we who are baptized may live as children of the light, producing in our lives every kind of goodness in righteousness and truth

That Jesus may be the good and gentle shepherd of all who suffer and are passing through a dark valley, giving them courage with the anointing of joy and grace

For our faithful departed ones, that Jesus, the light of the world, may raise them up to the realms of light and peace in heaven

**5th Sunday of Lent**

*Ezek 37:12-14, Ps 130, Rom 8:8-11,*
*John 11:1-45*

For the church, that she may put her trust in Jesus, the Resurrection and the Life, and believe in Him through all the seasons of life and death on her spiritual journey

For refugees, for the oppressed and abandoned, that God may settle them upon their own land, putting His spirit of life in them again

That we may give Jesus the sacred tribute of our faith, believing in Him even beyond the death of our hopes and of our loved ones

That our spirits may be alive because of righteousness, giving room to the divine Spirit of Jesus to work marvels of grace and peace in our souls

For those who suffer, whose dreams lie in the tomb, that the divine promise to open all graves and raise the dead may be active, bringing them healing and hope

For our beloved dead, that Jesus, who wept at the loss of His friend Lazarus, may raise them up to the abundant life of heaven, and console those they have left behind

# HOLY WEEK

## Palm Sunday

*general intentions*

For the whole church, uniting with one heart and voice to escort our Savior with palms and praises to the Holy City as He enters to meet His painful destiny, that we may follow Him faithfully to the end

For individuals, groups, and nations who, like Jesus, have been cruelly betrayed by a false gesture of peace, that the greedy betrayers may come to repentance and that true peace be restored through the Master's redemption

For all who bear the role of prophet in the church, that with the Master they may have a well trained ear and words that can rouse the weary, and never turn back in the face of persecution

That we may allow grace to bring us with Jesus to the loving obedience that empties us out into our own inevitable cross at His side, so that with Him we too may be raised on high by the Father

For the courage to look long and steadily at our crucified God, who is speaking His whole word of redeeming solidarity and humble divine love in the pain-filled silence of His cross

For all the intentions we bring in our hearts to this Holy Sacrifice, for all who have asked for our prayers, and for our beloved departed ones who have passed through the doors of death with Jesus

### Holy Thursday

*Exod 12:1-8, 11-14, Ps 116, 1 Cor 11:23-26, John 13:1-15*

For our Holy Father, our bishops and priests, whose ordination was instituted at the Last Supper, that their consecrated lives of priestly service may continue to flow from the Eucharist, which they offer in the person of Christ

For peace, that the blood of the divine Lamb may keep the destructive blow of war and oppression from us, and that each of us may partake of the Lamb with staff in hand, ready for the journey that justice will demand of us

For all of us in every capacity of loving service that we give to each other, that our Lord's humility and self-emptying, symbolized in the foot washing, may continue in our mutual reverence and devotion

For our loved ones who are far from the sacraments, for the sick and addicted, the imprisoned and abused, the lonely and the poor, that this night of love and suffering may draw them into communion with Jesus who has the remedy for their wounds

For all of us who share this Eucharist, remembering most vividly that hour when Jesus showed us the very depths of His love, that we might express our gratitude to Him by being faithful in all that He asks of us

For our faithful departed loved ones, who ate the Divine Bread and drank the Holy Cup and proclaimed the death of the Lord while on earth, that they may now share His victory over death in heaven

### Good, Friday

*Solemn Intercessions Only*

*see general intentions in* The Roman Missal, Third Edition

## SEASON OF EASTER

### Paschal Vigil

*general intentions*

For the whole Church on this night of the Lord's triumph, that the resurrection fire kindled this night might spread through the darkness of an unbelieving world with irresistible power

That God, who created the order and harmony of the earth out of a formless void may in the renewal of this paschal mystery bring peace out of selfish power struggles and restore reverence for every human being made in His image and likeness

That broken relationships in marriage and friendship may be exposed to God's example of total fidelity and generous forgiveness, and built up again in the precious stones of His grace and peace

For all who are still in the darkness of ignorance, sin, addiction, and unresolved pain, that the Risen One, who calls the light and it obeys Him, may make them shine for joy in His presence with all His holy ones

For all who are reborn tonight and for all of us consecrated to Jesus, washed in the living water from His pierced side, that we may all truly die to sin in Him, trusting also that we will share His triumph

That Jesus, who is our paschal sacrifice, the Lamb upon our altar, may in this Eucharist create in each of us a new heart and a new spirit, perfectly attuned to His own heart, which ever rises to the Father, both in suffering and in glory

### Easter Sunday

*Acts 10:37-43, Ps 118, Col 3:1-4,*
*John 20:1-9*

For the successors to the apostles in the church today, commissioned to preach to the people, that like Peter, they may boldly proclaim the resurrection of Christ and the forgiveness of sins in His name

That Jesus, the great cornerstone, may not be rejected by the builders of our society, but that the right hand of the Lord may be exalted in Him, building nations with life, justice, morality, and peace

For all of us, that our life may be hidden with Christ in God, and that we may seek what is above, celebrating this feast with the unleavened bread of sincerity and truth

That all Christians may offer to the Paschal Victim their thankful praises today, renewing their vows to Him with joy and gratitude for His victory of divine love

For all who suffer, who grieve, who are distressed in mind and heart, that Jesus, who brought unexpected exultation to Mary Magdalene and the apostles on that first Easter Sunday, may give them also a share of His rising to new life

For all our faithful departed ones, who were signed with the cross of Jesus, that the power of His glorious resurrection may bring them rejoicing into the wedding banquet of heaven

### 2nd Sunday of Easter

*Acts 2:42-47, Ps 118, 1 Pet 1:3-9,*
*John 20:19-31*

For the church, that we may continue to devote ourselves to the teaching of the apostles, to the breaking of bread, and to the prayers, praising God and earning the favor of all the people

That Jesus, who on the first Easter Sunday met His apostles with the beautiful greeting of peace, may turn the hearts of national leaders to the acts of justice that will lead to peace in the world

That we may obtain the blessing of those who believe without seeing Jesus, as we proclaim Him to be our Lord and our God

That Jesus, who gave His apostles the power to forgive sins, may renew and purify us on this Mercy Sunday with all the cleansing power of His paschal sacrifice

For those who are suffering through various trials, whose faith is being tested in the fire, that through Jesus they may emerge stronger and happier in His service

For our faithful departed ones, that through the resurrection of Jesus they may be brought into the inheritance that is imperishable, undefiled, and unfading in heaven

### 3rd Sunday of Easter

*Acts 2:22-33, Ps 16, 1 Pet 1:17-21,*
*Luke 24:13-35*

For our Holy Father, our bishops and priests, that a new outpouring of the Holy Spirit may give them power to announce the dying and rising of Jesus with St. Peter's bold conviction

That the Lamb who has ransomed us from the futile ways of war and oppression by His own blood may raise up leaders with the wisdom and patience to negotiate for peace

For all of us, guests at the table where Jesus offers and blesses the signs of His sacrifice, that we too may recognize Him in the breaking of the bread, and build up our brothers and sisters with the witness of our joy

That we may conduct ourselves with reverence during the time of our sojourning on earth, placing our faith and hope in God alone

For all who have been sorely tried by pain and loss, particularly the sick and the bereaved, that Jesus may join them on the road and help them interpret what has happened, making their hearts burn again with faith and love

For our faithful departed ones, that God may show them the path to life, and give them abounding joy in His presence and delights at His right hand forever

## 4th Sunday of Easter

*Acts 2:36-41, Ps 23, 1 Pet 2:20-25,*
*John 10:1-10*

For our holy shepherds in the church, that they may keep watch at the gate of the Lord's sheepfold, not allowing thieves and robbers to harm the flock, and welcoming the Lord when He comes to call His own

For those who suffer for doing good and speaking up for the sanctity of life and the balance of justice, that their patient witness may be an effective grace before God in the world today

For all who bear the role of shepherd, especially parents of families and superiors of religious communities, that this day of celebration may bring them our gratitude for all their loving care

For those who have gone astray like sheep, especially our own loved ones, that the shepherd and guardian of their souls, our Lord Jesus Christ, may find them and bring them home

For those who are walking in a dark valley, that the Good Shepherd may give them courage and lead them beside the restful waters of healing and peace

For our faithful departed ones, that Jesus, who came that we may have life, may take them into the abundant and eternal life that is heaven

## 5th Sunday of Easter

*Acts 6:1-7, Ps 33, 1 Pet 2:4-9, John 14:1-12*

For the church, that we may be a holy nation, a people God can call His own, as we announce the praises of the One who called us out of darkness into His own wonderful light

That the Lord, whose word is upright and whose works are trustworthy, may inspire leaders of nations with justice and right reason in their decisions and plans

For the deacons of the church, that they may be filled with faith and the Holy Spirit as they proclaim the Word of God and work diligently for God's kingdom

That we who have seen the Father in Jesus may do the works that Jesus has done, becoming upright and virtuous and powerful in our love and service

That those who are in distress and pain may not allow their hearts to be troubled, but put their faith in God and in Jesus, who is the way that guides them, the truth that consoles them, and the life that revives them

For our faithful departed ones, that Jesus, who has prepared a place for each of them in the Father's house, may now welcome them home into heavenly joy

## 6th Sunday of Easter

*Acts 8:5-8, 14-17, Ps 66, Pet 3:15-18, John 14:15-21*

For our Holy Father, our bishops and priests, that the Advocate, the Holy Spirit, may be with them in their work of teaching and preaching the gospel

That those who feel paralyzed or hampered in their work for peace and justice may be freed and given the power of the Risen One and His Holy Spirit

That each of us may always be willing and ready to share with others the reason for our hope, speaking gently and with reverence, and witnessing to Jesus by the power of a clear conscience in the sight of all

For all those preparing to marry, to be ordained, to receive First Communion or Confirmation, that the Holy Spirit may fall on them with grace and blessing at the threshold of these great sacraments

For all who have asked us to pray for them, for the sick, the poor, the bereaved, the struggling, that each one may have cause to say: "Blessed be God who refused me not my prayer or His kindness!"

For all our beloved departed ones who kept the commandments of Jesus on earth, that the Lord may now reveal Himself to them in the glory of heaven

## The Ascension of the Lord, Vigil

*general intentions*

For the whole church, anticipating the Ascension, that our glorious Lord and Savior may fill her heart with His paschal joy

That leaders of countries that have been evangelized may acknowledge the Lordship of Jesus in their decisions and policies, and that God may grant us His peace

That we who celebrate the bodily Ascension of Jesus into heaven may follow Him in our thoughts and desires, seeing everything on earth from the standpoint of eternity

For all who receive this Eucharist, that we may understand that Jesus will never leave us orphans, and that His presence has passed into the sacraments for our consolation and joy

For all who need the comfort of prayer today in a time of mourning, pain, or weakness, that the power of this Holy Sacrifice will lift them up to new realms of grace and hope

For our dear ones who have died, that they may be where Jesus has gone before us, safe in the place He has prepared for them, rejoicing in His love

## Ascension of the Lord

*Acts 1:1-11, Ps 47, Eph 1:17-23,*
*Matt 28:16-20*

For the apostles of the church today, that they may stir up within themselves and the whole church the power they received when the Holy Spirit was given to them in the grace of their ordination

That Jesus, who mounted His throne amid shouts of joy, may establish His rule over the hearts of world leaders, leading them into the ways of life, justice, morality, and peace for the exultation of all the peoples

That God may give us all His Spirit of wisdom, so that we may know and understand the hope of our calling and the riches of His glory that we will inherit as His holy ones

For the missionary outreach of the church, that we may all support by our prayers and financial resources the final mandate of Jesus: to make disciples of all nations

For all who are suffering, who think Jesus has left them behind, that they may come to know that He seems to hide himself in heaven only to send the Holy Spirit of grace, healing, and courage upon them

For our faithful departed ones, that Jesus, whom the Father raised from the dead and seated above every authority and power, may use His dominion to bring them to eternal life in heaven

## 7th Sunday of Easter

*Acts 1:12-14, Ps 27, 1 Pet 4:13-16,*
*John 17:1-11*

For the church, that through her teaching and preaching ministry she may bring all her children to eternal life by knowing the true God and the one whom He has sent, our Lord Jesus Christ

That those whom the Father has given Christ out of the world may shine throughout the nations in their witness to a culture of life and a civilization of love

That we may devote ourselves to prayer in faith and hope for the gift of God, His promised Holy Spirit, in the blessed company of Mary, the Mother of Jesus

For all who are made to suffer because they are Christians, that they may have the insight to see how blessed they are, and that the Spirit of glory and of God rests upon them

For the poor, the sick, the grieving, the depressed, and all who have asked our prayers as they share in the sufferings of Jesus, that the Lord may support them and console them by His union with them in their time of trial

For our faithful departed ones, that they may be dwelling in the house of the Lord and contemplating His loveliness in the kingdom of heaven

## Pentecost Vigil

*general intentions*

For the whole church, groaning in labor pains as she longs for the coming of the Holy Spirit, that this divine Paraclete may respond to our yearning with the gift of holy fire

That all creatures and all the world may be filled with peace and all good things as the Lord opens His hand and sends out His Spirit

That the Spirit may come to the aid of our weakness, interceding for us in our prayer according to God's loving will

That our faith in Jesus may be strong so that living water may flow from within us, refreshing and renewing everyone we meet

For all who have asked our prayers and all who are in need of loving intercession, that the Spirit may be poured upon them in grace and joy

For our beloved departed ones, who possessed the first fruits of the Spirit in this life of hope and struggle, that they may now be rejoicing in the Spirit amid the bliss of heaven

## Pentecost Sunday

*general intentions*

For the whole church on this day of Pentecost, as the glorified Christ lets fall His promised Holy Spirit, that the strong wind of His coming may surge through the Upper Room where we have waited, to kindle in each of us His holy fire

For the lay faithful, commissioned by the Spirit to be a ferment in society for the kingdom of God, that the Spirit's gift of fortitude may make them strong friends of Christ, able to stand up for the demands of justice, life, and peace

For all who are experiencing new stirrings in their lives— calls to change and growth, movements of repentance, even earthquakes of divine disturbance— that they may not quench or sadden the loving Spirit who awakens within them

That our Communion with Jesus in this holy sacrifice may intensify the presence of His Spirit in our hearts, and spread all around us the sweet fragrance of His gifts and fruits in our lives

That the Spirit may be an anointing of comfort to the sorrowful, healing to the sick, calm to the anxious, forgiveness to sinners, and refreshment to us all on our pilgrim way

For our faithful departed ones, that the Lord may send forth His Spirit into their souls, so that they may be placed in eternal life as His new creation

# ORDINARY TIME

## 2nd Sunday in Ordinary Time

*Isa 49:3, 5-6, Ps 40, 1 Cor 1:1-3,
John 1:29-34*

That grace and peace from God our Father
may rest upon the church, in all her ranks
of ministers and in all her faithful

That Jesus, who was raised up to be a light
for all the nations, may be glorified by the
Lord when national leaders make their
decisions according to His wise and life-
giving laws

That God may raise up in the church
prophets, who, like John the Baptist,
recognize and point out the work of the
Spirit and the person of Jesus Christ

That each of us who follow Jesus may, like
Him, make it our delight to do God's will
freely and fully in the unfolding of our lives

For those who are weary and find life
burdensome, who carry a burden of
sickness or poverty, that they may find
solace in the love of the servants of Jesus
and in His interior consolation

That Jesus, anointed Son of God, may
raise up our faithful departed loved ones,
purifying them of all sin and welcoming
them into His heavenly home

## 3rd Sunday in Ordinary Time

*Isa 8:23–9:3, Ps 27, 1 Cor 1:10-13, 17,
Matt 4:12-23*

For all preachers of the Gospel, that they
may preach not with human eloquence
but with the power of their example and
their proclamation of the cross of Christ

For all oppressed people, those who suffer
under the yoke of war and civil unrest,
that the yoke that burdens them may be
smashed by the Lord through national
leaders who truly care for justice

That there may be no divisions among the
followers of Christ, but that we may all
agree in what we say, and be united in the
same mind and the same purpose

That Jesus' message of repentance may be
heard and heeded in our own day, and that
the Lord may call new disciples to become
fishers of souls

For all who are suffering and living in a land
of darkness, that through prayer and love
and the power of God, their anguish may
take wing and their gloom may be dispelled

For our faithful departed, who have waited
for the Lord with courage, that they may
now see His bounty in the land of the living
for all the days of eternity

### 4th Sunday in Ordinary Time

*Zeph 2:3, 3:12-13, Ps 146, 1 Cor 1:26-31, Matt 5:1-12*

For unity among the disciples of the Lord, that all who are in Christ Jesus may have righteousness, sanctification, and redemption in the fullness of the faith and the sacraments

For the peacemakers, those statesmen who pursue diplomatic relationships to avoid conflict, and the prophets who speak up from among the people for the right to life and justice for all

That we may be among the remnant of the Lord who truly seek justice and humility, who speak no lies, and who take refuge in the name of the Lord

That we may aspire to live the beatitudes with which Jesus inaugurated His great Sermon on the Mount, becoming gentle, merciful, and poor in spirit, and accepting persecution in our path of discipleship

For those who mourn, who are suffering, lonely or ill, for all who are bowed down, that they may be comforted and raised up by the love of God and those who care for them

For our faithful departed, that God who keeps faith forever and sets captives free, may unbind them from all sin and bring them into the promised land of His eternal kingdom

### 5th Sunday in Ordinary Time

*Isa 58:7-10, Ps 112, 1 Cor 2:1-5, Matt 5:13-16*

For the shepherds of the church, that their proclamation may be given with a demonstration of the Spirit and power, supported by the holiness of their own lives

That the powerful of the earth may remove oppression and turn to satisfy the afflicted, so that the glory of the Lord may be over the nations and His blessing upon the peoples

That our good and loving deeds may shine before the world like a light and lift up peoples' vision like a city on a mountain, so that our heavenly Father may be glorified for His grace

That all Christians may be gracious and merciful and just, sharing their goods with the poor and trusting with firm hearts in the Lord

For those who live in weakness and fear and trembling, who understand Jesus crucified through their own sufferings, that Jesus may lift them up with Himself in the power of His resurrection

For our faithful departed, that the wounds of their sins may quickly be healed, and the Lord's vindication may go before them into His kingdom of light and joy

## 6th Sunday in Ordinary Time

*Sir 15:15-20, Ps 119, 1 Cor 2:6-10,*
*Matt 5:17-37*

That the Holy Spirit, who scrutinizes everything, may fill the church with holy wisdom, leading our shepherds to act upon and teach the commandments of God with respect and joy

For leaders of nations, that God who understands their every deed may inspire and enable them to make the choice for life, obedience, and justice for all

For the grace to control anger, that we may never be insulting or rude to one another, but instead may learn to live at peace, reconciling with our opponents before offering any gifts to God

For purity of life, that we may be the first to cut off from our lives whatever causes us to sin, reverencing our marriage partners and keeping our speech honest and true

For all who need our special prayers today: the sick, the poor, the imprisoned and addicted, the grieving and depressed, that joy and grace and healing may return to them through the power of this Holy Sacrifice

For our faithful departed, that they may soon possess as their portion "what eye has not seen nor ear heard, that portion which God has prepared for those who love Him."

## 7th Sunday in Ordinary Time

*Lev 19:1-2, 17-18, Ps 103, 1 Cor 3:16-23,*
*Matt 5:38-48*

For the church, the temple of God, that her holiness may shine out in the world, especially the witness of her universal love

For those who are wise in this age, the powerful and the influential, that they may be given the grace to understand God's wisdom, and turn their efforts to justice, life, and peace

For our enemies, for our persecutors, for those who press us into service and take what is ours, that we may have the grace to return more good to them than the evil they have done to us

That Jesus, who has taken us far beyond the provisions of the Old Law, may have the joy of seeing us become perfect as our heavenly Father is perfect

For all who are suffering and heavily burdened, that the Lord may heal all their ills, redeeming their life from destruction, crowning them with kindness and compassion

For our faithful departed, that the Lord, who has compassion on His children and puts our sins as far from us as the east is from the west, may make them pure and ready for life in His heavenly kingdom

### 8th Sunday in Ordinary Time

*Isa 49:14-15, Ps 62, 1 Cor 4:1-5,*
*Matt 6:24-34*

For the servants of Christ: our bishops and priests, that in their role as stewards of the mysteries of God, they may be found trustworthy and faithful

For the judges of human tribunals, that in their decisions they may remember that they themselves will be judged by the Lord, and so uphold life and justice in our land

That we may live without anxiety as followers of Jesus, knowing that we have a Father who clothes the wild flowers in splendor and feeds the smallest birds, and who will not fail to take care of our needs

For mothers who have had no tenderness for the children within their wombs, that God who is faithful even if a mother should forget her infant, may enlighten, forgive, and heal them

For all who are in a period of tribulation at this time, who are sick or grieving, that they may have the joy of experiencing that God is their safety and glory, the rock of their strength

For our faithful departed, that they may be at rest in God, undisturbed in the protection of His heavenly kingdom

### 9th Sunday in Ordinary Time

*Deut 11:18, 26-28, Ps 31, Rom 3:21-25,*
*Matt 7:21-27*

For the church, that she may ever come to understand anew that by herself she cannot please God, but that everything depends on faith in Him

That there may be no consequence of a curse on the disobedient actions of those in power among the nations, but that all world leaders may be careful to observe the statutes and decrees of the Lord

That we may be wise builders in our spiritual lives, setting our houses solidly on the rock of putting the words of the Lord into practice in our daily lives

For those who call upon the name of the Lord without doing the will of the Father, that they may see the division in their lives and return to a full and free obedience

For all who are discouraged, sick, poor, imprisoned, or addicted, and all who need our prayer today, that they may take courage and be stouthearted, hoping in the mercies of the Lord which are coming to meet them

For our faithful departed ones, who obeyed the law of the Lord while on earth, that they may now be reaping the rewards of their faithfulness in heaven

## 10th Sunday in Ordinary Time

*Hos 6:3-6, Ps 50, Rom 4:18-25,*
*Matt 9:9-13*

For the church and her holy shepherds, that they may never fail to reach out to those the world considers lost and hopeless, imitating the mercy of the Lord

That God, who shows His saving power to the upright, may raise up men and women in our day who will speak out for the oppressed, restoring the balance of justice in our world

That Jesus, who did not come to call the righteous but sinners, may cast His divine glance on our fallen away brothers and sisters, inviting them with power and tenderness to a change of heart

For the elderly, that like Abraham they may be strengthened by faith, giving glory to God whose promises never fail and whose love never falters

For those who are sick or suffering in any way, that this Holy Sacrifice may bring the light of God's coming into their lives and the spring rain of divine grace into their hearts

That Jesus, who was handed over for our transgressions and raised for our justification, may free our faithful departed ones from all sin and bring them rejoicing into heaven

## 11th Sunday in Ordinary Time

*Exod 19:2-6, Ps 100, Rom 5:6-11,*
*Matt 9:36–10:8*

For the church, the special possession of God, a kingdom of priests, a holy nation, that she may always hearken to His voice and keep the covenant He has made with her in a spirit of grateful love

For the shepherds of the nations, that God who claims all the earth as His own may direct them in the paths of justice, life, and peace

For the apostles of our own day, sent by the compassion of Christ into the harvest, that God may raise up many new laborers to help them and keep them strong in their ministry

That we who have received the love of God without cost, being justified by the blood of Christ, may give without cost and without stint to all who are troubled and abandoned in life

For those who feel enslaved to suffering and far from God, that the Lord, who released the Israelites from the slavery of Egypt, may bear these little ones up on eagles' wings and bring them to Himself in joy and grace

For our faithful departed ones, that as they have been reconciled to God by the death of His Son, they may now be saved by His life and brought into the joys of paradise

## 12th Sunday in Ordinary Time

*Jer 20:10-13, Ps 69, Rom 5:12-15,*
*Matt 10:26-33*

For the whole church, that we may go out to meet the inevitable reality of persecution on earth for the name of Jesus, because we have seen in advance the reward that our loyalty will bring us

That those who work and suffer for life and for peace may refuse to be intimidated, but speak the truth with justice in the name of God

For those who are feeling the pressure of divine testing in their lives as God probes their motives and their actions, that they may let themselves be converted

That we may have the courage to acknowledge Jesus before others, so that He will recognize us before the face of His heavenly Father

For those who are caught in abuse, neglect, illness; for the forgotten lowly ones who fall to the ground unnoticed like the sparrows, that they may be comforted by those who realize how precious they are in God's sight

For our faithful departed ones, that the grace of God and the gracious gift of Jesus Christ may overflow for them, purifying them and bringing them rejoicing into heaven

## 13th Sunday in Ordinary Time

*2 Kgs 4, Ps 89, Rom 6:3-4, 8-11,*
*Matt 10:37-42*

For the church and her holy leaders, that we may all think of ourselves as dead to sin, and living for God alone in Christ Jesus

That rulers of the nations may walk in the light of God's countenance and be exalted through His justice as they obey His command to uphold life and create justice

For the prophets of our own day, that they may be honored and received with obedience so that God's blessings may descend on those who hear them

That we may be worthy of Jesus, loving Him more than father and mother, more than son or daughter, more than our own life, taking up our cross and following Him faithfully

For those who long for children, for the sick, the oppressed and the grieving, that God, whose kindness and faithfulness are confirmed in the heavens, may grant them the blessings they desire on the earth

For our faithful departed ones, that Jesus, over whom death no longer has power, may raise them up to live for God in the heavenly kingdom

## 14th Sunday in Ordinary Time

*Zech 9:9-10, Ps 145, Rom 8:11-13,
Matt 11:25-30*

For the church, that those among us who are wise and learned and prudent in the ways of the world may be converted and take their place among the little ones who understand the heavenly Father

That Jesus, who holds all power hidden in His peacefulness, may calm and pacify the hearts of the powerful, inclining them to thoughts of justice and reverence before the gift of human life

That we who follow the just savior, who is gentle and humble, yet whose dominion shall be from sea to sea, may imitate His lowliness and rejoice in His salvation

For our dear ones who are far from the grace of God and His holy sacraments, that our prayers and love may bring them back to the Lord who willingly lifts up those who are falling

That the Lord, who is gracious and merciful, slow to anger and of great kindness, may come to the aid of those who need Him most in their time of illness and distress

For our dear departed ones, in whom the Spirit of the One who raised Jesus from the dead once dwelt by their baptism, that through the same Spirit they may enter into new life in the kingdom of heaven

## 15th Sunday in Ordinary Time

*Isa 55:10-11, Ps 65, Rom 8:18-23,
Matt 13:1-23*

For the members of the church, that they may endure the suffering of the present time with fortitude, waiting in hope for their sure revelation as children of God

That God may visit the lands and peoples of the world and water them with truth and wisdom, making every soul reverent before His gift of life and the demands of His justice

That we may respond fully to the Master's work, receiving the seed of His word in hearts that understand it, and bearing fruit with love and gratitude

For creation, our beautiful world, which is yet enslaved to futility, that we may respect it as God's gift and redeem it by our holy lives

For all who are groaning in the labor pains of anxiety, illness, financial setbacks, unemployment, and all the troubles of life, that redemption may come in a lifting of their burdens

For those who have preceded us beyond the horizon of death, that their eyes may be blessed with the sight of God and their souls filled with His beatitude in heaven

### 16th Sunday in Ordinary Time

*Wis 12:13, 16-19, Ps 86, Rom 8:26-27,*
*Matt 13:24-43*

For the church, the precious yeast in the dough of all humanity, that we may lighten and leaven the world by the witness of our love and fidelity to the Lord

That God, whose might is the source of justice, may show His mastery over all things by raising up world leaders obedient to His just and perfect laws

That we, who have grown up from good seed, yet have the enemy's sowing growing up alongside us, may patiently persevere in our good deeds until the harvest

That the kingdom of heaven, which on earth looks small and unimportant like a tiny mustard seed, may shelter many souls in its branches of truth and peace

For all who are living through a period of distress and suffering, that the Holy Spirit might come to the aid of their weakness, interceding for them according to God's will, obtaining grace and strength

For our faithful departed ones, that God, who is merciful and gracious, abounding in kindness and fidelity, may forgive their sins and lift them up to the joy of His heavenly kingdom

### 17th Sunday in Ordinary Time

*1 Kgs 3:7-12, Ps 119, Rom 8:28-30,*
*Matt 13:44-52*

For our teachers in the church, instructed in the kingdom of heaven, that they may bring from the storerooms of their wisdom both the old and the new for the edification of God's people

For the nations, that God may grant them leaders who wish to possess an understanding heart, that they may judge their people rightly and distinguish right from wrong

That we may understand the joy we have in our hidden treasure, our precious pearl of the kingdom of God, gladly selling all we have to possess it fully

That we may love the commands of God, making it our part to keep His words and observe His decrees, allowing His law to be our delight

For all who are in a season of suffering who have asked for our prayers, that all things may work for their good through God's tender and powerful providence

For our faithful departed ones, predestined and called to be conformed to the image of Jesus, that they may now be justified in Him and glorified with Him in heaven

## 18th Sunday in Ordinary Time

*Isa 55:1-3, Ps 145, Rom 8:35, 37-39,*
*Matt 14:13-21*

For the church, that neither death nor life, nor anguish, nor distress may keep us from conquering evil overwhelmingly because of the love of Christ Jesus our Lord

That the Lord, who is just in all His ways and holy in all His deeds, may lift the minds and hearts of world leaders to the ways of integrity, life, and peace

For all who feel powerless to help their brothers and sisters in need, that they may have the courage to bring to Jesus what little is available, so that His power to multiply may bless their efforts

For all of us sharing this Eucharist, who come without paying to a divine banquet, that no fragment of this feast be lost, but shared freely with all who are in need of God

For all who have asked for our prayers in a time of suffering, that our eyes may look hopefully to the Father on their behalf, and that He may open His hand and satisfy their desire for healing and strength

For our beloved departed ones, that they may be brought into the banqueting hall of heaven and delight in the rich fare of the face to face vision of God

## 19th Sunday in Ordinary Time

*1 Kgs 19:11-13, Ps 85, Rom 9:1-5,*
*Matt 14:22-23*

For the church, that we may learn to discern the voice of God, not in wind and earthquake and fire, but in the gentle whisper that announces His passing by

That God's proclamation of peace may be a reality for the nations, that kindness and truth may meet and justice look down from heaven on obedient hearts

That we may not faint and fail in our faith when we see how strong the wind is during the storms of life, but keep our eyes on Jesus, confident that in His power we also can walk on the waters

For the children of Israel, who can claim the covenants and the giving of the law, the worship and the promises, that they may also come to recognize their Messiah in Jesus Christ the Lord

For all who are fearful, anxious, depressed, or grieving, that they may hear the firm and kind voice of Jesus saying to them: "Take courage, it is I, do not be afraid"

For our faithful departed ones, that they may be with God on the mountain of His glory, pure and peaceful in His sight

## 20th Sunday in Ordinary Time

*Isa 56:1, 6-7, Ps 67, Rom 11:13-15, 29-32,*
*Matt 15:21-28*

For the church, God's miracle of mercy, gathered from all nations and made acceptable at His altar, that she may be the faithful sacrament of mercy to all

That we, as citizens of a free land, may take seriously our duty to speak out for our moral principles, doing our part to preserve the order that supports the gift of peace

For vocations to the priestly and religious life, that willing men and women may be brought to God's holy mountain and made joyful with us in His house of prayer

For our dear young people who sometimes seem demon-troubled in their lonely desperation, that loving parental hands may reach out to Jesus in earnest intercession for them

That our faith may be great as we pray for all who are in need of the healing and mercy of our Lord Jesus Christ

For our faithful departed ones, that God may have pity on them and bless them, and let His face shed its light upon them in the kingdom of heaven

## 21st Sunday in Ordinary Time

*Isa 22:19-23, Ps 138, Rom 11:33-36,*
*Matt 16:13-20*

For our Holy Father, successor to St. Peter and keeper of the keys of the kingdom, that His faith and the inner support of the heavenly Father may be His strength

That the depths of the riches and the wisdom and the knowledge of God may influence and judge the thoughts of the powerful, moving them to decisions based on justice and respect for life

That we may be challenged by the direct question of Jesus: "Who do you say that I am?" and that our answer may determine our thoughts, words, and actions before His face

For our bishops and priests and deacons, that they may be fathers over the new Jerusalem, holding a place of honor in the church with integrity and devotion

For the weak and the lowly, those who are sick or impoverished and lacking in resources, that through our calling upon the Lord for them He may build up their strength

For our faithful departed ones, that they may be quickly purified to sing the praises of the Lord in the presence of the angels

## 22nd Sunday in Ordinary Time

*Jer 20:7-9, Ps 63, Rom 12:1-2,*
*Matt 16:21-27*

For our holy leaders and teachers in the church, that they may think as God does, showing us the path to life in truth, even when it means the road of suffering

For the prophets of our own day, who receive derision and reproach from the powerful ones, that they may be strong and persevering, relying on God's power within

That we may be transformed by the renewal of our minds, discerning what is good and pleasing and perfect before God, and acting upon what we see

That we may take our place among the disciples of Jesus, willing to deny ourselves, to take up our cross and follow Him, knowing that the Father will repay us according to our faithfulness

For those who are in distress, that they may come to see that they are under the shadow of God's wings, upheld by His right hand, and take courage to cling fast to Him

For our faithful departed ones, that they may soon be in God's sanctuary, satisfied with the riches of heaven's banquet

## 23rd Sunday in Ordinary Time

*Ezek 33:7-9, Ps 95, Rom 13:8-10,*
*Matt 18:15-20*

For our Holy Father, our bishops and priests, who have been entrusted with a prophetic role, that they may speak out bravely against any evil that destroys and wounds Christ's followers

For the conversion of the powerful who have wandered far from God's law of love, especially when that law demands respect for life and the justice due to all

For all of us at the delicate times when we need to speak the truth honestly to those closest to us, that we may do it as Jesus told us: discreetly and respectfully, with the good of the other as our goal

That Jesus may not encounter in us hard and resistant hearts, but only our reverence before Him and our willingness to let Him be Master as well as Friend

For those who have asked for our prayers in a time of distress, that we may unite together lovingly to intercede for them, knowing that our united prayer is irresistible to our Heavenly Father

For our faithful departed ones, that they may soon be purified to sing joyfully to the Lord, coming into His divine presence with thanksgiving in the kingdom of heaven

### 24th Sunday in Ordinary Time

*Sir 27:30–28:7, Ps 103, Rom 14:7-9,*
*Matt 18:21-35*

For the church, for forgiveness and mercy within her ranks, that anger may be put aside and love for one another may prevail

For the forgiveness of national debts, especially those of poverty stricken countries who have no way of paying them back

For all of us, debtors to our Lord and Master and owing Him everything, that we may see the little debts that are owed us in their true proportion, and forgive as we have been forgiven

That we may no longer live for ourselves but for our Master Jesus, who died and came to life in order to be Lord of the dead and of the living

For the suffering little ones who endure sickness and poverty, that God may redeem their life from destruction and crown them with kindness and compassion

For our faithful departed, that God may put their transgressions from them as far as the East is from the West, and welcome them, purified and holy, into His kingdom

### 25th Sunday in Ordinary Time

*Isa 55:6-9, Ps 145, Phil 1:20-27,*
*Matt 20:1-16*

For our shepherds in the church, that for them Christ may be magnified in all things, as they give Him their fruitful labor for the benefit of the faithful

That God, whose thoughts are far above our thoughts, may direct the minds of world leaders to decisions for life, justice, morality, and as a result, peace

For the conversion of those who have wandered far from God, especially those among our loved ones, that they may turn to the Lord for mercy, and to God, who is generous in forgiving

That we may not begrudge God His generous mercy with the latecomers to His vineyard, but rejoice together with them that we have found such a good Master

For all who need our prayers in a time of sickness, poverty, hardship, or bereavement, that our gracious and merciful Lord may show them His compassion in healing and strength

For our faithful ones who have departed this life, that they may be with Christ in the kingdom of love and joy that is heaven

## 26th Sunday in Ordinary Time

*Ezek 18:25-28, Ps 25, Phil 2:1-11,
Matt 21:28-32*

That we may complete the joy of our holy leaders in the church by our unity of mind, doing nothing out of selfishness, and looking out for the interests of one another

For the powerful of the world, that they may turn from the practices of a civilization of death to do what is right and just before the God of life

That we may be doers of the Father's will, matching our actions with our words when we agree to obey Him, or if we have at first refused, changing our minds in the end

For the conversion of sinners, that they may turn from wickedness to righteousness in the sight of God, that they may live without shame in His presence

For all who have asked for our prayers in a time of distress, that they may know solace in our love, encouragement in Christ, and God's compassion and mercy in their troubles

For our faithful departed, that they may be among the blessed ones who joyously proclaim that Jesus Christ is Lord in the kingdom of His Father

## 27th Sunday in Ordinary Time

*Isa 5:1-7, Ps 80, Phil 4:6-9, Matt 21:33-43*

For the whole church, God's vineyard, tended faithfully by our Holy Father, our bishops and priests, that it may bear an abundant harvest of grace and holiness

For world leaders, that they may follow what is true, honorable, just, and worthy of praise, especially in the area of human life and dignity, so that there may be peace

For the conversion of all who return God no yield for His gracious cultivation, before the arrival of the hour of judgment between the Lord and His vineyard

For all who are suffering, that the church may help them with her prayers and relieve them of anxiety with her love, so that God's peace may stand guard over their hearts in Christ Jesus

That this Eucharist may be a sign and pledge of the harvest God expects of each of us, as we are united with the divine first fruits in our Lord Jesus

For our faithful departed ones, that through this Holy Sacrifice their purification may be quickly accomplished, and they may be welcomed into the kingdom of heaven

## 28th Sunday in Ordinary Time

*Isa 25:6-10a, Ps 23, Eph 1:17-18,*
*Matt 22:1-14*

For the church, for her leaders and teachers, servants of the great king who are sent to summon all to the banquet of His mercy, for their holiness and their courage

For a more just distribution of the goods of the earth, that everyone will have a share of life's banquet

That we may learn the secret of being content in abundance as well as in need, in humble circumstances as well as in wealth, doing everything peacefully in the One who strengthens us

That all Christians, clothed in the shining garment of their baptism, may one day be united at the wedding table of the Lord

For those who have asked us to remember them in God's presence, that in answer to our earnest prayer, the Father will wipe away the tears of their struggles

That the Lord who will destroy death forever may bring our faithful departed to the feast of eternal life

## 29th Sunday in Ordinary Time

*Isa 45:1-6, Ps 96, 1 Thess 1:1-5,*
*Matt 22:15-21*

For the church, that the Gospel may be preached in her assemblies with power and in the Holy Spirit and with much conviction

For the nations, that God may raise up leaders like Cyrus, grasping their right hand, giving them light and power to make decisions for life, justice, morality, and peace

That we may live justly, giving to Caesar what is Ceasar's, but that we may remember that there is no other God than the Father of Jesus, and give Him the glory of lives in which He is truly the Lord

For our school children, that their teachers may be truthful models of God's integrity who have their best interest at heart

For the sick, the elderly, the unborn, the handicapped, and all who give us the chance to be compassionate because of their weakness, that we may not lose hearts that are sensitive and respectful of all life

For our faithful departed, who labored in love and showed endurance in the hope of our Lord Jesus Christ, that they may now be rejoicing with Him in heaven

## 30th Sunday in Ordinary Time

*Exod 22:20-26, Ps 18, 1 Thess 1:5-10, Matt 22:34-40*

For the church, that we may be imitators of the Lord, receiving the word faithfully even in the midst of affliction, and experiencing the joy that comes from the Holy Spirit

For the nations of the world, that they may not molest or oppress aliens, wrong widows, or kill unborn children, thus risking the wrath of the Holy One

That the greatest commandment in the law may be the first priority of our lives, as we strive to love the Lord our God with our whole heart, soul, mind, and strength

For the grace to understand the importance of the second commandment, treating our neighbors as we would want to be treated, with justice and compassion

For all who have asked our prayers in a season of distress and suffering, that the Lord may be for them a rock of refuge, a shield and a stronghold of help and powerful kindness

For our faithful departed, that Jesus, whom God raised from the dead, may deliver them from all evil and bring them into His glorious heaven

## 31st Sunday in Ordinary Time

*Mal 1:14-2:8-10, Ps 131, 1 Thess 2:7-13, Matt 23:1-12*

For all who carry on the work of the first apostles, that they may be gentle in their personal relations with those to whom they minister, so that the Word they preach may be recognized and received as God's

For leaders of nations, that they may not break faith with one another and with their people, but keep the covenant of loyalty that is written in every human heart

That we may all come to acknowledge Christ as our one Master and God as our Father, humbling ourselves to become servants to one another as Jesus commanded

That this Eucharist may envelop us in the peace of God's little children, stilled and quieted in the arms of the One who shares with us His very self

That those who have been brought low by illness or misfortune may have the faith and the courage to rely on the divine law that exalts the lowly and fills the sorrowful with joy

For our faithful departed ones who have been humbled by death and judgment, that they may be purified quickly and exalted with Jesus in the blessed kingdom of heaven

### 32nd Sunday in Ordinary Time

*Wis 6:12-16, Ps 63, 1 Thess 4:13-18,*
*Matt 25:1-13*

For the church, that she may be ready to go into the wedding feast at any time, with her lamp shining and glowing before the Bridegroom

That those who rule the nations may learn to seek Wisdom, keeping vigil in their desire for prudent understanding, rejoicing in her resplendent and unfading light

That we may not be foolish in our preparations to meet our Savior but have our supply of faith and love ready to withstand the long vigil of waiting for His joyful appearance

For all who have become confused and disoriented in the changing currents of life, that the trumpet of God may resound in their ears, calling them from death to the unchanging and eternal life of heaven

For all whose lives have become parched, lifeless and without water, that God may cover them with the shadow of His wings and satisfy them with the riches of His grace and healing

For those who have fallen asleep and those who grieve them, that the Word of the Lord may be their hope and the promise of the risen Christ be their joy

### 33rd Sunday in Ordinary Time

*Prov 31, Ps 128, 1 Thess 5:1-6,*
*Matt 25:14-30*

For the church, that she may be like the worthy wife of today's reading, active and watchful, diligent and compassionate, fruitful in every good work

For world leaders, that they may not count on the appearance of peace and security, but build their nations on the rock foundation of a culture of life, morality, and justice

For all of us, the children of the light and of the day, that we may be alert and sober, ready for the day of the Lord which, we know, will come unexpectedly, like a thief in the night

For those who have received only one talent, who are tempted to bury the Master's money and coast through life without effort, that they may realize that their modest gifts are not their own, and that God expects them to work their resources with diligence and care

For all who are in need of compassionate intercession and loving care, especially the sick, those in financial difficulty, the oppressed and imprisoned, the lonely and grief-stricken

For our faithful departed ones, who were trustworthy with the talents they had received in this life, that they may now share the Master's joy in heaven

**34th Sunday in Ordinary Time, Christ the King**

*Ezek 34, Ps 23, 1 Cor 15:20-28, Matt 25:31-46*

For our shepherds in the church, that they may diligently look after and tend God's sheep, bringing back the strayed, binding up the injured, healing the sick, shepherding us rightly

That all sovereignties, authorities, and powers that are in opposition to God may be brought under subjection to Christ the King, that God may be all in all

That we who know in what the final judgment of God will consist may be the first to treat Christ in the hungry, the thirsty, the stranger, the sick, and the imprisoned with compassion and reverence

That we who have the Lord as our shepherd, who want for nothing under His care, may reach out to those who do not yet know God as Savior and Friend, leading them to Jesus

That those who are going through a dark valley of sickness, poverty, oppression, or grief may feel the guiding press of the divine Shepherd's staff, leading them to restful waters and the anointing of joy and grace

For our faithful departed ones, that Christ, the first fruits of those who have fallen asleep, may bring all who belong to Him rejoicing into His Father's kingdom

## SOLEMNITIES OF THE LORD DURING ORDINARY TIME

**Holy Trinity**

*Exod 34:4-9, Dan 3, 2 Cor 13:11-13, John 3:16-18*

For our holy leaders in the church, that like Moses they may be ever ready to ascend God's holy mountain with the commandments of God's law in their hands and in their hearts

That the witness of Christians to the communion that has its origin in the Holy Trinity may be an inspiration to the nations to do everything they can to live in peace

That we may come to understand the Holy Trinity as a mystery of mercy and graciousness, a God who is slow to anger and rich in kindness and fidelity to us, His children

For unity among the followers of Jesus, that we may learn to live in agreement, mending the ways of arrogance and pride, greeting one another with respect in a spirit of fellowship

For those who are perishing, who are sick, hungry, poor, imprisoned, or grieving, that God, who loved the world and sent His Son so that we might not perish, may show them His tender mercy

For our faithful departed ones, who believed in the name of Jesus, that they may be caught up in the embrace of the three Divine Persons in the bliss of heaven's joy

## Corpus Christi

*Deut 8, Ps 147, 1 Cor 10:16-17,*
*John 6:51-58*

For the whole church, keeping this solemnity in honor of the Body and Blood of Jesus, that we may renew our gratitude to our Heavenly Father, who provides for our journey with the bread that is His own Son

For peace, for the justice that undergirds peace; that we may share our bread with our hungry brothers and sisters in the same generous spirit that Jesus shares Himself as Bread with us

That we may come to a renewed awareness of who it is who feeds our souls in such self-effacing silence, and begin to show the same love in our relations with one another

For unity in the church, that all who partake of the one loaf may be truly one body, healed and whole in a communion of truth and love

For all who are suffering, that the broken Body and spilled Blood of Jesus may be a cup of blessing for them as it brings them the companionship of the Lord

For our faithful departed ones, who ate the Bread of Life in faithful obedience, that the Master's repeated assurance that He will raise them to new life may become for them a living reality in heaven

## Sacred Heart

*Deut 7:6-11, Ps 103, 1 John 4:7-16,*
*Matt 11:25-30*

For the church, that we, the people sacred to the Lord in His merciful fidelity, may be faithful to the covenant of love that binds us to Him

For peace, that peace may be the result of the sincere love toward one another that shows respect and works for justice

That this feast consecrated to the divine and human love of our Savior may bring us before Him rejoicing in His mercy and never forgetting the personal price He paid to be the expiation for our sins

For all of us sharing the banquet of love in this eucharistic sacrifice, that we may come to an ever deeper knowledge of God's love through the love we offer one another in His name

For those who labor and are burdened, who are bereaved or in any distress, that they may be among the meek and humble of heart whom God comforts by revealing the secrets of His love

For our beloved dead, that our merciful God may redeem them from destruction and crown them with kindness and compassion in His heavenly kingdom

# PROPER OF TIME

## SUNDAYS, SOLEMNITIES, FEASTS
# YEAR B

## SEASON OF ADVENT

### 1st Sunday of Advent

*Isa 63:16b-17, 19b, 64:2-7, Ps 80,*
*1 Cor 1:3-9, Mark 13:33-37*

For the church, that God who is faithful may keep her firm to the end, lacking for no spiritual gift, and irreproachable on the day of our Lord Jesus Christ

That the Shepherd of Israel, the Lord of Hosts, may rouse His power among the nations, giving new light and strength to their leaders to make decisions of life, morality, and justice

For all who have wandered far from God and hardened their hearts, that this Advent may bring them the grace to return to Him through the sacrament of reconciliation

That we may be watchful and alert, waiting for the Lord of the house to return, conducting ourselves as His good servants while we wait

That God our Father, the divine Potter who shapes our lives, may hear our prayers for the poor, the sick, the homeless, and the grieving, and return to them with healing and grace

That the Lord may work awesome deeds for our faithful departed, freeing them from all sin and making them worthy to stand in His divine presence in the glory of heaven

### 2nd Sunday of Advent

*Isa 40:1-5, 9-11, Ps 85, 2 Pet 3:8-14,*
*Mark 1:1-8*

For our leaders in the church, who like John the Baptist have the mission to prepare the way of the Lord, that their holiness of life may give power to their words, and their humility serve to raise up the divine Redeemer

That God may again comfort and speak tenderly to the poor and downtrodden of our world, and that the anticipation of the Lord's day of judgment shake every heart loose of indifference and greed, so that there may be peace in our time

That the fervent and humble reception of the sacrament of reconciliation may be an indispensable part of every Catholic's effort to clear a straight path for the Lord's coming during this Advent

For the dying, for all those who find their lives leveling out into a direct road homing toward the Lord, that He may come, gentle as a Shepherd who carries His lambs in His bosom and leads them with tender care

For all who are in special need of prayer: the sick, those in financial straits, the imprisoned and homebound, the refugees and the homeless, that our compassionate intercession may comfort them, and that many Christian hearts reach out to help them

For those who have died, that they may be found without spot or blemish, at peace before the Lord in heavenly glory

## 3rd Sunday of Advent

*Isa 61, Magnificat, 1 Thess 5:16-24,*
*John 1:6-8, 19-28*

For our Holy Father, our bishops and priests, who baptize with water and make straight the way of the Lord, that their ministry may be blessed and fruitful among God's holy people

That the Prince of Peace, who came to bring glad tidings to the poor, to release prisoners, and to heal the brokenhearted, may instruct the hearts of world leaders in His ways

That on this Advent Sunday dedicated to the spirit of joy, we may be given the grace to rejoice always in the spirit, like a bride bedecked with her jewels and ready to meet the divine bridegroom and accept His gift of salvation

That the humility of John the Baptist may descend upon us, helping us to see ourselves in the truth and to lift up and glorify the Lord

For all who are passing through a time of distress, illness, loneliness, or financial difficulty, that they may discover reasons for joy in an unexpected windfall of divine blessing and the respectful love of the followers of Christ

For our faithful departed, that the God of peace may make them blameless and perfectly holy, worthy to behold Him face to face in the heavenly kingdom

## 4th Sunday of Advent

*2 Sam 7, Ps 89, Rom 16:25-27,*
*Luke 1:26-38*

For the church, heir of the house of David in the person of her head, Jesus the eternal king, that she may be for God a noble temple in which He can show forth His glory and His love

For the commanders and leaders of the nations, that they may be like David, a man after God's own heart, who will do all that He commands

That the prudence and purity of the lowly virgin of Nazareth may be our model and inspiration in our relationship with God

That we may be brought with Mary into the obedience of faith, allowing God to accomplish His designs of love and goodness in our lives

For all who are lonely, ill, or grieving, that the One who can strengthen and console us may be active and watchful in our lives

That God, for whom nothing is impossible, may receive our faithful departed with mercy, forgiving and purifying them for entry into His glorious kingdom

## SEASON OF CHRISTMAS

### Nativity of the Lord, at the Vigil

*Isa 62:1-5, Ps 89, Acts 13:16-17, 22-25,*
*Matt 1:18-25*

For the church, God's chosen people, His virgin bride, that her rejoicing may be in her bridegroom, who took flesh in Jesus and came to dwell among us

That God's covenant of love may stand firm with all nations as they again seek to know His justice, obey His laws, and experience His peace

That we may imitate St. Joseph's faith and obedience, as He quietly left behind His own doubts and took Mary into His home, giving Jesus His name and the shelter of protecting love

That we may greet the birth of our divine Savior with the humility of John the Baptist, and herald His new coming into our lives with reverent joy

For those who are forsaken and desolate, that they may be called by a new name, and become a glorious crown in the hand of the Lord as He fills them with His joy

For all who have completed their course, who have passed beyond the gates of death, that they may be celebrating this Christmas in the exultation of the heavenly kingdom

### Nativity of the Lord, Mass at Midnight

*Isa 9:1-6, Ps 96, Titus 2:11-14,*
*Luke 2:1-14*

For the whole church, celebrating the birth of Jesus with abundant love and great rejoicing, that all darkness may be illuminated by the great light she now presents to the world

For peace, that in the mastery of the child that is born to us, every unjust yoke may be smashed, every tool of war destroyed, and the deliberations of world leaders be ruled by the Prince of Peace

For the grace of hospitality, that we may see Jesus in the least of His brothers and sisters, and especially that no expectant mother be refused the comfort and shelter she needs to bear her child

That Mary, our mother, may show her Divine Child to everyone that comes in wonder to the manger, and lay Him to rest in our hearts as we approach this Eucharist

For those who keep a lonely watch in the night, those who have no one to care for them, that with the shepherds they may also know of angels who will bring them tidings of great joy in the name of Jesus

For our dear ones who have died, that they may see the final appearance of their blessed hope, the glory of the great God and of Jesus our Savior, in the clear light of heaven

## Christmas Mass at Dawn

*Isa 62:11-12, Ps 97, Titus 3:4-7,*
*Luke 2:15-20*

For the shepherds of the church, our bishops and priests, that as they lead us today in glorifying and praising God for the birth of the Savior, they themselves may be renewed in His joy

For the governments and leaders of the world, that the message of the angels may be realized in every effort they make to avoid armed conflict and promote peace

For all who are in pain in body, mind, emotions, or spirit, that this holy day may be a blessing of peace and light on their journey

That Jesus, who in His birth as one of us has made every human joy His own, may be at the heart of our family festivities, our gift giving, and every lovely custom we keep in His honor

That Mary, our Mother, may show her divine child to every wondering heart that approaches the manger, and lay Him to rest in each of us as we approach this Eucharist

For our beloved dead, that they may be celebrating this Christmas amid the joys and splendors of heaven

## Nativity of the Lord, Mass during the day

*Isa 52:7-10, Ps 98, Heb 1:1-6,*
*John 1:1-18*

For the church on this great feast of Christmas, that her whole soul may be consumed in praise as she sings to the Lord with melodious song for His great mercy in giving us our Savior

That God may be king among the nations, so that the feet of those who bring glad tidings may be beautiful upon the mountains as they bear good news and announce peace

That as the Lord comforts His people and redeems Jerusalem, we too may bring comfort and joy in the name of Jesus to all those whose lives we touch

That with the angels of God we may gladly worship the firstborn Son who has come into the world, and spread the good news of His redemption

For all who are still in the darkness of loneliness, depression, illness, or grief, that the great light who is Jesus may enlighten them and they may know the joy of our love in His name

For our dear ones who have died, that they may be soon brought into heaven, where Jesus has His seat at the right hand of the Majesty on high

## Holy Family

*general intentions*

For our Holy Father, head of the family that is the Body of Christ, that He may be held in honor within the church

For peace in our families, forgiveness of grievances, harmony of roles, and that our children may be safe and loved within the home, so that our nation and every nation may be built up in peace

That our families may be protected from the special dangers of our age: from abortion and euthanasia, from the inroads of materialism and violence; that faith and prayer and mutual love may keep them together in the Lord

For families in exile, for families that have lost their children, for families of the unemployed and the poor, that the Holy Family, which experienced all these situations, may be their comfort and hope

For the gift of vocations, that the Christian life of our families may flower in young lives consecrated to the Lord, whose ministry will serve in turn to strengthen the families of the future

For our loved ones who have died, for our elders who have gone before us, that they may rest in peace and help their beloved families with their prayers

## Blessed Virgin Mary, the Mother of God

*Num 6:22-27, Ps 67, Gal 4:4-7, Luke 2:16-21*

For the whole church, that God's wisdom may strike root among us in the person of Jesus, making us a glorious people, the portion of the Lord, and the company of His holy ones

That God, who sends forth His command to the earth, may enable world leaders to keep His word, so that He may grant peace in our borders

For all of us as we celebrate this Christmas season, that the eyes of our hearts may be enlightened, and we may know what is the hope that belongs to our call in Christ Jesus

That the Word who was made flesh may give all those who believe in His name power to become children of God, shedding His light in the world by their lives of faith and good works

For all who are abandoned and forgotten in their need and suffering, that our prayer and our love may encircle them with joy and new beginnings of life

For our faithful departed ones, that God may bless them in Christ with every spiritual blessing in His heavenly home, giving them eternal rest and peace

## Second Sunday after Christmas

*Sir 24:1-2, 8-12, Ps 147, Eph 1:3-6, 15-18, John 1:1-18*

For the whole church, that God's wisdom may strike root among us in the person of Jesus, making us a glorious people, the portion of the Lord, and the company of His holy ones

That God, who sends forth His command to the earth, may enable world leaders to keep His word, so that He may grant peace in our borders

For all of us as we celebrate this Christmas season, that the eyes of our hearts may be enlightened, and we may know what is the hope that belongs to our call in Christ Jesus

That the Word who was made flesh may give all those who believe in His name power to become children of God, shedding His light in the world by their lives of faith and good works

For all who are abandoned and forgotten in their need and suffering, that our prayer and our love may encircle them with joy and new beginnings of life

For our faithful departed ones, that God may bless them in Christ with every spiritual blessing in His heavenly home, giving them eternal rest and peace

## The Epiphany of the Lord, Vigil

*general intentions*

For our leaders and teachers in the church, that they may be the first to worship at the manger and present their gifts of mind and heart to the Lord

That the Christmas grace of peace may radiate out into the whole world, exercising its gentle influence on the hearts of world leaders and turning their thoughts to the poor and the lowly

For all of us, represented by the foreigners who brought their adoration and their gifts to Jesus, that we may do all we can to spread the Good News and bring the whole world to His manger

That the faith and persevering search of the magi may inspire us during the dark times of our journey, when only the light of a great star leads us on through the night

For all who are suffering and poor and abandoned during this joyful season, that in memory of the Holy Family sheltered in a stable, we may reach out to them in love

For our loved ones who have gone before us marked with the sign of faith, that they may now see their Savior, unveiled in all His glory in heaven

## Epiphany

*Isa 60:1-6, Ps 72, Eph 3:2-3, 5-6,*
*Matt 2:1-12*

For the church, gathered as never before from all nations, that her holiness may shine out as a guiding star to bring to Jesus those who are still in the great darkness

For world leaders, that God may endow them with His judgment, so that they may govern His afflicted ones with justice and respect for the human dignity of each person

That wise men of every country and every religious background may come to understand the truth that Jesus alone is God made flesh and the Savior of the world, and place their gifts gratefully at His feet

That we who live in power and safety like Jerusalem of old may not miss the star rising over our heads, leading those with eyes to see down to humble Bethlehem with its hidden King

For all who travel a dark path through sickness, poverty, oppression, and every form of misery, that they may be overjoyed to find a star of guidance leading them to the mercy of the Lord

For our beloved departed ones, that they may come to rest in the radiant presence of the Savior whom they sought in the shadows of this passing world

## Baptism of the Lord

*Isa 55:1-11, Isa 12, 1 John 5:1-9,*
*Mark 1:7-11*

For the ministers of the Word of God, that by their preaching and example God's word may not return to Him void but achieve the end for which it was sent: the sanctification of God's people

That the leaders and commanders of nations may seek the Lord while He may be found, forsaking power and greed for life, morality, justice, and peace

For all who are thirsty for fullness of life, that they may come to the divine bounty and delight in the rich fare that God wishes to give freely and fully to us all

That we who have the Spirit's testimony to Jesus, who came to save us through water and blood, may keep His commandment of love out of gratitude and praise

For the poor, the sick, the grieving, the oppressed and the homeless, that they may come to believe that God is their Savior, their strength, and their courage through the love shown to them in His name

That Jesus may baptize with the Holy Spirit all our faithful departed, freeing them from all stain and making them worthy of a place in His heavenly kingdom

## SEASON OF LENT

### 1st Sunday of Lent

*Gen 9:8-15, Ps 25, 1 Pet 3:18-22,*
*Mark 1:12-15*

For the whole church driven by the Spirit
into the desert of this holy season of Lent,
that we may faithfully keep our Savior
company in His trials, and let Him give us
life in the realm of the Spirit

For world leaders, that they may not yield
to the temptations of power and greed,
but work for justice and the rights of each
human being

For all of us sharing this Eucharist, encircled
by the rainbow of God's covenant and kept
safe in the ark of holy church, that we
may go forth bearing the olive branch of
peace to all

For those preparing for baptism during
this holy season, that the full light of truth
may shine in their hearts, and that their
parish communities may support them on
the journey

That God, whose compassion and love are
from of old, may show His kindness and
goodness to the sick, the poor, the suffering,
and all who have asked for our prayers

For our faithful departed ones, that after
their time of testing and trial in the body,
they may know the ministry of the angels
in heaven

### 2nd Sunday of Lent

*Gen 22:1-2, 9a, 10-13, 15-18, Ps 116,*
*Rom 8:31-34, Mark 9:2-10*

For our holy shepherds in the church, that
they may help us listen to the beloved Son,
transfigured in the Father's glory today

For God's prophets and patriarchs, all who
follow His way, that they may be a light and
a sign in the world, a source of blessing for
all the nations

That the obedience of Abraham may be our
own, even to the utmost sacrifice, so that
we may receive God's abundant blessing
as our portion

For all who have tasted the delights of
the mountaintop, who want to stay there
forever with Jesus, that they may be
willing to follow Him also in the flatlands
of everyday life, content that Jesus alone
is with them

For all who are in want or misery, who
are sick or grieving, that God, who did not
spare His own Son but gave Him up for us
all, may now give them everything they
need along with Jesus

For our faithful departed ones, that by the
divine mercy they may walk before the Lord
in the land of the living, rejoicing forever
in heaven's transfiguration

### 3rd Sunday of Lent

*Exod 20:1-17, Ps 19, 1 Cor 1:22-25,*
*John 2:13-25*

For our Holy Father, our bishops and priests, that zeal for the Father's house may consume them as it did Jesus, so that they may be faithful ministers at His altar

For those who are strong and wise in the ways of the world, that they may become aware of the superior power and the greater wisdom of Christ crucified, and begin to give Him their loyalty

That the holy commandments of God may again become the standard of each human life, and that those who have seriously broken these laws may return to God through the sacrament of reconciliation

That we may keep our interior temples free of commerce and noise and injustice, that they may truly be houses of prayer and reverence on the earth

That Jesus, who understands human nature and its weakness under the burden of suffering, sickness, and grief, may comfort and heal those who bring their needs to this Holy Sacrifice

For our faithful departed loved ones, that Jesus, who was raised from the dead, may raise them up to life, joy, and peace in his eternal kingdom

### 4th Sunday of Lent

*2 Chron 36, Ps 137, Eph 2:4-10,*
*John 3:14-21*

For the church, that we may live the truth, doing all our works in God, and welcoming the light into our lives

That world leaders might be like Cyrus, the King of Persia, aware of God and obedient to His commands, building by their deeds a house of worship and reverence for God upon the earth

That we who have been saved by grace through faith by the gift of God, who is rich in mercy, may show that same generosity to those who are still dead in their transgressions

For the catechumens of the church, that God's holy light may find them eager and watchful, and that they may know the loving support of their parish communities

For those who sit and weep by the waters of affliction, whose joy has been silenced, that our humble prayers may give them cause to sing again the song of the Lord's goodness

That God, who so loved the world that He gave His only Son for us to have eternal life, may raise up our faithful departed ones to that blessed life with Him in heaven

## 5th Sunday of Lent

*Jer 31:31-34, Ps 51, Heb 5:7-9,*
*John 12:20-33*

For the church, that Jesus, who became the source of eternal salvation for all who obey Him may have the loyalty and gratitude of all His followers

That God may place His law within the hearts of our national leaders, that they may come to know Him and obey His wise and life-giving inspirations

That we may be willing, like our Master, to be grains of wheat falling to the ground and dying in order to produce much fruit and be His true servants

That Jesus, who experienced anguish of spirit in the face of His passion, may help those who are threatened by persecution to glorify God by their faith and witness

For those who with Christ are learning obedience from what they must suffer, that their prayers may share in His reverence and their lives come to perfection before the Father's face

For our faithful departed ones, that Jesus, who was lifted up to draw everyone to Himself, may draw the departed forth from every shadow that binds them and set them free in heaven's glory

# HOLY WEEK

## Palm Sunday

*general intentions*

For the whole church, uniting with one heart and voice to escort our Savior with palms and praises to the Holy City as He enters to meet His painful destiny, that we may follow Him faithfully to the end

For individuals, groups, and nations who, like Jesus, have been cruelly betrayed by a false gesture of peace, that the greedy betrayers may come to repentance and that true peace be restored through the Master's redemption

For all who bear the role of prophet in the church, that with the Master they may have a well trained ear and words that can rouse the weary, and never turn back in the face of persecution

That we may allow grace to bring us with Jesus to the loving obedience that empties us out into our own inevitable cross at His side, so that with Him we too may be raised on high by the Father

For the courage to look long and steadily at our crucified God, who is speaking His whole word of redeeming solidarity and humble divine love in the pain-filled silence of His cross

For all the intentions we bring in our hearts to this Holy Sacrifice, for all who have asked for our prayers, and for our beloved departed ones who have passed through the doors of death with Jesus

## Holy Thursday

*Exod 12:1-8, 11-14, Ps 116, 1 Cor 11:23-26, John 13:1-15*

For our Holy Father, our bishops and priests, whose ordination was instituted at the Last Supper, that their consecrated lives of priestly service may continue to flow from the Eucharist, which they offer in the person of Christ

For peace, that the blood of the divine Lamb may keep the destructive blow of war and oppression from us, and that each of us may partake of the Lamb with staff in hand, ready for the journey that justice will demand of us

For all of us in every capacity of loving service that we give to each other, that our Lord's humility and self-emptying, symbolized in the foot washing, may continue in our mutual reverence and devotion

For our loved ones who are far from the sacraments, for the sick and addicted, the imprisoned and abused, the lonely and the poor, that this night of love and suffering may draw them into communion with Jesus who has the remedy for their wounds

For all of us who share this Eucharist, remembering most vividly that hour when Jesus showed us the very depths of His love, that we might express our gratitude to Him by being faithful in all that He asks of us

For our faithful departed loved ones, who ate the Divine Bread and drank the Holy Cup and proclaimed the death of the Lord while on earth, that they may now share His victory over death in heaven

## Good, Friday

*Solemn Intercessions Only*

*see general intentions in* The Roman Missal, Third Edition

## SEASON OF EASTER

### Paschal Vigil

*general intentions*

For the whole Church on this night of the Lord's triumph, that the resurrection fire kindled this night might spread through the darkness of an unbelieving world with irresistible power

That God, who created the order and harmony of the earth out of a formless void may in the renewal of this paschal mystery bring peace out of selfish power struggles and restore reverence for every human being made in His image and likeness

That broken relationships in marriage and friendship may be exposed to God's example of total fidelity and generous forgiveness, and built up again in the precious stones of His grace and peace

For all who are still in the darkness of ignorance, sin, addiction, and unresolved pain, that the Risen One, who calls the light and it obeys Him, may make them shine for joy in His presence with all His holy ones

For all who are reborn tonight and for all of us consecrated to Jesus, washed in the living water from His pierced side, that we may all truly die to sin in Him, trusting also that we will share His triumph

That Jesus, who is our paschal sacrifice, the Lamb upon our altar, may in this Eucharist create in each of us a new heart and a new spirit, perfectly attuned to His own heart, which ever rises to the Father, both in suffering and in glory

### Easter Sunday

*Acts 10:37-43, Ps 118, Col 3:1-4, John 20:1-9*

For the successors to the apostles in the church today, commissioned to preach to the people, that like Peter, they may boldly proclaim the resurrection of Christ and the forgiveness of sins in His name

That Jesus, the great cornerstone, may not be rejected by the builders of our society, but that the right hand of the Lord may be exalted in Him, building nations with life, justice, morality, and peace

For all of us, that our life may be hidden with Christ in God, and that we may seek what is above, celebrating this feast with the unleavened bread of sincerity and truth

That all Christians may offer to the Paschal Victim their thankful praises today, renewing their vows to Him with joy and gratitude for His victory of divine love

For all who suffer, who grieve, who are distressed in mind and heart, that Jesus, who brought unexpected exultation to Mary Magdalene and the apostles on that first Easter Sunday, may give them also a share of His rising to new life

For all our faithful departed ones, who were signed with the cross of Jesus, that the power of His glorious resurrection may bring them rejoicing into the wedding banquet of heaven

### 2nd Sunday of Easter

*Acts 4:32-35, Ps 118, 1 John 5:1-6,*
*John 20:19-31*

For the whole church, recalling today the gift of forgiveness that Jesus gave on that first Easter with the breath of His Holy Spirit, that all may come to this fountain of mercy

That like the first followers of Jesus, the rich may bring their surplus to be distributed according to the needs of those who have nothing

For all who question and doubt the reality of the risen Christ, and who, like Thomas, let their despondency become stubbornness, that Jesus may invite them into His wounds and restore their faith

For the newly baptized and for us all, begotten of God and filled with the faith that conquers the world, that the power of faith may show itself in our obedient love

For all who are in a season of suffering, for the loved ones we carry in our hearts, that the joyful power of this Easter may become strength, light, and healing in their lives

For our faithful departed ones, that Jesus, who came through water and the blood of His loving sacrifice on their behalf, may bring them rejoicing into heaven

### 3rd Sunday of Easter

*Acts 3:13-19, Ps 4, 1 John 2:1-5,*
*Luke 24:35-48*

For our holy shepherds in the church, that they may always have the courage to confront sin in God's people as Peter did, and call them to repentance with compassionate understanding

That Jesus, the expiation for the sins of the whole world and our Advocate with the Father, may open the hearts of world leaders to keep His commandments, leading us into the paths of peace

For children receiving their First Communion, for those being ordained to the priesthood or making the loving commitment of matrimony, that these sacraments may be a blossoming in their lives that will bear good fruit

That we may consent to be taken into the mystery of the One who entered into glory only through the gates of suffering, and give ourselves to Him who gives Himself to us in this Eucharist

For all who are in pain of body or soul, especially our loved ones and those who have asked our prayers, that God may relieve their distress and put gladness into their hearts again

For our faithful departed ones, that Jesus, the victorious Author of Life, may stand before them with His radiant greeting of peace, and welcome them to the dwelling He has prepared for them in heaven

## 4th Sunday of Easter

*Acts 4:8-12, Ps 118, 1 John 3:1-2,*
*John 10:11-18*

For our shepherds in the church, that they may be imitators of Jesus, ready and willing to lay down their lives for their sheep

For the leaders of the people and the elders of the nations, that they may build their decisions on the one divine cornerstone, working for life, for justice, and for morality in the world

For unity in the church, that all the sheep may hear the voice of Jesus in true doctrine and practice, so that there will be one flock and one Shepherd

That we who are known intimately by Jesus our Good Shepherd may allow Him to teach us to know the Father, and to obey Him with love and reverence

For those who are suffering, that through the power of this Holy Sacrifice, they may have cause to give thanks to the Lord for His goodness and His everlasting mercy

For our faithful departed, who were God's children in this earthly life, that they may now be like God, seeing Him as He truly is

## 5th Sunday of Easter

*Acts 9:26-31, Ps 22, 1 John 3:18-24,*
*John 15:1-8*

For the church, that she may be at peace, being built up and walking in the fear of the Lord, and enjoying the consolation of the Holy Spirit

That God may raise up for the nations impassioned souls like Saul, who will speak up boldly for the cause of life, justice, and morality in the world today

For all of us, branches on the Lord's vine, that we may remain firmly united to Him in faith and love, and glorify the Father with an abundant fruit of holiness

That we may love, not just in word or speech, but in deed and in truth, thus reassuring our hearts in confidence before our Heavenly Father

For those who are being pruned through sickness, poverty, or grief, that our loving prayers may support them till the Lord brings forth in their lives an increased yield of joy and grace

For those who sleep in the earth, our faithful departed ones, that their souls may live exultantly before the face of the Lord in His glorious kingdom

## 6th Sunday of Easter

*Acts 10, Ps 98, 1 John 4:7-10,
John 15:9-17*

For the successor of Peter, for all the shepherds of the church, that they may be ready to welcome the action of the Holy Spirit wherever He chooses to pour Himself out for the glory of the Father

That in every nation there may be statesmen and leaders who fear God and act uprightly, making themselves acceptable to Him as Cornelius once did

That we who have been designated by Jesus as His friends may remain in His love by keeping His commandment of love

That we may understand how powerless we are to choose God unless He first chooses us and appoints us to bear fruit, and that we may follow Jesus with humility and gratitude for this surpassing grace

For all who are in need of prayer today in their struggles and sufferings, that our love may be active in prayer for them, and that God, who is love, may reach out to them and help them with great power

For our faithful departed ones, that God may win the victory of transforming love for them, and that they may sing to Him a new song for His saving power

## The Ascension of the Lord, Vigil

*general intentions*

For the whole church, anticipating the Ascension, that our glorious Lord and Savior may fill her heart with His paschal joy

That leaders of countries that have been evangelized may acknowledge the Lordship of Jesus in their decisions and policies, and that God may grant us His peace

That we who celebrate the bodily Ascension of Jesus into heaven may follow Him in our thoughts and desires, seeing everything on earth from the standpoint of eternity

For all who receive this Eucharist, that we may understand that Jesus will never leave us orphans, and that His presence has passed into the sacraments for our consolation and joy

For all who need the comfort of prayer today in a time of mourning, pain, or weakness, that the power of this Holy Sacrifice will lift them up to new realms of grace and hope

For our dear ones who have died, that they may be where Jesus has gone before us, safe in the place He has prepared for them, rejoicing in His love

## Ascension of the Lord

*Acts 1:1-11, Ps 47, Eph 1:17-23 or*
*Eph 4:1-13, Mark 16:15-20*

For our missionaries, that the final commission of Jesus to proclaim the Gospel to every creature may be the power that moves their prayer and work in the world

For the nations of the world over which Jesus sits enthroned, that they may submit to His divine authority, and thus come to know His peace

That we may wait with joy for the power we will receive when the Holy Spirit comes upon us to make us witnesses to Jesus in the sight of all

That the unity of the Spirit may be preserved in the bond of peace among the followers of Jesus, as we live in all humility and gentleness and patience with one another

For those who are suffering, that Jesus, who Himself suffered along with us, may fill them from within with courage, healing, and grace

For our faithful departed ones, that Jesus, who mounted His heavenly throne to shouts of joy, may now lead them into the realms of rejoicing and happiness in heaven

## 7th Sunday of Easter

*Acts 1:15-26, Ps 103, 1 John 4:11-16,*
*John 17:11-19*

For all who share in the apostolic ministry, chosen by God who knows the hearts of all, that they may be loyal followers of Jesus and strong in their witness to His truth

That the Lord, whose throne is in heaven and who rules over all, may raise up on earth leaders of the nations who will do His will and stand up for His values in this world

That we may come to know and to believe in the love that God has for us, remaining in love ourselves, so that God will be in us and we will be in Him

For young people graduating from our Catholic schools, for First Communicants and those receiving Confirmation, that they may be consecrated in truth by the Word of God and open to His will for their lives

For those who are frail and failing under the burdens and pressures of life, that Jesus may protect them in the name of His Father, guarding them so that nothing will be lost, but all will work together for their good

For our faithful departed ones, that they may share completely in the joy of Jesus, established forever in the kingdom of heaven

## Pentecost Vigil

*general intentions*

For the whole church, groaning in labor pains as she longs for the coming of the Holy Spirit, that this divine Paraclete may respond to our yearning with the gift of holy fire

That all creatures and all the world may be filled with peace and all good things as the Lord opens His hand and sends out His Spirit

That the Spirit may come to the aid of our weakness, interceding for us in our prayer according to God's loving will

That our faith in Jesus may be strong so that living water may flow from within us, refreshing and renewing everyone we meet

For all who have asked our prayers and all who are in need of loving intercession, that the Spirit may be poured upon them in grace and joy

For our beloved departed ones, who possessed the first fruits of the Spirit in this life of hope and struggle, that they may now be rejoicing in the Spirit amid the bliss of heaven

## Pentecost Sunday

*general intentions*

For the whole church on this day of Pentecost, as the glorified Christ lets fall His promised Holy Spirit, that the strong wind of His coming may surge through the Upper Room where we have waited, to kindle in each of us His holy fire

For the lay faithful, commissioned by the Spirit to be a ferment in society for the kingdom of God, that the Spirit's gift of fortitude may make them strong friends of Christ, able to stand up for the demands of justice, life, and peace

For all who are experiencing new stirrings in their lives— calls to change and growth, movements of repentance, even earthquakes of divine disturbance— that they may not quench or sadden the loving Spirit who awakens within them

That our Communion with Jesus in this holy sacrifice may intensify the presence of His Spirit in our hearts, and spread all around us the sweet fragrance of His gifts and fruits in our lives

That the Spirit may be an anointing of comfort to the sorrowful, healing to the sick, calm to the anxious, forgiveness to sinners, and refreshment to us all on our pilgrim way

For our faithful departed ones, that the Lord may send forth His Spirit into their souls, so that they may be placed in eternal life as His new creation

# ORDINARY TIME

## 2nd Sunday in Ordinary Time

*1 Sam 3:3-10, Ps 40, 1 Cor 6:13c-15a,
17-20, John 1:35-42*

For our holy leaders and priests, that they may be familiar with the ways of the Lord and able to teach the young how to listen for and respond to God's call, as Eli did with Samuel

That God's justice may be announced in the vast assembly of the nations, so that morality and respect for life may re-emerge and prevail

For vocations; that from the midst of families sensitive to God's will, young people may emerge who know they are looking for Jesus, who stay with Him and follow His call

For purity of life and conduct, especially among the young, that each Christian may guard and respect His body as a temple of the Holy Spirit

That Jesus may intervene in the lives of the poor, the sick, the grieving and oppressed, sending His followers to help them and supporting them in their hearts

For our faithful departed, who tried to keep their ears open to obedience while they walked on this earth, that God may purify them and reward their devotion with the joys of paradise

## 3rd Sunday in Ordinary Time

*Jonah 3:1-5, 10, Ps 25, 1 Cor 7:29-31,
Mark 1:14-20*

For the church, that her preachers may be ready and waiting for every mission when the Word of the Lord comes to them in the needs of the people

That stubborn and self–centered nations, or those who promote violence and discord, may, like Niniveh, learn to believe God and turn from their wicked ways

That we may live in the world with our eyes fixed on the coming of God's kingdom, using its goods, but not fully, knowing that the world in its present form is passing away

For the grace of good and holy families in the church, and that from them the Lord may call the young to be fishers of men in our own time

For all who have asked our prayers, who are passing through a time of sickness, impoverishment, or grief, that the Lord, whose compassion is from of old, may remember them in kindness and grace

For our faithful departed, for whom all earthly joys and sorrows have disappeared and who now see the full picture of life in God's living presence, that they may be at peace in His sight

## 4th Sunday in Ordinary Time

*Deut 18:15-20, Ps 95, 1 Cor 7:32-35,*
*Mark 1:21-28*

For the grace of unity among the disciples of Jesus, that all may be one under the authority of the Lord, who has power to drive out all the evil of the ages

That leaders of nations may not harden their hearts before the Lord, but worship Him by their decisions to respect life and to guarantee dignity and justice to all

That we may understand that Jesus is the great prophet promised by God, one like us, yet having God's words in His mouth, and that we may truly listen to Him with reverence and obedience

For vocations to the consecrated life of virginity, that many more young women may see the joy and freedom of a life that is intent solely on pleasing the Lord

That the Lord may cast out the forces of evil which bind our dear ones with injustice and grief, and grant healing and grace to all who have asked our prayers

For our faithful departed ones, that they may soon be purified and ready to come into the presence of the Living God with thanksgiving and joy

## 5th Sunday in Ordinary Time

*Job 7:1-4, 6-7, Ps 147, 1 Cor 9:16-19,*
*22-23, Mark 1:29-39*

For those who have been entrusted with stewardship in the church, that they may preach the Gospel willingly and freely, adapting themselves to all so as to win over as many as possible

For the oppressed, and those peoples who are without hope and resources, that the international community may come to their aid and help them recover and thrive again

That Jesus, who drove out demons throughout Galilee, may show His supremacy against the evil forces which oppress His holy people today

For doctors and medical personnel who continue the work of Jesus in their healing ministry, that the grace of His divine power may anoint their efforts to restore the sick to health

For those whose lives on earth are a drudgery, who are in misery and restlessness, illness or grief, that through the Lord's mercy they may see happiness again

For our faithful departed, that God who heals the brokenhearted and binds up all their wounds may purify them quickly for a place in His glorious kingdom

## 6th Sunday in Ordinary Time

*Lev 13:1-2, 44-46, Ps 32, 1 Cor 10:31–11:1, Mark 1:40-45*

For the priests, who once diagnosed leprosy and restored the lepers when they were cleansed, that today they may fearlessly point out sin and just as eagerly forgive and restore the repentant sinner

That the powerful and the influential may be men and women in whose spirit is no guile, upright of heart and resolute in their work for life and justice in the world

For all of us who follow Jesus, that we may be able to say to our brothers and sisters as St. Paul once did: "Be imitators of me, as I am of Christ."

For all those whose sin makes them unclean in God's sight and a danger to the community, that they may have recourse to Jesus for mercy and the beginning of a new life

That Jesus, who was moved with pity at the humble appeal of the leper, may again stretch out His hand and touch those who have asked our prayers in a time of sickness or great need

For our faithful departed, that all their faults may be taken away and their sin covered, so that they can be glad in the Lord and rejoice, exulting in the joy of heaven

## 7th Sunday in Ordinary Time

*Isa 43:18-19, 21-22, 24b-25, Ps 41, 2 Cor 1:18-22, Mark 2:1-12*

For our Holy Father, our bishops and priests, that their word may always be Yes to God and to His people, giving themselves in truth and love

For our civil leaders, that they may be men and women who are sustained by God because of their integrity, and who have regard for the lowly and the poor

For those who are paralyzed in their souls by the power of sin, that our faith and our persevering prayer may bring them to Jesus for forgiveness and peace

For those whose lives are paralyzed with sickness, poverty, addiction, financial difficulty, loneliness or grief, that the loving power of Jesus may intervene for release, healing, and joy

For all of us gathered around this Eucharistic table, that God who has anointed us and put His seal upon us may enable us to act according to the inspiration of His Holy Spirit

For our faithful departed, that God may do something new in their souls, purifying them and bringing them into His heavenly kingdom

### 8th Sunday in Ordinary Time

*Hos 2:16-22, Ps 103, 2 Cor 3:1-6,
Mark 2:18-22*

For the ministers of the new covenant; our present day apostles in the church, that with the qualification that comes from God they may preach in the Spirit and give witness by their holy lives

That world leaders may understand the covenant of love God has made with the human race, respecting it in their decisions to uphold a culture of life and foster a civilization of respect and justice

That we may allow Christ to be the bridegroom of our souls, espousing us in love, mercy, and fidelity, giving us intimate knowledge of the living God

That the fresh new wine of grace may be poured into our hearts made supple and flexible, new wineskins that can expand with its joy and hope

For those who are keeping a long fast, who are sick, poor, imprisoned, lonely, or depressed, that the Lord who has led them into the desert may now speak tenderly to their hearts, touching them with healing and delight

For our faithful departed ones, that they may soon be seated at the wedding banquet of their heavenly espousals with the Lord

### 9th Sunday in Ordinary Time

*Deut 5:12-15, Ps 81, 2 Cor 4:6-11,
Mark 2:23-3:6*

For the whole church, gathered around the Lord of the sabbath in worshipping communities all over the world, that this day dedicated to the refreshment of body and soul may be our gift of praise to God

For those who know no rest, who are still enslaved and oppressed by the unfeeling greed of others, that prophets of justice and mercy may arise to restore the withered substance of their lives and bring them peace

That God may share with us the glory shining on the face of Christ, and we may let His glory transfigure our lives

For all of us who carry the treasure of faith and grace in earthen vessels, that God uphold us in our weakness, glorifying His own power and love before all

For all those who are in distress, whose lives have been ravaged by tragedy, sickness, loss, and remorse, that as we cry out to God on their behalf, He may free them from the burden that weighs them down

For our faithful departed ones, that as they have shared in the dying of Jesus, they may be sealed with His glorious resurrection

## 10th Sunday in Ordinary Time

*Gen 3:9-15, Ps 130, 2 Cor 4:13-5:1,
Mark 3:20-35*

For the church, that through her ministers, grace may be bestowed in abundance on more and more people, causing thanksgiving to overflow for the glory of God

That nations and kingdoms may not be divided against themselves, but flourish strong and true in a culture of life

That Mary, the woman foretold in Genesis and the one who did the will of God without wavering, may obtain strength for each of her children to overcome evil and be faithful in their obedience to the Father

That Jesus, who was powerful against the unclean spirits and plundered the house of Satan, may cast out from our midst every shadow of evil and keep us strong in the Holy Spirit

For all who are discouraged, who feel their life wasting away, that they may also feel their inner self growing stronger and being renewed in the power of God's glory

For our faithful departed ones, whose earthly tent has been destroyed, that God, who raised up the Lord Jesus, may now raise them up and place them in His own divine presence amid all the joys of heaven

## 11th Sunday in Ordinary Time

*Ezek 17:22-24, Ps 92, 2 Cor 5:6-10,
Mark 4:26-34*

For the church, once planted by God on the mountain heights as a tender shoot, that she may grow in the power of the Lord, blooming and bearing fruit for His honor

That upright and just men and women may flourish among the nations like palm trees, vigorous and sturdy in their work for life, morality, and justice

That we may be courageous while we are away from the Lord, walking by faith rather than sight and aspiring to please Him in all we do

For the expansion of the kingdom of God in our midst; that it may sprout and grow quietly and inexorably, transforming our lives into an offering worthy of God

That the Lord's kindness and faithfulness may be with all who are sick and suffering, helping them to grow through this time of testing into a harvest of peace and joy

For our faithful departed ones, who have appeared before the judgment seat of Christ, that their recompense may be purity and joy in the heavenly kingdom

## 12th Sunday in Ordinary Time

*Job 38:1, 8-11, Ps 107, 2 Cor 5:14-17,
Mark 4:35-41*

For the church, the beginning of God's new creation, that the love of Christ may impel her holy ministers to preach and teach with the urgency of the first apostles

That God may bring to their desired haven all who are caught in the storms of war and oppression, raising up leaders of justice and compassion who will help them

That we may no longer live for ourselves, but for Jesus, who died for our sake and was raised up to bring us to new life

That we may never be terrified, no matter how turbulent our lives may become, but honor the power and compassion of Jesus with our faith

For those who feel they are perishing in the winds and waves of sickness, poverty, abuse, or addiction, that Jesus may awaken in their foundering boats and create a great calm of healing and peace

For our faithful departed ones, that Jesus may bring them safely to the other side, establishing them in His heavenly kingdom

## 13th Sunday in Ordinary Time

*Wis 1:13-15, 2:23-24, Ps 30, 2 Cor 8:7-15,
Mark 5:21-43*

For the church, that she may excel in faith, discourse, knowledge, all earnestness, in the love of her apostles, and in the gracious acts of kindness she extends to the poor

For the nations which have an abundance of material things, that they may supply the poverty of the deprived nations, so that there may be equality and a balance of justice in the world

For all those whose lives are being lost slowly in a flow of misfortune, that they may have the faith and courage to reach out and touch the cloak of Jesus, making contact with His restoring power

That we may not be afraid, knowing that God does not rejoice in the destruction of the living, but that we may trust Him even in the face of death

For the sick, the poor, those for whom weeping has entered in, that the Lord may be their helper and with the dawn bring them rejoicing

For those who have fallen asleep in death, that Jesus may take them by the hand, bidding them rise up to the blissful life of His heavenly kingdom

## 14th Sunday in Ordinary Time

*Ezek 2:2-5, Ps 123, 2 Cor 12:7-10, Mark 6:1-6*

That the Spirit may enter into our leaders in the church, setting them on their feet and opening their mouths to proclaim God's truth

That the voices rooted in God who speak up for the cause of life, of justice, and of peace may be heard even by the obstinate, and that rebellious hearts may come to know that there are prophets in their midst

That Jesus may never have cause to be amazed or distressed at our lack of faith, but that we may give Him the homage of our believing minds and attentive souls

For our missionaries, whose lot is often hardships, persecutions, and constraints for the sake of the Gospel, for their courage and joy

For all who are in a season of illness, financial difficulty, or emotional distress, that they may know the power of Jesus, which is made perfect in their weakness

For those who have gone before us through the doors of death, that they may encounter a Savior in Jesus, whose sacrifice has the power to cleanse them from all sin

## 15th Sunday in Ordinary Time

*Amos 7:12-15, Ps 85, Eph 1:3-14, Mark 6:7-13*

For our leaders in the church, that they may experience new energy to preach repentance, to heal and to drive out evil in the name of Jesus

For our leaders in the world, that they may have the courage to work for the arduous peace that is based on true justice, and built up on kindness and compassion

That we who have been sealed with the promised Holy Spirit may activate this anointing by our work for life, and peace in our world

For all of us gathered at this Eucharist, blessed with every spiritual blessing in the heavens, destined for adoption in Jesus, that we may live in gratitude to the praise of God's glory

For the healing of the sick and the driving out of demons, that God's anointing may give suffering ones health and freedom

That our beloved dead may have redemption from their sins and experience the fullness of their inheritance as God's adopted children

### 16th Sunday in Ordinary Time

*Jer 23:1-6, Ps 23, Eph 2:13-18,*
*Mark 6:30-34*

For the holy shepherds of the church, that they may tend God's flock with vigilance and integrity, so that no one need fear or tremble, and none will be missing in God's sight

For those who shepherd the nations, that they may be righteous, governing wisely, and doing what is just and right in their lands

That we who are led by restful waters, guided safely through the dark valley, anointed with fragrant oil, and given an overflowing banquet in this Eucharist, may respond with trust, obedience, and thanksgiving to the care of our God

For the lost sheep; those who have wandered far away from the life giving waters of the holy sacraments, that our prayers and our love and the gentle inspirations of the Holy Spirit may bring them back

For all who need our intercession: the sick, the poor, the hungry, the grieving, the most forgotten little ones in our midst, that Jesus may call them apart to rest for awhile at the feast of His loving compassion

That Jesus may be the peace of our faithful departed ones, breaking down every barrier of sin in His precious Blood, and leading them into the everlasting pastures of heavenly bliss

### 17th Sunday in Ordinary Time

*2 Kgs 4:42-44, Ps 145, Eph 4:1-6,*
*John 6:1-15*

For unity among the followers of Jesus Christ: that there may be one Lord, one faith, one Baptism, one Spirit bringing every soul into obedience to the truth in one church

That Jesus may be king of all nations, leading those who have resources to share with those who have nothing to eat

That we may live in a manner worthy of the divine call we have received; in humility, gentleness, patience, forgiveness, and love

That we may be generous in offering our loaves and fishes to Jesus for the common good, trusting Him to multiply our gifts for the satisfaction of all

For those whose eyes look hopefully to God in a time of sickness, poverty, grief, addiction, imprisonment or abuse, that He may open His hand and satisfy their desire for good things

For our faithful departed, that through our prayers and this Holy Sacrifice they may be seated at the feast on God's holy mountain in heaven

## 18th Sunday in Ordinary Time

*Exod 16:2-4, 12-15, Ps 78, Eph 4:17, 20-24, John 6:24-35*

For our priests, who bring down upon our altars the living presence of Jesus in the Holy Eucharist, that this divine bread may be their joy and their strength

For the thousands of innocent children who die every day from starvation, that we may come to their aid as God responded to the needs of the Israelites of old

For all who are enslaved to their illusions of happiness and the strong desire to grasp these illusions, that the process of corruption may be broken by the in-breaking of God's truth and freedom

That our eucharistic Christ, who found only disbelief and contentious demands when He spoke of Himself as the Bread of Life, may find in us adoring faith, humble gratitude, and reverent love

For all who are heavily burdened, that they may find their barren desert laden with divine dew, producing the nourishment they need, one day at a time

For our faithful departed who ate the Bread of Life on earth, that this divine life may be their joy in heaven

## 19th Sunday in Ordinary Time

*1 Kgs 19, Ps 34, Eph 4:30–5:2, John 6:41-51*

That the church may be a sacrificial offering to God, a fragrant aroma, by her imitation of God and her life of love

That those who are taught by God, who have listened and learned from the Father, may be bold in their work for life, for moral integrity, for justice, and for peace

For all of us, who are traveling the arduous path that leads to the mountain of God, that like Elijah we may gratefully eat the divine bread as strength for the journey

That none of us may grieve the Holy Spirit within us, but please God by our kindness, compassion, and mutual forgiveness

For all who are afflicted and distressed, who are sick and in grief, that the Lord may make them radiant with joy, and that His holy angel may encamp about them and deliver them

That Jesus, who promised that whoever eats the living bread from heaven will live forever, may raise up our faithful departed to the joys of His kingdom

## 20th Sunday in Ordinary Time

*Prov 9:1-6, Ps 34, Eph 5:15-20,
John 6:51-58*

For our leaders and teachers in the church, that they may live always in the house of wisdom, advancing in the way of understanding

That statesmen and people of influence in the world may live as the wise do, making the most of every opportunity to do good and trying to understand the will of the Lord

That we may be filled with the Spirit, singing to the Lord in our hearts, giving thanks always in the name of our Lord Jesus Christ

That Jesus, Who has given us His Flesh for food and His Blood for drink, may find us approaching Him with clean hearts, humble and thankful for such a divine gift

For all who are in distress; the sick, the poor, the grieving, the imprisoned and addicted, that they may seek the Lord and find that He is good, making them radiant with joy

For our faithful departed ones, that Jesus, who has life because of the Father, may give them new life forever in His Father's kingdom

## 21st Sunday in Ordinary Time

*Josh 24, Ps 34, Eph 5:21-32, John 6:60-69*

For the church, the spouse of Christ, that she might be cleansed and presented to Jesus without spot or wrinkle, holy and without blemish

That the Lord may raise up in our own day leaders of nations who will determine in their hearts to serve Him, working for life, for morality, for justice, and for peace

For Christian families, that the father and mother may love and respect one another, and bring up their children in holiness, creating the seedbed of religious vocations and new priests for the church

That with Peter we may say to Jesus, "You have the words of eternal life....You are the Holy One of God", and stay with Him even when others walk away

For all who are brokenhearted and crushed in spirit, that the Lord may rescue them from all their distress and deliver them from all their fear

That the Lord, who is Spirit and life, may raise up our faithful departed to the bliss of heavenly glory

## 22nd Sunday in Ordinary Time

*Deut 4:1-2,6-8, Ps 15, Jas 1:17-18, 21b-22, 27, Mark 7:1-8, 14-15, 21-23*

For the church, that we may be a people that not only honors God with our lips, but also with our hearts, keeping His commandments faithfully

That our nation may give evidence of its wisdom and intelligence by keeping close to God and to the Christian principles on which we were founded

That we may humbly welcome the word of God with its power to save our souls, and become doers of the word in our lives

For all who are defiled by the evil that comes from within, for the conversion of those who have wandered far from God and from His church, especially our own loved ones

For orphans and widows, for all who are in a time of affliction or sickness, for the imprisoned and the grieving, for all who have asked for our prayers

For our faithful departed, that the Father of lights, from whom all good giving and every perfect gift descends, may welcome them into His kingdom of light and peace

## 23rd Sunday in Ordinary Time

*Isa 35:4-7, Ps 146, Jas 2:1-5, Mark 7:31-37*

For our shepherds in the church, that their efforts in the demanding work of preaching may be united with those of Jesus, who also struggled at times to open the ears of the deaf to His Good News

For peace, that with the Lord we may sustain the fatherless and the widow, set the captives free, give food to the hungry and stand fast for justice for all who are oppressed

For the poor, chosen by God to be rich in faith and honored heirs of the kingdom, that we may show them in faith the respect that is their due

That Jesus, who takes each of us away from the crowd by ourselves when He comes to us in the hidden intimacy of His Holy Eucharist, may open our ears to His truth and give us voice to praise and love Him

For all those whose hearts are frightened, who are blind or deaf or lame in body or soul, that God may come with divine recompense to save them, making streams of joy burst out in their lives again

For our faithful departed ones, that through the merits of Jesus their souls may be cleansed for entrance into the blissful kingdom of heaven

### 24th Sunday in Ordinary Time

*Isa 50:5-9a, Ps 116, Jas 2:14-18,*
*Mark 8:27-35*

For our holy shepherds, that they may be the first to acknowledge Jesus as the Christ and His way of the cross as the road for all His followers

For all in a position of power and influence, that they may be concerned in an effective way for the life and dignity of each human being under their care

That we may learn to think as God does, following the example of Jesus, willing to lose our lives for Him and for the Gospel, in order to receive life in abundance from the Father's hands

For the gift of faith that expresses itself in good works, that the poor, the sick, the imprisoned and the grieving may be relieved through our loving deeds

For the prophets who must undergo persecution in order to remain faithful to the truth that God has shown them, that they may know that the Lord God is their help and upholds their right

For our faithful departed, that God may free their souls from death, and that they may walk in joy before the Lord in the land of the living

### 25th Sunday in Ordinary Time

*Wis 2:12, 17-20, Ps 54, Jas 3:16–4:3,*
*Mark 9:30-37*

That those who wish to be first in the church may begin from a position of servanthood, setting out to inspire and empower others in the humble following of Jesus

That people of our day may come to see clearly that wars and conflicts begin with their own unruly passions, and work instead to sow the fruit of righteousness and to cultivate peace

For the just ones who are being tested under the persecution of those who hate them for their goodness, that they may remain strong and faithful, knowing that God will vindicate them

For the gift of wisdom from above, so that we may be pure, gentle, and full of mercy and good fruits in the sight of our heavenly Father

For those who feel like they are the last of all: the sick and the poor, the imprisoned and the grieving, that we may receive and care for them as if they were Jesus Himself given into our hands

That Jesus, who accepted His death as the path to resurrection, may raise up our faithful departed ones to share His joy and glory in heaven

## 26th Sunday in Ordinary Time

*Num 11:25-29, Ps 19, Jas 5:1-6,*
*Mark 9:38-43, 45, 47-48*

For our elders in the church, those who preach in God's name, that the spirit of the Lord may come to rest on them, giving their words prophetic power

That among the wealthy and the powerful there may be those who are not against Jesus and His law of love, that justice may again flower upon the earth

That we may understand how serious are the consequences of our actions in time and in eternity, and cut out of our lives whatever causes us to sin

For our children, the little ones who believe in Jesus, that they may be protected from all that could lead them into temptation, so as to grow in their love for the Lord

For all who are counting on our loving intercession, who are passing through a season of illness, poverty, or emotional pain, that Jesus may reach out to them in healing and strength

For our faithful departed, that they may not lose their reward, but be safe from Gehenna and welcomed into heaven

## 27th Sunday in Ordinary Time

*Gen 2:18-24, Ps 128, Heb 2:9-11,*
*Mark 10:2-16*

For the preachers and teachers of the church, that they may have the courage to uphold the dignity of marriage between a man and a woman in a world filled with contrary currents of thought

That God may raise up world leaders after His own heart, who will uphold the sanctity of life, the morality of love, and the justice that leads to peace

For the children, loved and blessed by Jesus, that we may protect their innocence and imitate their simple way of accepting Jesus and His kingdom

For those who have endured the tragedy of divorce, for broken families, for single parent homes, for all domestic situations that need our prayers

For all those who are being made perfect through suffering, that as they share the cross of Jesus they may also be anointed with His joy and grace

That Jesus, who died to bring many children to glory, may deliver our faithful departed ones from all their sins and bring them into the light and peace of heaven

## 28th Sunday in Ordinary Time

*Wis 7:7-11, Ps 90, Heb 4:12-13,
Mark 10:17-30*

For the church, that the Word of God may be living and effective in her, discerning the reflections and thoughts of each of our hearts

That the spirit of wisdom may come upon world leaders to guide them in the difficult decisions they must make, and that they may prefer her to riches and power

For those who search for Jesus but whose souls are burdened with possessions, that His look of love and His wise demands may break the bonds of their attachments

For vocations; that many young people may discover within themselves the God-given strength to leave family and all human gain for the sake of Jesus and His holy Gospel

For all who have asked for our prayers in a time of sickness, unemployment, or grief, that God for whom all things are possible may heal and help them

For our faithful departed, who have come before the One to whom we all must render an account, that the Word of God may find them true and purify them quickly for the joys of heaven

## 29th Sunday in Ordinary Time

*Isa 53:10-11, Ps 33, Heb 4:14-16,
Mark 10:35-45*

For the priests of the church, especially those who feel the weight of their weakness, that Jesus, our compassionate high priest, may give them mercy and grace in their hour of need

For peace in our hearts and in the world, that our leaders may make their authority felt only in the service they provide with respect and justice

That Jesus, who redeemed us by suffering and bore our guilt, may call back to the sacraments of His mercy those who have abandoned their faith, especially those dear to us

For all of us sharing in this Eucharist, standing by the cross through which Jesus justified us, that we may receive Him humbly, ready to serve at His side

That the Lord may let His mercy be upon all who are drinking of His painful chalice, that their sufferings may be lightened and sweetened by the divine companion of their darkest days

That the kindness of the Lord may be upon our faithful departed ones who have put their trust in Him, bringing them into the joy of His kingdom

## 30th Sunday in Ordinary Time

*Jer 31:7-9, Ps 126, Heb 5:1-6,*
*Mark 10:46-52*

For our shepherds in the church, that they may deal patiently with the ignorant and the erring as they come to recognize their own weakness

That the Lord who brings back the captives and does great things for the lowly, may move the hearts of the powerful to compassion and guide them in the ways of justice and peace

That the prayer of Bartimaeus may become our own, and we may know how to cry out our need for Jesus with courage and insistence

For all of us gathered at this Eucharist, coming to Jesus because He has called us in His merciful love, that our faith may enable Him to open our eyes so that we, too, may follow Him on the way

For those who are journeying in tears: the blind and the lame, the sick and the grieving, the poor and the exiled, that the Lord may console and guide them, leading them to a level road of healing and joy

For all our faithful departed ones, that Jesus, the great High Priest, may offer on their behalf all the riches of His perfect sacrifice, and bring them rejoicing to the heavenly feast

## 31st Sunday in Ordinary Time

*Deut 6:2-6, Ps 18, Heb 7:23-28,*
*Mark 12:28b-34*

For our bishops and priests, men subject to weakness and yet called by God to share in the ministry of His Christ, that they may be upheld and protected from all evil

That nations may grow and prosper the more by keeping the commandments of the Lord which He has implanted in every heart

That we may offer a pleasing sacrifice in God's sight by our faithful observance of His law of love, giving Him our hearts, our understanding, and our strength and serving each other in His name

For our young people and our children, that through the leadership of good teachers and the grace of a solid family life, they may learn to live with understanding and hope

That those who feel their weight of sorrow or sickness may place all their confidence in Jesus, who is holy, innocent, undefiled, and always able to save those who approach God through Him

That Jesus, made perfect forever through His death and resurrection, may perfect our faithful departed and make them worthy of the heavenly kingdom

## 32nd Sunday in Ordinary Time

*1 Kgs 17:10-16, Ps 146, Heb 9:24-28, Mark 12:38-44*

That the church may always have great respect for the poorest and weakest in her midst, who are often the most generous in the sight of God

That with the Lord we may seek to secure justice for the oppressed, give food to the hungry, set captives free, and raise up all who are bowed down

That we may not hesitate to give to God and to His people, even when we feel like we have nothing left, thus earning the approval of our Savior

For the grace of strong Catholic families, and that parents may be generous with God when He asks for their children to consecrate themselves to the spread of the Gospel

That God may multiply the resources of those who are sick, lonely, and poor, of the aged and grieving, of all who are little and weak, as He did for the widow of Zarephath

For those who have died and have gone through their judgment, that the perfect sacrifice of this Holy Mass may follow them before God's throne, obtaining mercy and peace

## 33rd Sunday in Ordinary Time

*Dan 12:1-3, Ps 16, Heb 10:11-14, 18, Mark 13:24-32*

For our ministers and priests in the church, that they may be among the wise who shine brightly, leading the many to justice

That world leaders may be assisted by the guardian angels of their nations to promote the true justice that leads to peace

That we may live our lives in this passing world with our hearts set on the world to come, so that we may be among the elect gathered on the last day into the everlasting kingdom of Jesus Christ

For all of us sharing this Eucharist, the one offering which makes perfect forever those who are being consecrated, that we may unite ourselves to our great High Priest in thought, words, and actions this day

For all who are in a season of suffering and weakness at this time, that the Lord may be their allotted portion and their cup, raising them to joy and gladness of heart

For our faithful departed, that St. Michael may lead them into the eternal kingdom, and that Jesus may grant them the fullness of joys in His presence

### 34th Sunday in Ordinary Time, Christ the King

*Dan 7:13-14, Ps 93, Rev 1:5-8, John 18:33-37*

For the church, the kingdom created by Jesus and the people who are made priests for His God and Father, that we may offer ourselves with Him as an acceptable sacrifice

For all peoples, nations, and languages, that they may come to acknowledge the dominion of Jesus Christ, whose kingship is everlasting

That we may belong to the truth, hearing the voice of Jesus in obedience and following Him in freedom and love

That the Lord, who has freed us from our sins by His blood, may bring all His baptized people to repentance and reconciliation in the sacrament of penance, the fountain of joy and peace

That all who labor under a burden of suffering or grief may have the grace to carry their cross bravely in the footsteps of the King of Kings, and know His intimate consolation

That Jesus, whose kingdom does not belong to this world, may bring all whom He has called through the gates of death into the heavenly glory where He is truly King forever

## SOLEMNITIES OF THE LORD DURING ORDINARY TIME

### Holy Trinity

*Deut 4:32-40, Ps 33, Rom 8:14-17, Mt 28:16-20*

For our holy shepherds in the church, who continue the mission of baptizing all nations in the name of the Father, the Son, and the Holy Spirit, that they may know from personal experience that Jesus is with them always

For national leaders, that in their labors for the common good they may keep God's statutes and commandments, so that each nation may prosper in peace

For graduates, for newlyweds, for all men and women marking important transitions in their lives, that they may be supported by the loving divine energy that guides them in the ways of faithfulness and truth

That the Holy Spirit of adoption may give us the confidence to call on God as "Abba", taking hold of our inheritance as beloved children of the Most High

For the sick, the imprisoned, those who feel isolated from God, that we who are led by the Spirit of God may reach out to them and draw them into the divine communion of grace

For our faithful departed ones, that they may be in the heart and love of the blessed Trinity

## Corpus Christi

*Exod 24:3-8, Ps 116, Heb 9:11-15,*
*Mark 14:12-16, 22-26*

For the whole church, celebrating today
the solemnity of Christ's Body and Blood,
that our joy and thanksgiving may glorify
Him for His surpassing love

That those who are sealed with the blood
of the covenant God makes in accordance
with all His commands, may be the first to
stand up for life, for justice, and for moral
integrity in our world

For our priests, ministers of Christ's new
covenant which contains the promise of
everlasting life, that they may be holy and
reverent in their priestly service

For a return to the sacrament of
reconciliation; that God's people may
approach Holy Communion free of sin
and prepared for the divine intimacy of
immediate contact with the living Christ

For the sick, the anxious, the oppressed,
and all who have asked for our prayers,
that healing and grace may radiate from
the tabernacle into the lives of each one

For our faithful departed, whose death
was precious in the eyes of the Lord, that
through the offering of this Holy Sacrifice,
they may now be fully alive in His presence

## Sacred Heart

*Hos 11:1, 3-4, 8-9, Isa 12, Eph 3:8-12,*
*14-19, John 19, 31-37*

That the shepherds of our holy church
may be graced with gifts in keeping with
the riches of God's glory, so that they may
preach the unfathomable riches of Christ
with conviction and authority

That we may draw near in confidence to
God, imploring the gift of a return to the
culture of life for all the nations of the
world, and for that justice which brings
peace

That Jesus, who has drawn us with human
cords, with bonds of love, to His divine
heart, may have the joy of our ready and
willing response

For all who have asked our prayers when
they feel helpless before the trials of this
life, that the breadth and height and depth
of God's love may be revealed to them for
their comfort and joy

For vocations, that the loving Heart of our
Savior may conquer many hearts to the
point of total consecration and service in
His church

That our departed loved ones, who received
in the Eucharist the Blood that flowed from
the heart of Jesus, may now be purified in
that Blood and made ready for heaven's
wedding feast

# PROPER OF TIME

## SUNDAYS, SOLEMNITIES, FEASTS
# YEAR C

## SEASON OF ADVENT

### 1st Sunday of Advent

*Jer 33:14-16, Ps 25, 1 Thess 3:12–4:2,*
*Luke 21:25-28*

For our holy shepherds in the church, that they may be untiring in showing us how we should conduct ourselves in order to please God

That the Lord may raise up in our own days world leaders who will do what is right and just in the land, so that we may dwell in safety and security

That the Lord who is good and upright may show sinners the way back to Him, giving them the grace to approach the sacrament of penance for peace and reconciliation

For the vigilance and strength we need to stand before the Son of Man, never becoming drowsy with the anxieties of daily life, but ready to welcome Him with joy

That the paths of the Lord may be kindness and constancy for those who are experiencing tribulation, illness, abandonment, loneliness, or grief

That our faithful departed may be made blameless in holiness before our God and Father, ready for the kingdom of our Lord Jesus Christ

### 2nd Sunday of Advent

*Bar 5:1-9, Ps 126, Phil 1:4-6, 8-11,*
*Luke 3:1-6*

For the church, the New Jerusalem, that she may be named by God the peace of justice and the glory of God's kingdom, filled with her children returning from the east and from the west

That God may lead the nations by the light of His holy laws planted in every heart, with His mercy and justice for company

That our love may increase more and more, that we may be pure and blameless for the day of Christ, knowing what is of value, and filled with the fruit of righteousness

That the voice of John the Baptist may re-echo in the desert of our secular society, helping us to prepare the way of the Lord and to make straight His paths in our lives

For all those whose road is toilsome through illness, poverty, loneliness, or grief, that God may fill up the valleys of sorrow and lower the mountains of obstacles, showing those who toil His loving salvation

That God, who began a good work in the souls of our faithful departed may continue to complete it until they are fully ready for heavenly life in Christ Jesus

## 3rd Sunday of Advent

*Zeph 3:14-18, Isa 12:2-6, Phil 4:4-7,*
*Luke 3:10-18*

For the whole church, that we will let God sing His song of love over us today, harmonizing with Him in our own joy of heart, refusing to let any discordant notes into the beautiful music of redemption

That the joy of expected salvation may enable the rich and powerful to repent, sharing their food and clothing with the poor, abandoning oppression and indifference

That like John the Baptist we may humbly and fearlessly proclaim the majesty of our Savior by the witness of our lives, letting our kindness be known to all

For the grace to banish all anxiety from our hearts as we bring our intentions to the One who is coming to meet us, honoring Him with our thanksgiving and accepting His gracious gift of peace

For all who are discouraged, hungry, lonely, homeless, sick, or grieving, that on their behalf we may make our requests known to God, with thanksgiving for His sure and merciful response

For our faithful departed ones, that they may draw water with joy at the fountain of salvation as God removes every judgment against them and welcomes them into His kingdom of joy

## 4th Sunday of Advent

*Mic 5:1-4, Ps 80, Heb 10:5-10,*
*Luke 1:39-45*

For our shepherds in the church, that in the power of Jesus they may stand firm and shepherd His flock in the majestic name of God

That God may give new life to the nations, that they may call upon His name and He may rouse His power to save them from all evil

That with Jesus we may offer the Father a ready and obedient will, making with Him a new covenant of holiness and peace

That the blessing of those who believe may be ours as it was Mary's, and that we may join her in bringing a blessing to all those whom we encounter and serve

For all who suffer and who are losing hope, that the Expectant Virgin may visit each one, stirring up in them the gift of the Holy Spirit

For our faithful departed ones, that the new covenant consecrated in the body of Jesus Christ may open for them the joys of His heavenly kingdom

## SEASON OF CHRISTMAS

### Nativity of the Lord, at the Vigil

*Isa 62:1-5, Ps 89, Acts 13:16-17, 22-25,*
*Matt 1:18-25*

For the church, God's chosen people, His virgin bride, that her rejoicing may be in her bridegroom, who took flesh in Jesus and came to dwell among us

That God's covenant of love may stand firm with all nations as they again seek to know His justice, obey His laws, and experience His peace

That we may imitate St. Joseph's faith and obedience, as He quietly left behind His own doubts and took Mary into His home, giving Jesus His name and the shelter of protecting love

That we may greet the birth of our divine Savior with the humility of John the Baptist, and herald His new coming into our lives with reverent joy

For those who are forsaken and desolate, that they may be called by a new name, and become a glorious crown in the hand of the Lord as He fills them with His joy

For all who have completed their course, who have passed beyond the gates of death, that they may be celebrating this Christmas in the exultation of the heavenly kingdom

### Nativity of the Lord, Mass at Midnight

*Isa 9:1-6, Ps 96, Titus 2:11-14,*
*Luke 2:1-14*

For the whole church, celebrating the birth of Jesus with abundant love and great rejoicing, that all darkness may be illuminated by the great light she now presents to the world

For peace, that in the mastery of the child that is born to us, every unjust yoke may be smashed, every tool of war destroyed, and the deliberations of world leaders be ruled by the Prince of Peace

For the grace of hospitality, that we may see Jesus in the least of His brothers and sisters, and especially that no expectant mother be refused the comfort and shelter she needs to bear her child

That Mary, our mother, may show her Divine Child to everyone that comes in wonder to the manger, and lay Him to rest in our hearts as we approach this Eucharist

For those who keep a lonely watch in the night, those who have no one to care for them, that with the shepherds they may also know of angels who will bring them tidings of great joy in the name of Jesus

For our dear ones who have died, that they may see the final appearance of their blessed hope, the glory of the great God and of Jesus our Savior, in the clear light of heaven

## Christmas Mass at Dawn

*Isa 62:11-12, Ps 97, Titus 3:4-7,*
*Luke 2:15-20*

For the shepherds of the church, our bishops and priests, that as they lead us today in glorifying and praising God for the birth of the Savior, they themselves may be renewed in His joy

For the governments and leaders of the world, that the message of the angels may be realized in every effort they make to avoid armed conflict and promote peace

For all who are in pain in body, mind, emotions, or spirit, that this holy day may be a blessing of peace and light on their journey

That Jesus, who in His birth as one of us has made every human joy His own, may be at the heart of our family festivities, our gift giving, and every lovely custom we keep in His honor

That Mary, our Mother, may show her divine child to every wondering heart that approaches the manger, and lay Him to rest in each of us as we approach this Eucharist

For our beloved dead, that they may be celebrating this Christmas amid the joys and splendors of heaven

## Nativity of the Lord, Mass during the day

*Isa 52:7-10, Ps 98, Heb 1:1-6,*
*John 1:1-18*

For the church on this great feast of Christmas, that her whole soul may be consumed in praise as she sings to the Lord with melodious song for His great mercy in giving us our Savior

That God may be king among the nations, so that the feet of those who bring glad tidings may be beautiful upon the mountains as they bear good news and announce peace

That as the Lord comforts His people and redeems Jerusalem, we too may bring comfort and joy in the name of Jesus to all those whose lives we touch

That with the angels of God we may gladly worship the firstborn Son who has come into the world, and spread the good news of His redemption

For all who are still in the darkness of loneliness, depression, illness, or grief, that the great light who is Jesus may enlighten them and they may know the joy of our love in His name

For our dear ones who have died, that they may be soon brought into heaven, where Jesus has His seat at the right hand of the Majesty on high

## Holy Family

*general intentions*

For our Holy Father, head of the family that is the Body of Christ, that He may be held in honor within the church

For peace in our families, forgiveness of grievances, harmony of roles, and that our children may be safe and loved within the home, so that our nation and every nation may be built up in peace

That our families may be protected from the special dangers of our age: from abortion and euthanasia, from the inroads of materialism and violence; that faith and prayer and mutual love may keep them together in the Lord

For families in exile, for families that have lost their children, for families of the unemployed and the poor, that the Holy Family, which experienced all these situations, may be their comfort and hope

For the gift of vocations, that the Christian life of our families may flower in young lives consecrated to the Lord, whose ministry will serve in turn to strengthen the families of the future

For our loved ones who have died, for our elders who have gone before us, that they may rest in peace and help their beloved families with their prayers

## Blessed Virgin Mary, the Mother of God

*Num 6:22-27, Ps 67, Gal 4:4-7, Luke 2:16-21*

For the whole church, that God's wisdom may strike root among us in the person of Jesus, making us a glorious people, the portion of the Lord, and the company of His holy ones

That God, who sends forth His command to the earth, may enable world leaders to keep His word, so that He may grant peace in our borders

For all of us as we celebrate this Christmas season, that the eyes of our hearts may be enlightened, and we may know what is the hope that belongs to our call in Christ Jesus

That the Word who was made flesh may give all those who believe in His name power to become children of God, shedding His light in the world by their lives of faith and good works

For all who are abandoned and forgotten in their need and suffering, that our prayer and our love may encircle them with joy and new beginnings of life

For our faithful departed ones, that God may bless them in Christ with every spiritual blessing in His heavenly home, giving them eternal rest and peace

## Second Sunday after Christmas

*Sir 24:1-2, 8-12, Ps 147, Eph 1:3-6, 15-18, John 1:1-18*

For the whole church, that God's wisdom may strike root among us in the person of Jesus, making us a glorious people, the portion of the Lord, and the company of His holy ones

That God, who sends forth His command to the earth, may enable world leaders to keep His word, so that He may grant peace in our borders

For all of us as we celebrate this Christmas season, that the eyes of our hearts may be enlightened, and we may know what is the hope that belongs to our call in Christ Jesus

That the Word who was made flesh may give all those who believe in His name power to become children of God, shedding His light in the world by their lives of faith and good works

For all who are abandoned and forgotten in their need and suffering, that our prayer and our love may encircle them with joy and new beginnings of life

For our faithful departed ones, that God may bless them in Christ with every spiritual blessing in His heavenly home, giving them eternal rest and peace

## The Epiphany of the Lord, Vigil

*general intentions*

For our leaders and teachers in the church, that they may be the first to worship at the manger and present their gifts of mind and heart to the Lord

That the Christmas grace of peace may radiate out into the whole world, exercising its gentle influence on the hearts of world leaders and turning their thoughts to the poor and the lowly

For all of us, represented by the foreigners who brought their adoration and their gifts to Jesus, that we may do all we can to spread the Good News and bring the whole world to His manger

That the faith and persevering search of the magi may inspire us during the dark times of our journey, when only the light of a great star leads us on through the night

For all who are suffering and poor and abandoned during this joyful season, that in memory of the Holy Family sheltered in a stable, we may reach out to them in love

For our loved ones who have gone before us marked with the sign of faith, that they may now see their Savior, unveiled in all His glory in heaven

## Epiphany

*Isa 60:1-6, Ps 72, Eph 3:2-3, 5-6,*
*Matt 2:1-12*

For the church, gathered as never before from all nations, that her holiness may shine out as a guiding star to bring to Jesus those who are still in the great darkness

For world leaders, that God may endow them with His judgment, so that they may govern His afflicted ones with justice and respect for the human dignity of each person

That wise men of every country and every religious background may come to understand the truth that Jesus alone is God made flesh and the Savior of the world, and place their gifts gratefully at His feet

That we who live in power and safety like Jerusalem of old may not miss the star rising over our heads, leading those with eyes to see down to humble Bethlehem with its hidden King

For all who travel a dark path through sickness, poverty, oppression, and every form of misery, that they may be overjoyed to find a star of guidance leading them to the mercy of the Lord

For our beloved departed ones, that they may come to rest in the radiant presence of the Savior whom they sought in the shadows of this passing world

## Baptism of the Lord

*Isa 40:1-5, 9-11, Ps 104, Titus 2:11-14,*
*3:4-7, Luke 3:15-16*

For the ministers of the church, that they may continue to train us to reject godless ways and worldly desires, and to live justly and devoutly in this age as we await the appearance of Jesus

That the Lord God may rule with His strong arm over all the counsels and deliberations of the nations, guiding them into decisions for life, justice, and morality

That we who have been saved by the bath of rebirth and renewal by the Holy Spirit may accept the fullness of our mission upon the earth, even as Jesus did after His baptism

For all who have not been baptized, who have never heard of the name of Jesus or the kindness and generous love of the Father, that new missionaries may be raised up to bring the Good News to them

For all who are struggling through a rugged land and rough country on their journey through life, that the glory of the Lord may be revealed to them in mercy, healing, and grace

For our faithful departed ones, who became justified by grace and were made heirs in hope of eternal life by their baptism, that they may now enjoy that life forever

## SEASON OF LENT

### 1st Sunday of Lent

*Deut 26:4-10, Ps 91, Rom 10:8-13,
Luke 4:1-13*

For our holy priests, who receive the offerings of God's people and set them upon the altar, that their words and example may support the worship and faith of all

That all worship of the Evil One may cease in the world, that there will be no more human sacrifices to power and pleasure, and that instead we will return with our whole hearts to the service of God and a culture of life

That we may never put the Lord our God to the test, but with Jesus give Him our humble adoration and resist all temptation with the help of His loving power

That we who dwell in the shelter of the Most High and abide in the shadow of the Almighty, may keep this holy season of Lent as a time of prayer and penance, pleasing in His sight

For those who are afflicted, sick, or poor, that God may be their refuge and fortress, giving His angels command to guide and heal and deliver them

For our faithful departed, who confessed that Jesus is Lord and believed that God raised Him from the dead, that God may now raise them up with Jesus to the life of heavenly joy

### 2nd Sunday in Lent

*Gen 15:5-12, Ps 27, Phil 3:17–4:1,
Luke 9:28-36*

For our leaders in the church, that they may set such an example of fidelity to the cross of Christ that they will be able with St. Paul to ask others to imitate them

For the rulers of the nations, that they may be stouthearted in their reliance on the Lord and allow Him to be the light that guides their deliberations

That we who enter the cloud of the Father's presence as we participate in this Eucharist may listen to His beloved Son with all the reverence and obedience we can possibly bring to this divine encounter

For all those who, like Abraham, have only God's promises on which to rely, that they may honor God with their faith, even during their fearful vigils in the darkness, and thus deserve the covenant of His blessing

For our faithful departed ones, that Jesus Christ may show Himself to them as their Savior and that their citizenship may now be in heaven

### 3rd Sunday of Lent

*Exod 3, Ps 103, 1 Cor 10, Luke 13:1-9*

For the church and her holy leaders, that like Moses they may be faithful in their mission to lead us into the Promised Land in the name of the God of Abraham and Sarah, Isaac, and Jacob

That world leaders, especially leaders of Christian nations, may act with moral integrity before God in all their decisions, obedient to the Lord who secures justice and defends the rights of all the oppressed

For all the members of the church, who are exposed, Lent after Lent, to God's insistent call to conversion, and who experience the patient cultivation of the redeeming Christ, that each one may begin to bring forth the fruit Christ rightly expects

For all of us who approach the Eucharist today, that we may do so reverently as on holy ground, conscious that this Holy Bread conceals the One who once flamed out of the burning bush

For all who are suffering or anxious, sick or grieving, that they may be comforted by the Lord who heals all our ills and abounds in kindness and compassion

For our faithful departed ones, that God may redeem them from destruction and crown them with mercy and love in heaven

### 4th Sunday of Lent

*Josh 5:9-12, Ps 34, 2 Cor 5:17-21,
Luke 15:1-3, 11-32*

For the ambassadors of Christ— our Holy Father, our bishops and priests— that there may be a special blessing on their ministries of reconciliation and forgiveness

That the old order of violence, injustice, and exploitation in the world may pass away, and God may create something new upon the earth in a culture of life, peace, and love

That God, the generous and forgiving Father of all His prodigal children and also of His intolerant children, may give us hope in His mercy and grace to rejoice in the return of the sinner to His love

For all who have squandered their inheritance on a life of dissipation, that the prayers of their brothers and sisters may bring them back to the arms of the Father in the sacrament of reconciliation

For the poor ones who are in great distress: those who are sick, hungry, homeless, and in grief, that the Lord may hear their call for help, and give them cause to be radiant with joy

For our faithful departed ones, who once fed on the manna of the Eucharist with us, that they may now be feasting their eyes on the face of God in the Promised Land of heaven

## 5th Sunday of Lent

*Isa 43:16-21, Ps 126, Phil 3:8-14,*
*John 8:1-11*

For the church, that as she brings her catechumens to the moment of spiritual birth at Easter, she may be filled with praise of God who is always causing something new to spring forth in her midst

For the poor and oppressed of the earth, that God may restore their fortunes, and make what they sow in tears come to a harvest of rejoicing

For our young people, that by God's grace they may come to rate everything as loss so that they may gain Jesus and be found in Him

For all who have become aware of their sin in this Lenten season, that in the sacrament of reconciliation they may be released from their inner accusers by the Lord's compassionate and respectful forgiveness

For all who are suffering in mind, heart, and spirit, and for all who have asked for our prayers, that God may create a way through their desert and lead them to the waters of His consolation and grace

For our faithful departed who have finished their race on this earth, that as they shared Christ's sufferings they may now attain to the resurrection in God's glorious kingdom

# HOLY WEEK

## Palm Sunday

*general intentions*

For the whole church, uniting with one heart and voice to escort our Savior with palms and praises to the Holy City as He enters to meet His painful destiny, that we may follow Him faithfully to the end

For individuals, groups, and nations who, like Jesus, have been cruelly betrayed by a false gesture of peace, that the greedy betrayers may come to repentance and that true peace be restored through the Master's redemption

For all who bear the role of prophet in the church, that with the Master they may have a well trained ear and words that can rouse the weary, and never turn back in the face of persecution

That we may allow grace to bring us with Jesus to the loving obedience that empties us out into our own inevitable cross at His side, so that with Him we too may be raised on high by the Father

For the courage to look long and steadily at our crucified God, who is speaking His whole word of redeeming solidarity and humble divine love in the pain-filled silence of His cross

For all the intentions we bring in our hearts to this Holy Sacrifice, for all who have asked for our prayers, and for our beloved departed ones who have passed through the doors of death with Jesus

## Holy Thursday

*Exod 12:1-8, 11-14, Ps 116, 1 Cor 11:23-26, John 13:1-15*

For our Holy Father, our bishops and priests, whose ordination was instituted at the Last Supper, that their consecrated lives of priestly service may continue to flow from the Eucharist, which they offer in the person of Christ

For peace, that the blood of the divine Lamb may keep the destructive blow of war and oppression from us, and that each of us may partake of the Lamb with staff in hand, ready for the journey that justice will demand of us

For all of us in every capacity of loving service that we give to each other, that our Lord's humility and self-emptying, symbolized in the foot washing, may continue in our mutual reverence and devotion

For our loved ones who are far from the sacraments, for the sick and addicted, the imprisoned and abused, the lonely and the poor, that this night of love and suffering may draw them into communion with Jesus who has the remedy for their wounds

For all of us who share this Eucharist, remembering most vividly that hour when Jesus showed us the very depths of His love, that we might express our gratitude to Him by being faithful in all that He asks of us

For our faithful departed loved ones, who ate the Divine Bread and drank the Holy Cup and proclaimed the death of the Lord while on earth, that they may now share His victory over death in heaven

## Good, Friday

*Solemn Intercessions Only*

*see general intentions in* The Roman Missal, Third Edition

# SEASON OF EASTER

## Paschal Vigil

*general intentions*

For the whole Church on this night of the Lord's triumph, that the resurrection fire kindled this night might spread through the darkness of an unbelieving world with irresistible power

That God, who created the order and harmony of the earth out of a formless void may in the renewal of this paschal mystery bring peace out of selfish power struggles and restore reverence for every human being made in His image and likeness

That broken relationships in marriage and friendship may be exposed to God's example of total fidelity and generous forgiveness, and built up again in the precious stones of His grace and peace

For all who are still in the darkness of ignorance, sin, addiction, and unresolved pain, that the Risen One, who calls the light and it obeys Him, may make them shine for joy in His presence with all His holy ones

For all who are reborn tonight and for all of us consecrated to Jesus, washed in the living water from His pierced side, that we may all truly die to sin in Him, trusting also that we will share His triumph

That Jesus, who is our paschal sacrifice, the Lamb upon our altar, may in this Eucharist create in each of us a new heart and a new spirit, perfectly attuned to His own heart, which ever rises to the Father, both in suffering and in glory

## Easter Sunday

*Acts 10:37-43, Ps 118, Col 3:1-4, John 20:1-9*

For the successors to the apostles in the church today, commissioned to preach to the people, that like Peter, they may boldly proclaim the resurrection of Christ and the forgiveness of sins in His name

That Jesus, the great cornerstone, may not be rejected by the builders of our society, but that the right hand of the Lord may be exalted in Him, building nations with life, justice, morality, and peace

For all of us, that our life may be hidden with Christ in God, and that we may seek what is above, celebrating this feast with the unleavened bread of sincerity and truth

That all Christians may offer to the Paschal Victim their thankful praises today, renewing their vows to Him with joy and gratitude for His victory of divine love

For all who suffer, who grieve, who are distressed in mind and heart, that Jesus, who brought unexpected exultation to Mary Magdalene and the apostles on that first Easter Sunday, may give them also a share of His rising to new life

For all our faithful departed ones, who were signed with the cross of Jesus, that the power of His glorious resurrection may bring them rejoicing into the wedding banquet of heaven

## 2nd Sunday of Easter

*Acts 5:12-16, Ps 118, Rev 1,*
*John 20:19-31*

For the church, experiencing the distress and the endurance we have in Jesus, that we may also share in His victory as the risen and glorified Lord

That there may be joyful shouts of victory in the tents of the just as the resurrection of Jesus empowers them to conquer the obstacles thrown up by evil in the world today

That on this Mercy Sunday, we may experience the peace that Jesus offered to His apostles with the forgiveness of all their sins

That we may put our faith in Jesus, whom we have not seen, acknowledging Him as our Lord and our God, obtaining the blessing of His believing servants

For the sick and the distressed in mind or spirit, that the healing that flowed out from the apostles in Jesus' name may rejoice and strengthen them today

For our faithful departed ones, that Jesus, who holds the keys of death and the netherworld, and who lives forever and ever, may raise them up to be with Him in His glorious kingdom

## 3rd Sunday of Easter

*Acts 5:27-32, Ps 30, Rev 5:11-14,*
*John 21:1-19*

For our modern day apostles who experience scorn and persecution for their loyalty to Jesus, that they may rejoice that they have been found worthy to suffer dishonor for the sake of His name

That the One who sits on the throne and the Lamb that was slain may receive honor and glory from world leaders as they build a culture of life and establish a civilization of love

That with Peter we may answer "Yes" to the Lord's repeated interior question: "Do you love me?", and consent to follow Him faithfully, feeding the lambs He has entrusted to our care

For all who are working hard during a long night and catching nothing, that Jesus may fill their nets and provide for them a feast of refreshment and grace

For those who are suffering, who are in a netherworld of pain or grief, that the Lord may be their helper and change their mourning into dancing

For our faithful departed ones, that they may soon join the blessed ones around the throne, giving blessing and honor, wisdom and strength to their beloved Savior

## 4th Sunday of Easter

*Acts 13:43-52, Ps 100, Rev 7:14-17,*
*John 10:27-30*

For our holy shepherds in the church, that they may be a light to the nations, and an instrument of salvation to the ends of the earth

For national and civic leaders, that they may heed the witness of Christian prophets and apostles, upholding the dignity of human life and the justice due to all the children of the Heavenly Father

For those who are persecuted for their faith, that, like Paul and Barnabas, they may speak out boldly, giving witness to the Word of God as the Lord commands

That we may understand how firm and unshakable is our hope because of Jesus, our Good Shepherd, and that we may remain at peace in His hands, knowing that we are safe and loved

For those who are in a period of great distress, suffering from illness, depression, or poverty, that the blood of the Lamb, offered in this Mass, may strengthen and console them

For our dear ones who have died and those who grieve their passing, that God may lead the departed souls to springs of life-giving waters, and wipe away every tear from the eyes of those who remain here below

## 5th Sunday of Easter

*Acts 14:21-27, Ps 145, Rev 21:1-5,*
*John 13:31-35*

For the church, the new Jerusalem, that she may prepare for her ultimate meeting with the divine Spouse as a bride prepares for her husband, adorning herself with faith and works of love

For national and civic leaders, that the plans of their hearts may be conformed to the kingdom of God, who is always creating a new order of peace

For modern day apostles, that like Paul and Barnabas, they may continue to strengthen the spirits of the disciples and help them to persevere in the faith throughout life's hardships

That we may shine as followers of Jesus by the love we have one for another, even to the extent of the Lord's love, which drove Him to lay down His life for His friends

For all who are suffering from sickness, anxiety, poverty, or grief, that the Lord, who is gracious and merciful, may show them His great kindness and compassion in graces of healing and joy

For our faithful departed ones, that they may be in the kingdom where there is no more death or mourning, wailing or pain, where God wipes away every tear and makes all things new

## 6th Sunday of Easter

*Acts 15:1-2, 22-29, Ps 67, Rev 21,*
*John 14:23-29*

For the apostles and elders of the church today, that they may deliberate and address the problems that arise with the same power of the Holy Spirit that helped the first apostles

That the nations may have cause to be glad and exult as God rules them with equity and guides them through chosen leaders raised up by His mercy

That the vision of the perfect and beautiful heavenly Jerusalem, gleaming with God's splendor and lit by the radiance of the Lamb, may encourage us to be living stones worthy to be laid in a structure of such glory

That we may come to be a dwelling place for the Father by loving Jesus and keeping His word, thus enjoying the blessing of His peace

For the poor, the sick, the grieving, and the depressed, all whose hearts are troubled or afraid, that God may have pity on them and bless them, letting His face shine upon them in love and mercy

For our faithful departed ones, that Jesus may take them to be where He is, in the kingdom of His beloved Father

## The Ascension of the Lord, Vigil

*general intentions*

For the whole church, anticipating the Ascension, that our glorious Lord and Savior may fill her heart with His paschal joy

That leaders of countries that have been evangelized may acknowledge the Lordship of Jesus in their decisions and policies, and that God may grant us His peace

That we who celebrate the bodily Ascension of Jesus into heaven may follow Him in our thoughts and desires, seeing everything on earth from the standpoint of eternity

For all who receive this Eucharist, that we may understand that Jesus will never leave us orphans, and that His presence has passed into the sacraments for our consolation and joy

For all who need the comfort of prayer today in a time of mourning, pain, or weakness, that the power of this Holy Sacrifice will lift them up to new realms of grace and hope

For our dear ones who have died, that they may be where Jesus has gone before us, safe in the place He has prepared for them, rejoicing in His love

## Ascension of the Lord

*Acts 1:1-11, Ps 47, Eph 1:17-23 or*
*Heb 9:24-28, 10:19-23, Luke 24:46-53*

For the whole church, deriving life from the witness of the first apostles, that we may continue their work of preaching repentance to all the nations for the forgiveness of sins

For the nations of the world, that Jesus, who mounted His throne as ruler of them all, may raise up for the nations leaders after His own heart

For those who are far from the church and her sacraments, that the Holy Spirit promised by the Lord may be stirred up in them through our loving and fervent prayers

That the Father may give us the wisdom and insight to understand the fullness of the Lord, who fills the universe at every level, yet comes so humbly into our hearts in this Eucharist

For all who suffer, that Jesus, who raised His hands and blessed His disciples before parting from them, may bless them with grace, courage, light, and peace

For our faithful departed ones, that Jesus, who has gone before us into the sanctuary of heaven in order to prepare a place for each of us, may now welcome them home into their heavenly dwellings

## 7th Sunday of Easter

*Acts 7:55-60, Ps 97, Rev 22:12-20,*
*John 17:20-26*

For the church, that we may be among the blessed ones who wash our robes in the Blood of the Lamb, and who with the Spirit and the Bride cry out for the coming of the Lord Jesus

For modern day prophets, that they may be strong enough to witness fearlessly to their vision of Jesus and His will among the nations, and gentle enough to bear with forgiveness the price of their witness

For unity among all the followers of Jesus, that the world may believe the Father sent Him to bring us all to perfection in His love, which always creates oneness of mind and heart

That Jesus, who calls Himself the bright morning star, may rise in the hearts of the young, and attract irresistibly those whom He has called to consecration in religious life

For all who have asked our prayers in a time of distress, sickness, unemployment, poverty, or grief, that Jesus, who prayed so fervently for us all at His Last Supper, may obtain for them healing and grace and joy

For our faithful departed ones, that Jesus, who asked that those who believed in Him may be with Him and see His glory, may bring them into the clear vision of His heavenly kingdom

## Pentecost Vigil

*general intentions*

For the whole church, groaning in labor pains as she longs for the coming of the Holy Spirit, that this divine Paraclete may respond to our yearning with the gift of holy fire

That all creatures and all the world may be filled with peace and all good things as the Lord opens His hand and sends out His Spirit

That the Spirit may come to the aid of our weakness, interceding for us in our prayer according to God's loving will

That our faith in Jesus may be strong so that living water may flow from within us, refreshing and renewing everyone we meet

For all who have asked our prayers and all who are in need of loving intercession, that the Spirit may be poured upon them in grace and joy

For our beloved departed ones, who possessed the first fruits of the Spirit in this life of hope and struggle, that they may now be rejoicing in the Spirit amid the bliss of heaven

## Pentecost Sunday

*general intentions*

For the whole church on this day of Pentecost, as the glorified Christ lets fall His promised Holy Spirit, that the strong wind of His coming may surge through the Upper Room where we have waited, to kindle in each of us His holy fire

For the lay faithful, commissioned by the Spirit to be a ferment in society for the kingdom of God, that the Spirit's gift of fortitude may make them strong friends of Christ, able to stand up for the demands of justice, life, and peace

For all who are experiencing new stirrings in their lives— calls to change and growth, movements of repentance, even earthquakes of divine disturbance— that they may not quench or sadden the loving Spirit who awakens within them

That our Communion with Jesus in this holy sacrifice may intensify the presence of His Spirit in our hearts, and spread all around us the sweet fragrance of His gifts and fruits in our lives

That the Spirit may be an anointing of comfort to the sorrowful, healing to the sick, calm to the anxious, forgiveness to sinners, and refreshment to us all on our pilgrim way

For our faithful departed ones, that the Lord may send forth His Spirit into their souls, so that they may be placed in eternal life as His new creation

# ORDINARY TIME

## 2nd Sunday in Ordinary Time

*Isa 62:1-5, Ps 96, 1 Cor 12:4-11,*
*John 2:1-11*

For the church, rich in the variety of her gifts, that the expression of faith, wisdom, healing, prophecy, and discernment of spirits may give glory to the work of the Holy Spirit in her midst

That the families of nations may give the Lord the glory due His name, obeying His laws and pursuing His values of life, truth, human dignity, justice, and peace

That Mary's advice to the servants, "Do whatever He tells you," may be the watchword of our lives as we obey every divine command, which Jesus gives only to make our lives overflow with grace and glory

For married couples, showing forth in their lives the mystery of Christ's union with His Bride, the Church, that Jesus may provide for them a rich wine of generous and faithful love for one another and for their children

For those who are experiencing their lives as forsaken and desolate, that through God's merciful intervention they may again be called His delight as He unites their destinies to His own in a bond of union and joy

For our faithful departed, that they may be cleansed and made ready for the heavenly marriage banquet, drinking the new wine with Jesus in His glorious kingdom

## 3rd Sunday in Ordinary Time

*Neh 8:2-4a, 5-6, 8-10, Ps 19, 1 Cor 12:12-*
*30, Luke 1:1-4, 4:14-21*

That the Spirit of the Lord may be upon all those who minister in Christ's name, that they may be empowered to bring glad tidings to the poor, liberty to captives, and sight to the spiritually blind

That the fear of the Lord, which is pure, and the ordinances of the Lord, which are true and just, may be the guiding force in the lives of those who lead the nations on earth

That Sundays and all feasts which are holy to the Lord may be days of rejoicing, as we listen to His words and partake of His rich food in the Holy Eucharist, thus renewing our strength for the journey

For the Body of Christ, made up of many members yet one living organism with Christ as its Head, that each of us may be concerned for the other members, and each may act humbly and effectively according to the role God assigns them

For our suffering brothers and sisters, that as members one of another we may serve and pray for them as if for ourselves, and that God may grant them healing and grace

That Jesus, who came to let the oppressed go free, may liberate our faithful departed from any residue of sin and make them acceptable to the Lord in His holy kingdom

### 4th Sunday in Ordinary Time

*Jer 1:4-5, 17-19, Ps 71, 1 Cor 12:31–13:13, Luke 4:21-30*

For the leaders in the church, known and dedicated from the beginning, that they may be strong pillars in the fortified city that is the church

For the prophets appointed to the nations, that they may stand up and tell the powerful ones all that God commands them

For the most excellent gift of love, that we may be kind and patient, believing and hoping and enduring all things, practicing the greatest virtue that will last forever

For all who are persecuted for speaking the truth, that Jesus, who suffered the rejection of His own friends and relatives in Nazareth, may enable them to pass through the midst of their suffering with serenity and faith

For all who have asked our prayers or who need prayer because of sickness, financial difficulties, depression, loneliness, or grief, that they may experience God as their stronghold and refuge who brings them salvation

For our faithful departed ones, who practiced love while they were on earth, that they may now have perfect knowledge and love, seeing God face to face in heaven

### 5th Sunday in Ordinary Time

*Isa 6:1-8, Ps 138, 1 Cor 15:1-11, Luke 5:1-11*

For those whom the Lord has sent as prophets and ministers in His name, that their lips may be pure and their hearts clean by contact with the Lord and His holy angels

That all the rulers of the earth may give thanks to the Lord and govern according to His ways, defending life, fostering human dignity, and upholding justice

For the apostles and the missionaries of the church today who work hard and often catch nothing, that Jesus may inspire them to try yet one more time, and fill their nets with souls to be saved

That we may obey the Lord's command to launch out into the deep, leaving the safe seashores of a shallow spiritual life for the adventure He has in store for us

For those who are caught in weakness and fear, those who are feeble and sick, poor and oppressed, that God may complete the good work He has begun in them, building up strength within them for His glory

That Christ, who died for our sins, may purify the souls of all the dead and bring them rejoicing into His heavenly kingdom

## 6th Sunday in Ordinary Time

*Jer 17:5-8, Ps 1, 1 Cor 15:12, 16-20,*
*Luke 6:17, 20-26*

For the church, that her preachers may proclaim the blessedness taught by Jesus and have the courage to stand up for His countercultural values in a hostile world

That national leaders may be men and women who have learned to delight in the law of the Lord, meditating upon it and applying it in their decisions and laws

That we may be trees planted near the flowing waters of God's grace, placing our trust and hope firmly in the Lord, and even in the year of drought bringing forth good fruit

For those are persecuted for their faith and witness to Jesus, that they may have the grace and insight to rejoice in the knowledge that their reward in heaven will be rich and full

For those who are poor, who are weeping and hungry and sick, that those who are rich and filled may see them and come to their aid, and that our prayers may bring them solace

For those who have fallen asleep in Christ, that Jesus raised from the dead may give them fullness of life in the kingdom of heaven

## 7th Sunday in Ordinary Time

*1 Sam 26:2, 7-9, 12-13, 22-23, Ps 103,*
*1 Cor 15:45-49, Luke 6:27-38*

For the church, that we may follow the more difficult exhortations of Jesus, even in His encouragement to turn the other cheek and hand over more than is taken from us

For the anointed ones, the rulers of nations, that as they are protected by their position from all harm, so they may extend the shelter of protection to the unborn, the oppressed, and the vulnerable

For the grace to stop judging, to forgive, to give in goodly measure, to be generous and kind to one another and to everybody in Jesus' name

That as Christians, we may go beyond the law of doing good to those who do good to us, and begin to love even our enemies, imitating God's kindness to the ungrateful and the wicked

For all who have asked our prayers in their sickness or distress of any kind, that the Lord may redeem their life from destruction and crown them with love and compassion

For our faithful departed, who have borne the image of the earthly man, Adam, that they may now bear the likeness of the heavenly man, Jesus, in His holy kingdom

### 8th Sunday in Ordinary Time

*Sir 27:4-7, Ps 92, 1 Cor 15:54-58,*
*Luke 6:39-45*

For the church, that she may give thanks to the Lord and proclaim His kindness by the joy in her liturgies and the witness of her holy ones

For our leaders in the world, that their words may be honest and their deeds kind, with no husks of wickedness emerging in their decisions and actions

That we may be careful to attend to the splinters in our own eyes, keeping our souls clean and pure by frequent confession, thus seeing clearly enough to help those we love to amend their lives

For the grace to be cleansed down to our roots by the Lord's pruning, so that we may bear the good fruit of holiness in our words and deeds

For those who are being tested in the furnace of tribulation, that they may emerge just and upright before the Lord, healed and holy in His sight

For our faithful departed, that death may be swallowed up in victory for them, losing its sting as they enter the banquet of heavenly joy

### 9th Sunday in Ordinary Time

*1 Kgs 8:41-43, Ps 117, Gal 1:1-2, 6-10,*
*Luke 7:1-10*

For our preachers and teachers in the church, that they may be slaves of Jesus Christ, setting before us the whole Gospel with the fidelity of the angels

That all may honor the great name of the one God, even those who are not of His people, and that the prayers of all for justice, life, and peace may be answered

For a spirit of humility before the Lord, especially as we approach Him to take Him under our roof in Holy Communion

That the faith of the centurion may commend us to Jesus in all the needs we place before Him today

That God's kindness may be steadfast toward the poor and the sick, the depressed and grieving, and that His fidelity may bring them comfort and hope

For our faithful departed, who put their faith in the Gospel of the grace of Christ, that they may now be experiencing the reward of their loyalty in heaven

## 10th Sunday in Ordinary Time

*1 Kgs 17:17-24, Ps 30, Gal 1:11-19,*
*Luke 7:11-17*

For our prophets and teachers in the church, that they may be men and women of God, and that the word of the Lord may come truly from their mouths

That God may raise up among the nations leaders after His own heart, willing to fight for the right to life and justice, turning the mourning of the oppressed into dancing in the sight of the Lord

For vocations, that those who have been set apart and called through the grace of God for special consecration and ministry in the church may respond generously and with love

That the power and grace of prophecy may never be absent from the church, but that compassion and prayer may continue to triumph over the powers of death

That Jesus, who was moved with pity for the widow of Nain and raised her son to new life, may now stretch out His hands over all those who have asked for our prayers in a time of distress and pain

For our faithful departed ones, that the Lord may bring them up from the nether world and preserve them from those going down into the pit, welcoming them into the joys of heaven

## 11th Sunday in Ordinary Time

*2 Sam 12:7-10, Ps 32, Gal 2:17, 19-21,*
*Luke 7:36–8:3*

For our prophetic leaders in the church, that like Nathan they may have the courage to confront the sinful with the truth of their condition and the compassion to offer them the forgiveness of the Lord

That those who have faith in Jesus Christ may be the first to make their voices heard among the nations, working for justice, life, morality, and peace

For the women who follow Christ, who provide for Him out of their means and make themselves His disciples, that they may be respected for their gifts and honored for their faithfulness

For souls who have a gift for love but have used it in harmful or sinful ways, that they may understand the mercy of their Savior, and bring their alabaster flask and their tears to the feet of Jesus

For all who know their need for God in a time of suffering and trial, that the Lord may be their shelter, preserving them from distress, ringing them round with glad cries of freedom

For our faithful departed ones, that they may be among those to whom the Lord imputes no guilt, exulting and rejoicing in His heavenly kingdom

### 12th Sunday in Ordinary Time

*Zech 12:10-11, 13:1, Ps 63, Gal 3:26-29,*
*Luke 9:18-24*

For unity in the church, that there may no longer be divisions and disagreements, but that all the children of God may be one in Christ Jesus

That the prophetic voices raised in defense of life, of justice, and morality may be heard and heeded by the rulers of the nations, that we may be worthy of the blessing of God's peace

That God may pour out upon us all a spirit of grace and petition, that we may look upon the pierced One with grieving love, and come to Him as to a fountain that will purify us from all sin

That we may have the courage to take up our crosses every day and follow Christ, allowing our lives to be lost for His sake and believing we will find everything again in Him

For all who are suffering: the sick, the grieving, and the poor, that God's kindness may touch their lives, and they may have reason to shout with joy under the shadow of His healing wings

For our faithful departed ones, that God may fill their souls with the riches of His heavenly banquet, and they may praise Him exultantly in His glorious kingdom

### 13th Sunday in Ordinary Time

*1 Kgs 19:19-21, Ps 16, Gal 5:13-18,*
*Luke 9:51-62*

That the apostles in the church today may not be men of fire and brimstone, deserving the rebuke of Jesus, but rather those who speak the truth with loving and humble hearts

For the nations of the world, that they may not consume one another, biting and devouring in greed and thirst for power, but serve and help each other to prosper in peace

That we may be led and guided by the Spirit of God, not gratifying the desires of the flesh, but taking hold of the joyful freedom from sin, for which Christ has set us free

For those whom Jesus is calling to follow Him more closely, that they may not look back at what they are leaving behind, but gratefully consent to join His company and proclaim the kingdom of God at His side

For those who are in a season of anguish, pain, or grief, that God may be their allotted portion and their cup, filling them with strength and grace in the midst of their trials

For our faithful departed ones, that Jesus may show them the path to life and the fullness of joys in His presence

## 14th Sunday in Ordinary Time

*Isa 66:10-14, Ps 66, Gal 6:14-18,*
*Luke 10:1-12, 17-20*

For the apostles of the church today, that in the name of Jesus all evil may be subject to them, and they may have the secret joy of knowing that their names are written in heaven

That the peace which is the greeting of the Savior and His prophets may come to rest upon people of peace who live among the nations, spreading its blessing to all

That the marks of the sufferings of Jesus may be found in our lives, as we follow Him faithfully on the way of the cross

That the Master of the harvest may send out laborers to gather in the abundance of grace He has sown in many hearts, granting us priests and missionaries willing to spend their lives in this holy work

For those who are worn down by the trials of life, who are poor, sick, abused, and forgotten, that our loving prayers may keep vigil at their side, and they soon may have cause to bless God for His kindness

For our faithful departed loved ones, that they may be welcomed into the heavenly Jerusalem and find their comfort there

## 15th Sunday in Ordinary Time

*Deut 30:10-14, Ps 69, Col 1:15-20,*
*Luke 10:20-37*

For our Holy Father, our bishops and priests, that Jesus who is the head of the body, the church, may bless them with His power for truth and goodness in the sight of all

For the blessing of peace, that Jesus, who made peace by the blood of His cross, may give enemies the grace to come to mutual understanding and forgiveness

That we may never cross to the other side of the road to pass by anyone in need, but reach out with generosity and love to help them

That we may come to love the Lord with all our heart and all our strength, and obey His command to love others as we do ourselves, no matter what barriers of race or religion lie between us

That we who approach this table of love to share in the Body of Jesus may take from it the strength to live by His teaching and to obey His commands

For our beloved dead, that Jesus, the firstborn from the dead, may bring them to a place of light, joy, and peace

### 16th Sunday in Ordinary Time

*Gen 18:1-10, Ps 15, Col 1:24-28,
Luke 10:38-42*

That our holy shepherds in the church may proclaim the Lord Jesus in truth, teaching and admonishing everyone with wisdom, presenting each member of the church perfect in Christ

That leaders of nations may walk blamelessly and do justice, harming no one, and honoring those who fear the Lord, promoting respect for life and fostering peace

That our generous and reverent hospitality may extend to all, serving Jesus in His brothers and sisters, and obtaining from God the blessing of fruitfulness and grace

For those who have chosen the better part, who show their love for the Lord by attentive listening at His feet as His disciples, that He may find joy in them and His blessing may rest upon them

For all who are filling up in their flesh what is lacking in the sufferings of Christ, that as they help His church through their union with the Redeemer, they may find compassion and support in her members

For our faithful departed ones, that God may soon make known to them the riches of His glory in the divine hospitality of heaven

### 17th Sunday in Ordinary Time

*Gen 18:20-32, Ps 138, Col 2:12-14,
Luke 11:1-13*

For the church, that the Father in heaven may give the Holy Spirit to all of us in satisfying abundance, seeing our constant need of His power and grace

For the champions of the right to life, for those who are working to uphold justice and morality, for the peacemakers, that the blessing of God and the support of His holy people may be with them

That we may honor the goodness of God by asking Him for what we need, seeking and knocking at the door of His mercy, confident in Him as our heavenly Father

That we may imitate the persistence of Abraham in our prayer, and strive to be the faithful remnant for the sake of whom God is willing to spare the whole nation

For the lowly ones who walk amid sickness and distress, that the Lord may build up strength with them and give them cause to sing His praise in the presence of His holy angels

For our faithful departed ones, buried with Christ in baptism, that Jesus may cancel every bond that is still against them, nailing it to His redeeming cross

## 18th Sunday in Ordinary Time

*Eccl 1:2, 2:21-23, Ps 90, Col 3:1-5, 9-11,*
*Luke 12:13-21*

For our shepherds in the church, that they may help us to number our days aright, and to gain wisdom of heart by resolutely putting God first in our lives

For leaders of the nations, who labor with wisdom and knowledge and skill to attain their goals, that these goals may be precious and lasting in God's sight, so that He may prosper the work of their hands

That we may heed the warning of Jesus to guard against all greed in our lives, and become rich in what matters to God, so that our treasure will last forever

That we may willingly put to death in ourselves the immorality and evil desires that belong to our old selves, and become renewed in the image of our Savior, Jesus Christ

For all who are suffering in body, mind, or spirit, that our prayers may help them, and that God may fill them at daybreak with His kindness and take them into His gracious care

For our faithful departed ones, whose life is now hidden with Christ in God, that they may be shining with Jesus in His glory

## 19th Sunday in Ordinary Time

*Wis 18:6-9, Ps 33, Heb 11:8-19,*
*Luke 12:32-48*

For our leaders and ministers in the church, servants of a good Master and entrusted with great responsibility, that they may be worthy of their charge

For the powerful leaders of nations, that they may remember they are still servants of a divine Master whose law upholds justice, life, and morality

That we may all be vigilant and ready with lighted lamps to welcome the Lord when He returns, for we already have a foretaste of the banquet which He serves in this Holy Eucharist

For the gift of confidence, that we may be without fear, certain that the Father has given us the kingdom, and that we may place all our treasure and our hearts in heaven

For all who are suffering, who are sick or grieving, who are waiting for God to be their help and their shield, that the eyes of the Lord may be upon them for grace and healing

For our faithful departed ones, that they may soon be purified to stand with all the saints in the heaven; the city with foundations, whose architect and maker is God

## 20th Sunday in Ordinary Time

*Jer 38:4-6, 8-10, Ps 40, Heb 12:1-4,*
*Luke 12:49-53*

For the church, that there may be good men and women to speak up for her persecuted prophets and rescue them from harm

That we may have the courage to choose sides with Jesus in the division that His coming establishes on the earth, and that as we speak out for justice and human dignity in His name we may become worthy of His peace

That we may endure our crosses with hope, looking forward to the joy that lies before us, refusing to grow weary or lose heart in the struggles of life

That the fire that Jesus came to bring to the earth may be set ablaze in our hearts, consuming every obstacle to our complete dedication to His person and His service

For all who are afflicted and poor, who feel like they are in a pit of destruction, that our prayers and this Holy Sacrifice may give them a new song of deliverance and joy

For our faithful departed ones, that they may be quickly purified to join the great cloud of witnesses in heaven who help us with their example and their prayers

## 21st Sunday in Ordinary Time

*Isa 66:18-21, Ps 117, Heb 12:5-7, 11-13,*
*Luke 13:22-30*

For our priests and Levites, that they may bring their offerings in clean vessels to God's holy mountain, living with integrity and purity before Him

For the people of the east and west, north and south, and for their leaders, that they may return to a culture of life and a civilization of love, thus becoming worthy of a place at table in the kingdom of God

That by the grace and help of Jesus we may be strong enough to enter through the narrow gate, that the door of the kingdom may not be locked on us by the master of the house

That we may learn to endure our trials as the discipline of the Lord, rejoicing that He thinks of us as sons and daughters worthy of His divine training

For all who have asked our prayers in a season of loneliness, illness, poverty, or grief, that they may experience how steadfast is the kindness of the Lord and how truly His fidelity endures forever

For our faithful departed ones, that they may be among those chosen to see God's glory in the heavenly Jerusalem

## 22nd Sunday in Ordinary Time

*Sir 3, Ps 68, Heb 12:18-19, 22-24,*
*Luke 14:7-14*

For our priestly leaders in the church, that they may have the minds of holy sages and an attentive ear for divine wisdom

That the poor, the crippled, the lame, the blind, and the unborn may be welcome at the table of earth's plenty by the rich and the powerful of the world

For the grace of humility, that we may find favor with God, exalted by His right hand because we have humbled ourselves in His presence

That as we unite with the angels in their festal gathering under the sprinkled blood of the Savior, we may joyfully invite others to this divine banquet

For those who are sitting in the lowest place at life's feast: the poor, the sick, the lonely, and the abandoned, that they may hear the loving divine invitation to move up higher, as they are healed and restored

For our faithful departed ones, that they may soon be in the city of the living God, among the spirits of the just made perfect

## 23rd Sunday in Ordinary Time

*Wis 9:13-18, Ps 90, Phlm 9-10, 12-17,*
*Luke 14:25-33*

That the loving concern of St. Paul for His new convert Onesimus may be a model for today's apostles, as they put their hearts into their ministry on behalf of God's chosen ones

For world leaders, whose deliberations are mortal and timid and whose plans are unsure, that their paths may be set straight by the Holy Spirit from on high

That we may come to be true disciples of Jesus, because we have considered the cost carefully and decided that He is worth the loss of everything else

For the grace to shoulder our crosses without complaining, happy to follow the Master in bad times as well as good

For those caught in a dark night of pain and suffering and who have asked for prayer, that God may fill them at daybreak with His kindness, helping them with His gracious care

For our faithful departed ones, whose bodies have returned to dust, that their souls may spring up and live abundantly in God's blessed kingdom

### 24th Sunday in Ordinary Time

*Exod 32:7-14, Ps 51, 1 Tim 1:12-17,*
*Luke 15:1-32*

That our holy leaders in the church may be as effective as Moses once was, as they pray to God for their people

That God, who reconciled the world to Himself in Christ, may inspire the powerful of the earth to thoughts of peace and deeds of life and justice

For the prodigal children, who have wandered far from the Father, especially those among our own loved ones, that a great impulse of grace may draw them back to His welcoming love

For the faithful ones, that they may come to understand the Father's heart, and reach out to the lost ones as brothers and sisters worthy of honor and rejoicing

For those who have become disoriented through the heavy burdens and sufferings of life, that the divine shepherd may find them and carry them gently to healing and peace

For our faithful departed ones, that the grace of our Lord may be abundant for them, bringing them mercy and a place at the heavenly feast of reconciliation and joy

### 25th Sunday in Ordinary Time

*Amos 8:4-7, Ps 113, 1 Tim 2:1-8,*
*Luke 16:1-13*

For all who have been appointed preachers and apostles in the church, that they may proclaim the one God with courage and Jesus, the mediator between God and humanity, with love

That there may be no trampling upon the needy and destroying the poor of the earth among the nations, but that honest and upright leadership may lift them up

That we may be given the grace to lead a quiet and tranquil life with devotion and dignity, lifting up holy hands without anger or argument in prayer before God

That we may choose whom we will serve with prudence and conviction, trustworthy before God in small matters as well as great matters that last forever

For those who have been brought low through the ravages of sickness, poverty, depression, or grief, that God may lift them up from the dust and seat them with dignity and joy among the princes of His people

For our faithful departed ones, who served the Lord honestly upon the earth, that they may be rejoicing with Him in His holy kingdom

## 26th Sunday in Ordinary Time

*Amos 6:1-7, Ps 146, 1 Tim 6:11-16,*
*Luke 16:19-31*

For our Holy Father, our bishops and priests, that they may be men of God, holding fast to their noble confession of faith and love for Jesus Christ

That the wealthy nations may not become complacent, stretched comfortably upon their couches, but instead reach out to the poor nations that are on the verge of collapse

That we may base our actions on the law and the prophets, and on Jesus, the fulfillment of them all, especially when He makes known to us the consequences of selfishness in the life that lasts forever

For all of us receiving this Eucharist, that we may become more like Jesus, securing justice for the oppressed, giving food to the hungry, and raising up those who are bowed down

For those who are poor and sick, like Lazarus, that they may have the comfort of our compassionate love and our earnest prayer

For our faithful departed ones, that they may be rejoicing before the blessed and only Ruler who dwells in unapproachable light, and with His Son, our Lord Jesus Christ

## 27th Sunday in Ordinary Time

*Hab 1:2-3, 2:2-4, Ps 95, 2 Tim 1:6-8,*
*13-14, Luke 17:5-10*

For our holy leaders in the church, that they may stir into flame the gift of God and the spirit of power and love and self control received in their holy ordination

For the areas of the world in which there is destruction and violence, strife and clamorous discord, that the cries of the prophets may draw down God's compassion on the little ones

That we may bear our share of the hardship for the Gospel with the strength that comes from God, proud of our testimony to our Lord Jesus Christ

For all of us, unprofitable servants who never accomplish more than our duty before our Master, that our obedience may be full and loving in His sight

For all who are distressed or suffering in body, mind, and spirit, that our faith as we pray for them may be strong and effective, moving mountains of pain and bringing healing and joy

For our faithful departed ones, that the vision of their heavenly destiny may press on to fulfillment in peace and gladness

## 28th Sunday in Ordinary Time

*2 Kgs 5:14-17, Ps 98, 2 Tim 2:8-13,*
*Luke 17:11-19*

For the church, that the Word of God may never be chained in her assemblies, but that the salvation that is in Christ Jesus may be proclaimed by her holy apostles and preachers

That all the nations and their leaders may come to realize, as Naaman did, that there is no God in all the earth except the One who has revealed Himself in the history of Israel, and that they may give Him their worship and obedience

For grateful hearts, that we may bring to Jesus our most humble thanks for all His blessings, and never take any of His goodness for granted in our lives

For the gift of strong faith, sufficient to draw down the power of the Lord in our lives and in the lives of those we love, that we may attract His grace and help in every need

For those whose suffering or sickness have made them outcasts like the lepers in today's readings, that our compassion and prayer may reach out to Jesus for them, obtaining His gifts of healing and joy

For our faithful departed, who have persevered and have died with Christ, that they may now live and reign with Him in His heavenly kingdom

## 29th Sunday in Ordinary Time

*Exod 17:8-13, Ps 121, 2 Tim 3:14–4:2,*
*Luke 18:1-8*

For our holy leaders in the church, that like Moses they may keep their hands lifted up in prayer to God with the willing support of their people

That prayer may direct the course of human conflict in the world, and bring the opposing parties to negotiation, that a balance of justice may lead to peace

That we may be faithful to what we know and believe, formed by the Scripture, trained in righteousness, and equipped for every good work

For the followers of Jesus, that we may learn to pray always in faith, without becoming weary, knowing that God will respond and do justice for us at the right moment

For all who are suffering: the sick, the poor, the forgotten elderly, the abused and imprisoned, that the Lord may be their guardian and their shade

For our faithful departed ones, that our prayer and our faith may be efficacious for them, obtaining the purification necessary for their joyful entry into heaven

## 30th Sunday in Ordinary Time

*Sir 35:12-18, Ps 34, 2 Tim 4:6-8, 16-18, Luke 18:9-14*

For our Holy Father, our bishops and priests, that the Lord may stand by them and give them strength, so that through them His proclamation might be completed among the nations

That God, who hears the cry of the oppressed and the wail of the orphan, may direct the minds and hearts of the powerful to come to their aid

That we may never despise others nor be convinced of our own righteousness, but realize that we are all sinners before God, much in need of His mercy

That the prayer of the lowly and the suffering may reach the Most High, and that He may respond, judging justly and affirming the right

For all who are brokenhearted and crushed in spirit, that they may experience how the Lord redeems the lives of His servants and saves those who hope in Him

For our faithful departed, who have finished the race and kept the faith, that they may now receive the crown of righteousness in the heavenly kingdom

## 31st Sunday in Ordinary Time

*Wis 11:22–12:2, Ps 145, 2 Thess 1:11–2:2, Luke 19:1-10*

For the church, that God may make us worthy of our calling and powerfully bring to fulfillment our every good purpose and every effort of faith

That the Lord, who is gracious and merciful and compassionate toward all His works, may awaken compassion in the hearts of the powerful, especially for the poor and the helpless unborn

That salvation may come to the houses of those who have strayed far from God, that they, like Zacchaeus, may be given the grace to desire to see who Jesus is and experience His salvation

That we may respond with Zacchaeus to the invitation of the Lord, coming down from our self exaltation in our projects and plans, and receiving Jesus with joy into our hearts

For all who are weary and lonely, depressed or sick, abused or imprisoned, that God, who lifts up the falling and raises those who are bowed down, may come to their aid

For our faithful departed, in whom is the imperishable spirit sent by the Lord, that God, the lover of souls, who has mercy on all, may purify them of sin and bring them home to heaven

### 32nd Sunday in Ordinary Time

*2 Macc 7:1-2, 9-14, Ps 17, 2 Thess 2:16–3:5, Luke 20:27-38*

For our leaders and preachers in the church, that the word of the Lord may speed forward and be glorified through their ministry, and that they may be delivered from the perverse and the wicked

For the kings and rulers of the earth, that they may understand clearly that this passing life will end with a divine reckoning of their decisions and deeds

For all the disciples of Christ, that we may be willing to die rather than transgress God's laws, like the heroic brothers in the book of Maccabees

That the Lord, who has given us everlasting encouragement and good hope through His grace, may direct our hearts to the love of God and the endurance of Christ

For all who have asked our prayers in a time of suffering and distress, that God may hold them as the apple of His eye and keep them safe under the shadow of His wings

For our faithful departed ones, that they may be made as pure as the angels, singing the praise of the God of the living in His glorious kingdom

### 33rd Sunday in Ordinary Time

*Mal 3:19-20, Ps 98, 2 Thess 3:7-12, Luke 21:5-19*

For our Holy Father, our bishops and priests, that like St. Paul they may present themselves as models for the faithful, worthy of imitation in every virtue

That leaders of nations, the powerful and influential, may be among those who fear God's name, that the sun of justice may arise in the world with its healing rays

For all Christians, that they may work diligently in this passing world, eating their own food by their quiet labor, yet keep the glorious coming of the Lord ever in the resilience and enthusiasm of their hope

For all who are being persecuted, who are led before tribunals of power because of the name of Jesus, that they may be supported by His wisdom in their speech and by His endurance in their sufferings

For those whose lives are in ruins, with not one stone upon another, who are sick, poor, oppressed, exiled, or in deep mourning, that the Lord may come into their hearts with grace and healing

For our faithful departed ones, for whom the day of the Lord has already arrived, that they may soon be purified to partake of the full joy of His heavenly kingdom

### 34th Sunday in Ordinary Time, Christ the King

*2 Sam 5:1-2, Ps 122, Col 1:12-20, Luke 23:35-43*

For our leaders in the church, that they may preach Christ and Him crucified; our heavenly King, the power and wisdom of our God

For those who shepherd the peoples, who are the commanders of the nations, that like King David they may be anointed with the will to rule in justice and truth

That God, who has delivered us from the power of darkness and transferred us into the kingdom of His beloved Son, may hold us safe in His grace until the day of Christ Jesus

That the saints, our brothers and sisters, the holy ones who live in light, may come to our help in our struggles for life and morality, seeking to build the kingdom of heaven on the earth

For struggling families, for strained marriages, for those whose lives are devastated by sickness or poverty, for those who are sinking under a weight of discouragement, for all who need our prayers

For our faithful departed ones, that Jesus may remember them now that He has come into His glorious kingdom

# SOLEMNITIES OF THE LORD DURING ORDINARY TIME

### Holy Trinity

*Prov 8:22-31, Ps 8, Rom 5:1-5, John 16:12-15*

For all who preach and minister in the name of the Trinity, that the Holy Spirit who sends them forth may also guide them into all truth

That the perfect peace that is the Holy Trinity may overflow into our world, creating a community of love between individuals, families, and nations

For all Christians, that Jesus, in whom we have gained access by faith to the grace in which we now stand, may make us one in truth and love

That the wisdom of God who is Jesus, through whom all creation came into being, may fill our hearts with a profound respect for the earth on which we all live

For all who are enduring affliction in mind, body, or spirit, that their faith may bring them God's peace even in this testing time of their endurance

For our faithful departed ones, that they may soon be caught up in the embrace of joy, love, and communion that is the most blessed Trinity

### Corpus Christi

*Gen 14:18-20, Ps 110, 1 Cor 11:23-26,
Luke 9:11-17*

For the whole church on this solemnity of the Body and Blood of Christ, that our faith in His personal presence under the veil of bread and wine may fill us with a spirit of adoration and loving gratitude

For the hungry nations, that we may bring our loaves and fishes to be blessed by Jesus, and obey His command to begin the distribution, even when the task seems impossible

For all our priests of God Most High, that the anointing which has sealed their souls forever may make them fervent and holy ministers of God's mysteries

For children who are receiving the Body and Blood of Christ for the first time, that they may begin a relationship of love with the Lord and rejoice His heart with their innocence

For those who are in pain, who feel the death of the Lord in their own lives, that as we gather their suffering into union with this Holy Sacrifice, their darkness may be eased by the Lord Jesus

For our faithful departed, who proclaimed the death of the Lord as they received His Body in this life, that they may now know the life of the Lord in the joys of heaven

### Sacred Heart

*Ezek 34:11-16, Ps 23, Rom 5:5-11,
Luke 15:3-7*

For all the shepherds of the church, all who care for the flock of Christ, that they may shepherd them rightly, leading them to good pastures of truth and goodness

For peace; that God may raise up leaders after His own heart, who will do what is fair and just in His sight

That we may be the hands of Jesus reaching out to heal the sick and bind up the injured, but especially to seek out the strayed and the lost, and bring them home to the Father in jubilation with our Savior

For all who are in need of God's loving kindness, especially those who have asked for our prayers in a difficult time, that the love of God may be poured out in their hearts through the Holy Spirit

That we may offer to our Savior the courtesy of our firm belief in the love of His Sacred Heart, and return to Him the consecration of our own hearts to works of love in His name

For our faithful departed, who have been justified by the blood of Jesus, that He may now share His life with them in everlasting joy

# PROPER OF TIME

## WEEKDAYS

## SEASON OF ADVENT

### Advent Week 1, Monday

*Isa 2:1-5, Ps 122, Matt 8:5-11*

For the church, as the prophecy of all nations coming to the Lord's mountain is fulfilled, that the genius and gifts of each nation may be welcome in her midst

That swords may be beaten into plowshares and spears into pruning hooks, and our world may know the blessing of peace

That we may be given the faith and the humility of the centurion, drawing out from Jesus His power of miracles on behalf of our loved ones

For all who are sick or paralyzed in any way like the centurion's servant, that they may have friends who will approach Jesus on their behalf to obtain healing and peace

For our beloved dead, that they may go up to the house of the Lord and set foot joyfully within the gates of the heavenly Jerusalem

### Advent Week 1, Tuesday

*Isa 11:1-10, Ps 72, Luke 10:21-24*

For the church, the Body of Christ, that with Him she may be filled with the Spirit of wisdom and understanding, counsel and strength, knowledge and holy fear

That Isaiah's vision of perfect peace may begin to be fulfilled on this holy mountain, where we offer the sacrifice of reconciliation and receive into our hearts the Prince of Peace

That we may change and become like little children, to whom the Father reveals His secrets, taming the violent forces of our world with the power of the Lord

For the poor, the sick, the needy and afflicted ones, that there will be men and women of justice who will hear them when they cry out and decide aright for their needs

For our beloved departed ones, that they may know the Father face to face and be blessed in what they see, through the merits of Jesus our Savior

## Advent Week 1, Wednesday

*Isa 25:6-10a, Ps 23, Matt 15:29-37*

For our priests, who see themselves with such limited resources in the face of tremendous need, that the Lord who has pity on the people may multiply and bless their efforts in His name

That God may raise up world leaders after His own heart, so that He can provide for all nations a feast of material abundance and spiritual freedom and peace

That fallen away Catholics may feel their need of a Savior, and during this holy season return to the sacraments and to God's grace, letting Him lead them to good pastures where they can be at rest

For the sick, the dying, the homebound, those who have no one to remember them with love, that through our prayer and the love of many hearts, God may wipe the tears from their faces

For the faithful departed, who looked to God as Savior in this life, that they may rejoice and be glad in His saving work in the kingdom of heaven

## Advent Week 1, Thursday

*Isa 16:1-6, Ps 118, Matt 7:21, 24-27*

For our Holy Father, our bishops and priests, who come to us in the name of the Lord and who bless us from the house of the Lord, that their holy lives may give us light

For our country, that it may be a nation that is just, one that keeps faith, and is rewarded with peace because of its firm purpose to work for the good of all

That many more young men and women will see the gates of holiness opening and enter them, grateful to spend their lives for God and His holy people

That we who acknowledge Jesus as Lord may be careful to act on His word, building our house on solid rock

For our beloved departed ones, that God whose mercy endures forever may purify them quickly and show them His divine salvation

### Advent Week 1, Friday

*Isa 29:17-24, Ps 27, Matt 9:27-31*

For the church, that it will ever be a place where the lowly can find joy in the Lord and the poor rejoice in God's love

For peace, that the tyrant may be no more, and all who are alert to do evil will be cut off, and that the threat of war may be kept from us by the Prince of Peace

For all those who feel engulfed in the world's misuse of Christmas, that through Advent liturgies, penance services, and special practices in Church and home they may be steadied and sustained in their spiritual preparation

For all who seek healing from the Lord Jesus and pursue Him with their longing, that they may have the confidence He asks in order to work His miracles

That our beloved departed ones may be purified quickly and be free to gaze on the loveliness of the Lord and receive His bounty in the land of the living

### Advent Week 1, Saturday

*Isa 30:19-21, 23-26, Ps 147, Matt 9:35–10:5a, 6-8*

For the church during this holy season as she seeks out her own who have become lost, for the spiritual success of penance services and "Come Home for Christmas" programs

For peace; that world leaders may hear and heed the voice of the Divine Teacher who points out the right way in the depths of their hearts

That laborers may be sent into the Lord's harvest with authority over evil and the power to heal and bless

For all who are in need of compassionate intercession: the sick, the brokenhearted and those who weep, that the Lord may be gracious to them and bind up their wounds of soul and body

For our loved ones who have completed their long season of Advent with the end of their earthly pilgrimage, that they may see face to face the One they have always desired

## Advent Week 2, Monday

*Isa 35:1-10, Ps 85, Luke 5:17-26*

For our Holy Father, our bishops and priests, that as they proclaim the prophets who foretell the flowering of the parched land, they themselves may exult and bloom in God's sight

For world leaders, that in their decisions, they may be at the meeting place where justice and peace shall kiss and truth shall spring out of the earth

For all who are paralyzed by sin or indifference to God, that faith-filled and loving souls may bring them to the feet of Jesus and obtain from Him forgiveness and mercy

For all who are in a time of physical or spiritual distress, who feel frightened and weak, that with divine recompense God may come to save them

For our beloved departed ones, that they may walk on the holy way and enter Zion singing, crowned with everlasting joy

## Advent Week 2, Tuesday

*Isa 40:1-11, Ps 96, Matt 18:12-14*

For our leaders in the church, that they may be heralds of the glad tidings that God is coming with power and compassion again

That world leaders may imitate the way the Lord will rule the earth, with justice and constancy, with mercy and peace

For the sheep that have gone astray, for all those under the burden of expiating guilt, for the little ones who are in danger of getting lost, that we may rejoice the heart of God by helping Him to tenderly reclaim them

For all the intentions recommended to our prayer, that God may come with power into every need and create new reasons for each one to rejoice again

For our beloved departed ones, that they may meet the One who gathers them into His arms and leads them with a shepherd's care to the perfect pastures of the heavenly kingdom

### Advent Week 2, Wednesday

*Isa 40:25-31, Ps 103, Matt 11:28-30*

For the church and her leaders, that God may uphold her hope as with eagle's wings, helping us all to run in His ways and not grow weary

That the vague and unspoken longings for peace that surface with the approach of Christmas may blossom into acts of compassion, becoming a way of life

That Christians may seize upon the grace that enables them to give pardon for iniquity and healing for injuries, not reacting to others according to their sins, but being agents of kindness and redemption

For all who are weary and find life burdensome with its deceptive promise of happiness in material things, that they may be drawn to Jesus, and exchange their heavy load for His light burden

For those who have departed this mortal life, that their purification may be swift and their welcome into the kingdom of heaven assured

### Advent Week 2, Thursday

*Isa 41:13-20, Ps 145, Matt 11:11-15*

For our shepherds in the church, that they may have the power of Elijah to motivate God's people to be strong and energetic in their pursuit of the kingdom of heaven, taking it by force

That the Lord, who is compassionate towards all His works, may stir up in the hearts of world leaders desires and initiatives that will lead to peace

That God's people may experience His saving help as He turns their inner deserts into rivers and plants their wastelands with flowering trees, showing everyone His gracious salvation

For the poor and destitute, those living on the street, those who suffer most from the winter's cold and the coldness of human hearts, that loving hands may reach out to them in the name of Jesus

That our dear departed ones may rejoice in the Lord and glory in the Holy One of Israel, experiencing the grace of His full salvation in heaven

## Advent Week 2, Monday

*1 Sam 15:16-23, Ps 50, Mark 2:18-22*

For the church in all her members, that each baptized soul may be a new wineskin, capable of receiving all the truth and grace that the Lord wishes to pour in

For the powerful, who like Saul are tempted to take for themselves the resources that God has put at the service of all, that they may be converted to obedience and generosity

For all who twist and interpret God's commands to fit their own will, that those who see more clearly may have Samuel's courage to speak up and lead them back to humble submission

For those whose lives are a long fast, afflicted with sickness, poverty, pain, addiction, or grief, that the Bridegroom may return and bring the joy of the wedding feast again

For our dear ones who have passed away, who went along the right way of obedience in this life, that they may now see the salvation of God in His divine light and glory

## Advent Week 2, Tuesday

*1 Sam 16:1-13, Ps 89, Mark 2:23-28*

That the Spirit of the Lord may rush upon the anointed ministers of Christ, stirring up the grace of their ordination for the salvation of all

That the Lord who looks into the heart may choose and anoint rulers of nations who will do His will, pursuing justice, protecting life, upholding morality, and fostering peace

That Jesus, who defended his disciples from the attacks of the Pharisees, may uphold and defend believers who are attacked for their faith

That God, Father, Rock, and Savior of His suffering little ones, may assist all who have asked our prayers in their needs

That our loved ones who have gone before us may soon be seated at the sacrificial banquet in God's presence and with His saints

## Advent Week 2, Wednesday

*1 Sam 17:32-33 etc., Ps 144, Mark 3:1-6*

That the church may take the part of David, relying completely on the Lord in every conflict with the powers of evil

That Christians may do all they can to exert their influence for the cause of gospel morality, justice, concern for the poor and for the planet, and peace

That we may never remain silent when there is a question of preserving life or destroying it, but always let our voices be heard bravely on the side of the God of the living

That God may be a refuge and a fortress, a stronghold and deliverer to those who call upon His name in their sickness, poverty, and grief

That our beloved dead may soon be singing a new song of deliverance and victory in the presence of the Lord in His heavenly kingdom

## Advent Week 2, Thursday

*1 Sam 18:6-9, 19:1-7, Ps 56, Mark 3:7-12*

For our leaders and teachers in the church, for those who heal and nourish God's people, for our priests, that they show Christ's love in word and deed

For leaders of nations, that they may not act out of anger or jealousy, but let themselves be persuaded into honorable and peace-keeping actions

That Christ may be powerful in us, the members of His body, to drive out evil in all its forms, and to bring healing to those who are oppressed by dark forces of mind and soul

For those who are in distress, whose tears are stored in God's flask, that they may know that God is with them through the loving actions of those who help and console them

For our beloved dead, that they may be purified quickly through this holy sacrifice, to walk before God in the light of the living

## Advent Week 2, Friday

*Isa 48:17-19, Ps 1, Matt 11:16-19*

For the church, that we may follow the teaching of the Lord, our God, who leads us on the way we should go, so that our posterity in His kingdom will last forever

For world leaders, that they may not follow the counsel of the wicked, but delight in the law of the Lord, making decisions for life, justice, and peace

That Jesus may make us His sensitive followers, ready to follow His lead whether He approaches us in austerity or abundance, knowing that He is wise in all His works

For the sick, for those who mourn the loss of a loved one, for those in financial difficulties, for prisoners, for the lonely and the elderly, for all who need loving intercession and compassionate reverence

For those who have gone before us marked with the sign of faith, that the fruit they bore while planted near the running waters of grace may now be their key to God's heavenly kingdom

## Advent Week 2, Saturday

*Sir 48:1-4, 9-11, Ps 80, Matt 17:9a, 10-13*

For our leaders in the church, that they may appear like a fire at the head of the people, speaking the prophetic word like Elijah and John the Baptist

That the Prince of Peace may bless us with the gift of national leaders who respect the dignity of each human person

That we may be ready to suffer for God as John the Baptist and Jesus did before us, taking strength from our contact with the Lord in this Eucharistic banquet

For all who have asked our prayers and all who need compassionate hearts to relieve their burdens at this time, that the blessing of Jesus and the love of His followers may console them

That the Shepherd of Israel may shine forth from His cherubim throne upon all our faithful departed, bringing them into new life in his own kingdom

**Advent Week 3, Monday**

*Num 24:2-7, 15-17a, Ps 25, Matt 21:23-27*

That the soul of the church may continue to be formed and guided into all truth by the one Divine Star, our Lord Jesus Christ, who advances to meet our Advent longing

That prophetic voices raised in our world, when they are found to be the utterances of those whose eyes are true, may be taken seriously, so that there may be peace

For the conversion of those who resist the authority of Christ in their lives, that our prayer and fasting, joined to this holy sacrifice, may win for them renewal of heart

For the sick, the poor, the lonely and forgotten prisoners and street people, that God, whose compassion and kindness are from of old, will remember them and inspire many to help them

For our dear departed loved ones, that they may be free from all stain of sin and behold the beauty of the Lord, enraptured and with eyes unveiled

**Advent Week 3, Tuesday**

*Zeph 3:1-2, 9-13, Ps 34, Matt 21:28-32*

For our Holy Father, our bishops and priests, that they may teach us the way of righteousness by word and example

That God may change and purify the lips of all peoples, making us upright and just in our dealings with one another, so that there may be peace

For the whole church as she undergoes continual judgment and conversion, that she may be found humble and lowly, taking refuge in the name of the Lord

For those who are in a season of distress: financial difficulties, sickness, loneliness or emotional pain, that the Lord who is close to the brokenhearted may let them experience the power of His salvation

That our faithful departed may be brought quickly through all purification and stand, radiant with joy, in the Lord's presence

## Advent Week 2, Friday

*1 Sam 24:3-21, Ps 57, Mark 3:13-19*

For our Holy Father, our bishops and priests, successors to the first apostles and personally chosen by Jesus, that they may be faithful to the mission He has entrusted to them

For the oppressed, for the helpless unborn, for all who are pursued and hunted down by the mighty, that God may grant them justice beyond the reach of the powerful ones

That we may treat our enemies with the high mindedness and generosity that David showed to Saul, that the Lord may take our part and keep us from harming our own souls with revenge and hatred

For the poor, the sick, victims of natural disasters and conflicts, that God may send them His mercy and faithfulness and give them refuge under the shadow of His wings

For all who have gone before us, that they may come to know God's mercy personally as He purifies them and welcomes them into heaven

## Advent Week 2, Saturday

*2 Sam 1:1-4 etc., Ps 80, Mark 3:20-21*

For the church, that Mary, her model and Mother, may assist each baptized soul to be faithful to Jesus through all the changes of life

For nations who try to seek the solution of their issues in war and violence, that the international community may give an example of negotiation and peaceful means to resolve issues

For those who are dear friends to one another, as Jonathan was for David, that their unity and loyalty may remain unshaken

For all who have asked our prayers and for those most in need of prayer today, that their distress may be relieved by the power of love in this Holy Sacrifice

For the dead and those who mourn for them, as David did for Saul and Jonathan, that the souls of the deceased may find rest, and those who are left behind may find comfort

### Advent Week 3, Monday

*2 Sam 5:1-7, 10, Ps 89, Mark 3:22-30*

That the church may never become a house divided against itself, but that all parties may put their faith in Jesus to work in their efforts to remain strong and united in love

That those who lead the peoples out and bring them back may be anointed by the Lord as He once anointed David, with power to govern wisely and well

For the gift of discernment of spirits, that the Holy Spirit may guide and direct us in our assessment of what is good and what is evil

That God's faithfulness and mercy may be with the sick, the poor, those suffering from war and natural disasters, and all who need His help today

That our dear departed ones may be brought into the New Jerusalem, the stronghold of the Lord, with splendor and rejoicing

### Advent Week 3, Tuesday

*2 Sam 6:12-15, 17-19, Ps 24, Mark 3:31-35*

That the King of Glory, throned upon the cherubim, may find a permanent resting place in the church, honored and exalted with joy by her members

That our world leaders may be as devoted to God as David was, so that they too may be able to bless their people with life, justice, and peace

That we may take our place with Mary as loyal disciples of Jesus, earning the right to be in His intimate family circle by our faithful obedience and love

For all who are suffering, lonely, depressed, imprisoned, or ill at this time, that this Holy Sacrifice may have the power to bring them healing and grace

That the ancient portals of heaven may open to allow our beloved dead to enter, crowned with everlasting joy

## Advent Week 3, Wednesday

*Isa 45:6c-8, 18, 21c-25, Ps 85,
Luke 7:18b-23*

For our shepherds in the church, that they may teach the truth about Jesus in all its fullness, so that no one may find a stumbling block in their approach to Him

For those in a position of power and influence in the world, that they may act in kindness and truth, so that justice and peace may prevail

For all of us, waiting for justice to descend like gentle rain and for the earth to open and bud forth a Savior, that God may enlarge our desire and answer it with His own divine coming

For the sick, the poor, those who are oppressed with evil spirits, that Jesus, who cured diseases and afflictions in His own day, may respond to our prayers on their behalf

That Mary, model of holy expectation during these Advent days, may welcome into God's kingdom our loved ones who have gone before us marked with the sign of faith

## Advent Week 3, Thursday

*Isa 54:1-10, Ps 30, Luke 7:24-30*

That the church may have the joy of being obliged to enlarge her tent to accommodate the abundance of her new offspring

For world leaders, that they may work for life and justice, so that God may remake with us His covenant of peace

For all who feel far from God, who have an image of Him as forbidding and severe, that they may hear Him calling them tenderly, removing every reproach

For all who are in special need at this time from sickness, financial distress, or emotional pain, that through the power of prayer, God may change their mourning into dancing again

For our departed loved ones, that their Advent longing may come to fulfillment in the kingdom where Jesus reigns as Savior, Master, and Lord

## Advent Week 3, Friday

*Isa 56:1-3a, 6-8, Ps 67, John 5:33-36*

For the whole church, that she may be a lamp set afire and burning brightly for all who seek God in the darkness of the modern world

That God may make His ways known upon the earth and in all nations through the blessing of upright leaders who will rule the peoples in equity, working for peace

For all of us whom the Lord has brought to this holy mountain and made joyful in this house of prayer, that our sacrifices may be acceptable to Him as we unite ourselves with His only Son

For all who are in special need at this time, and those who have asked our prayers, that they may find that their burdens are lightened

For those whose Advent time of longing is over, who have seen the Lord, that they may be quickly purified to live with Him forever in heaven

*For Saturday of the Third Week of Advent and weekdays of the Fourth Week of Advent, use the intercessions for the appropriate date on the following pages.*

### Advent Week 3, Wednesday

*2 Sam 7:4-17, Ps 89, Mark 4:1-20*

For the church, the house of the Lord, built of living stones, that each of us may be dedicated to His honor and to the building of His kingdom upon the earth

That world leaders may make it their first priority to build up their nations in justice, truth, and peace, so that God will make each country and dynasty stand fast in His favor

That we may receive the seed of God's Word on good soil, not allowing persecution, the lure of riches, or the wiles of Satan to choke it off, so that we may bear good fruit in joy and praise

For those who are struggling to grow amid the thorns of illness or tribulation, that our love and prayers and the gracious power of Jesus may help them to thrive again

For our dear ones who have gone before us, that God will establish His covenant of love with them in the heavenly kingdom that will stand firm forever

### Advent Week 3, Thursday

*2 Sam 7:18-19, 24-29, Ps 132, Mark 4:21-25*

For our Holy Father, our bishops and priests, keepers of the house built for the Lord by His Son Jesus Christ, that they may be its strong guardians worthy of the Lord's blessing

That world leaders may keep God's covenant and decrees, which He teaches them through an upright conscience, so that God may establish and prosper their authority upon the earth

For all of us who are entrusted with the lamp of faith, that we may reveal the One Who lies hidden in our hearts through the radiance of our words and actions

For those who have asked our prayers in a time of struggle, grief, and distress in their lives, that God may grant them His blessing of health and grace and hidden joy

For all the dead whose faith is known to God alone, that they may be purified to become shining lights in the kingdom of light and beauty which is heaven

**Advent Week 3, Friday**

*Isa 56, 1-3, 6-8, Ps 67, John 5:33-36*

For the whole church, that she may be a lamp set afire and burning brightly for all who seek God in the darkness of the modern world

That God may make His ways known upon the earth and in all nations through the blessing of upright leaders who will rule the peoples in equity, working for peace

For all of us whom the Lord has brought to this holy mountain and made joyful in this house of prayer, that our sacrifices may be acceptable to Him as we unite ourselves with His only Son

For all who are in special need at this time, and those who have asked our prayers, that they may find that their burdens are lightened

For those whose Advent time of longing is over, who have seen the Lord, that they may be quickly purified to live with Him forever in heaven

*For Saturday of the Third Week of Advent and weekdays of the Fourth Week of Advent, use the intercessions for the appropriate date on the following pages.*

## December 17

*Gen 49:2, 8-10, Ps 72, Matt 1-17*

For the whole church, drawing nearer now to the radiant coming of Jesus in the flesh, that with her leaders she may be sustained in joy and hope

That God may endow with judgment the leaders of nations, that they might govern their peoples with justice

That the genealogy of Jesus may encourage us with the reality of His human nature, and we may understand that it is a brother of ours who comes with divine power to save us

For all who have asked our prayers during a time of distress and pain, that God may defend the afflicted among the people, and save the children of the poor

That our Blessed Mother, who kept the secret of the first Advent in her adoring heart, may bring into the full light of glory all whom the Father has called from this world

## December 18

*Jer 23:5-8, Ps 72, Matt 1:18-25*

For our Holy Father, our bishops and priests, that like St. Joseph they may be righteous in their decisions and docile to the divine influence of grace in their lives

That the Lord may raise up in our time leaders who will reign and govern wisely, and do what is just and right in the land, so that there may be peace

That Mary may keep watch over the hidden awakenings of grace in us all, even as she guarded with her adoring silence the secret of the Incarnation in her womb

For all who are in a season of sickness, loneliness, or abandonment, that Joseph and Mary may bring the treasure of their firstborn Son into their lives

For our beloved dead, that the Lord who alone does wondrous deeds may cleanse them of all sin and bring them rejoicing into His kingdom of light and joy

## December 19

*Judg 13:2-7, 24-25, Ps 71, Luke 1:5-25*

For our shepherds in the church as they make the journey to Christmas with their parish communities, that they may arrive at the feet of Jesus in peace and reconciliation

That war may be averted from our world, and that our leaders may be given clear-sighted wisdom from the Prince of Peace

For the holiness of our families, for parents who are just in the eyes of God, that from their youth will arise vocations consecrated to God

For the gift of a strong faith, which does not doubt or question God's action in our lives, so that we may never be mute in our praise or slow in co-operating with His gracious design

For all who have asked our prayers, for all who have need of loving intercession, and for our dear departed loved ones, that our prayer may be heard for their joy and gladness

## December 20

*Isa 7:10-14, Ps 24, Luke 1:26-38*

For our consecrated ministers, who ascend the mountain of the Lord and stand in His holy place, that their hands may be sinless and their hearts clean, and that they may have the joy of intimacy with God

For peace; that as the Prince of Peace takes flesh in the womb of the gentle virgin, He may inspire world leaders to be sincere in their respect for every human life from its very conception

For Mary's surrender in our hearts, that we may accept with complete loving trust and humility every initiative of God in our lives, always saying, "Be it done to me according to your word"

That the suffering and the oppressed may experience the power of the unexpected and the miraculous in their lives, a sign that the Lord Himself is answering our prayers for them

For those who have died, that Mary, who found favor with God, may intercede for them and bring them into His kingdom of heaven rejoicing

## December 21

*Song 2:8-14 or Zeph 3:14-18a, Ps 33, Luke 1:39-45*

For the whole church, waiting for the imminent approach of her beloved Savior and Bridegroom, that she may soon hear His voice rejoicing over her with gladness and renewing her in His love

That our nation may learn to be a people whose God is the Lord, a people in whose midst the plan of the Lord takes precedence, so that He may bless us with His peace

That the love which impelled Mary to bring Jesus to her cousin under the humble guise of family service may be the same impetus that supports all our actions during this holy season

For all who are suffering in body, mind or spirit, that the expectant Virgin may visit them and surprise them with her joy

For our dear departed ones, that they may find that the winter is past for them, that the divine lover is calling them to arise and enter the eternal bliss of heaven

## December 22

*1 Sam 1:24-28, 1 Sam 2:1, 4-5, 6-7, Luke 1:46-56*

For our Holy Father and our bishops and priests, who have been dedicated to the Lord for as long as they live, that their self sacrifice may be pleasing in His eyes and an inspiration for all His people

That world leaders may be willing to raise the needy from the dust and to lift up the poor, working for life, for justice, and for peace

That Mary's song of praise may find an echo in our hearts; that we may celebrate God's wonderful ways of lifting up the lowly, filling the hungry with good things, and coming to our help in all our needs

That those who suffer and have asked our prayers may have cause to sing their own Magnificat, as God remembers His promise of mercy for each of them

For those who have died, that God who casts down to the nether world and raises up again may give them life with Himself in His glorious kingdom

## December 23

*Mal 3:1-4, 23-24, Ps 25, Luke 1:57-66*

For our Holy Father, our bishops and priests, that they may be purified ever more in the refining fire of God's love, so that they may offer His divine sacrifices in a way most pleasing to him

That the King of all nations, the Keystone of the arch of humanity, our Lord Jesus, may bring peace to all the troubled areas of our world

For those whose hearts and tongues have been bound in distrust and apathy before God, that a new experience of His mercy may open their mouths in gratitude and praise

That we who share in this Eucharist, who are visited suddenly in our interior temple by the Lord whom we seek, may welcome all His work in our hearts today

For the intentions of all who are suffering, lonely, or at the mercy of the winter weather, for all who need our prayer, and for our beloved dead

## December 24

*2 Sam 7:1-5, 8b-12, 14a, 16, Ps 89,*
*Luke 1:67-79*

For the whole church on this eve of the Savior's birth, that our Blessed Mother, who kept the first Advent with such immaculate purity and expectation, may guide our final preparations

That the One who is the dawn from on high may break upon us and guide our feet into the ways of peace

That God, who built an enduring dynasty for King David, may build up in each of our hearts a throne for Himself that will stand firm forever

For all who are sick, grieving, poor, lonely, or in financial distress on this Eve of Christmas, that in Jesus' name hearts and hands may reach out to them in respect and love

For our faithful departed, that they may spend this Christmas rejoicing in heaven with the angels and the One who came to save us all

# SEASON OF CHRISTMAS

*See Proper of Saints for December 26–28, pp. 412–13.*

## December 29

*1 John 2:3-11, Ps 96, Luke 2:22-35*

For all who are consecrated to the Lord by the bonds of holy priesthood, that all their sacrifices may be offered with the reverence of Joseph and Mary as they offered Jesus in the temple

That we who pray for peace in response to the angelic greeting "Peace on Earth", may remember that it was promised to those of good will, and bring every resource of prayer, sacrifice, and action to the work of peace

For the elderly, who wait wordlessly for some hidden promise of hope to be fulfilled before they feel ready to accept death, that God may come to them in reconciliation, joy, and love

For all who have a sorrowful destiny in life, whose hearts are pierced, that Mary, who once shared their troubles, may intercede to lighten their burdens

That we who have come to know Jesus through intimate contact with Him in the Holy Eucharist may keep His new commandment of love, walking in the light of His truth

For our departed loved ones who have gone in peace, that their eyes may see the salvation God has prepared for us all in Jesus

## December 30

*1 John 2:12-17, Ps 96, Luke 2:36-40*

For the church, that her leaders may still proclaim fearlessly the all-importance of God in a world of profit and pleasure, which only dazzles and deceives and then passes away

That in these days when we celebrate the arrival of the Prince of Peace God may awaken in our leaders the goodwill to which His angels promised peace on earth

For the anawim of the church—the widows who haunt her temples, and those who know the ways of fasting and prayer—that their insights and gentleness may serve to build up the church and renew her hope in Jesus

That our families may be strong in faith, and that their children may grow in grace and strength, filled with wisdom and the favor of God

For the sick and those who are near death, that the loving Father who has drawn them away from the passing scene of this world may let them taste His sweetness and know His compassion

That our dear departed loved ones may come to know Him who is from the beginning, seeing the Father face to face in heaven's vision

## December 31

*1 John 2:18-21, Ps 96, John 1:1-18*

For the whole church, cherishing its anointing that comes from the Holy One, that with her leaders she may grow into all knowledge and truth

For world leaders, that on this eve of the world day for peace they may make and keep resolutions to uphold justice, life, and the dignity of each human person, creating the climate for true peace

That there may be many young and enthusiastic souls who will, like John the Baptist, give testimony to the true Light which has come into the world

That we may be among those who accept Jesus into our lives freely and fully, so that He may give us power to become children of God shining in a darkened world

For all who have need of prayer today: that they may receive grace upon grace from the fullness of the Savior

For our beloved departed ones, that they may come to see God and the only begotten Son who is at the Father's side in heaven

## January 1

*For January 1, use the intercessions for the Solemnity of the Blessed Virgin Mary, the Mother of God on pp. 6, 42, or 78.*

### January 2 before Epiphany

*1 John 2:22-28, Ps 98, John 1:19-28*

For our leaders in the church, that they may always be voices who urge us to make straight the ways of the Lord

For our leaders in the world, that their decisions may make known the salvation of the Lord by choosing the pathways of justice, life, and peace

For all of us receiving this Eucharist, that we may remain in Jesus and allow His anointing to teach and guide us

For all who are in a period of great need or distress, that the Lord may show them His kindness and His faithfulness and raise up friends to help and console them

For our beloved dead, that the promise of eternal life offered to those who remain in Jesus may become a radiant reality for them in the heavenly kingdom

### January 3 before Epiphany

*1 John 2:29–3:6, Ps 98, John 1:29-34*

For the church; for prudence, order, and harmony among her ministers and for loyalty and respect in her members, so that she may be blessed with unity

That through the efforts of Christians who have heard the Gospel and live by it, all the ends of the earth may see the salvation of God mirrored in justice and built up in peace

For all of us on whom the Spirit has come down and remained because of our baptism, that with John the Baptist we may witness to Jesus by our holiness of life

For the sick, for the dying, for the elderly, the handicapped, and all who bear in their flesh and in their spirit a share in the passion of Jesus

For those who have died but are not yet pure, that our loving prayers and this Holy Sacrifice may cleanse them and bring them into heaven where they may see God as He is

### January 4 before Epiphany

*1 John 3:7-10, Ps 98, John 1:35-42*

For all our leaders in the church, that they may always find that they are rediscovering Christ, staying with Him, and proclaiming Him to others

For those in power in the world, that through their words and decisions they may allow the Lord to rule the earth with justice and the peoples with equity

For the Sisters of Charity, founded by St. Elizabeth Ann Seton, for their ministries in the church, their personal intentions, their holiness, and the grace of new vocations to their company

That all of us may act out of our union with Jesus in this Holy Eucharist, showing forth to each other and to those in greatest need His holiness and loving kindness

That the Lamb of God may shepherd our dear departed loved ones to the heavenly kingdom which His sacrifice has won for them

### January 5 before Epiphany

*1 John 3:11-21, Ps 100, John 1:43-51*

For our Holy Father, a man without guile and a true follower of Jesus, that His labor and effort may be rewarded with rich spiritual fruit

For the balance of justice, with those who have enough of this world's good opening their hearts to the brothers and sisters who are in need

That we who receive in Communion the One who laid down His life for us may truly come to understand love and put it into practice in deed and in truth

For all who are suffering or grieving at this time, especially those who have asked our prayers, and those who have no one to remember them before God

That the angels of God who ascended and descended on the Son of Man may come with Him now to escort our deceased loved ones into His heavenly kingdom of love and light

## January 6 before Epiphany

*1 John 5:5-13, Ps 147, Mk 1:7-11*

For our leaders and teachers in the church, that like John the Baptist they may be humble before the majesty of the one whom they proclaim as the Christ

For the nations of the world, that the Lord may grant peace to their borders as a result of their earnest efforts to uphold the dignity of human life and the cause of human justice

That we who possess God's testimony and know that we have eternal life in Jesus may live our lives in a spirit of gratitude and reverence towards our Savior

For the poor, the sick, the imprisoned, the grieving, the addicted, that they each may be granted a new revelation of God's mercy in this Christmas season

For our faithful departed, that they may be given the capacity to see Jesus in His glory, anointed by the Spirit and possessing the Father's favor

## January 7 before Epiphany

*1 John 5:14-21, Ps 149, John 2:1-11*

For our holy shepherds, that they may have the discernment to know the One who is true, and help us to be on our guard against every form of idol

For the mercy of peace in every conflicted and oppressive situation in our world today

For sinners, especially our loved ones who are estranged from the church, that God who hears our prayers may bring them back to His mercy

That our Blessed Mother may intercede for us and for all who are suffering, so that the wine of God's joy may be given us as a sign of His power and His love

For our loved ones who have gone before us in faith, that God may protect them from the power of the Evil One and bring them safely home to heaven

### Monday after Epiphany

*1 John 3:22–4:6, Ps 2, Matt 4:12-17, 23-25*

For the church, that she may be faithful to the Spirit of God who acknowledges Jesus come in the flesh, and that she may give witness to Him at all times

That the kings and rulers of the earth may give heed and serve the Lord with fear, keeping His ways of justice, life, and peace

That the repentance demanded by Jesus may be in our hearts as we continually turn from the ways of the world to the dominion of the Gospel

That Jesus, who cured every disease and illness among the people of His own time, may hear our prayers for all those who need His healing touch today

For our beloved dead, that as they remained in Jesus during this passing life, they may now see Him face to face in the life that has no end

### Tuesday after Epiphany

*1 John 4:7-10, Ps 72, Mark 6:34-44*

For the church, proclaiming that God is love according to the Gospel, that she may show forth this love in all her actions, making God present in the world

That God may endow the powerful ones with judgment, that they may govern the peoples with justice, defend the afflicted, and save the children of the poor, preparing the way for peace

That the hunger of our brothers and sisters may be appeased by Jesus who asks us for the resources we can bring Him to help Him in this task

That Jesus, whose heart was moved with pity for the needy crowd, may sustain with His mercy the sick, the poor, the afflicted little ones whom we bring Him today in our prayer

That God, who sent His Son as expiation for our sins, may release our faithful departed ones from every burden and bring them rejoicing into His heavenly kingdom

## Wednesday after Epiphany

*1 John 4:11-18, Ps 72, Mark 6:45–52*

For the church, battling the winds that rise against her, that Jesus may once again get into the boat of St. Peter, giving courage and strength

The those in positions of power and influence may have pity for the lowly and the poor, working for the causes of justice, life, and peace

That we who have experienced the love of God and know that He remains in us may become perfect in our love for one another

For all who have recommended themselves to our prayers, that Jesus may say to each one in the midst of life's storms: Take courage, it is I; do not be afraid

That those who have gone before us may have confidence on the day of judgment, allowing perfect love to cast out all fear in God's presence

## Thursday after Epiphany

*1 John 4:19–5:4, Ps 72, Luke 4:14-22*

That in union with our Holy Father, our bishops, and our priests, we may always live in the victory that conquers the world, which is our faith

That world leaders may imitate Jesus in His vocation to bring glad tidings to the poor and liberty to captives of oppression and injustice

For all of us in the community of faith, that we who profess our love of God may obey His command to love our brothers and sisters in deed and in truth

That Jesus, who was anointed for grace and healing, may touch and heal the sick, the distressed, the imprisoned, and all who need His gentle hand upon their lives

For our dear departed loved ones, that as they were begotten of God by baptism in this life, so also they may come to the fullness of divine life in the bliss of heaven

### Friday after Epiphany

*1 John 5:5-13, Ps 147, Luke 5:12-16*

For our holy shepherds in the church, that their ministry of faith and healing may be supported by deep prayer

That God may bless the children within the borders of all nations through the efforts of their leaders to promote the dignity of each human life

That we who possess the threefold testimony—the water of our Baptism, the Blood of the Eucharist, and the indwelling Spirit—may believe that we also possess eternal life in Jesus Christ

For all who are afflicted, sick, or depressed, especially those who count on our prayers, that they may be given faith in the Lord's will to reach out to them in compassion and power

That God, who gave us eternal life in His Son, may reveal this life in our loved ones who have completed their time on earth, and bring them into His heavenly kingdom

### Saturday after Epiphany

*1 John 5:14-21, Ps 149, John 3:22-30*

For the whole church, that she may give glory to the grace of being begotten by God in her life of loving prayer and humble service

That we may take hold of the confidence we have in God that He hears us if we ask according to His will, and that we may boldly request that our civil leaders walk in the ways of life, morality, justice, and peace

For vocations to the priestly and religious life; that the Bridegroom may have many friends whose joy consists in preparing His way and listening for His voice

That the Lord who loves His people and adorns the lowly with victory, may hear our prayers for all those who are in a season of distress and suffering, giving them cause to exult in glory again

That Jesus, true God and eternal life, may receive our loved ones who have departed this earthly existence into the glory and joy of His kingdom

## SEASON OF LENT

### Ash Wednesday

*Joel 2:12-18, Ps 51, 2 Cor 5:20–6:2, Matt 6:1-6, 16-18*

For our Holy Father, our bishops and priests, that as ambassadors for Christ they may fearlessly proclaim the need for repentance and reconciliation with God during the acceptable time of Lent

For the leaders of Christian nations, that through the grace of this holy season they may be given clarity of heart and vision, and be sustained with a willing spirit to work for justice and peace

That we who accept the sign of ashes as a confession of our mortality and of our faith in the life-giving power of God, may make room for that divine life to grow by our hidden deeds of penance and mercy

That we may no longer avoid the effort to change, but that all our powers be gathered into the assembly of the Lord, acknowledging our offenses and begging for a clean heart and a steadfast spirit

For the sick, the forgotten poor, the imprisoned, and the lonely, that the softening of hearts may begin to loosen their bonds as love begins to flow to them in Jesus' name

For the dead, that the One who became sin for their sake may cleanse them of all stain, and share with them His joy in the glorious kingdom

### Thursday after Ash Wednesday

*Deut 30:15-20, Ps 1, Luke 9:22-25*

For our leaders in the church as we take our first steps into the holy season of Lent, that they may be men and women of God, challenging the community as Moses did to choose God's ways in truth

For our civil leaders, that they may refuse to follow the counsel of the wicked, but delight rather in the law of the Lord, choosing life and peace

For the conversion of sinners and those who have blindly chosen the curse that comes from the vanishing path of evil, that our fervent prayer may help them turn from the way of self destruction

For those who are enduring suffering, rejection, and abuse, for all those whose lot was chosen by Jesus as His own, that we may accompany them with love in their time of trial

For our dear departed ones, who took up their cross in this world, that their willing loss of life into Jesus may now blossom in His glorious resurrection

### Friday after Ash Wednesday

*Isa 58:1-9, Ps 51, Matt 9:14-15*

For the whole church on this day of special penance and fasting, that our poor brothers and sisters may benefit from our self denial as we share their daily portion

That Christians may take the lead in setting free the oppressed, releasing those bound unjustly, and sheltering the homeless, so that there may be peace

That we may humbly admit our sinfulness and be given the great grace of a deep conversion to God during this holy season

For all who are suffering in body and soul, especially those who have asked us to pray for them, that the inner bonds that afflict them may be broken and their wounds healed

For our beloved dead, that their time of purification may be shortened, and they may rejoin the Bridegroom at the wedding banquet of heaven

### Saturday after Ash Wednesday

*Isa 58:9-14, Ps 86, Luke 5:27-32*

For the leaders of the church, reaching out to the beloved sinners as Jesus did and inviting us all to a change of heart, that their efforts may bear fruit in a great return to God

That the Christian leaders of powerful and wealthy nations may take the lead in removing oppression and assisting the afflicted, so that the restored balance of justice may bear its fruit of peace

For the restoration of the honor that is due to the Lord's day, and that all other interests and pursuits may yield to the worship, reflection, and rest that our souls require for strength and renewal

For all who are in need of loving intercession in their distress, for the imprisoned and the poor who are so easily forgotten, that God may gladden the souls of those who cry to Him

That Jesus who came to call not the righteous but sinners, may forgive the offenses of all our departed, and bring them into the banquet of His joy in their salvation

## Lent Week 1, Monday

*Lev 19:1-2, 11-18, Ps 19, Matt 25:31-46*

For our Holy Father, our bishops and priests, that they may continue to call upon God's people to be holy

For world leaders, that they may respect the basic code of upright living that is planted in everyone's heart

That our charity may be sincere and effective and that the judgment upon our works may bring us everlasting life

For all the intentions recommended to our prayers, especially for the sick and suffering and those who mourn the loss of a loved one

For our beloved departed, that our prayers may help them as they stand before the Lord and see Him as He is in the moment of judgment

## Lent Week 1, Tuesday

*Isa 55:10-11, Ps 34, Matt 6:7-15*

That God's Word may not be void in His holy Church, but may do His will, watering the earth of our souls and making them fertile and fruitful

For the brokenhearted, for the defenseless, for the oppressed, for the unborn, that God may raise up leaders and prophets who will speak for them and help them

That our prayer may be one of confidence in a Father who knows all our needs, and be filled with submission to His will and forgiveness of our enemies

For those who have asked for the help of prayer in a season of illness, trial, or grief, that God may again make them radiant for joy because of their faith in him

For those who have gone before us, who often had the Lord's Prayer upon their lips and in their hearts, that they may now behold the forgiving Father

### Lent Week 1, Wednesday

*Jonah 3:1-10, Ps 51, Luke 11:29-32*

For our leaders in the church, that they may fearlessly proclaim the need to reform, no matter how enormously large the task seems to be

For the leaders of the world, that like the King of Nineveh and the Queen of the South, they may respond to the message of the prophets of our time who cry out in God's name for justice, life, and peace

For all who have wandered far from Christ and His church, that He may create a clean heart in them and renew in them a steadfast spirit

That Jesus may raise His sign of hope and healing over the sick, the poor, the imprisoned, the addicted, and all who are in need of our prayer

For all the faithful departed, that they may be purified of every trace of sin and brought rejoicing before the God of all the saints

### Lent Week 1, Thursday

*Est C:12, 14-16, 23-25, 12, 14-16, 23-25, Ps 138, Matt 7:7-12*

For our shepherds in the church, who are at times alone in their witness against a hostile environment, that they may, like Queen Esther, have recourse to the Lord in fervent and efficacious prayer

For our world leaders, that the King of Gods and Ruler of every power may build up strength within them to work for true peace and human dignity in His name

That our Lenten fasting may serve to help those who must fast by necessity, and our small experiences of their daily lot make our hearts humble and compassionate

That encouraged by the words of Jesus we may learn to ask, knock, and seek with more persistence and confidence in our prayer for all the intentions that have been recommended to us

For our beloved dead, that God may turn their mourning into gladness and their sorrows into wholeness in His heavenly kingdom

### Lent Week 1, Friday

*Ezek 18:21-28, Ps 130, Matt 5:20-26*

For the church, that the special penance and reconciliation services held by parishes during Lent may be a turning point in the lives of all who participate in them

That those who walk in the ways of iniquity and have violence in mind to disrupt the good order of any nation may turn from their evil course to the ways of righteousness and peace

For each person who knows that another has something against him, that this season of Lent may be the time when the hard work of reconciliation is done

For all who have asked for our prayers in a time of distress or illness, and for our loved ones who need a special grace to return to the sacraments

For those who have died, who are imprisoned in the process of their own purification, that this Holy Sacrifice may bring them the joy of release into God's blissful kingdom of love

### Lent Week 1, Saturday

*Deut 26:1-9, Ps 119, Matt 5:43-48*

For our Holy Father, our bishops and priests, that they will continue to form a people sacred to the Lord in a holy covenant of mutual loyalty and devotion

For peace in the world, and especially in the land where Jesus walked and taught the fulfillment of the Hebrew covenant in the perfect command of love

For our enemies, for our persecutors, for those who hold us in contempt, that we may release them from any bonds of resentment and bitterness, and pray for their healing and happiness

For the sick, the elderly, the addicted, the imprisoned, the homeless, and the refugees, and all who are in need of special prayer today

For our dear departed loved ones, that this Holy Sacrifice may make them perfect even as the Father is perfect, and enable them to enter the heavenly kingdom

## Lent Week 2, Monday

*Dan 9:4b-10, Ps 79, Luke 6:36-38*

For the church and her ministers, that she may never cease to admit her sinfulness before God, acknowledging His justice and pleading for His mercy

That the rulers of this age may heed the prophetic voices that cry out for the life of the unborn, justice for the oppressed, and peace for all

That today's Gospel message, direct and powerful as it is, may change our lives; and we may become merciful and forgiving even as our heavenly Father is merciful

For all who are brought very low, especially for the prisoners whose sighing comes before the Lord, and for all who have asked our prayers

For those who have gone before us, that the measure of their good gifts may be shaken down and overflowing in the kingdom of heaven

## Lent Week 2, Tuesday

*Isa 1:10, 16-20, Ps 50, Matt 23:1-12*

For our leaders in the church, that they may truly be servants of the servants of God, and thus merit the first places in His kingdom

For world leaders, that they make justice their aim, redressing the wronged, hearing the orphan's plea and defending the widow, promoting peace in our time

For all those whose sins are like scarlet, that through a great grace of conversion they may becoming willing to obey God again

That we who receive Jesus under the humble appearance of ordinary bread may learn to be one with Him in His humility of heart

For all the intentions recommended to our prayers, for the sick, the unemployed, the homeless, and for our beloved dead

## Lent Week 2, Wednesday

*Jer 18:18-20, Ps 31, Matt 20:17-28*

For our leaders in the church, who have been invested with authority in order to serve the needs of all, that they may be true to the desires of the Master in the exercise of their mission

For peace in the world, that leaders may arise who will speak on behalf of those who suffer most from armed conflict, and turn away the wrath that threatens them

For all of us who drink the chalice of the Lord in this Eucharist, that He may give us strength for the share of His bitter chalice that is part of our earthly destiny, so that it may become a communion of love with Him

For all who are approaching their Jerusalem where suffering will take hold of their lives, that Jesus may walk at their side and raise them up in His compassion

For those who have died and have commended their spirits into the hands of a faithful God, that their destiny may be His glorious kingdom

## Lent Week 2, Thursday

*Jer 17:5-10, Ps 1, Luke 16:19-31*

For our Holy Father, our bishops and priests, that they may faithfully hold up the Law and the Prophets, which point the way of salvation to all who choose to hear

For world leaders, that they may not seek their strength in human beings, but trust in the Lord and flourish like a tree beside the running waters of life, justice, and peace

For those who are dried up in spirit through neglect of God and His life-giving way, that the Lord who alone probes the heart will attract them in secret ways back to himself and to the sacraments

For the poor and neglected suffering ones of our own day, that we may have eyes to see them and compassion for their wounds

For our beloved dead, that their purification may be shortened through our loving prayer, and that they may soon find a place with Lazarus in the bosom of Abraham

### Lent Week 2, Friday

*Gen 37:3-4, 12-13a, 17b-28a, Ps 105, Matt 21:33-43, 45-46*

For the church on this journey of Lent, that our prayer and penance, and our listening to God's word may deepen our love for our Savior and our gratitude for His pain-filled redemption

For peace, that God who softened the hearts of Reuben and Judah toward their brother Joseph may change and soften the enmity of hearts today

That we who receive Jesus in this Eucharist may make Him the capstone of our lives, entering into His sufferings so as to share His glory

For all who have been sold or forced into slavery, for all who suffer oppression under the hatred or greed of others, that Jesus, who shared their fate, may become their divine liberator

For our faithful departed, that as they bore good fruit in the Lord's vineyard in this life, so now they may drink the new wine of His glory in the next

### Lent Week 2, Saturday

*Mic 7:14-15, 18-20, Ps 103, Luke 15:1-3, 11-32*

For the church, gathered around the table of our merciful Father, welcomed, robed, ringed, and forgiven, that we may glorify Him with our grateful love

That world leaders may give evidence of God's compassion when dealing with victims of poverty and disease

For the prodigal sons and daughters, especially those among our loved ones whom we carry in our hearts, that they may respond to the grace that urges them to come home to their loving Father

For those who are returning painfully to the Father through the realms of sickness, financial hardship, loss, and grief, that they may find loving hearts and hands to help them

For those who have gone before us in death, that they may be welcomed into the Father's house with a celebration of rejoicing

## Lent Week 3

*alternative readings: Exod 17:1-7, Ps 95, John 4:5-42*

For our leaders in the church, who must respond to the demands of the people, that God may stand with them as He did with Moses, providing the waters of life in the church through their ministry

That the peoples of the earth may not test and tempt God with immorality and injustice, but listen to His voice and respond with reverence and obedience

That we may give Jesus the cool water of our faith and our love, and that we may understand the gift of God, knowing that Jesus is the One who gives us the living water of everlasting life

That Jesus, who gently led the Samaritan woman to salvation, may reach out to all the sick and sinful souls who need to come home to His love during this holy season

For our dear departed loved ones, the harvest of the Lord, that they may be Jesus' hidden food, the joy of His heart, which only wishes to save and glorify us in heaven

## Lent Week 3, Monday

*2 Kgs 5:1-15, Ps 42, Luke 4:24-30*

For the church, her leaders, her teachers, and her faithful, who know Jesus more intimately than the world, that He may not be without honor among His own

For all people who are unjustly oppressed and enslaved, that like Naaman's slave girl, they may by their return of good for evil open the way for the healing of the oppressor

That more souls may feel their thirst for the waters of the living God, and be attracted by His light and faithfulness to the mountain whereon He dwells

For all who suffer in mind or body, that through the compassionate ministry of Christians who fulfill their prophetic role of witness to a saving God, they may find release and strength

For our beloved dead who still thirst for the face of the living God, that they may soon behold Him in the beauty of heaven

### Lent Week 3, Tuesday

*Dan 3:25, 34-43, Ps 25, Matt 18:21-35*

That our princes, prophets, and leaders in the church today may have contrite hearts and humble spirits, guiding us in the ways of repentance and unreserved following of the Lord

That God may make known to our world leaders His ways, guiding them in His truth and teaching them to work for life, for justice, and for peace

That we may forgive our brothers and sisters from our hearts, realizing clearly the pittance of their debts and the consequences before God of refusing forgiveness

For those who are brought low by sickness, unemployment, bereavement, imprisonment, or addiction, that our sacrifice in God's presence today may bring light and sweetness to them

For those who have gone before us, who have come before the King as He settles accounts with His servants, that they may be set free from their debts in mercy

### Lent Week 3, Wednesday

*Deut 4:1, 5-9, Ps 147, Matt 5:17-19*

That the church may never forget the great things God has done for her, never get used to grace, and that her gratitude may find expression in obedience

That our great nation may give evidence of its wisdom and intelligence among the nations by resolutely observing the God-given laws upon which it was founded

For all who find it difficult to obey, for whom law is an impersonal and negative reality, that they may come to understand that the God of love can only legislate for the fullness of life in His children

For all who have asked for our prayers, and for those most in need of prayer, that healing, strength, and guidance may come to them through the power of this Holy Mass

For our dear departed loved ones, who while on earth obeyed and taught the commands of Jesus, that they may now enjoy the fruits of their obedience in heaven

**Lent Week 3, Thursday**

*Jer 7:23-28, Ps 95, Luke 11:14-23*

For our holy shepherds in the church, that during this acceptable time of repentance, they may be zealous in gathering in those who have become scattered, who have lost the word of God in their lives

For world leaders, that they may not harden their hearts to the inner voice that guides their steps into the ways of peace

For the conversion of sinners, for the softening of hardened hearts, for a return to God in the sacrament of reconciliation for many souls this Lent

That through the power of Jesus the forces of evil may be driven out of the lives of those who are held bound, and their tongues may be loosed in praise of our saving God

For all the faithful departed, that the kingdom of God may come upon them with all the joys of heaven

**Lent Week 3, Friday**

*Hos 14:2-10, Ps 81, Mark 12:28-34*

For the church, as the greatest commandment is proclaimed today in all her assemblies, that every idol may be cast out before this living God who alone is worthy of our adoring devotion

That leaders of powerful Christian nations may do their part to relieve the poor of their burden and to rescue those in distress, walking in the straight paths of the Lord

That our compassionate God may heal the defection of those who have wandered far from Him, helping them to take root and blossom beside the waters of His forgiving mercy

That the cleft rock of the Heart of Jesus, pierced for our sins and yet filling us with honey and the finest wheat, may make us capable of returning love in the face of every injury we receive

That the mercy of Jesus may be like the dew for our departed loved ones, and that they may blossom like the lily in the courts of our God in heaven

### Lent Week 3, Saturday

*Hos 6:1-6 , Ps 51, Luke 18:9-14*

For the whole church, that what is proud in her may be humbled, and that each of her members identify honestly with the sinner who admits His wrong and asks for mercy

For world leaders, that they may strive to know the Lord, and that for them His judgment may shine forth as the light of day, creating peace

That God who desires love and not sacrifice may find that our piety remains and grows in His presence through the action of His saving grace

For all who are in a period of distress of mind, body, or spirit and whose hearts are humbled by suffering, that they may be exalted in joy and healing

For our beloved dead, that God may raise them up to live in His presence in the joy and peace of heaven

### Lent Week 4, Monday

*alternative readings, Mic 7:7-9, Ps 27, John 9:1-41*

For our leaders in the church, that they may be men and women who see clearly and worship Jesus with all their hearts, helping others to come to Him for healing and sight

For the oppressed and the helpless little ones of the world, that the Lord may take up their cause and establish their rights in the sight of the powerful

For those preparing for baptism, that like the man born blind they may now be able to see the truth and believe in Jesus who gives them their spiritual sight

For those who are suffering in soul or body, that our prayers may bring them relief, and help them to wait for the Lord with courage until they see His bounty in the land of the living

For our faithful departed ones, that Jesus, the light of the world, may raise them up to the realms of light and peace in heaven

**Lent Week 4, Monday**

*Isa 65:17-21, Ps 30, John 4:43-54*

For the church, that God may not let her enemies rejoice over her, but may increase the light of her witness in the world, especially during these privileged days of Lent

That Isaiah's vision of a new heaven and a new earth may begin to come to fruition through the work of world leaders who labor for justice and peace

That we may gladden the Heart of Jesus with our strong faith in His power and in His love, not needing to see signs and wonders in order to believe

For those who are weeping, for those who are sorely tried, that the Lord may return and have pity on them, changing their mourning into dancing

For our beloved departed ones, that God may create rejoicing and happiness in their purified souls as He leads them into heaven

**Lent Week 4, Tuesday**

*Ezek 47:1-9, 12, Ps 46, John 5:1-6*

For the ministers of the altar, that as they channel the life-giving waters of the sacraments into our hearts, they themselves may be refreshed and healed by their contact with this saving stream

For peace, that the salt sea of embittered nations and peoples may be sweetened and made fresh by God's grace and the loving forgiveness of Christian hearts

That the free flowing presence of grace in our lives may be the cause of our growth and thanksgiving at all times, but especially during this holy season of Lent

For the sick and those paralyzed by addiction and poverty, who wait for a helping hand, that in the person of His followers Jesus may again show the mastery of His loving power in their lives

That our beloved dead may be freed from any impurity that still clings to them and be made ready to appear with joy before the face of the Lord

### Lent Week 4, Wednesday

*Isa 49:8-15, Ps 145, John 5:17-30*

For our leaders in the church, that like the Divine Shepherd they may guide God's people to good pasture and living water with compassion and truth

For our leaders in the world, that the distress of present conflicts may impel them to turn with greater determination to find every way possible to create and preserve peace

For mothers who have been without tenderness for the children in their womb, that they may come to a change of heart

That the Lord, who is near to all who call upon Him in truth, may support and comfort all who feel their need for Him in a season of stress, sickness, unemployment, or anxiety

For all our beloved dead, that they may hear the voice of the Son of Man calling them into new life

### Lent Week 4, Thursday

*Exod 32:7-1, Ps 106, John 5:31-47*

For the church and her ministers, that like Moses they may be people pleasing to God and capable by their prayer of turning the divine anger into mercy

For peace, especially in the lands made holy by the patriarchs, the prophets, and the saving work of Jesus

That we may be as John the Baptist, with the lamps of our faith and love burning and shining as a testimony to the world

For all who have asked for our prayers in a time of illness or distress, that through this Holy Sacrifice God may again do great deeds and wondrous works of healing and grace for them

For the faithful departed who believed in the One whom God had sent to save us, that they may now hear the voice and see the form of the Father in the heavenly places

## Lent Week 4, Friday

*Wis 2:1, 12-33, Ps 34, John 7:1-2, 10, 25-30*

For the ministers of the church, that they may continue to proclaim the divine origin of Jesus Christ in their words and in the reverence of their liturgical actions

For the gift of peace, that a renewed purity of heart may enable world leaders to understand the hidden counsels of God and the primacy of human rights

For all who are persecuted for their faith and their goodness of life, that God may be close to them when they are brokenhearted and crushed in spirit, and raise them up as He did His Christ

For all the intentions recommended to our prayers, for our loved ones who are in a season of distress at this time, that God may deliver them out of all their troubles

For those who have gone before us marked with the sign of faith in the suffering Messiah, that Jesus may cleanse them from all sin and raise them up in His glorious kingdom

## Lent Week 4, Saturday

*Jer 11:18-20, Ps 7, John 7:40-53*

For our priestly shepherds in the church, that they may be like Nicodemus who defends Christ before His enemies with the power of truth

That our national and international leaders may be men and women of justice, leading their people under God's protection in the ways of peace

For all who are in danger of persecution because of their prophetic witness to the truth, that they may entrust themselves in their innocence to the salvation of the Lord, who judges the hearts of all

For the sick, the unemployed, the poor, the imprisoned and addicted little ones who stand most in need of mercy, that God may be a saving shield before them, granting them light and grace

For our dear ones who have departed the land of the living, that they may be quickly purified to enjoy the delights of eternal life in heaven

## Lent Week 5

*alternative readings: 2 Kgs 4, Ps 17,
John 11:1-45*

For the church, that she may walk in the light of Christ during the short day of this earthly life, following Jesus wherever He goes

That the power and witness of God's prophets may prevail among the nations who need to hear His truth in order to rebuild a culture of life and a civilization of love

That like Martha and Mary we may come to Jesus with our sorrows and give Him our faith, so that His power may become active for rejuvenation and peace

For all who grieve in the face of death, that Jesus, who wept for His friend Lazarus, may summon them to new life and joy

For our dear departed ones, that Jesus, the Resurrection and the Life, may reward their faith in Him by calling them forth into new life in His holy kingdom

## Lent Week 5, Monday

*Dan 13:1-9, 15-17, 19-30, 33-62, Ps 23,
John 8:12-20*

For our shepherds, our bishops and priests, as they prepare for Holy Week, for their spiritual strength and fervor

That God may raise up prophets like Daniel who will point out to world leaders where the will of God lies, so that the innocent may be spared

That we may never be eager to cast the first stone or to judge others in any way, but remember our own sins and weaknesses and imitate the divine patience and mercy

For all who are walking through a dark valley of illness, unemployment, addiction, or abuse, that they may feel the guidance of the Good Shepherd leading them to waters of rest and peace

That Jesus, who would not condemn the woman caught in adultery, may forgive the sins of our faithful departed and free them from all suffering, bringing them into the light and joy of His kingdom

## Lent Week 5, Tuesday

*Num 21:4-9, Ps 102, John 8:21-30*

For the church, that she may always be willing to lift up the cross for the healing of the people

That the time of fear and destruction may soon come to an end for all oppressed and war-torn areas of our world

For those who stand most in need of the grace of forgiveness, who are in danger of dying in their sins, that they may have the light to approach the sacrament of reconciliation, to be met there by the mercy of the Son of Man

For all who are passing through a time of distress, especially those who have asked for our prayers, that they may experience the face of God turning to them in grace and healing

For all those who have died, that with Jesus they may experience the all-pervading presence of the Father in the face-to-face vision of heaven

## Lent Week 5, Wednesday

*Dan 3:14-20, 91-92, 95, Dan 3:52-56, John 8:31-42*

That the church may be imbued with the prophetic spirit that inspired the three youths in the fiery furnace, willing to face martyrdom rather than draw back from their witness to God

That like King Nebuchadnezzer, the leaders of the nations may be able to recognize and acknowledge God's power and His rights in the world

That we may allow Jesus to set us free, believing in Him with all our hearts and giving His word the freedom to have all the room in our lives

That through the power of this Holy Sacrifice, Jesus, the beloved Son, may free those who are chained by sin, poverty, sickness, grief, or any other distress in this land of exile

That those who have gone before us may join all the blessed in singing God's praises as they behold Him forever, throned upon the cherubim

**Lent Week 5, Thursday**

*Gen 17:3-9, Ps 105, John 8:51-59*

The Abraham, our father in faith, may keep the church and her holy ministers faithful to God's covenant in our own age

That those in positions of power and influence may keep God's judgments before them as a covenant of life and of peace

That Jesus, who reveals His divine name to us in today's Gospel, may enable us to keep His word and glorify Him by our faithful obedience

For all who have asked for our prayers and for those who are most in need of prayer at this time, that our loving intercession and the offering of this Mass may gain them healing and grace

That Jesus, who promised that those who keep His word will never see death, may free our departed loved ones from every bond of sin and bring them into the kingdom of the living

**Lent Week 5, Friday**

*Jer 20:10-13, Ps 18, John 1:31-42*

For our Holy Father, our bishops and priests, that in all the great and small persecutions they face they may be true to their loyalty to Jesus

That the Lord may be with the prophets of our own age like a mighty champion, helping them to speak out for the right to life and to human dignity for all God's children

That our Eucharist today may unite us to Jesus who is in the Father, and enable us to abide in Him and bring forth the good works that He desires to perform through us

For the sick, the poor, the bereaved, the oppressed and persecuted, for all who are suffering, that God may be for them a rock of refuge and a stronghold of hope

That Jesus, the Father's beloved Son, may take into His care all our dear ones who have died, bringing them into the Father's presence as the trophies of His victory

### Lent Week 5, Saturday

*Ezek 37:21-28, Jer 31 canticle,*
*John 11:45-57*

For the grace to keep loyal and fervent company with our Redeemer during this coming Holy Week, as He courageously goes up to the Passover to suffer and die for our redemption

That the covenant of peace promised by God to His people may spread as a blessing of peace to all the troubled areas of our world today, especially to the land of Israel

For Christians, assembled from all the nations into the flock of the Good Shepherd, that the one who makes us holy may continue to lead us into full unity

For all who suffer, whose powers of body and soul are dispersed and scattered by pain, that Jesus may call everything together again by His healing might

For our beloved dead, that Jesus, who died so that the whole nation would not be destroyed, may bring them to the city of peace which is the heavenly Jerusalem

# HOLY WEEK

### Holy Week, Monday

*Isa 42:1-7, Ps 27, John 12:1-11*

For our leaders in the church, that they may guide us with the gentleness that does not break the bruised reed, and the firmness that will make the church a light for all nations

For the victory of justice in our world, that God may raise up and form leaders after His own heart, so that there will be peace

For all who pour out their lives as precious nard upon the feet of Jesus, giving them their entire love, that the fragrance from their sacrifice will rejoice the whole house of the church

For all those in a season of grief, pain, or illness, that our prayers may uphold them to wait for the Lord with courage

For our beloved dead, that they may see the bounty of the Lord in the land of the living

## Holy Week, Tuesday

*Isa 49:1-6, Ps 71, John 13:21-33, 36-38*

For our priests, especially those who feel they have toiled in vain and spent their strength for nothing, that they may find everything again in the hands of the glorified Christ, anointed with His victory

For the prophets, the sharp-edged swords, the polished arrows of God who speak out for the right to life and human dignity, that they may be heard and heeded by our world leaders

For all who are devastated by the betrayal of friends, co-workers, and family members, that Jesus, who understands their distress from personal experience, may sustain and comfort them

For all of us who in this Eucharist come into living contact with the heart of Christ like the beloved disciple, that Jesus may feel free to confide in us and know that we will be faithful

For all the intentions recommended to our prayer and for our dear departed ones, that the grace of the paschal mystery may absorb and transform everything it touches in our lives with its healing and its glory

## Holy Week, Wednesday

*Isa 50:4-9, Ps 69, Matt 26:14-25*

For the priests of God, that they may accept from Him the gift of a well-trained tongue, and be open to His word and fearless of its consequences

For those who work for peace, for the right to life, for justice, that God may uphold their cause and never let them be put to shame

For all who are suffering persecution, especially those most bereft of sympathy and comfort, that they may experience how faithful God is to His own who are in bonds for His sake

That the fruit of our Communion with Jesus today may be the grace to follow Him into the winepress of His passion with resolute love, knowing that we will share His victory

For all who are in a period of distress and in need of prayer, for the repose of the souls of our faithful departed, that all the lowly ones may be glad and feel their hearts reviving because of the Lord's redeeming love

# SEASON OF EASTER

## Easter Octave, Monday

*Acts 2:14, 22-33, Ps 16, Matt 28:8-15*

For our Holy Father, our bishops and priests, that with St. Peter they may preach the truth of Jesus and His glorious resurrection boldly and without fear, impelled by the Holy Spirit

For peace, that the holy greeting of Jesus to His beloved disciples and friends may spread its grace over the whole world

For all who have been entrusted with the good news of Jesus' triumph over sin and death, that they may make the proclamation by their words and by their actions

For all those for whom the cross is still their portion, that they may experience the comfort of knowing that their pain, united to that of the Lord, will end in His radiant victory

For our beloved dead, that the grace of the resurrection may be comfort and speedy entrance into the exulting company of heaven

## Easter Octave, Tuesday

*Acts 2:36-41, Ps 33, John 20:11-18*

For all who have inherited the role of proclamation from the first preacher, St. Peter, that with Him they may speak the truth boldly and that God may work through them to save His people

For the newly baptized, who rejoice the church and swell the ranks of her faithful, that they may also join in her battles for life, peace, and human dignity with all the energy of their newfound joy

For all true lovers of Jesus, who like Mary Magdalene regard even angelic apparitions as nothing without Him, that their persevering and ardent devotion may be rewarded by a sudden encounter with the Beloved

For the sick, the poor, the imprisoned, all who need the intercession of compassionate hearts, that Jesus, risen and victorious, may bring them the grace of their own rising to new life

That our dear departed ones may come to their personal meeting with their risen Savior, and hear Him call each one lovingly by name

## Easter Octave, Wednesday

*Acts 3:1-10, Ps 105, Luke 24:13-35*

For our leaders in the church, that they may be filled with the spirit of wisdom that spoke in Jesus when He explained the Scriptures to His own, kindling the fire that the first disciples felt burning inside them

That those who are distressed and despairing may be met with the respect and compassion that walks with them until their hope is restored and peace is made possible

For the sick in body or soul who sit begging while so many pass them by, that there may be for them Christians like Peter and John, who see them, stop, and give them what they have in the name of Jesus

For all of us sharing this Eucharist, that we may come to know our risen Lord in the breaking of this bread, and be ready to get up and spread the Good News, unafraid of the darkness

For all those whose day of life is practically over, and for all who have died, that Jesus may give them hope in the glory that waits for us all on the other side of the cross

## Easter Octave, Thursday

*Acts 3:11-26, Ps 8, Luke 24:35-48*

That the church may continue to proclaim a suffering Messiah and the need to unite with Him in His trials in order to emerge with Him in His glory

For our political leaders, that they may be willing to be guided by the holy and righteous ones who point out the ways that lead to justice and peace

That Jesus, who is still our living companion hidden in the Holy Eucharist, may give us the grace to truly build our lives around His life giving presence

For all who have asked our prayers and all who stand in need of prayer today, that the Lord may grant them a time of refreshment and grace

For our faithful departed, who participated with us in the breaking of the bread, that they may now be feasting with the Lord, recognized and adored, in His holy kingdom

## Easter Octave, Friday

*Acts 4:1-12, Ps 118, John 21:1-14*

That the church may continue to proclaim the salvation found only in Jesus, the cornerstone of our faith

That the world may not lack apostles and prophets who will speak out in the name of truth, for the cause of life, justice, and peace

For all of us who so often toil in vain to fill our nets, that we may listen to the mysterious voice of the Lord who directs our efforts to a great catch

That we who partake of the meal provided by Jesus in this Eucharist may bring Him the urgent intentions of the poor, the sick, the addicted, the imprisoned, and all those whom we love

For our departed loved ones, who have come ashore with Jesus on the other side of His passion and death, that they may soon be pure and ready to enter the kingdom of joy that He won for us

## Easter Octave, Saturday

*Acts 4:13-21, Ps 118, Mark 16:9-15*

For our shepherds in the church, who continue Peter and John's ministry by speaking and teaching in the name of Jesus, that they may be as fearless in their witness as were the first apostles

That the witness of Christian prophets, who proclaim the right to human dignity for all in Jesus' name, may be heard and heeded by world leaders

That we may never hear the Lord's rebuke for unbelief and hardness of heart, but respond generously to His command to take the Good News to every creature

That Jesus may continue to show His power in the lives of ordinary men and women who will be recognized as His companions by their joy, courage, and power to heal hearts in His name

For all the intentions recommended to our prayer, for the loved ones we hold in our hearts, and for our dear ones who have entered the mystery of death, that the resurrection of Jesus may be grace and life for them all

### Easter Week 2, Monday

*Acts 4:23-31, Ps 2, John 3:1-8*

For the priests, teachers, and preachers of the church, that they may be filled with the Holy Spirit and speak the word of God with boldness

For the nations of the world, who at times still gather together against the Lord and His will to life and justice, that the Father may in His powerful providence raise up Jesus as our King of Peace

For the newly baptized, begotten from above, that they may be strong in their faith and grow in works of love and grace

For all the intentions recommended to our prayers, that Jesus the anointed one may be powerful in His loving mercy toward the needs of each

For our beloved dead, that each one who was reborn of water and the spirit may now taste the full delight of the kingdom of God

### Easter Week 2, Tuesday

*Acts 4:32-37, Ps 93, John 3:7b-15*

For the apostles of today: our Holy Father, our bishops and priests, that they may continue to bear witness with great power to the resurrection of the Lord Jesus

That the Lord, whose throne stands firm from of old and whose decrees are worthy of trust, may direct world leaders in accord with those decrees into the ways of justice and peace

For all of us sharing this Eucharist in which Jesus is again lifted up, that we may lift up our love for each other as a sign to attract all to the One who has come down from heaven for love of us

For the sick, the terminally ill, and those whose disabilities or advanced age bring loneliness of heart, that there may be sons of encouragement and daughters of charity who lay their resources of time and compassion before them

For our dear departed ones, that the risen Lord may complete their purification in a powerful gift of grace, and lead them rejoicing into eternal life

## Easter Week 2, Wednesday

*Acts 5:17-26, Ps 34, John 3:16-21*

For the apostles and prophets of the church today who suffer under persecution, that they may rely on God's power to open the doors of every prison

For world leaders, that their deeds may be worthy to be exposed to the light, as they labor in the ways of peace

For young people graduating from high school and college, that they may seek the Lord who can deliver them from all their fears and make them radiant with joy

For all who are afflicted in mind, body, or spirit, that they may have the grace to call upon the Lord who can free them from distress

For our dear departed ones, who believed in Jesus, that they may not be condemned, but that God who so loved the world may bring them rejoicing into His kingdom

## Easter Week 2, Thursday

*Acts 5:27-33, Ps 34, John 3:31-36*

For the leaders of the church, that they may have the compassion and courage to confront those who do wrong, and thus offer them the opportunity to receive the great grace of repentance

For the prophets of our own time who speak out in the cause of human dignity, that they may be heard and heeded by those in a position of power and influence

For vocations, that many may accept the testimony of Jesus deep in their hearts and give themselves to Him in life and death

For those who are experiencing the troubles of the just in distress of mind, body, or spirit, that they may experience how the Lord delivers them

For our beloved dead who believed in the word of the Son of God, that they may now taste and see how good the Lord is

## Easter Week 2, Friday

*Acts 5:34-42, Ps 27, John 6:1-15*

For our leaders in the church who suffer dishonor for the sake of the Gospel, that they may have the grace to rejoice as the apostles did and keep on proclaiming Jesus as the Lord

For leaders of wealthy nations, that they may not allow the poorer nations to go away hungry, but share their resources for the sake of justice and peace

For vocations, that generous hearts may seek only to dwell in the house of the Lord all the days of their life, and to do His work in this world

That we may offer the Lord our small gifts of loaves and fishes, trusting in His power to multiply what we give Him for the sake of all who need compassion and help in their needs

For our beloved departed ones, that they may soon see the bounty of the Lord in the land of the living

## Easter Week 2, Saturday

*Acts 6:1-7, Ps 33, John 6:16-21*

For our leaders in the church, still engaged in steering her through the turbulent waters of our own day, that their labors may move the Savior to manifest Himself in the grace of courage and strength

That the Lord, who loves justice and right, may raise up leaders after His own heart to keep us in the ways of peace

For deacons, that God may continue to grace them with prudence and deep spirituality and prosper their ministry in the church

For the poor, the sick, the imprisoned, and addicted, and all who have asked for our prayers, that the eyes of the Lord may be upon them for healing and renewal

For our faithful departed, that they may hear the words of the Lord, "It is I. Do not be afraid," as He welcomes them into heaven

## Easter Week 3, Monday

*Acts 6:8-15, Ps 119, John 6:22-29*

For the leaders of the church and especially for her deacons, that they may all be filled with grace and power and speak with the wisdom that comes from the Holy Spirit

For our civil leaders, that they may choose the way of truth and open themselves to understand God's commandments, so that they may lead us in the ways of peace

For all who are looking for Jesus, even if only to receive His favors, that the Lord may raise them to the faith which perceives the seal of God upon Him, even when His words are challenging and difficult

That the intentions of all those for whom we have been asked to pray may be laid at the feet of Jesus during this Holy Sacrifice, to be blessed and answered in His love

For our loved ones who have passed on, who ate the food that endures for eternal life while they were on earth, that eternal life in heaven may now be their portion

## Easter Week 3, Tuesday

*Acts 7:51–8:1, Ps 31, John 6:30-35*

For our shepherds in the church, that like Stephen they may give fearless witness in the Holy Spirit to the teachings of Jesus, even at the risk of persecution

For all the war-ravaged areas of our world, for those who suffer the results of terrorism and genocide, for the great blessing of peace

That we may stand firm in Jesus, our bread of life, coming to Him that we may never hunger, believing in Him that we may never thirst

For all the intentions recommended to our prayers, for all who are in a time of testing and distress, that the Lord may hide them in the shelter of His presence and let His face shine upon them

For all our beloved dead, who fed on the Bread of God in this passing world, that they may quickly be purified to see the Lord Jesus in the heavenly kingdom

## Easter Week 3, Wednesday

*Acts 8:1-8, Ps 66, John 6:35-40*

For the whole church, especially where she is harassed and persecuted, that her suffering may be the seed of healing and rejoicing in the souls of those to whom her ministers are scattered

That the initiatives to bring about peace and respect for all human life may be blessed, giving us a new reason to sing praise for the tremendous deeds of God among the peoples

For all who have wandered far from Jesus, the bread of life, and have become famished and vulnerable to the poisonous nourishment of sin, that they may return to their Savior

For the poor, the sick, the addicted and oppressed, the imprisoned and those who grieve, that Jesus, who never rejects anyone who comes to Him, may grant them mercy, healing, and peace

That our faithful departed, who believed in Jesus during this mortal life, may now be raised up by Him to eternal life

## Easter Week 3, Thursday

*Acts 8:26-40, Ps 66, John 6:44-51*

For our Holy Father, our bishops, priests, and deacons, that they might be as responsive to the movement of the Spirit as Philip was, letting themselves be placed wherever souls are searching for the Lord

For peace; that we may all be taught by God to come to Jesus as the model for all truth, justice, and courageous self-sacrifice to give life to the world

For all of us sharing this Eucharist, feeding upon the Flesh of the Lord, that we may be willing to give our lives generously for one another as He did

That God may not refuse our prayer or His kindness for all the special intentions we bring to this Holy Sacrifice

For those who have died, that Jesus, who will raise us all on the last day, may open to them the gates of heaven in welcome and joy

## Easter Week 3, Friday

*Acts 9:1-20, Ps 117, John 6:52-59*

That our ministers in the church may be like Ananias, willing to respond to the Lord's directions at all times, giving healing and new life in His name

That Christians may be today's outspoken witnesses to the justice and respect for the dignity of each human being, bringing back to our world the tranquility of order that is peace

For the conversion of all who persecute Jesus in His members, that like Saul they may be brought to their own Damascus encounter with Him

For our Christian brothers and sisters who are not yet able to take in the full mystery of the Eucharist, that they may be given the grace to understand clearly the words of the Lord

For all the intentions recommended to our prayers, for the healing of the sick among us, and for our beloved departed ones

## Easter Week 3, Saturday

*Acts 9:31-42, Ps 116, John 6:60-69*

For our leaders in the church, that like Peter they may decide always to remain with Jesus, even when His words of spirit and life are hard to understand and follow

For the gift of peace, that peace may be restored to troubled nations, and that we may all be built up in peace of heart and the consolation of the Holy Spirit

For the paralyzed and impoverished, the sick and lonely people in our midst, that Christians sensitive to the movement of the Spirit may come to them with healing and life

That with Jesus we may have the grace to speak the truth, even when it means we will lose companions and supporters

For our beloved dead, who believed the words of Jesus and shred in His Eucharist, that the Spirit of the Lord may raise them to eternal life

### Easter Week 4, Monday

*Acts 11:1-18, Ps 42, John 10:1-10*

For the shepherds and pastors of the church, who keep watch at the gate over the flock of Jesus, that they may allow no thief to damage and steal His own

For world leaders, that God may send forth to them His light and His fidelity, and that they themselves may faithfully guide us in the ways of justice and peace

For the unconverted and those estranged from God and His church, especially our own loved ones, that God may grant them life-giving repentance

That we who know the vigilant and tender care of the Good Shepherd, may by our prayers obtain the same blessing for all who have asked our prayers

For our loved ones who have died, who thirst to go and behold the face of the living God, that Jesus may shepherd them to the running waters of God's mercy

### Easter Week 4, Tuesday

*Acts 11:19-26, Ps 87, John 10:22-30*

That our ministers in the church may be men filled with the Holy Spirit and faith, helping us to remain faithful to the Lord in firmness of heart

That those who glory in the name of "Christian" may be the first to stand up for the life and dignity of every child of God

That we who are among the flock of the Good Shepherd may listen to His voice, following Him faithfully wherever He may lead

For the poor, the sick, the imprisoned and addicted, the oppressed and those who grieve, that the hand of the Lord may be with them in healing, strength, and grace

That Jesus, who gives His sheep eternal life and does not allow them to perish, may take our faithful departed into His hands and bring them to His Father

## Easter Week 4, Wednesday

*Acts 12:24–13:5a, Ps 67, John 12:44-50*

That the Holy Spirit may never cease to send forth our holy preachers to proclaim the word of God and spread the Gospel of Jesus

That the peoples on the earth may be ruled with equity and the nations be guided by leaders who fear the Lord

That the words of Jesus may be for us the way out of darkness into God's brilliant light, because we accept them and put them into practice in our lives

For all who are in a time of distress of mind or body, who are anxious about their loved ones, who are in mourning, that our loving prayers and this holy sacrifice may be light and joy for them

For those who have gone before us, that God may let His face shine upon them and bring them quickly into His glorious kingdom

## Easter Week 4, Thursday

*Acts 13:13-25, Ps 89, John 13:16-20*

That the church might always be faithful to her mission of proclaiming the Good News of Jesus and the need for repentance in His name

That God, who raised up David as a holy and just king, may raise up in our own day leaders and people of influence and power who do what is just and right in His sight

That we may follow the Master's example as He washes the disciple's feet, by our humble service of one another and of all who come to us in His name

That God's faithfulness and His mercy may be with all who suffer, and that through His name their strength may be exalted

That our departed loved ones may have reason to sing the goodness of the Lord and to exalt His faithfulness at the wedding banquet of heavenly joy

## Easter Week 4, Friday

*Acts 13:26-33, Ps 2, John 14:1-6*

For our leaders in the church, that they may be strong witnesses, proclaiming Jesus as the Way, the Truth, and the Life

That the rulers of the earth may serve the Lord in truth, giving their peoples reason to rejoice before Him in the ways of peace

For vocations, that generous hearts may follow in the footsteps of St. Paul, eager to preach the good news of Jesus Christ

For all who are distressed by sickness, unemployment, bereavement, and all the misfortunes of life, that God may give them the grace not to let their hearts be troubled or afraid, but to be firm in their trust

For our departed ones, especially those near and dear to us, that Jesus will bring them into the dwelling He has prepared for them in His heavenly kingdom

## Easter Week 4, Saturday

*Acts 13:44-52, Ps 98, John 14:7-14*

For the church in her holy ministers, that like Paul and Barnabas they may speak the word of God and words of truth fearlessly especially in times of opposition

For leaders of nations that are known to be formed by centuries of Christian tradition, that they may radiate the light of Christian values to the watching world

That our words and deeds may be a true reflection of the work of the Father, and that we may be filled with joy and the Holy Spirit

For all the intentions that weigh heavily on our hearts, that we may glorify the Father in the Son by believing that if we ask for help with confidence in the name of Jesus, He will do greater deeds than we know how to expect

For our faithful departed ones, that Jesus may show them the face of the Father unveiled in the clear light of heaven

## Easter Week 5, Monday

*Acts 14:5-18, Ps 115, John 14:21-26*

For the preaching of the Gospel, that no one may look for honor but only preach the truth about the living God, giving all glory to Him

That the Holy Spirit, the Advocate, may be with Christians who must stand up and be counted for the moral values of the church, giving them courage and teaching them what they must speak

That we may be made worthy to become the dwelling place of the Father by our love for Jesus and our obedience to His commandments

For all who have asked for our prayers and for those who are most in need of prayer at this time, for the forgotten and oppressed people of our world

That our dear departed loved ones may be quickly purified, so that Jesus may reveal Himself to them in the full glory of heaven

## Easter Week 5, Tuesday

*Acts 14:19-28, Ps 145, John 14:27-31*

For our leaders in the church, that they may strengthen the spirits of Christ's disciples and exhort them to persevere in the faith

For peace, that Jesus' farewell gift to us may stand guard over our hearts and enable us to be a leaven of peace in the world

That we may not allow our hearts to be troubled or afraid, no matter what trial or persecution may come, but trust in Jesus through everything that happens in our lives

For all who are in need of prayer, especially the poor, the sick, the imprisoned and addicted, and those who are grieving the loss of a loved one

For our beloved dead, that they may be introduced into the glorious splendor of God's kingdom

## Easter Week 5, Wednesday

*Acts 15:1-5, Ps 122, John 15:1-8*

For the church as she faces her areas of dissension, which began even in apostolic times, that the work of the Spirit may be recognized and the elders meet to look into the issues of our own day

For the work of the prophets who speak up and witness for the culture of life and the civilization of love

For all of us united with the living and True Vine through our Holy Communion with Jesus, that we may glorify the Father by the good fruit of love and service we bring forth in our lives

For the barren branches that have been pruned off the vine, that by our prayers and sacrifices they may be re-grafted and take root in Jesus again

For the living who are going through a dark tunnel of pain or depression, and for the dead who are united to us by the bonds of love and faith, that Jesus may bring them light and peace

## Easter Week 5, Thursday

*Acts 15:7-21, Ps 96, John 15:9-11*

For our leaders in the church, that they may discern their way through the issues that confront the church today with the same attention to the movement of the Spirit that characterized the apostles

For the nations, that among them the Lord may be king, and direct their leaders to govern in equity, so that they may be worthy of the blessing of peace

That with the first Gentiles, our hearts may be purified by the Holy Spirit and faith, so that we may bear joyful witness to the salvation Jesus has won for all

For those who are suffering in body, mind, or spirit, that they may receive the grace to remain in the love of Jesus in the midst of their trials, so as to have comfort and peace of heart

For our beloved dead, that their purification may be completed through the merits of this Holy Sacrifice, and their joy made complete in heaven

## Easter Week 5, Friday

*Acts 15:22-31, Ps 57, John 15:12-17*

That the Holy Spirit may continue to move in the church today, creating unity and peace among her members

That the church may be a beacon of moral uprightness in the world, and that her light may be welcomed by those in positions of power and influence

That we, who have been called friends by our Lord Jesus Christ, may truly understand His Heart and keep His commandment to love each other

That Jesus, who called us and appointed us to go forth and bear fruit, may accept our prayer on behalf of our suffering brothers and sisters, and bring them healing, grace, and strength

That God, whose mercy towers to the heavens and whose faithfulness is higher than the skies, may welcome our deceased loved ones into His holy kingdom

## Easter Week 5, Saturday

*Acts 16:1-10, Ps 100, John 15:18-21*

That the Spirit of Jesus may continue to direct the expansion of the church and inspire new vocations for her missionary efforts

For those who are persecuted on account of their witness to the teachings of Jesus and to the moral values of His church, that they may continue to speak the truth in love

That we may rejoice to be like our Master, sharing His sufferings so as to share His glory

That the Lord, whose kindness endures forever, may show His faithfulness to all who are suffering, who are oppressed and hungry, who need love and understanding

That our faithful departed may be purified to come before the Lord with joyful song in His divine kingdom

### Easter Week 6, Monday

*Acts 16:11-15, Ps 149, John 15:26–16:4*

For the church, that the Spirit who bears witness on behalf of Christ may make her witness strong even in the face of persecution

That Christians may reach out to praying hearts, as Paul did to Lydia, that the number of people who stand up for the right to justice and to human dignity may increase in the world

That we who have been with Jesus from the beginning of our lives may testify to Him as Lord by our faith, our moral truth, and our joy

For all who are suffering, especially those who have asked for our prayers, that they may experience the divine love and healing that will bring a new song of praise and exultation into their hearts

That our beloved dead may sing to the Lord a new song of praise in the assembly of the faithful enrolled in heaven

### Easter Week 6, Tuesday

*Acts 16:22-34, Ps 138, John 16:5-11*

That many may rejoice at coming to faith in God through the ministry and the living witness of His holy ministers

That God may build up strength within all those who work for the cause of justice and of peace in our world, that their light may shine brilliantly before all

For the coming of the Advocate, the Holy Spirit, into the church and into the hearts of each of us, to energize and enlighten us with His power and grace

That all who call upon the name of the Lord in their suffering of body or soul may experience the Lord's salvation in their lives

For our dear departed ones, that they may be purified quickly, and come to sing God's praises in the presence of the angels in heaven

### Easter Week 6, Wednesday

*Acts 17:15, 22–18:1, Ps 148,
John 16:12-15*

For the church and her leaders, that the example of St. Paul's apostolic zeal may invigorate the new evangelization and bring generous hearts to place their lives at the service of the Gospel

For the deep conversion that our world needs in order to engage in a culture of life, so that the peace which is the fruit of justice and mutual respect may be restored to us

For all who are still searching for an Unknown God, and yet trying in vain to find Him in the works of their own genius and art, that God may open their hearts to the humility of faith

For all those who are still unable to bear the fullness of truth, that the Spirit of truth sent by Jesus may strengthen their hearts and open their eyes to see His glory

For all who have asked for our prayers, for those we hold in our hearts, and for our beloved dead

### Easter Week 6, Thursday

*Acts 18:1-8, Ps 98, John 16:16-20*

For our Holy Father, our bishops and priests, and especially for our missionaries, that as they continue the work of proclamation with all its challenges, they may have the joy of help in their work and the conversion of many

For peace, that the Lord will again reveal His salvation and justice among the nations by raising up leaders after His own heart

For all who have come to a dead end in their lives, as Paul did in the city of Athens, that they may not allow the defeat to paralyze them, but move on in the strength of the Lord

For all who are in a period of distress, who with the disciples of Jesus have to weep and mourn in illness or great loss, that their sorrow may also be turned into joy

For those who have died, who for a little while are separated from us, that the power of Jesus' resurrection may overcome any obstacle to their full communion with the Father

**Easter Week 6, Friday**

*Acts 18:9-18, Ps 47, John 16:20-23*

That the church may go on speaking in the name of Jesus and refuse to be silenced, knowing that the Lord is with her

That God, who mounts His throne amid shouts of joy, may give to the rulers of the earth the light and strength to follow His ways of justice and life

That we may come before the throne of grace with confidence, carrying all the intentions of our hearts, knowing that the Father will do anything we ask for in Jesus' name

For all who are in labor during a time of darkness and pain, that Jesus may bring them the joy which no one can take from them

That our faithful departed may see Jesus in the kingdom of heaven, and that no one may be able to take this joy away from them

**Easter Week 6, Saturday**

*Acts 18:23-28, Ps 47, John 16:23-28*

For our leaders in the church, that they may with an ardent spirit speak and teach accurately about Jesus

That those who have come to believe in Jesus through grace may be at the forefront of every battle for the right to life, justice, and human dignity in our world

That Jesus, who came from the Father into the world and now leaves the world to return to the Father, may prepare for us a new outpouring of the Holy Spirit

That the Father, who already loves us to the point of giving us His only Son, may glorify Jesus by granting all the petitions we bring to this Eucharist in our hearts

That the power of this Holy Sacrifice may free those who have died in Christ to take their place in the kingdom of His joy

## Easter Week 7, Monday

*Acts 19:1-8, Ps 68, John 16:29-33*

For all who have consecrated their lives and labors to Jesus, that in their struggles and sufferings they may have courage in His power to conquer the world

That God, whose title is father of orphans and defender of widows, who leads forth prisoners and gives a home to the forsaken, may arise in the spiritual strength of all who work for life, justice, and peace

For those who do not yet know the Holy Spirit, who have never felt His powerful interior movements or the joy of His prophetic spirit, that He may be revealed to them through the inspired and loving preaching of modern day apostles

For our dear ones who suffer from terminal illness and its progressive diminishments, that the Spirit's coming may enrich them with His fruits of patience, long suffering, and mildness, making them icons of the redeeming Christ in our midst

For our faithful departed ones, that the fiery Spirit of divine love may soon purify them and make them fit for the kingdom of love which is heaven

## Easter Week 7, Tuesday

*Acts 20:17-27, Ps 68, John 17:1-11a*

For the whole church waiting and praying for the coming of the Holy Spirit, that His gift to us may be the true knowledge of God and the One sent by God, Jesus Christ

For all those whom the Spirit compels to face hardships and persecutions for the sake of the truth and justice upon which peace is built, that they may be faithful

For the missionaries of the church, that like St. Paul they may serve the Lord in humility in the midst of their trials and sorrows, and have the courage to insist on true repentance and strong faith

For all who are struggling and suffering in the trials of life, that the prayer of Jesus may enable them to give glory to the Father by finishing with love all that He asks of them

For our beloved dead, that Jesus may give them eternal life and share with them the glory which is His by right

**Easter Week 7, Wednesday**

*Acts 20:28-38, Ps 68, John 17:11b-19*

For the shepherds of the church, who continue to guide the flock won by the Blood of Jesus, that they may be docile to the Holy Spirit in all His demands upon their vigilance and hard work on behalf of the flock

For all who work for justice, those who raise prophetic voices against the structures of sin that destroy human dignity, that the greater joy that comes from giving may be their portion

For Christians whose mission compels them to remain in the midst of the world's temptations, that the Lord's prayer for them may be heard: not that they be taken out of the world, but that they may be kept safe from the Evil One

That the Holy Spirit may pray in us for the needs and intentions that He knows better than we do, and that He may make us receptive to God's response

For those who have gone before us, consecrated in the truth by the Word of Jesus, that the Father may bring them into perfect unity in the glory of heaven

**Easter Week 7, Thursday**

*Acts 22:30, 23:6-11, Ps 16, John 17:20-26*

For unity in the church, in religious communities and parish families, and for a return to full unity for all of us who are brothers and sisters in Christ

That God may inspire our local and national leaders to determine the truth about the issues that plague our society, and give them the courage to rescue the most threatened, as the commander did with St. Paul

That many may choose the Lord as their allotted portion and their cup, that they may know the counsel of the Holy Spirit as they set the Lord before them as their one love

That as we keep vigil with Mary in the Upper Room, our communion with Jesus in this Eucharist may prepare us to accept with docile and responsive hearts the downflow of His promised Spirit

For our loved ones who have died, that their souls may not be abandoned to the nether world, but be raised up with Jesus to the fullness of joy in God's presence

## Easter Week 7, Friday

*Acts 25:13b-21, Ps 103, John 21:15-19*

For our leaders in the church and in religious and parish communities, that the Spirit's coming may inflame their love for Jesus, increasing their capacity to feed His beloved flock

For all who can come to the aid of those who suffer from violence and injustice, that they may follow the voice of the Spirit who urges them to make the sacrifices demanded by love

For all of us who continue to prepare for the Feast of Pentecost, that our prayerful vigil of waiting for the descent of the Holy Spirit may create a channel of longing, attracting His fire into the heart of the church

That the Holy Spirit may be healing to the sick, strength to the weary, truth to the wandering, joy to the sorrowful, and the unction of forgiving peace to those who feel their weight of sin

For our faithful departed ones, that the Lord may put their sins away, as far as the east is from the west, and lead them rejoicing into His heavenly kingdom

## Easter Week 7, Saturday

*Acts 28:16-20, 30-31, Ps 11, John 21:20-25*

For the whole church, waiting with Mary on this final day of vigil and prayer for the renewal of the Spirit's coming, that we may soon feel the press of His response in joy and grace

That the Lord, whose searching glance rebukes violence in all its forms, may grant repentance to all who have caused injustice or oppression, even if only by their indifference, so that there may be true peace

That the Holy Spirit may again renew the face of the earth, watering our dryness, cleansing hearts, counseling the unsure, bringing all hearts to the Father

For all who are suffering, those we love and those who are most forgotten, that the waves of light and healing that radiate impelled by the Spirit of Love may break upon the shore of every desolate heart

For our beloved dead, who followed Jesus in this life, that they may now follow Him into His glorious kingdom of light and love

# PROPER OF TIME

## WEEKDAYS OF ORDINARY TIME
# YEAR I

### Week 1, Monday

*Heb 1:1-6, Ps 97, Mark 1:14-20*

For the Church and her holy leaders, that they may continue the proclamation of the Gospel of God that Jesus began, inviting all to repentance and faith

For the rulers of the earth, that justice and judgment may be the foundation of their power, and that they may work for the cause of human life, especially the most weak and vulnerable

For vocations, especially to the priestly life; that many more young men will feel the Lord's call and abandon everything to follow Him

For the poor, the sick, the lonely and depressed, the imprisoned and addicted, and all who have asked our prayers, that the power of Jesus, God's only begotten Son, may be healing, strength, and guidance for each one

For our faithful departed, that they may soon be worthy to contemplate Jesus above all the angels, at the right hand of the Majesty on high

### Week 1, Tuesday

*Heb 2:5-12, Ps 8, Mark 1:21-28*

That the proclamation of Jesus, crowned with glory and honor because He suffered death, may go forth from the heart of the church, whose members have a share in this suffering and in this glory

That our national and world leaders may have great respect for the dignity of each human being, whom God has made little less than the angels

That the unclean spirits of our own day may flee before the power of Jesus as we invoke Him in this holy sacrifice

For all who have asked our prayers in a time of physical, mental, or emotional distress, that Jesus, who is making them perfect through suffering, may support and uphold them in peace

That Jesus, who by the grace of God tasted death for everyone, might bring to life and glory those who have gone before us marked with the sign of faith

## Week 1, Wednesday

*Heb 2:14-18, Ps 105, Mark 1:29-39*

For our leaders and teachers in the church, that like Jesus they may find their power and inspiration in persevering prayer

That the Lord may make His judgments prevail in the hearts of the leaders of the world and turn their thoughts to the justice that fosters true peace

For all who are being tested through suffering, that Jesus who was also tested through what He suffered, may help them as a merciful and faithful high priest

For the sick who have been recommended to our prayers, that Jesus may reach out His hands of healing over them as He did outside the house of Simon Peter

For our beloved dead, that Jesus who defeated death may guide them through every final purification into the joy of His Father's kingdom

## Week 1, Thursday

*Heb 3:7-14, Ps 95, Mark 1:40-45*

For the whole church, that we may encourage one another so that no one may grow hardened by the deceit of sin, but we may all follow Jesus in newness of heart

That the world may enter into God's rest through the God-fearing actions of those in a position of power and influence, creating a climate of justice and peace

That we who are the people God shepherds and the flock He guides, may devote all our energies to hearing His voice and following His life-giving laws

For all who wish to come to Jesus through the power of prayer when they are sick, troubled, unclean, or depressed, that they may experience His gentle mercy and the touch of His healing hand

For our brothers and sisters who followed the Master in this life and have gone before us in death, that they may now enter into God's rest

## Week 1, Friday

*Heb 4:1-5, 11, Ps 78, Mark 2:1-12*

For the church, whose ministers have been given power to forgive sins on earth, that an earnest return to the sacrament of penance may purify and restore her to life and full vigor

That world leaders may keep their hearts steadfast and their spirits faithful to the natural law God has planted in each heart, so that nations may enjoy the blessings of peace

That we who surround the table of this Eucharist may be united in faith and resolute in our loving response to God, so that in spite of every earthly trial, we may know the blessing of His rest

For all who are paralyzed by poverty, sickness, or the pain of unforgiven sin, that our faith as we bring them to Jesus in this Eucharist may be their healing

For our beloved dead, that they may hear the voice of Jesus saying to each one: "Child, your sins are forgiven", so that they may be free to enter His heavenly kingdom

## Week 1, Saturday

*Heb 4:12-16, Ps 19, Mark 2:13-17*

For our leaders and teachers in the church, that they may faithfully proclaim God's word as living and effective, sharper than a two-edged sword, and filled with salvation

For peace and the courage to take the steps needed for peace, that the words and thoughts of world leaders may be such as to find favor before the God of peace

That we may imitate Jesus in His outreach to those who are far from God, especially to our loved ones who have abandoned the practice of their faith

For all who are in a period of testing by poverty, sickness, or any kind of suffering, that Jesus, who was tested in every way that we are, may keep them from sin and bring them triumphantly through the trial

For our beloved departed ones, that they may now confidently approach the throne of grace to receive mercy and to be united with God forever in heaven

## Week 2, Monday

*Heb 5:1-10, Ps 110, Mark 2:18-22*

For unity among the followers of Jesus, that we who are offered the new wine of the kingdom may present God with new wineskins, ready to expand with the energy of His love and reconciliation

For world leaders, that the princely power with which they have been invested may be used to show respect and compassion for every human being under their care

That the call of the Bridegroom may enchant the hearts of the young, and that many may choose to prefer His love to earthly goods, fasting from everything except Him

For all who are learning obedience through suffering, that they may persevere through the test by the power of Jesus

For all our beloved dead, that Jesus who is the source of eternal salvation for all who obey Him may welcome them into the wedding banquet of heaven

## Week 2, Tuesday

*Heb 6:10-20, Ps 111, Mark 2:23-28*

For the great gift of unity among the disciples of Jesus, that illumined by the truth we may allow God to multiply and bless us under one faith and one baptism

For peace in our hearts, our homes and our world, that God may send deliverance to all the people who cry to Him in their great need

For the grace of hope, that we who have God's oath as an anchor of the soul, sure and firm, may through faith and patience inherit all that He has promised

For all the special needs that have been entrusted to our prayers, that Jesus, who defended His disciples in their need, may make himself the merciful Lord of every distressing situation

For our beloved departed ones who died in hope, that their purification may be shortened through the merits of this Holy Sacrifice, and they may soon be with Jesus beyond the veil

### Week 2, Wednesday

*Heb 7:1-3, 15-17, Ps 110, Mark 3:1-6*

For the church, that under the direction of her righteous King of Peace, she may walk in unity and in holiness

For our political leaders, that they may see clearly that it is better to save life than to destroy it, and take the steps needed to respect the lives of all

For vocations to the priesthood, that many young men will come forward to bear upon their souls the mark of one who is a priest forever, according to the order of Melchizedek

For all who have asked for our prayers and for those in special need of prayer, that Jesus may restore what is withered in their lives

For those who have died and gone before us into the unveiled presence of God, that their judgment may be merciful and that they may be at peace in His sight

### Week 2, Thursday

*Heb 7:25–8:6, Ps 40, Mark 3:7-12*

That the church of Jesus Christ may be blessed with unity and peace through His ministry as our great High Priest, and that all His followers may be made holy in spirit and in truth

That leaders of nations and those in a position of power and influence may have ears open to obedience to the law of life and justice written on every human heart

For the holiness of families, that their delight may be to do the will of God, and that from these families God may choose those who will announce His justice in the vast assembly in the roles of priesthood and religious life

For all who are sick or troubled by unclean spirits of emotional illness, addiction or depression, that they may approach Jesus with confidence to touch Him and be healed

That Jesus, minister of the sanctuary and the true tabernacle of heaven, may welcome into God's presence our loved ones who have gone before us marked with the sign of faith

## Week 2, Friday

*Heb 8:6-13, Ps 85, Mark 3:13-19*

For the grace of unity in the church, that God's laws of love and forgiveness may be in our minds and written upon our hearts

For world leaders, that they may champion the cause of life, so that kindness and truth can meet in our society, and there may be true justice and peace

For apostolic vocations, that Jesus may summon those whom He wants and send them forth to preach and to have authority over all that is evil

For all who are suffering and going through a period of testing and trial, that through our loving intercession, God may establish a new covenant of life and healing with them

That Jesus, who is mediator of a new covenant founded on new and better promises, may welcome those who have gone before us into His kingdom of light and love

## Week 2, Saturday

*Heb 9:2-3, 11-14, Ps 47, Mark 3:20-21*

For unity among all the followers of Christ, that the damage of the centuries may be repaired, and that all who follow Jesus may profess one faith

That God, who is king of all the earth and who reigns over the nations, may guide world leaders into the truth of the dignity of each human life that comes forth from His creating hands

That Jesus, our great High Priest, may by the blood of His sacrifice cleanse His followers from dead works and make us worthy to worship the living God in the beauty of holiness

For the poor, the sick, the overburdened, the unemployed, the prisoners, the addicted, and all who need our prayers, that our Communion with Jesus today on their behalf may bring them relief and new hope

For our beloved dead, that Jesus, who has passed through the greater and more perfect sanctuary on their behalf, may welcome them into God's presence, cleansed and rejoicing in His sight

### Week 3, Monday

*Heb 9:15, 24-28, Ps 96, Mark 3:22-30*

For the peace and unity of the church, founded by Jesus, blessed by the Father, and inspired in all things by the Holy Spirit, that she may continue to announce God's salvation, day after day

For the kingdoms and nations of the world, that they may not be divided against themselves and that they may work together to build a just and lasting peace

For the grace of a great respect for the person and the work of the Holy Spirit in the life of the church and in the personal journey of each one of us

That Jesus, who has entered heaven so that He might appear before God on our behalf, may answer our prayers for all our brothers and sisters who labor under a load of suffering

For our departed loved ones, who have died and have undergone judgment, that Jesus may return to bring them salvation and a place in the kingdom of heaven

### Week 3, Tuesday

*Heb 10:1-10, Ps 40, Mark 3:31-35*

For the church, consecrated through the offering of the Body of Jesus Christ, for her holiness and unity under the direction of her pastors

For peace, that national leaders may work to establish justice and respect for the life and dignity of all God's children

That we may merit the title brother and sister and mother of Jesus by our earnest efforts to do the will of God in our daily lives

For those who are waiting for the Lord in a time of trial, sickness, loneliness, or grief, that through our loving prayers, He may stoop toward them and put a new song into their hearts

That those who have gone before us may have cause to proclaim God's justice, faithfulness, and salvation, as He brings them into His promised kingdom

## Week 3, Wednesday

*Heb 10:11-18, Ps 110, Mark 4:1-20*

For our priests, who stand daily at their ministry, offering the one sacrifice of Jesus to take away sins, that they may realize the dignity and power of their holy office

That the balance of justice may be restored in our world, especially justice for the most vulnerable and oppressed, so that we may be blessed with God's peace

That we may be good soil for the hearing of God's word, bearing fruit in patience and gratitude for such a great gift

For those who have asked our prayers, and for all those in need of loving intercession: the sick, the poor, the addicted, the grieving, and the imprisoned, that they may find relief in God's merciful kindness

For our loved ones who have died, that by the consecration of their baptism and the mercy of God, they may be made perfect forever and ready to stand in God's presence

## Week 3, Thursday

*Heb 10:19-25, Ps 24, Mark 4:21-25*

For the church, that she may be a lamp set on a lamp stand and shining brightly, so that all who are in the world may see Jesus lifted up and glorified in her witness

That the cause of life, justice, and peace may be advanced in our time by men and women who have sinless hands and clean hearts, able to stand fast on the mountain of the Lord

That we may hold unwaveringly to our confession of faith that gives us hope, and rouse one another to love and good deeds, encouraging each other as the day of the Lord draws near

For all who stand in need of prayer today, who are in a time of testing and pain, that they may receive a blessing from the Lord, bringing healing and grace

For those who have died, that they may have confidence of entrance into the sanctuary of heaven through the new and living way Jesus opened through His own flesh

## Week 3, Friday

*Heb 10:32-39, Ps 37, Mark 4:26-34*

For all who are charged with the mission of evangelization in the church, that they may plant the Gospel with detachment and patience, convinced of God's power to make the seed grow and bear fruit

For secular leaders on every level of society, that they may truly place their trust in the Lord and do works of justice and peace in His sight, especially for those who are the most vulnerable

For all who are undergoing a great contest of suffering and who are tempted to give in to self pity and despair, that they may not surrender their confidence

For all who need endurance to do the will of God in a time of sickness, grief, depression, or financial distress, that their faith may grow like a mustard seed to draw down God's grace and healing power

For all who have gone before us into the mysterious realm of eternity, that they may soon be purified of every stain, and brought into the eternal life earned by their faith

## Week 3, Saturday

*Heb 11:1-2, 8-19, Luke 1: 69-75, Mark 4:35-41*

For our Holy Father, our bishops and priests, that they may lead us in the fruitful obedience of faith

For peace, that men and women of strong faith and clear vision may be raised up as leaders in our time

For holy and dedicated families in which faith and love are nourished and practiced, and from which vocations can be harvested

For all who are struggling with the storms of life, that they may realize they have Jesus with them in their boat and that He has the power to calm the wind and the waves

For our beloved departed ones, that by God's mercy they may be set free from every bond that keeps them from being holy and righteous in his sight and worthy of the heavenly homeland

## Week 4, Monday

*Heb 11:32-40, Ps 31, Mark 5:1-20*

For the church in her holy leaders and pastors, who have to struggle against unclean spirits in our own day, that through the power of Jesus they may be victorious

For those engaged in the cause of life, of justice, of peace, that the Lord may clear away before them the evil influences that oppose their loving efforts in His name

For all who are persecuted for their faith or for their moral convictions, that they may be brave and persevering, and win through to the prize of life

For all who feel in their anguish of body or spirit that they are cut off from the Lord's sight, that the sound of our pleading on their behalf may bring them into the healing shelter of God's presence

For our dear departed loved ones, who by faith did what was just, that they may now obtain the promises they hoped for in the kingdom of heaven

## Week 4, Tuesday

*Heb 12:1-4, Ps 22, Mark 5:21-43*

For the Church, inspired by her cloud of witnesses, both ancient and modern, that each of us may persevere in running the race with our eyes fixed on Jesus

That all the ends of the earth may remember and return to the Lord, for just and peaceful solutions to the grievances of nations, for an end to terrorism and for a great respect for life

For all those who feel their strength flowing out of them, that they may approach Jesus in their time of need and experience the power that goes out from Him

For all the sick, especially our friends and benefactors, that fear may be put aside for them, and that faith may be aroused, which draws on the healing of Jesus

For all our beloved dead, that Jesus, who has taken His seat at the right hand of God, may bring them quickly into His joy and console those who grieve for them

## Week 4, Wednesday

*Heb 12:4-7, 11-15, Ps 103, Mark 6:1-6*

For theologians and biblical scholars in the church, that in their study of the human Jesus they may never lose sight of His divine origin

For those who struggle against sin and injustice of all kinds, and for all who are tested and tried in their efforts to uphold God's values, that peace may crown their striving

For the conversion of sinners, especially those have sprung up as a bitter root and cause trouble in the church, that they may return to the grace of God in humility and goodness

That the mighty deeds wrought by the hands of Jesus may be repeated in the lives of the poor, the sick, the imprisoned, and the addicted, through the humble prayer that comes from our faith

For the faithful departed whose bodies are returning to dust, that their souls may experience the kindness of the Lord who has compassion on those who fear him

## Week 4, Thursday

*Heb 12:18-19, 21-24, Ps 48, Mark 6:7-13*

For the church, sprinkled with the blood of Jesus, that we may allow Him to make our spirits perfect, so that we may be ready to stand in heaven's festal assembly with all the saints in light

That God, whose right hand is full of justice, may guide world leaders on the road to peace

For apostolic vocations in the church, that many generous hearts may learn the ways effectively to preach repentance and drive out the evils of our time

For all who have asked for our prayers in a time of special distress or illness, that our humble intercession may connect them with the power of the Savior to be an anointing for their every need

For our beloved departed ones, that they may be welcomed into the assembly of the firstborn enrolled in heaven

## Week 4, Friday

*Heb 13:1-8, Ps 27, Mark 6:14-29*

For our Holy Father, our bishops and priests, who speak the word of God to us, that their work may bear fruit, and that they may know of our respect and gratitude for their leadership of faith

For all who suffer, like John the Baptist, for their outspoken witness to the truth and God's values of life, holiness, and justice, that they may persevere in their witness to the end

That we who follow Jesus may be filled with love, hospitality, and solidarity with those who are imprisoned and ill treated, and be ever ready to proclaim the Gospel of truth

For the sick, the poor, and all who are beset with fear, that through our prayers the abode and shelter of God's protection and blessing may become real for them

For those who have died, who seek the Lord's presence in the direct vision of heaven, that they may be purified quickly and admitted to God's banquet of rejoicing

## Week 4, Saturday

*Heb 13:15-17, 20-21, Ps 23, Mark 6:30-34*

For all the members of the church, that they may bring joy to the hearts of their leaders by their good deeds, generosity, obedience, and praise

That the God of peace may furnish those who labor for peace, for life, and for human rights with all they need to carry out His will

That through Jesus the great Shepherd of the sheep, and through Mary His mother, our heavenly Father may carry out in us all that is pleasing to Him

For all who need the gentle care of the Good Shepherd: the sick, the elderly, the ignorant, that His Heart may again be moved to pity for them

That Jesus, who invited His disciples to come away and rest awhile, may grant eternal rest to those who have died marked with the sign of faith

### Week 5, Monday

*Gen 1:1-19, Ps 104, Mark 6:53-56*

For the church in its moments of chaos and darkness, that the mighty wind of the Holy Spirit may sweep again over the dark waters

That God, who created the light and saw how good it was, may enlighten our lawmakers to see the dignity of all human life and to work for peace in God's beautiful creation

For all Christians, that we may bring forth the fruit of good deeds, as nature produces every tree that bears its yield of sweetness and refreshment

For all the sick recommended to our prayers, especially those suffering from cancer, that they may feel the healing power of the tassel of Jesus' cloak

For the dead who have gone before us from this lovely earth, that they may be purified and ready to return to the One who first called them forth to live before His face

### Week 5, Tuesday

*Gen 1:20–2:4, Ps 8, Mark 7:1-13*

For the church, that she may never lose sight of God's commandments for the sake of any human tradition, but keep her heart close to the Lord

That our leaders in the world may come to respect the dignity of man and woman created in the divine image, and to work for life, justice, and peace

That the human race may exercise its dominion over God's wonderful creation with care and with reverence, acting as co-workers with the divine Creator of all things

That God, who found His whole creation to be very good, may repair the ravages of disease, poverty, and addiction in the lives of His children, especially those for whom we pray

For our deceased loved ones, created little less than the angels, that they may now be enjoying the company of the angels in the kingdom of heaven

## Week 5, Wednesday

*Gen 2:5-9, 15-17, Ps 104, Mark 7:14-23*

For the church, for her purity of heart: that what emerges from her members may be wholesome and kind

That God, who formed man out of the clay of the ground and blew into His nostrils the breath of life, may help all leaders of nations to hold every human life in reverence

For all who cultivate the land, that they may care for it as God intended and not allow greed to permanently damage its natural resources

For all who are languishing in the shadow of death: the sick, the afflicted and oppressed, that through our prayers God may send forth His spirit into them and renew the face of the earth

For our beloved dead, that the fruit of the tree of life may be their portion in the land of the living

## Week 5, Thursday

*Gen 2:18-25, Ps 128, Mark 7:24-30*

For the church, that the power of her faith may be such as to cast out demons in our own time

That national leaders and all in a position of influence in the world may uphold the nobility and goodness of family life, through which the children of the future are brought to us all

For the rights and dignity of women, bone of man's bone and flesh of His flesh, that her role and her worth may be upheld with reverence

For all who have been recommended to our prayers in a time of sickness, family problems, or financial difficulty, that we may approach Jesus with confidence and persistence on their behalf

For those who have died in the peace of Christ, that the Lord may bless them as they enter the realm of eternity, and that they may see the heavenly Jerusalem in gladness and joy

### Week 5, Friday

*Gen 3:1-8, Ps 32, Mark 7:31-37*

For the Church and her leaders, feeling the effects of the sin of Adam and Eve, that she may close her ears to all temptation and persevere in obedience to God

For those who hold power in the world, that they may be men and women in whose spirit is no guile, acting blamelessly in the cause of justice and peace

That Jesus may invoke God's power over any deafness in our listening to His word, and open our mouths to praise and thanksgiving in His presence

For those enduring a time of stress through sickness, financial difficulty, addiction, or poverty, that God may be their shelter and ring them round with glad cries of freedom through the energy of love

That our loved ones who have died may have no reason to hide themselves from the Lord God, but come before Him singing for joy

### Week 5, Saturday

*Gen 3:9-24, Ps 90, Mark 8:1-10*

That our leaders and teachers in the church may help us to number our days aright in wisdom of heart and submission to God

For the cause of life, of justice, and of peace in our world, and for those who fight for these values in the face of great opposition

That Mary, the mysterious figure of Genesis whose offspring would crush the serpent's head, may be our leader and our model in the struggle against evil in our own day

That Jesus' heart may again be moved with pity for those who have asked for our prayers in time of special need, and that we may be willing to share our resources to help them

For our beloved dead, that through the sacrifice of Jesus the way to the tree of life may be opened for them in the kingdom of heaven

## Week 6, Monday

*Gen 4:1-15, 25, Ps 8, Mark 8:11-13*

For our Holy Father, our bishops and priests, and all the people of God, that we may never test the Lord but obey Him with faith and love

For peace, that the slaying of our brothers and sisters may cease upon the earth, and that the murderers may repent and turn back to God

For mothers distressed by the evil actions of their children, for mothers whose children have died untimely deaths

For the sick who have been recommended to our prayers, and for all those who are most forgotten and who must suffer alone, that they may be upheld and comforted

For all our beloved dead and those who mourn their loss, that the mercy and love of God may envelop each one in peace

## Week 6, Tuesday

*Gen 6:5-8, 7:1-5, 10, Ps 29, Mark 8:14-21*

For the church, that each disciple of the Lord may have eyes to see, ears to hear, and a heart that understands Him

That the God of glory may thunder in the hearts of world leaders, moving them powerfully to works of justice, life, and peace

That we may never grieve the heart of God by unworthy thoughts and deeds, but be found truly just in His eyes as Noah was

For all who have asked our prayers, for the suffering and the oppressed and the weary, that our loving intercession may lighten their burdens today

That our dear departed loved ones may quickly be purified of every stain, adoring the Lord in holy attire in the company of His angels

### Week 6, Wednesday

*Gen 8:6, 13, 20-22, Ps 116, Mark 8:22-26*

For the church, that she may offer to the Lord a sacrifice of sweet fragrance in the immolation of her Head and the holiness of her members

For peace, that the dove which our prayer and faith send forth over the floodwaters of terrorism and war may return with a sign of serenity and hope

For all who are spiritually blind, who see only violence as an answer to violence, who do not yet know how to conquer evil with good, that Jesus may take them aside and slowly restore their sight

For the sick, the homeless, the hungry, the imprisoned, the abused, that our prayer and love for them today will bring a little warmth and joy back into their lives

That our faithful departed, who took up the cup of salvation and called upon the name of the Lord in this life, may now be rejoicing with Him forever in the next

### Week 6, Thursday

*Gen 9:1-13, Ps 102, Mark 8:27-33*

For our leaders in the church, that they may think as God does, guiding us through the Paschal mystery of death and resurrection with confidence and faith

That God who will demand an accounting for human life may prosper the labor of those who work for the care of all His children

That each of us may answer the question, "Who do you say that I am?" by acknowledging Jesus as our anointed Savior, and follow His way of the cross with courage

For all men and women, made in the image of God, who are ignored and oppressed in their suffering, that our reverent love and our prayer may restore their dignity and their joy

That those who have died may abide in God's presence, purified and at peace in His sight

## Week 6, Friday

*Gen 11:1-9, Ps 33, Mark 8:34–9:1*

For the church, that she may never be ashamed of Jesus or of His words in this generation, but shine forth as His living witness in a darkened world

That we may be a nation whose God is the Lord, a people He has chosen for His own inheritance because of our conversion to a culture of love

For all of us, that we may be eager to deny ourselves and take up our crosses and follow Jesus, knowing that this is the way to preserve our life and our joy

For all who are troubled or afraid, suffering and lonely, that God who fashioned the heart of each of us may hear our prayers for them and come quickly to console them

For all who have tasted death and have gone before us, that they may see the Kingdom of God come in power in the glory of heaven

## Week 6, Saturday

*Heb 11:1-7, Ps 145, Mark 9:2-13*

For our Holy Father, our bishops and priests, that they may be well attested through their faith and thus be a shining example for all God's people

For peace, that God may show us again the way to peace and give us the courage to take the steps that lead to this great blessing which only He can give

That our sacrifice of praise this day may be made acceptable through the faith we place in our God, hoping to please Him`

For our dear ones and those who have asked our prayers in a season of suffering, that the transfigured Jesus may bring light and meaning into their darkness

For our loved ones who have departed from this world, that they may look up and see only Jesus, ready to welcome them home

### Week 7, Monday

*Sir 1:1-10, Ps 93, Mark 9:14-29*

For our spiritual leaders, that God may lavish His spirit of wisdom upon them as His friends, so that prudent understanding may always be present in the church

For our temporal leaders, that they may make decisions that are wise and respectful of the gifts of God, especially the gift of our earth and the gift of human life

That the Lord Jesus may help our unbelief, so that our prayer for the intervention of His divine power may release those who are bound and tormented in body and spirit

For the sick, the poor, the addicted and imprisoned, the refugees and the homeless, that the Lord who is girt about with strength may come to their aid with authority and compassion

For our dear departed ones, that Jesus may take them by the hand and raise them up to eternal life in His presence

### Week 7, Tuesday

*Sir 2:1-11, Ps 37, Mark 9:30-37*

For our Holy Father, our bishops and priests, that they may continue to pursue their special vocation as the servants of God

For the children, beloved by Jesus who identifies Himself with them, and especially for the most helpless of the children, the unborn little ones

For all who walk in the ways of God, that we may trust Him, love Him, and hope for lasting joy and mercy from His hands

For all who are being tested and purified in the crucible of trial, that their faith may not fail, and that they may emerge as pure gold in God's sight

For our faithful departed, who trusted in the Lord and did good in their lifetime, that they may now abide forever in the everlasting inheritance of heaven

## Week 7, Wednesday

*Sir 4:11-19, Ps 119, Mark 9:38-40*

For the church, that she may keep the precepts and the decrees of the Lord and thus claim His promise of everlasting life

That our world leaders may be among those who are not against the Lord, and that they may be of the company of those who work for human dignity, for justice and peace

That we may seek the ways of wisdom and allow her to prove and test us, so that we may win her favor and inherit the Lord's blessing

For all who have asked for our prayers in a time of trouble, sickness, poverty, or unhappiness of any kind, that this Holy Sacrifice may bring them grace and comfort

For those who have gone before us, who long for the salvation of the Lord, that their souls may live to praise Him in the kingdom of heaven

## Week 7, Thursday

*Sir 5:1-8, Ps 1, Mark 9:41-50*

For our Holy Father, our bishops and priests, that they may do everything to prevent the tragedy of the loss of innocence in one of God's little ones

For the dominant nations of the world, that they may not rely on their wealth or their power, but fear God and act according to His will

That we may be counted among those who delight in the law of the Lord, who will accept any loss rather than delay our full conversion to our God

For all who have asked for our prayers, who are in a time of distress of mind or body, that they may know the comfort of the running waters of God's mercy and healing

For our beloved dead, especially those who need our prayers for their purification, that they may yield the fruit of righteousness in due season

### Week 7, Friday

*Sir 6:5-17, Ps 119, Mark 10:1-12*

For our leaders and teachers in the church, that they may uphold Jesus' clear and difficult teaching on marriage as the way God set up human nature from the beginning

That the poor, the oppressed, and the unborn may find a friend in lawmakers as well as in those who fight for their cause

In thanksgiving for the gift of true friendship in our lives, and that we may be strong and faithful friends of God

That the sick, especially those among our benefactors and dear ones, may be given patience and strength, and if God so wills it, the touch of His healing power

For those who have died, who have treasured God's commands and delighted in His statutes, that they may now taste the abundant fruit of their faithfulness in heaven

### Week 7, Saturday

*Sir 17:1-15, Ps 103, Mark 10:13-16*

For the church, living in God's everlasting covenant, that she may discern the wonder of His deeds and proclaim the truth of His holy laws

For those who have power in the world, that wisdom and knowledge may be given them, and that they may have ears to hear the prophetic voices that cry out for justice and peace

For children, that they may be treated with reverence and love as those to whom the kingdom of heaven belongs, and for us, that we may accept the kingdom of God as little children

For all those who are most forgotten in their distress, the poor, the homebound, the imprisoned, the addicted, and the refugees, that they may be seen and heard in Jesus' name

For our faithful departed, whose days of blooming on earth are over, that the Lord may remember that they are but dust, forgive them their sins, and bring them to life everlasting

## Week 8, Monday

*Sir 17:19-27, Ps 32, Mark 10:17-27*

For our Holy Father, our bishops and priests, that they may persevere in leading us on the ways of conversion and repentance, encouraging all those who are losing hope

For the rich and powerful of this world, who have the hardest time entering the kingdom of heaven, that by God's power their hearts may be softened in compassion and generosity

For vocations, that upright men and women may accept the grace and invitation to sell what they have and come to follow only Jesus in their lives

For the faithful who are experiencing times of stress and the overflow of deep waters in sickness, unemployment, grief, and any hardship, that our loving prayers may help them

For our beloved dead, that God may be their shelter, preserve them from distress, and ring them round with glad cries of freedom in His kingdom of peace and light

## Week 8, Tuesday

*Sir 35:1-12, Ps 50, Mark 10:28-31*

For our bishops and priests, that their holiness of life and good example may rise as a sweet fragrance in God's presence

For world leaders, that they may have the light to avoid injustice and refrain from evil, and that every impulse to war that is not fully justified may be sacrificed to God as a peace offering

For vocations, that many more generous souls will joyfully put aside everything for the sake of Jesus and the Gospel

For all of us sharing this Eucharist, that we may not appear before the Lord empty-handed, but pay Him homage with the free-will gifts of our service and love

For all who are in need of our prayer at this time, who are living with the reality of sickness, danger, poverty, oppression, or death, and for our loved ones who have died and are still in need of our prayers

## Week 8, Wednesday

*Sir 36:1, 5-6, 10-17, Ps 79, Mark 10:32-45*

For those who exercise leadership in the church, that after the example of Jesus they may willingly serve others, giving their lives as a ransom for many

That the God of the universe may come to our aid and put all the nations in dread of him, fulfilling the prophecies of those who cry out for life, for justice, and for peace

That we may be willing to drink of the cup and be immersed in the mystery of the cross of Jesus, that we may also know the power and glory of His resurrection

For all who are brought very low by pain, financial distress, grief, displacement, or addiction, that God's compassion may quickly come to them through this Holy Sacrifice

That Jesus, who willingly gave His life that we might live, may extend the grace of His redemption to our dear ones who have died

## Week 8, Thursday

*Sir 42:15-25, Ps 33, Mark 10:46-52*

For the church, that she may proclaim the wonders of God's works, from the spark and the fleeting vision to the great grace of redemption in Christ Jesus

That the Lord, who loves justice and right, may turn the hearts of world leaders to uphold human dignity, so that the earth may again be filled with His kindness

For all of us in our areas of spiritual blindness, that we may cry out insistently for the mercy of Jesus, so that our faith may save us, and we may follow Him wherever He goes

That all who put their trust in our prayers may know the kindness of the Lord through the power of this Holy Sacrifice

That all who have gone forth from this world marked with the sign of faith may now rest in eternal peace

## Week 8, Friday

*Sir 44:1, 9-13, Ps 149, Mark 11:11-26*

For our Holy Father, our bishops and priests, and all the leaders in the church, that they may be godly persons whose virtues may not be forgotten, and whose glory lights up the church

For peace, especially where people are most enslaved and oppressed, that the Lord may again adorn the lowly with victory

For a renewal of our faith in prayer and our willingness to forgive in order to be forgiven

For all the souls from whom Jesus comes looking for fruit, that He may find there the ripe yield of grateful love

For all the intentions recommended to our prayer, for those who are sick, unemployed, grieving, or distressed, and for our beloved dead

## Week 8, Saturday

*Sir 51:12-20, Ps 19, Mark 1:27-33*

For the church, teaching and working with the divine authority of Jesus, that she may persevere in the face of misunderstanding as Jesus did

For those in a position of power and influence, that they may heed the divine law written in their hearts with its clear precepts of justice and respect for all human life

That we may be lovers of divine wisdom, cultivating her until she yields her harvest of ripening joy for our hearts

For all who are experiencing times of trouble and distress, for all who have asked for our prayers and for those who have no one to remember them today

For those who kept the Lord's ordinances and lived in His holy fear while they lived on earth, that they may receive the reward of their fidelity in heaven

## Week 9, Monday

*Tob 1:3, 2:1a-8, Ps 112, Mark 12:1-12*

That the church and her holy ministers may raise up in our own day an upright generation, worthy of God's blessing and becoming a light for the world

That the example of Tobit who defied the authorities for His religious convictions and practices may inspire many to stand up and be counted for the moral and doctrinal teaching of the church

That we who have inherited the vineyard of the Lord may bring forth a rich harvest for His joy and His glory

For all the intentions we bring in our hearts to this Eucharist, and for all who have asked for our prayers, that grace and mercy may be their portion

For all who have suffered violent deaths and for all our loved ones who have died in peace, that the Blood of Jesus may cleanse them of all sin and bring them into the glory of heaven

## Week 9, Tuesday

*Tob 2:9-14, Ps 112, Mark 12:13-17*

That our leaders in the church may show us how to give to God what belongs to God by their reverence and their truthful teaching

That we may give our government all that is due to them, and love our country enough to defend the moral values on which it was founded

That we may follow the example of Jesus and be truthful people who are not concerned with anyone's opinion, but live our faith lovingly and fully

For the sick, the poor, the imprisoned, the addicted, the oppressed, the grieving, and all who need our special prayers today

That this Eucharist may be powerful in releasing the souls of those who have died from any bond of sin, so that they may be welcomed to the wedding feast of heaven

## Week 9, Wednesday

*Tob 3:1-11a, 16-17a, Ps 25,
Mark 12:18-27*

That the church may always glorify the holy and honorable name of God, making known His deeds of justice, truth, and mercy

For peace, for the courage to take the steps needed for peace by upholding justice and defending the dignity of human life

For the despondent, those who like Tobit and Sarah pray for death, that their tears may be brought before God, and that His angel may be sent for their healing

That God, whose kindness and compassion are from of old, may hear our prayers for all those who have entrusted their sufferings to our intercession

That the God of the living may raise up our brothers and sisters who have gone before us, releasing them from every impurity and making them worthy of the clear light of heaven

## Week 9, Thursday

*Tob 6:10-11, 7:1bcde, 9-17, 8:4-9a, Ps 128,
Mark 12:28-34*

That the church may always uphold the sanctity of marriage and its primary purpose: the rearing of children for God's kingdom

That we may obtain the blessing of those who fear the Lord by our steady and Spirit-led work to uphold the dignity of every human being, especially the most vulnerable

That our sincere and total love for God and for one another may place us among those who meet with the approval of our Savior, those who understand Him and welcome His kingdom

For newlyweds, for those who are contemplating marriage, for those in troubled marriages, for all who need the support of our loving intercession in their married life

That our dear departed ones may see the prosperity of the heavenly Jerusalem, purified, blessed, and favored before the Lord

### Week 9, Friday

*Tob 11:5-17, Ps 146, Mark 12:35-37*

That the archangel Raphael may accompany Our Holy Father, our bishops and priests, and all who journey in God's name, bringing with them the blessing of God's comfort and the grace of His good news

That God, who secures justice for the oppressed, gives food to the hungry, and sets captives free, may find every Christian active in these same good works

For the safety of all who travel, that through His holy angels, God may grant them successful journeys and a blessed return to those who love them

That God's gift of healing may console the sick, that sight may be granted to the blind, freedom to the addicted and the imprisoned, and salvation and hope to all

That Jesus, Lord of David, may bring into heaven our friends, relatives, and benefactors who have gone before us, marked with the sign of their faith

### Week 9, Saturday

*Tob 12:1, 5-15, 20, Tob 13:2 ff [24],*
*Mark 12:38-44*

For the whole church of Jesus Christ, that we may be generous with our praise to God's glory and our alms to His poor

For world leaders, that they may give what is due to every human being, working for the justice that promotes peace

That we who receive in this Eucharist the very God of glory before whom the angels present our prayers, may give Him the widow's full sacrifice of adoration and service today

For those who are being tested in suffering as Tobit was tried, for all who need the assistance of our loving prayer and the powerful healing that flows from the sacrifice of this altar

For our faithful departed, that they may rest in the peace of Jesus and enter with the angels into the glory of the Lord

## Week 10, Monday

*2 Cor 1:1-7, Ps 34, Matt 5:1-12*

For the church, that she may hunger and thirst for righteousness in all her members, and especially in her leaders and teachers

For the peacemakers, those who labor to obtain justice for all, those who stand up for the dignity and life of every human being, that God may prosper their work upon the earth

For the persecuted, that God's encouragement may overflow in their hearts, enabling them to endure their sufferings with a joyful heart

For those who mourn, for those who are sick or imprisoned or suffering the chains of addiction, for all who need our prayers, that they may be comforted and healed

That the angel of the Lord may encamp around our dear ones who have died, delivering them from all sin and escorting them to God's heavenly kingdom

## Week 10, Tuesday

*2 Cor 1:18-22, Ps 119, Matt 5:13-16*

For the whole church, anointed by God and sealed with the Holy Spirit, that under the direction of her leaders she may always say "Yes" to the Father

For peace, that we who are called to be prophets of peace, justice, and life may let our light of truth and love shine brightly before the world

That our loyalty to God's commands may make our footsteps steady according to His promise of life and salvation

For all who have asked our prayers in a time of suffering or grief, for all who are in need of prayer and have no one to intercede for them, that they may know God's comfort and peace

That through this holy sacrifice God's countenance may shine upon those who have gone before us, purifying them and giving them eternal life

## Week 10, Wednesday

*2 Cor 3:4-11, Ps 99, Matt 5:17-19*

For all engaged in the ministry of righteousness, especially our Holy Father and our bishops and priests, that the glory of God may shine upon their faces and in their deeds

For peace, that world leaders may work for the justice that is the foundation of true peace, and for the right to life that is the foundation of all human dignity

That we may deserve the title of greatness in the kingdom of heaven by our fidelity to the smallest of God's commands

That the poor, oppressed, and suffering little ones of our own day, especially those who count on our prayers, may be consoled and uplifted through this Holy Sacrifice

For all those who have kept God's law during their sojourn on earth, that they may now receive the glory of His holy kingdom in heaven

## Week 10, Thursday

*2 Cor 3:14–4:1, 3-6, Ps 85, Matt 5:20-26*

For our leaders in the church, that they may never preach themselves but only Jesus, making themselves true servants for His sake

For peace, that we may listen to God as He proclaims peace for His people, that truth may spring out of the earth and justice meet with kindness for all people

For the power of forgiveness and the grace to settle with our brothers or sisters who have anything against us before we approach the Lord in prayer or sacrifice

For all the intentions recommended to our prayers, for all who are in distress of mind or body, that the freedom that comes from the Spirit of the Lord may be their healing

For those who have gone before us marked with the sign of faith, that they may be gazing on the Lord with unveiled faces in His glorious kingdom of peace and joy

## Week 10, Friday

*2 Cor 4:7-15, Ps 116, Matt 5:27-32*

For the church, holding the treasure of grace in poor earthen vessels, that God's surpassing power may be made manifest in her frailty

For the prophets of life, justice, and peace in our world, that they may speak the truth in love, and that those in a position of power and influence may listen to their witness

For all who are entangled in the snares of adultery, that they may be given the light of truth and the strength of grace to break out of their chains

That those who are carrying the dying of Jesus in their lives through sickness, grief, or any affliction, may also know the life of Jesus through peace and healing

For our dear departed ones, that God who raised up the Lord Jesus will raise them up also with Him, and place them at His side in His glorious kingdom

## Week 10, Saturday

*2 Cor 5:14-21, Ps 103, Matt 5:33-37*

That the love of Christ may impel our holy ministers in the church, making them ambassadors of God's reconciliation in our own day

That Mary, Queen of Peace, may lead us all in the ways of justice and life, teaching us by prayer and sacrifice how to obtain the great grace of true peace in our own day

That our "Yes" may mean yes, and our "No" may mean no, and that our deeds may be truthful and upright before our God

That God may crown with kindness and compassion all who have put their trust in our prayers, granting them health, grace, and strength

That Christ, who became sin for us, may help our loved ones who have died to become the righteousness of God through the power of this Holy Sacrifice, leading them to heaven

### Week 11, Monday

*2 Cor 6:1-10, Ps 98, Matt 5:38-42*

For all ministers of God, whose difficult mission makes them a sign of contradiction for our age, that they may meet the challenges of their ministry with a firm and joyful faith

For peace, that those who have been taken advantage of, pressed into service, and subjected to violence may be able to disarm their persecutors by their own greatness of spirit

For all those who seem to have received the grace of God in vain, that our prayers and love may awaken this precious gift in them while the time is still acceptable for salvation

For all who are enduring hardships, afflictions, and constraints through life's trials, that patience and kindness in the Holy Spirit may also be given to them through the power of God

For our beloved dead, that they may see the salvation by our God, winning victory over all their sins and bringing them rejoicing into heaven

### Week 11, Tuesday

*2 Cor 8:1-9, Ps 146, Matt 5:43-48*

That those who can may be generous in the help they give to the churches that are new or struggling, under the direction of our pastors who oversee and direct these gracious actions

That the Lord, who sets captives free and raises up those who were bowed down, may prosper the work of all who labor for justice, life, and peace

That we may be perfect as our heavenly Father is perfect by loving our enemies and praying for those who persecute us

For all who are enduring a severe test of affliction, that they may also know the abundance of joy that God grants to sustain them

That Jesus, who became poor so that we might become rich, may take into the riches of His divine kingdom our loved ones who have gone before us

## Week 11, Wednesday

*2 Cor 9:6-11, Ps 112, Matt 6:1-6, 16-18*

For our Holy Father, our bishops and priests, that they may be first of all men of interior prayer, so that their visible acts of ritual may have a deep foundation

That our secret alms and our quiet fasting may uphold the cause of life and obtain the gift of peace

That we may be cheerful and generous givers, confident that God will make every grace abundant for us and enrich us in every way

For all who have asked our prayers in a time of distress in sickness, economic hardship, or grief, that our loving intercession and the power of this Holy Sacrifice may bring them relief

For all who have died, that as they enter the mysterious realm of God's hidden kingdom they may receive their reward in abundant joy forever

## Week 11, Thursday

*2 Cor 11:1-11, Ps 111, Matt 6:7-15*

For our leaders in the church, that they may possess the intensity of St. Paul's concern for His converts, calling each baptized soul to a sincere and pure commitment to Christ

For our national and world leaders, that their works may be faithful and just, reliable in truth and equity

For graduates, for newlyweds, for all who are in a time of new beginnings, that the Father who knows what we need before we ask may accompany them with grace and light

For all the intentions commended to our prayers, for all who are in anguish of mind or body at this time, that God may deliver them from evil

For our departed loved ones, that they may be presented to Christ purified and worthy to enter heaven at His side

### Week 11, Friday

*2 Cor 11:18, 21-30, Ps 34, Matt 6:19-23*

That the church may rejoice in the holy ministers of Christ, who are willing to suffer and who are truly concerned for her life and growth

That the prophets of our time, who speak out for the dignity of every human being, may be heard and heeded by our world leaders

That we may be eager to store up heavenly treasure, our eyes filled with God's light and our hearts set upon the things that last forever

For the afflicted ones who call out to the Lord from a situation of illness, grief, economic hardship, or any kind of oppression, that they may be saved and restored to radiant joy

For those who have gone before us marked with the sign of faith, that they may be quickly purified and find in heaven a treasure of love and peace in the Lord

### Week 11, Saturday

*2 Cor 12:1-10, Ps 34, Matt 6:24-34*

That God's power may be made perfect in the hearts of our bishops and priests, who in spite of their weakness trust Him for the grace to lead His holy people

For world leaders, that they may turn aside from money and power to serve God and work for justice and peace

That with our Blessed Mother, we may leave to God the care of our human concerns, and seek first His kingship over our lives

That the angel of the Lord may encamp around those for whom we pray in all their needs and intentions, and that they may taste and see how good God is in their lives

That those who have died may be made worthy to be caught up into paradise to hear and see the ineffable things that await us all at the end of our journey

## Week 12, Monday

*Gen 12:1-9, Ps 33, Matt 7:1-5*

For our Holy Father, our bishops and priests, who have been called by God to be a blessing for all the communities of the earth, that they may be faithful and obedient like Abraham of old

That God may raise up world leaders who will do what is just and right in His eyes, following the law He has placed in the hearts of all His children

That each of us may obey the Lord's injunction not to judge, attending to what needs correcting in our own lives before we point out the faults of others

For all who suffer, who feel their weakness and loneliness, that the kindness of the Lord may be upon them who wait in hope for His merciful help

For our beloved dead, who have been called forth from the land of their kinsfolk, that God will show them a new land in His own kingdom of promise and blessing

## Week 12, Tuesday

*Gen 13:2, 5-18, Ps 15, Matt 7:6, 12-14*

For the church and her holy ministers, that we may have the courage to take the constricted road that leads to life, avoiding the broad road that leads to destruction

That the Lord's injunction to do to others what we would have them do to us may be the guiding light for the decisions of our national leaders, creating a climate of peace

That like Abraham we may allow others to take the best portion, knowing that in the end God's blessing rests upon the one who gives everything away

For the poor, the sick, the abandoned and oppressed, the imprisoned and addicted, and all who need our loving intercession, for their help and healing

For those who have passed through the narrow gate of death, that they may find themselves in the eternal kingdom of abundant life and joy

### Week 12, Wednesday

*Gen 15:1-12, 17-18, Ps 105, Matt 7:15-20*

For our leaders in God's assembly, that the good fruit they bear may attract many to the living vine that is Jesus Christ and His holy church

For deliverance from the false prophets of our own day, and that God may raise up many true prophets to show us the way to justice and peace

That like Abraham we may put our faith in God no matter how circumstances seem to obscure His promises, that we may be holy and righteous in His sight

For all those who have recommended themselves to our prayers in a period of distress or illness, that they may be comforted

For our beloved departed ones, that this Holy Sacrifice may release them from the residue of their sins and bring them rejoicing into heaven

### Week 12, Thursday

*Gen 16:1-12, 15-16, Ps 106, Matt 7:21-29*

For our leaders in the church, that they may know Christ more deeply than simply performing mighty deeds in His name, but give the faithful an example of fidelity to His doctrine

For the people of the Middle East, many of whom have inherited the ancient rivalry of Isaac and Ishmael, that they may know at last the great gift of peace

For all God's people, for the grace to build their spiritual homes on the bedrock of Christ and His teachings, so that no storm of this world will have the power to bring them down

For all the special intentions remembered at this Mass, for all who are in need of loving intercession for their spiritual and temporal needs, for the dear ones we hold in our hearts

For our beloved dead, that they may be visited with the saving help of God, and come to rejoice in the joy of His people and glory in His heavenly inheritance

## Week 12, Friday

*Gen 17:1, 9-10, 15-22, Ps 128, Matt 8:1-4*

For the church, her ministers, and her faithful, that she may walk in God's presence and be blameless in her ways

For all those who work for the right to life and dignity of every child of God, for justice and the rights of the oppressed, for moral integrity, and for peace

For our faith in God, that it may extend even into impossible situations like that of Abraham and Sarah, that we may trust in the promise of divine intervention in spite of all appearances

That Jesus, who was moved with compassion at the appeal of the leper, may allow His Heart to be touched by our fervent petitions for all who have asked our prayers

That the Lord may cleanse our faithful departed ones of all their sins, purifying them for entrance into His eternal and glorious kingdom

## Week 12, Saturday

*Gen 18:1-15, Luke 1, Matt 8:5-17*

For those in authority in the church as the centurion was in today's gospel reading, that their influence among God's people may be for the up-building of His church in grace and love

That Mary, queen of peace, who sang God's divine reversals of power and riches in her Magnificat, may obtain for us the grace to be on the side of the smallest and most vulnerable in our society today

For all of us receiving this Eucharist, that our hospitality may be generous to our divine Guest, and our humility genuine in His presence

That those who appeal to the Lord Jesus through our prayers for help in a time of sickness, poverty, or family problems may have the centurion's faith to obtain His gracious response

That Jesus may say the word and release our dear departed loved ones from all their sins, giving them the power to rise and enter the kingdom of His love

### Week 13, Monday

*Gen 18:16-23, Ps 103, Matt 8:18-22*

That the humble yet insistent intercession of Abraham may be the model for all prayer in the church, especially when our holy leaders speak to the Lord

For a return to the culture of life and moral uprightness in our own nation, that we may offer the Lord a spectacle of innocent men and women in His sight

For all of us as we determine ever more faithfully to follow Jesus, that we may be willing to imitate His poverty and leave even our dear ones behind for His love

That the Lord may crown with graciousness and compassion all who have recommended themselves to our prayers, hoping for His mercy

That God may show His surpassing kindness to all who have died, redeeming their lives from destruction and bringing them safely into His heavenly kingdom

### Week 13, Tuesday

*Gen 19:15-29, Ps 26, Matt 8:23-27*

For the church riding the rough seas of unrest and challenge on all sides, that we may remember the power we have in Jesus, who will never forsake us

That a return to obedience to the Lord and fidelity to upright moral principles may be the safety of our country; that we may find mercy and peace

That we may walk in integrity and truth, submitting to the Lord's testing in firmness of heart and counting on His mercy

For all who are caught in the storms of life, who feel that they are perishing, that they may have the faith to call upon Jesus and be rewarded with a great calm

For our faithful departed, that like Lot they may be saved from the destruction of the wicked and brought to a place of safety, light, and peace

## Week 13, Wednesday

*Gen 21:5, 8-20, Ps 34, Matt 8:28-34*

For our Holy Father, our bishops and priests, that the fear of the Lord may be the sure foundation of their holiness, and the gift of wisdom may be its crown

For all races and peoples who suffer rejection and exile, that their cries of distress may draw down God's merciful intervention in their need

For our brothers and sisters who feel compelled to self destructive behaviors and violence towards others, that the power of Jesus may restore them to sanity and peace

For the sick, the poor, the disabled, the imprisoned, the grieving, and all who need our prayers, that Jesus may intervene in their lives, driving out all evil and bringing them healing and grace

For our beloved dead, that this Holy Sacrifice may be their release into the heavenly realms of light and rejoicing

## Week 13, Thursday

*Gen 22:1-19, Ps 115, Matt 9:1-8*

For confessors, for penitents, for all who still make contact with the power of Christ to forgive sins, that the use of the sacrament of penance may prevent evil from paralyzing spiritual progress

That no idols of silver and gold, no greed or personal gain, may be sought by those invested with temporal power, but that they may use their influence in the cause of justice and peace

For those entrusted with the healing of soul, mind, and body, that they may let themselves be used as channels by the One who cures both spiritual and physical sickness

That the Father, who did not spare His divine Son upon the mount of sacrifice, may grant to all who suffer the grace to see and submit to His saving and restoring will

For our faithful departed, that God's angel may come to them as He did to Abraham with the good news of the reward of their obedience in the kingdom of heaven

### Week 13, Friday

*Gen 23:1-4, 19, 24:1-8, 62-67, Ps 106, Matt 9:9-13*

For the church, whose members live in the tension of a promised homeland that is already among us and yet is still to come, that our faith may bear fruit in deeds that foreshadow the kingdom of God

For world leaders, that they may observe what is right and steadfastly do what is just, so that we may live in the blessing of peace

For sinners; for recovering sinners who know how helpless they are without the Lord, for sinners who suffer from the blindness of their own pride, that each one may have ears to hear the Lord's merciful command: "Follow Me"

For young people in love, for married couples, that like Isaac and Rebecca, they may find solace in one another and grow together in the Lord's ways

For our beloved dead, that they may rejoice in the joy of God's people who are in heaven, and glory in their inheritance among the just

### Week 13, Saturday

*Gen 27:1-5, 15-29, Ps 135, Matt 9:14-17*

For our priests, who minister to us in God's name and impart to us His special blessing, for their holiness, their ministry, and all their personal intentions

For the grace to make a culture of life and a society based on justice our aim, under the direction of Mary, Queen of Peace

That we may be fresh wineskins to receive the new wine of God's kingdom with all its energy of grace and redemption

For those who are in a time of fasting, undergoing sickness, poverty, imprisonment or grief, that the Bridegroom Christ may show Himself to them in the secret of their hearts, bringing them joy in His love

That the holy patriarchs who live in God's presence may welcome our deceased brothers and sisters into the company and assembly of the redeemed in heaven

## Week 14, Monday

*Gen 28:10-22, Ps 91, Matt 9:18-26*

For those who guard the church, the awesome shrine which is the abode of God and the gateway to heaven, that they may be reverent and faithful

That all the nations of the earth may find blessing in those who are working for life, justice, moral integrity, and peace

For all those who feel their life draining away within them, that they may approach Jesus in a spirit of faith and experience His healing

That we may trust in God's faithfulness to us in all our journeys and all our sorrows, drawing out His power by our humble and loving expectation

For our loved ones who have fallen asleep, that they may meet Jesus face to face and know His mercy for their souls

## Week 14, Tuesday

*Gen 32:23-33, Ps 17, Matt 9:32-38*

For the shepherds of the church, that they may come to the rescue of those who are troubled and abandoned, teaching them, and driving out demons as Jesus did

For those who wrestle with God in earnest prayer and obedient action, that they may obtain grace and mercy for the oppressed and those who are longing for the blessing of peace

For vocations, that we may obtain from the master of the harvest good and holy laborers to gather in the abundance of souls thirsting for God's kingdom

That the Lord may continue His battle with evil in the hearts of all those who are suffering from illness, heartbreak, or emotional hardship, saving and curing them

That Jesus' heart may be moved with pity for our dear ones who have died, and that He may purify them quickly to come into His glorious kingdom

### Week 14, Wednesday

*Gen 41:55-57, 42:5-7a, 17-24a, Ps 33, Matt 10:1-7*

For the church and her holy ministers, who hold the key to the divine nourishment, that they may be faithful and generous in their distribution of grace and mercy

For our political leaders and those in a position of influence in the world, that they may be men and women of justice and concerned for the rights and dignity of all

For the lost sheep; those who have wandered far away from the faith of their fathers, that our prayer and sacrifice and reaching out to them in love may work the miracle of their return

That Jesus' power to drive out unclean spirits and to cure every disease and every illness may be active today for the sick and for those who are oppressed in spirit

That the kingdom of heaven may be at hand for all the faithful departed, and that they may enter into a place of light and peace

### Week 14, Thursday

*Gen 44:18-21, 23-29, 45:1-5, Ps 105, Matt 10:7-15*

For our leaders in the church, that the word of the Lord may prove them true and make them strong in their proclamation of the Gospel

For peace, that the blessing of peace we offer in Christ's name may at last find a resting place in hearts and homes and in our world

For all who have suffered betrayal and hatred from those closest to them, that like Joseph they may come to see what good God can bring out of it for themselves and even for those who wronged them

For all who are in a famine time of their lives, that they may find a Joseph who by God's grace has kept blessings in reserve to sustain them until the rains come again

For those who have died and come through their own day of judgment, that God's mercy may purify them to be worthy of a place at the heavenly banquet

## Week 14, Friday

*Gen 46:1-7, 29-30, Ps 37, Matt 10:16-23*

For the church, that God may make of her a great nation, going and coming with His people in all the stages of the journey

For the prophets of our own day, that they may be shrewd as serpents in knowing how to deal with those who oppose them, and simple as doves in their testimony

For those who are persecuted for their witness to Jesus, that the Holy Spirit may speak through them and uphold them in their faith

For the sick, the poor, those who grieve, the imprisoned and the addicted, and those who suffer financial hardship or any kind of oppression, that Jesus may come to them in healing, freedom, and peace

For those who have gone before us marked with the sign of faith, that through this Holy Sacrifice the doors of heaven may be opened for them

## Week 14, Saturday

*Gen 49:29-32, 50:15-26a, Ps 105, Matt 10:24-33*

For the disciples of Jesus, especially those who carry His trust as ministers of His church, that we may all become like our Teacher and resemble our holy Master

That we may acknowledge Jesus before the world by our fidelity to moral integrity, and by our prayer and work for life, justice, and peace

For those who are persecuted, that they may see, as Joseph did, that God can bring good out of evil, and have the strength to forgive those who do them wrong

That God, who has counted every hair of our heads in omnipotent and loving fidelity, may banish fear from the hearts of those who suffer, and enable them to trust Him for the gift of new life

For all who have passed through the dark portals of death, that they may now speak their praise and thanksgiving in the brilliant light of heaven

### Week 15, Monday

*Exod 1:8-14, 22, Ps 124,*
*Matt 10:34–11:1*

For the whole church, that we may accept the challenge set forth by Jesus, taking up our cross and following after Him even when our loved ones oppose us in our faith

For all for whom life has been made bitter by the rich and the powerful, that their plight may be seen by those in positions of influence who can help them in their distress

That we may receive the prophets and the righteous ones with respect and generosity, sharing in their mission and in their reward

For vocations, that God may choose among our young people and give them the gift of being willing to lose their lives completely for the sake of Jesus, knowing that they will find a richer and fuller life in Him

For our beloved dead, that they may be purified through the offering of this Holy Mass, and made worthy to enter the kingdom of heaven

### Week 15, Tuesday

*Exod 2:1-15a, Ps 69, Matt 11:20-24*

For our Holy Father, our bishops and priests, for their holiness, their personal intentions, and their ministry in the church

That God, who worked to save Israel through Moses, may now raise up leaders in the world to uphold human dignity and the rights of the little ones who are most oppressed and forgotten

That through our work for a culture of life we may draw out from the water the helpless infants and the unborn who are under the shadow of death

That we may never take God's mighty deeds for granted, but accept our need for repentance so as not to have to face a severe judgment in the end

For those who have gone before us marked with the sign of faith, that they may be purified quickly and made ready for the joys of heaven

## Week 15, Wednesday

*Exod 3:1-6, 9-12, Ps 103,*
*Matt 11:25-27*

For all of us in the church, that we may realize that the place where we stand is holy ground, and how awesome is the God and Father of our Lord Jesus Christ

That God may raise up new leaders like Moses for the oppressed and the suffering, to lead them out from under tyranny into the realm of His peace

That we may be counted among the childlike to whom the Father desires to reveal His beloved Son

For our families and our communities, for the grace to truly love and respect one another, and that this Eucharist may be the bond that unites us in Christ Jesus our Lord

For our faithful departed, that the angel of the Lord may come to them and lead them to the joys of paradise

## Week 15, Thursday

*Exod 3:13-20, Ps 105, Matt 11:28-30*

For the elders of the church: our Holy Father, our bishops and priests, that they may be faithful messengers of God's revelation and open channels of His love

For all whose rights to life, liberty, and the pursuit of happiness are so easily thwarted by the powerful, that God may again raise up prophets to champion their cause

That we may learn from Jesus to be gentle and humble of heart, sharing His yoke with Him and finding it easy and light

For all who labor and are burdened, that they may come with confidence to Jesus and accept the gift of His divine rest

For those who have died, that God may lead them into a good land, flowing with milk and honey; the heavenly homeland that He has prepared for them

**Week 15, Friday**

*Exod 11:10–12:14, Ps 116,*
*Matt 12:1-8*

That Jesus, who defended His apostles against every attack, may uphold and defend our leaders in the church today

That God, who desires mercy and not sacrifice, may prosper the work of those who stand up for life, for justice, for moral values, and for peace

For all of us partaking of the true Passover Lamb in this Holy Eucharist, that the Blood of Jesus may be our safety against every destructive blow, and that we may be ready for the journeys on which the Lord will lead us

For all in distress of mind or body, for all who feel caught in the problems that life can bring, that God, who freed the Israelites from oppression, may bring them to their Passover feast of liberty and joy

For our dear ones who have gone before us through the gates of death, that this Holy Sacrifice may free them from all sin, and that they may be brought rejoicing into God's heavenly kingdom

**Week 15, Saturday**

*Exod 12:37-42, Ps 136, Matt 12:14-21*

For the church, the new Israel of God, that she may be freed from all servitude and follow Jesus through the desert in freedom and strength

That God may raise up world leaders after His own heart, who will not contend or cry out, but will work to bring justice to victory in our own day

That we who feast on the unleavened bread of this Holy Eucharist may take hope and vigor for our pilgrimage from the grace that Jesus freely offers us in His living contact with our souls

For the bruised reeds and smoldering wicks, for those so beaten down by their trials that they have almost lost hope, that Jesus may lift them up with gentleness and power

For our beloved dead, who keep vigil for the Lord beyond the grave, that their purification may be swift and their entry into the promised land certain

## Week 16, Monday

*Exod 14:5-18, Canticle from Exodus 15, Matt 12:38-42*

For the church, that she may not fear her enemies as Israel once feared the Egyptians, but stand her ground and wait for the victory the Lord will win for her

For the men and women of integrity to speak up for God's commandments and values in the midst of an evil and unfaithful generation, for their courage and faithfulness

For all of us who listen to the words of Jesus, who is greater than Jonah and greater than Solomon, that we may take His words to heart and produce good fruit in His sight

For those who are passing through a time of great trial and pain, that through our loving intercession they may be given the grace to let the Lord fight for them, keeping their souls quiet in peace and confidence

That the powerful right hand of the Lord may raise up our dear ones who have died, saving them from all evil and leading them into heaven's promised land

## Week 16, Tuesday

*Exod 14:21–15:1, Exod 15, Matt 12:46-50*

For holy leaders like Moses in the church today, who follow closely all that God commands and who mediate His power in our midst

For the defeat of oppression and the drowning of all evil tyranny in our world, for the triumph of justice and peace

That we may be among the mothers, brothers, and sisters of Jesus because of our firm desire to do all that the heavenly Father wills

For all who are in a time of distress, grief, sickness, or interior darkness, that God may open up a path through the mighty waters for them, and lead them safely to the other side

For our beloved dead, that they may be brought in and planted upon the mountain of the Lord's inheritance and given a place in His holy sanctuary

### Week 16, Wednesday

*Exod 16:1-5, 9-15, Ps 78, Matt 13:1-9*

For our leaders in the church, who mediate between God and His sometimes discontented people, that in answer to their prayers God may be generous in His response to our needs

That national leaders will make prudent and effective decisions in their efforts to uphold human dignity and take care of the most vulnerable in the world today

For all of us sharing in this Eucharist, where the glory of the Lord appears not in a cloud but under the appearance of bread and wine, that we, too, may be ready to serve others with humility

For all who have asked us to pray for them, for the gift of good discernment in those pursuing vocations, for a generous response from all souls to God's initiative of sowing His word in our hearts

For our departed dear ones, that through our prayers their purification may be complete and they may eat the bread of angels at the heavenly banquet

### Week 16, Thursday

*Exod 19:1-2, 9-11, 16-20, Dan 3, Matt 13:10-17*

For our Holy Father, our bishops and priests, who are the ones privileged to speak directly to God on behalf of the people, that they may be holy enough to be summoned to the top of the mountain of divine encounter

For the gift of peace, the fruit of listening to the voice of God and putting into practice all that He commands

That we may have eyes blessed with seeing and ears blessed with hearing in the presence of our Divine Master, Jesus

That God, who sits upon His throne above the cherubim, may look into the depths of the human need and suffering that we bring before Him, and grant healing and grace

For all who have gone before us into eternity, who have seen God in the temple of His holy glory, that they may soon take their place in the company of the saints

## Week 16, Friday

*Exod 20:1-17, Ps 19, Matt 13:18-23*

For the holy ministers who serve in the church, that they may not tire of sowing the good seed of the Gospel, no matter what kind of soil they encounter on their way

That Christians may stand up for the countercultural values they have received from God, cultivating justice which is the basis of peace

That in our fast-paced, hard-working society, souls may be found that insist on the place of the Sabbath rest, and make holy a portion of their daily life by prayer and reflection

For all who are in a season of suffering, tension, grief, or sickness, that through our prayers and this Holy Sacrifice they may again have enlightenment in their eyes and rejoicing in their hearts

For all who have tried to keep God's commandments until they were called from this world, that the harvest they bring before the Lord may be pleasing in His eyes and worthy of heaven

## Week 16, Saturday

*Exod 24:3-8, Ps 50, Matt 13:24-30*

For all the ministers of the covenant in the church, who seal the agreement between God and men in the blood of the Lamb, that they may be worthy of their holy calling

That leaders of Christian nations may be careful to heed and do all that the Lord has told us in His commandments, showing other nations the way to peace

For patience with the growth of the wicked seed in the midst of all that is good, for courage to persevere in bearing good fruit, waiting for the Lord's harvest

That our Blessed Mother may see to the needs of all who have asked for prayer, consoling the sorrowful, healing the sick, restoring hope to the weary, and bringing us all to Jesus

For our dear ones who have come to the end of their lives and are passing through the doors of death, that God's angel harvesters may collect them as good grain into heaven

### Week 17, Monday

*Exod 32:15-24, 30-34, Ps 106,*
*Matt 13:31-35*

For those who have authority in the church, that they may never set up idols according to the pressure of society, but remain faithful to the true God

That the law given to Moses and inscribed on the tablets of every human heart may be the guiding light of men and women invested with power in the world

That the kingdom of heaven may grow in us like yeast in the dough, leavening our heaviness, gently raising us up to the Father

That Jesus, who came to announce what was hidden, may open the secret of peace, grace, and healing to those who have asked our prayers

That God's angel may go before the souls of our departed loved ones, leading them into the promised land of heaven

### Week 17, Tuesday

*Exod 33:7-11, 34:5b-9, 28, Ps 103,*
*Matt 13:36-43*

That the column of cloud, the presence of God, may stand guard over all the prayers of our holy leaders in the church, and that they may always have the respect of their people

That the Lord who secures justice and the rights of the oppressed may revitalize His holy commandments in the hearts of world leaders, so that peace may prevail in our own day

That we may trust in the revelation of the Lord as a merciful and gracious God, rich in kindness, fidelity, justice, and goodness, and live in His presence with obedience and joy

For all who must suffer and endure the sight of weeds among their wheat, that they may have the patience to wait for the harvest when God will sort out everything with justice and truth

For our beloved dead, that God may put their transgressions from them as far as the east is from the west, showing them the compassion of a loving Father

## Week 17, Wednesday

*Exod 34:29-35, Ps 99, Matt 13:44-46*

For our leaders in the church, that they may be the Lord's intimates as Moses was, meeting Him behind the veil of their personal prayer and witnessing to His glory by the radiance of their lives

That all the troubled and desperate people of our world may be anointed this day with peace and touched by the loving kindness of many hearts

That Christians may rediscover the joyful treasure they have in the Good News of Jesus and be willing to sell off all their selfish sadness to enter into this joy

For all who have asked for our prayers, especially the sick and those who are lonely or afraid, that the pearl of great price may be their hidden wealth and Jesus their great hope

For those who have gone before us marked with the sign of faith, that they may be purified through this Holy Sacrifice and released for the joys of heaven

## Week 17, Thursday

*Exod 40:16-21, 34-38, Ps 84, Matt 13:47-53*

For our Holy Father, our bishops and priests, that like Moses they may do exactly as the Lord commands them and set up a worthy dwelling place of God among His people

For world leaders, that they may have the grace of true discernment to know what God wishes them to do, and carry out what they have come to see

For vocations, that young people may be attracted to the threshold of the house of God and seek to build their nests near His altar

For all who are in a time of distress, illness, confusion, or pain, that through our prayers and this Holy Sacrifice they may find that the Lord is truly their strength

For our beloved dead, that they may be among the righteous separated out and carried in joy by the angels into the presence of the Lord

### Week 17, Friday

*Lev 23:1, 4-11, 15-16, 27, 34b-37, Ps 81, Matt 13:54-58*

That the Lord's feast of unleavened bread and His holy Passover may be offered by our priests under the new covenant, with blameless hearts

That the harvests of the world may be dedicated to the Lord by sharing part of them with the poor and the needy little ones

That the day of atonement may live in the hearts of Catholics who make faithful use of the sacrament of reconciliation

That our prayer of faith my prevail upon Jesus, our beloved prophet, to work mighty deeds among those who have need of our intercession today

That Jesus, Son of Mary, may heed the earnest request of His holy Mother on behalf of all who have crossed over into the realm of eternity

### Week 17, Saturday

*Lev 25:1, 8-17, Ps 67, Matt 14:1-12*

That the church may bravely and consistently teach her rich doctrine of social justice, which applies God's inspired word to the signs of our own times

That the movement to remit the debts of the poorer nations may continue to grow, restoring on earth a balance of justice and compassion

For all who are persecuted, like St. John the Baptist, for their uncompromising witness to the law of God in a lawless world, that they may hold out to the end

That our Blessed Mother may be the advocate of all who are in need of her help; the sick, the poor, the grieving, the addicted, and the imprisoned, obtaining grace and mercy for each one

That those who have died may be brought through their day of atonement into the great jubilee of heavenly joy

## Week 18, Monday

*Num 11:4-15, Ps 81, Matt 14:13-21*

For our holy leaders in the church, who carry the burden of the people's need, that each moment's demands may bring them to prayer, and God may find them faithful channels of His response

For those who shape policy in the political realm, that they may be more sensitive to the hunger of the many than to the profit of the few, and create the balance of justice needed in our world today

That all who are engaged in the ministry of the Eucharist may more and more resemble the Holy Bread they distribute, becoming themselves food for the needs of God's people

For those who hunger for food, employment, security, love, and understanding, that those others whose hunger is for holiness may be for them God's compassionate answer in their need

That our departed dear ones may be purified to take their place in heaven, filled with honey from the rock which is Jesus Himself

## Week 18, Tuesday

*Num 12:1-13, Ps 51, Matt 14:22-36*

For God's holy ministers and priests, who bear God's trust throughout the church, that He may come to their defense whenever they are spoken against

That Christian politicians and statesmen may take the lead in listening to and following the moral teachings of the church, which like Moses speaks in the name of God

For all who are struggling in God's service and under His command, rowing against the wind, making no progress, seemingly deserted, that the God who tests them may also comfort them

For our sick and sorely tried loved ones, that they might be brought to Jesus to be healed of every affliction

For all who have gone before us, that they may have clean hearts and steadfast spirits before the divine judge and merciful Father

### Week 18, Wednesday

*Num 13, Ps 106, Matt 15:21-28*

For our Holy Father, our bishops and priests, that they may be the first to show an invincible trust in the Lord especially in times of difficulty

For world leaders, that they may navigate the terrain of diplomacy with realism but believe that God will be on their side if they follow His divine laws

That we may approach the Lord with humility, persistence, and faith, as did the Canaanite woman, in our deep need for His mercy

For all those who have asked for our prayers in their urgent needs and intentions, that through the power of this Holy Sacrifice they may receive healing and grace

For our deceased loved ones, that the Lord may quickly purify them and welcome them into His blissful heaven

### Week 18, Thursday

*Num 20:1-13, Ps 95, Matt 16:13-23*

For pastors and superiors, who at times share the distressing lot of Moses, that God, the source of all patience and encouragement, may keep them faithful in showing forth His glory

For all who speak out for the cause of life, of justice, of morality in the face of angry opposition, for their strength and support

That we may always proclaim and defend the faith that was first given voice by St. Peter, acknowledging Jesus as the Son of the living God

For the poor, the sick, the unemployed, the imprisoned, and the addicted, that by the Lord's mercy they may have reason to sing joyfully to Him, acclaiming Him as the rock of their salvation

For our loved ones who have died, that the keys kept by St. Peter may unlock the kingdom of heaven to them

## Week 18, Friday

*Deut 4:32-40, Ps 77, Matt 16:24-28*

For the church, the new people of God, who hear His voice not in the midst of fire but from the mouth of Jesus, that she may consent to be saved by keeping God's covenant

For the leaders of nations, that they may keep God's statutes and commandments in order to give long life to their people

That we may accept the invitation of Jesus to take up our cross and follow Him, consenting to lose our lives in order to really save them

For all who are passing through a season of distress or oppression, that God, who delivered the Israelites from the power of Egypt, may bring them into a place of peace and prosperity

For those who have gone before us marked with the sign of faith, that they may soon be ready to stand before the Son of Man and His holy angels in the Father's glory

## Week 18, Saturday

*Deut 6:4-13, Ps 18, Matt 17:14-20*

For our Holy Father, our bishops and priests, that they may be men of faith for whom nothing is impossible as they battle the evils of our day

For those who rule Christian countries, that they may never forget the Lord, but fear Him and serve Him in their policies and decisions

That all Christians may take to heart the command to love the Lord with all their heart, soul, mind, and strength, serving Him in their neighbor as God desires

That Jesus may continue to drive out the demons that cause torment today, and that our faith may be strong enough to win His intervention for all who have asked for our prayers

For our beloved dead, that they may soon be brought by the Lord and by our Blessed Mother into the promised land of the heavenly kingdom

### Week 19, Monday

*Deut 10:12-22, Ps 147, Matt 17:22-27*

For our leaders in the church, that they may never be afraid to exhort God's people to love and serve the Lord and to keep His ways without compromise

For our leaders in the world, that God who has no favorites and accepts no bribes may help them to be upright and to befriend the aliens, the orphans, and the widows of our own day

That Jesus, who describes Himself as One who dies and rises, may draw us into the rhythm of this graced movement in our own lives

For all the intentions recommended to our prayers, especially for the sick and dying, for those facing financial crises or life-changing decisions, and for those discerning God's call in their lives

That the gates of heaven may be opened for the souls for whom we pray, that peace may be their portion and the vision of God may be their joy

### Week 19, Tuesday

*Deut 31:1-8, Ps 32, Matt 18:1-5, 10, 12-14*

For our Holy Father, our bishops and priests, that like Joshua they will be firm and steadfast as they lead the people of God into His promised homeland

That leaders of nations may remember that it is the Lord who has set up the boundaries of the nations, and follow His will toward justice and peace for all

For the little ones of Christ's flock, especially the lost sheep among our own families and friends, that the will of the Father may be fulfilled so that none of them may be lost

For all of us sharing in this Eucharist, that we may approach our union with the Savior with the hearts of little children, converted and humble in His sight

For all the intentions we bring to this liturgy, all who have asked us to pray for them, and for our beloved dead

## Week 19, Wednesday

*Deut 34:1-12, Ps 66, Matt 18:15-20*

That those who take the place of Moses in the church today may be granted a glimpse of the heavenly homeland promised to us all, so that they will guide us with vision and enthusiasm

That heads of nations may be filled with wisdom as Joshua was, to lead us in a culture of life and moral integrity

That the difficult task of mutual correction may be carried out in the church with the delicacy of love and the fortitude of truth

For all the intentions we bring to this altar, that Jesus may see us united in prayer, and that the Father may be gracious to our requests

For our dear ones who have died, that we who are gathered in Jesus' name may obtain mercy and release for their souls

## Week 19, Thursday

*Josh 3:7-10a, 11, 13-17, Ps 114, Matt 18:21–19:1*

For the church, that her covenant with God, symbolized in the holy ark, may have power over all obstacles in her way to her promised homeland

That nations who are in debt to God for the abundance of their material riches may be ready to show compassion to the less fortunate nations in their debts

That we may place no limits on our forgiveness of our brothers and sisters, giving them seventy times seven chances to begin again

For all those who have asked our prayers in a time of sickness or distress, that they may know there is a living God in their lives by His powerful intervention on their behalf

For all the souls still in debt to God and waiting to be purified before they may enter heaven, that this Holy Mass may obtain for them forgiveness and peace

### Week 19, Friday

*Josh 24:1-13, Ps 136, Matt 19:3-12*

For the church, that her teaching on the sanctity of marriage in an age of hardness of heart may be clear and strong

For the elders, the judges, and the officers of all nations, that they may live in the holy fear of the Lord and respect His covenant of life with every human being

For those who have renounced marriage for the sake of the kingdom of God, for those who are being called to marriage, that they may shine brightly because of their joy in the Lord

For those in troubled marriages, for single parents, for all who struggle with hardship or illness, for all the intentions we bring in our hearts to this Eucharist

That God whose mercy endures forever may purify and welcome our loved ones who have passed out of this life into the peace and joy of His kingdom

### Week 19, Saturday

*Josh 24:14-29, Ps 16, Matt 19:13-15*

For the whole church, that the members of each household in her ranks may choose with all their hearts to serve the Lord in gratitude for all His gifts

For the leaders of nations, that they may cast out the strange gods of greed and hostility, oppression and war, and follow the way of justice and peace

For children, for the littlest ones, to whom the kingdom of heaven belongs, that they may be protected and loved and brought to Jesus for His blessing

That our Blessed Mother may obtain health for the sick, refuge for the fearful, joy for those in grief, inner freedom for the imprisoned, and salvation and grace for all

For all our beloved dead, who have come for judgment before the holiness of God, that they may soon be purified to share in His joy and bliss in heaven

## Week 20, Monday

*Judg 2:11-19, Ps 106, Matt 19:16-22*

For the pastors and judges of the church, raised up by God with the power and insight to liberate His people from sin and its oppression of the human heart, that they may be firm and steadfast in their mission

That unborn children may no longer be sacrificed to the false gods of money and pleasure, but that our society may again learn to value the dignity of every human life

For vocations, that young men and women who wish to be perfect may generously sell all and follow Jesus with their whole hearts

For all who have asked our prayers in a time of illness or distress, that the Lord may take pity on their affliction and raise them up to life and health again

For our beloved dead, who wished to gain eternal life, that our prayers and this Holy Sacrifice may hasten their purification and bring them rejoicing into God's presence

## Week 20, Tuesday

*Judg 6:11-24, Ps 85, Matt 19:23-30*

For our priests, who have given up everything to follow Jesus, that the promised hundredfold of joy may be their portion along with eternal life

For our leaders in the world, that in their plans and policies they may co-operate with God's desire to have kindness and truth meet, so that justice and peace may grow

That as we lay out our offerings before God and receive the Body of Christ we may allow the fire of His love to take possession of our thoughts and actions

For those who are physically, mentally, financially, or emotionally distressed at this time, that God, for whom nothing is impossible, may bring them comfort and strength

For our beloved dead, that God's angel may come to them and lead them through the portal of purification to the joys of heaven

### Week 20, Wednesday

*Judg 9:6-15, Ps 21, Matt 20:1-16*

That those who labor in the Lord's vineyard, our Holy Father, bishops, priests, and deacons, may work cheerfully in His service, attracting souls to God by the witness of their joy

That we may carefully select those who will rule over us in a spirit of justice and good faith, choosing leaders who will promote life and peace

That we may grow accustomed to the world of Jesus where the last is first and the first, last, and where the Father astounds us with His generosity

That God may gladden with the joy of His face all those who are brought low through sickness, unemployment, or grief, blessing them with His presence

For those who have come forward to receive the recompense of their labors at the end of the day of this short life, that they may be amazed at the liberality of the heavenly Harvest Master

### Week 20, Thursday

*Judg 11:29-39, Ps 40, Matt 22:1-14*

That the Spirit of the Lord may come upon our holy ministers and shepherds in the church, that they may inflict a great defeat upon the power of evil in our own days

That the prophetic voices who take the part of justice, morality, and peace may be heard and heeded in our world today

That we may be among the chosen who willingly leave everything behind when we are summoned to the wedding banquet of the heavenly King

For all the intentions recommended to our prayers, for all the needs we bring in our hearts to this Eucharist, that the Master of the wedding banquet may be gracious to us all

That those who have gone before us in death may come before God dressed in the wedding garment of His grace and favor

## Week 20, Friday

*Ruth 1:1, 3-6, 14b-16, 22, Ps 146,*
*Matt 22:34-40*

That the church may always uphold the precept of love of God and love of neighbor on which the law and the prophets depends

That the command to love our neighbor that is written on every human heart may lead those in a position of power to respect the dignity of each human being under their care

That the devoted love shown by Ruth to Naomi may be the inspiration of marriages and friendships and all the ties that bind us to one another

That Jesus, who gave us the great commandment of mutual love, may lead the way in love by granting our requests for all who have appealed to us for prayer in a time of need

That the Lord, who sets captives free and who raises up those who are bowed down, may free our dear departed ones from all that holds them back from the full enjoyment of His heavenly kingdom

## Week 20, Saturday

*Ruth 2:1-3, 8-11, 4:13-17, Ps 128,*
*Matt 23:1-12*

For our Holy Father, our bishops and priests, servants of the servants of God, that they may always follow the Master in His teaching and His example

That bonds of love and care may be forged between peoples, after the example of Ruth, who because of her love became the ancestress of Jesus

That we may never perform our religious and charitable acts to be seen, but take our place with Mary among the humble who are lifted up by the Lord

For all who, like Naomi, have known grief and loss, sickness and trial in their lives, that they may be comforted as she was by human love, and granted new life by our compassionate Father

For the souls who have departed this life, who have entered the humiliation of death, that they may be exalted now in the presence of Jesus

### Week 21, Monday

*1 Thess 1:2-5, 8-10, Ps 149, Matt 23:13-23*

For our pastors in the church, that their preaching of the Gospel may prove to be not a matter of mere words but of power, because of their conviction and holiness of life

That world leaders may turn to the Lord from the idols of power and privilege, to serve the living and true God in justice and truth

That we may never deserve Jesus' frightening words to the scribes and Pharisees, but keep our perspective accurate, serving God in humility and love

That God who adorns the lowly with victory may raise up and console the sick and the overburdened who have recommended themselves to our prayers

That Jesus, who delivers us from the wrath to come, may receive the souls of our dear ones who have died and bring them through every purification to the realms of light and love in heaven

### Week 21, Tuesday

*1 Thess 2:1-8, Ps 139, Matt 23:23-26*

For the church, that in her teaching and practice she may always insist on the weightier things of the law: judgment and mercy and fidelity

That God may raise up in our own day prophets and rulers after His own heart, who will build up a culture of love and justice

For missionaries who suffer and are insolently treated, that they may draw courage to speak the Gospel in a way that pleases God rather than men

That those who suffer from sickness, financial hardship, or addiction may find us as gentle with them as a nursing mother is with her little ones, and that our prayers for them may be effective

That God who has probed every soul and knows each one, may grant to those who have gone before us the gift of forgiveness, light, and peace in His kingdom

## Week 21, Wednesday

*1 Thess 2:9-13, Ps 139, Matt 23:27-32*

For our Holy Father, our bishops and priests, who constantly encourage us to make our lives worthy of the God who calls us to His kingship and glory, that they may have the joy of a full response

That Christian political leaders may make their conduct upright, just, and irreproachable, taking the message of the Gospel as truly the word of God and living by it

For all of us sharing this Eucharist, that we who are filled from within with the presence of Jesus may bring His light and love to all whom we meet today

For all who are in a time of distress and suffering, that God may give them the strong faith to see that the night shines as the day when it is held in His loving providence

For the souls of all who have died, that God's hand may guide them and His right hand hold them safely on their course to the mansions of heaven

## Week 21, Thursday

*1 Thess 3:7-13, Ps 90, Matt 24:42-51*

For our leaders in the church, that they may be encouraged by our faith, and help us in turn to be blameless in holiness before our God and Father

That world leaders may have the perspective of the Lord in all their doings, so that He may prosper the work of peace in their hands

For the grace to be vigilant as we await the return of the Lord, so that He will find us waiting and ready to welcome Him

For all the intentions recommended to our prayers, especially for those in a time of serious need, that the gracious care of the Lord may be with each one for whom we pray

For our beloved dead, that this Holy Sacrifice may speed their purification, making them ready to stand blameless in holiness before our God and loving Father

### Week 21, Friday

*1 Thess 4:1-8, Ps 97, Matt 25:1-13*

For the church and each faithful soul within her care, that we may keep our lamps of faith and love supplied and burning, waiting in hope for the return of the Bridegroom

For those who work for the upholding of human dignity, that their voices may be heard and heeded by our national leaders

For holy Christian families, knit together in respect and love, with the Holy Spirit as the lamp of godliness burning to light the way

For the poor, the sick, the imprisoned, the addicted, and the grieving, that the grace and healing contained in this Eucharist may overflow into their lives

For our dear departed ones who have heard the midnight summons of the Bridegroom calling them from this life, that they may surround Him in joy with lamps alight in His heavenly kingdom

### Week 21, Saturday

*1 Thess 4:9-12, Ps 98, Matt 25:14-30*

For our priests, the stewards who administer the sacramental treasures of a Master whom they have never seen, that when He comes they may bring Him the fruits of their labors with confidence

For peace, that political leaders may not be selfish in their outlook, but instead imitate God who rules the world with justice and the peoples with equity

For all of us who have received the precious talent of baptism, that we may invest the grace we have been given by making ever greater progress in our love for one another

For teachers and students at this time of the beginning of the new school year, that God may prosper their studies and instruct every young heart in His ways

For those who have gone before us into the time of accounting with the Master, that this Holy Sacrifice may supply their need and hasten their purification

## Week 22, Monday

*1 Thess 4:13-18, Ps 96, Luke 4:16-30*

For the church, that our hope in the resurrection of the dead may be firm, and that we may look forward with joy to our meeting with the Lord and our reunion with our loved ones

That by our work for justice, life, and peace we may tell among the nations God's glory and His wondrous deeds

That we who have grown up in the spiritual company of Jesus may never let familiarity dim His divine stature in our eyes

That Jesus, who came to proclaim liberty to captives, sight to the blind, and freedom to the oppressed, may console and strengthen our dear ones who are experiencing trouble or illness

For those who have fallen asleep, that Jesus who died and rose from the dead may bring them rejoicing into the realm of His heavenly glory

## Week 22, Tuesday

*1 Thess 5:1-6, 9-11, Ps 27, Luke 4:31-37*

That the preachers of the church may speak with authority and power, knowing that they are bearers of the Word of God to the children of the light

That world leaders may be alert and sober, with hearts that have been brought into submission to the law of God

That Jesus may again manifest His power against the forces of evil, casting them out and not allowing them to do any harm to God's holy people

For the sick, the poor, the grieving, and the oppressed, that they may wait for the Lord with courage, knowing that He will show them love and mercy

That our departed loved ones and all the souls who are undergoing purification may soon see the bounty of the Lord in the land of the living

### Week 22, Wednesday

*Col 1:1-8, Ps 52, Luke 4:38-44*

For our holy shepherds, that they may take time to be by themselves in prayer as Jesus did, receiving the guidance they need in their ministry

That Jesus may cast out every demon that works against a culture of life, enlightening our national and world leaders to see the dignity of every human being

For missionaries, that they may carry the Word of truth with joy and courage, making it grow and bear fruit in the whole world

That like Peter we may intercede with Jesus for those who are sick or in need of any kind of healing, drawing out His mercy and His power

That the hope reserved for us in heaven, which inspires our faith and our love, may become a blessed reality for those who have gone before us marked with the cross of Jesus

### Week 22, Thursday

*Col 1:9-14, Ps 98, Luke 5:1-11*

For our leaders in the church, that they may be endowed with the courage they need to stand fast on the difficult moral issues of our day

That world leaders may be filled with knowledge of God's will, bearing fruit in every good work for life, justice, integrity, and peace

For vocations; that more willing hearts may be amazed at the way in which obedience to the word of Jesus makes their lives overflow, then leave everything to follow Him

For all who are in a time of great distress, who have nothing to show for their labors and sufferings, that Jesus may surprise them with a gift of abundance and joy

For our beloved dead, that they may be delivered from the power of darkness and transferred to the kingdom of the beloved Son

## Week 22, Friday

*Col 1:15-20, Ps 100, Luke 5:33-39*

For our Holy Father, our bishops and priests, that they may always point to Christ Jesus in their preaching as the image of the invisible God and the One in whom all things hold together

For world leaders, that Jesus, Master of thrones, dominions, principalities and powers, may be master of their thoughts and decisions

For all the faithful, that we may be fresh wineskins into which the joy and grace of the Savior may be safely poured

For all who are in a season of suffering, bereavement, or emotional turmoil, that Jesus, in whom all things hold together, may make peace for them through the Blood of this Holy Sacrifice

For our dear ones who have died, that the Lord may make them enter His gates with thanksgiving and His heavenly courts with praise

## Week 22, Saturday

*Col 1:21-23, Ps 54, Luke 6:1-5*

For the church, that she may persevere in the faith, firmly rooted, stable, and not shifting from the hope of the Gospel

That Mary, Queen of peace and Mother of all the living, may gather all our prayers and work for life and justice into a fragrant offering, powerful for good

That Jesus, Lord of the Sabbath and Master of all wisdom, may inspire and direct our actions according to His flawless and loving will

For all the intentions we bring to this Eucharist, especially to obtain healing and help for our friends, relatives, and benefactors

For those who have gone before us, that they may be presented holy, without blemish, and irreproachable before the throne of the Father

### Week 23, Monday

*Col 1:24–2:3, Ps 62, Luke 6:6-11*

For our holy leaders in the church, who labor and struggle in accord with the power of God urging them, that they may have the joy of presenting everyone perfect in Christ

For those in a position of power and influence in the world, that they may work to save life rather than destroy it, upholding human dignity in all their efforts

That we may have knowledge of the mystery of Christ, in whom are hidden all treasures of God's wisdom and love

For those who are filling up in their flesh what is lacking in the afflictions of Christ, that they may have the light and grace to offer all for the sake of His Body, the Church

For our departed loved ones, friends, and benefactors, that they may be at rest in God, their stronghold and their salvation

### Week 23, Tuesday

*Col 2:6-15, Ps 145, Luke 6:12-19*

For the church, that she may be rooted and built up in Christ, growing ever stronger in faith and filled with gratitude

That the empty, seductive philosophies that corrupt our world today may be revealed for what they are by those who stand up fearlessly for God and for His commandments

That Jesus may summon and call new apostles to proclaim His kingdom, and grant the gift of many new religious vocations in His holy church

That power may go out from Jesus and cure all whom we bring to Him in this Holy Eucharist; the sick and the distressed whom we enfold in our prayer

That all those who died believing in the power of God who raised Jesus from the dead may now experience new life in company with Christ

## Week 23, Wednesday

*Col 3:1-11, Ps 145, Luke 6:20-26*

For our Holy Father, our bishops and priests, that they may lead us in setting our hearts on things above as we help them fight the grave moral battles of our day

For world leaders, that God whose dominion endures through all ages may raise up voices of conscience who will speak for His kingdom of peace

For the grace of conversion from all forms of sin, even the most hidden, that the old self may be buried and Christ come to full life in each of His members

For the poor, the hungry, the suffering, those who weep, and those who are persecuted, that God may fill their souls with the joy of hope brought by His Gospel

For those who have died, whose life is hidden from our eyes with Christ in God, that they may know the fullness of joy in God's heavenly kingdom

## Week 23, Thursday

*Col 3:12-17, Ps 150, Luke 6:27-38*

For all God's chosen ones, holy and beloved, that we may put on heartfelt compassion, kindness, humility, gentleness, and patience in our dealings with one another

That the peace of Christ may control the hearts of those who have control over the policies and plans that can lead to world peace

That we may have the light and grace to stop judging and love our enemies, blessing those who curse us and overcoming evil by the power of free and humble goodness

That God's kindness and mercy may be given to those who have asked for our prayers in a time of trial or illness, that they may be healed and consoled

For the souls of our dear departed ones, that they may be forgiven, and that good gifts may be poured into their lap in the kingdom of love which is heaven

## Week 23, Friday

*1 Tim 1:1-2, 12-14, Ps 16, Luke 6:39-42*

For all those whom God has considered trustworthy and appointed to the ministry of the grace of Christ, that they may be found faithful

That the grace of our Lord may be abundant to support all those who work for the right to life and justice for the oppressed and hungry in our world

That we may be careful to keep our eyesight free and clear, humbly accepting lifelong discipleship under our one teacher, Jesus the Lord

For all who are in need of healing and consolation, that through this Holy Eucharist they may experience the fullness of joys in God's presence

For those who have gone before us marked with the sign of faith, that grace, mercy, and peace may be theirs from God the Father and from Christ Jesus our Lord

## Week 23, Saturday

*1 Tim 1:15-17, Ps 113, Luke 6:43-49*

For our Holy Father, our bishops and priests, that they may be true servants of the Lord, praising His name in word and deed

For our leaders in the world, that they may be good in their hearts and produce as their fruit the works of justice and peace

That we may be among those who take Jesus' words to heart and build our lives upon them, so that we may stand firm in the storms of adversity and temptation

For all who are in need of God's mercy and the prayers of His people: the sinners, the sick, the addicted, the unemployed, and all who are in a season of suffering at this time

For our beloved departed ones who had faith in Jesus Christ, that they may now gain everlasting life in His blessed presence

## Week 24, Monday

*1 Tim 2:1-8, Ps 28, Luke 7:1-10*

For the heralds and apostles of the truth, who teach the nations in Jesus' name, that like St. Paul, they may be clear and incisive in their message

That our prayers, petitions, and intercessions on behalf of civil authority may be effective, and that Christians may be able to lead a life of piety and dignity in the world

That we may imitate the humility of the centurion in our encounter with Jesus who enters our house in this Holy Eucharist

That our faith on behalf of the sick and all those who have asked our prayers may be strong and pleasing to Jesus, that He may work for them His miracles of healing

For our dear departed ones, and for all the souls who still undergo purification to be worthy of God's heavenly kingdom

## Week 24, Tuesday,

*1 Tim 3:1-13, Ps 101, Luke 7:11-17*

For our bishops, priests, and deacons, that they may fit the description offered by St. Paul today and bring honor to the church

That God may raise up men and women of integrity as national leaders who are willing to work for justice, life, and true peace

That we may hold fast to the mystery of the faith with a clear conscience, and be temperate and hospitable in our deeds, so as to attract others to the Gospel

That Jesus, who worked a miracle of compassion and love for the widow of Naim, may respond to our fervent prayers for the sick and for those who grieve

For those who have gone before us marked with the sign of faith, that Jesus may complete in them the work of purification and bring them into His heavenly kingdom

## Week 24, Wednesday

*1 Tim 3:14-16, Ps 111, Luke 7:31-35*

For the church of the living God, pillar and foundation of truth, that she may hold fast to her destiny as the sacrament of salvation for the whole world

That the light shed in the world by the teaching magisterium of the church may guide the nations in the ways of justice and peace

That we may be children of wisdom, seeing Jesus as the way to the Father and following His teaching and His example in our lives

For all those who have asked for our prayers in a time of sickness, unemployment, grief, or trial, that the grace of this Holy Sacrifice may be light and hope in their lives

That Jesus, who was manifested in the flesh and vindicated in the spirit, may take into His glory our brothers and sisters who have died

## Week 24, Thursday

*1 Tim 4:12-16, Ps 111, Luke 7:36-50*

For our leaders in the church, that they may not neglect the gift given them in the laying on of hands, but be a continuing example of love, faith, and purity to believers

For the poor nations, who are blocked from development by crippling debts, that their creditors may be merciful and allow them to have a new chance

For all who are conscious of their sinfulness, that they may imitate the woman who repented at the Lord's feet and gave Him an anointing of her great love

That we who receive Jesus in this Eucharist may draw from Him the fruits of His healing and grace upon all those for whom we pray

For those who have died, that they may meet their Savior with the love that shows their sins have been forgiven, and that He may surround them with the hospitality of His heavenly kingdom

## Week 24, Friday

*1 Tim 6:2c-12, Ps 49, Luke 8:1-3*

For the leaders in the church, that they may pursue righteousness, devotion, faith, love, patience, and gentleness

That world leaders may not be blinded by the trap of greed and power, but work with integrity for the lasting values of life, justice, and peace

That we who follow Jesus may experience the great gain of religion with contentment, and instead of pursuing riches share our resources with Him like the holy women of the Gospel

For all who are troubled with evil spirits, crippled by illness, and hemmed in by addiction, that Jesus may proclaim to them the good news of the kingdom of God by His miracles of healing and power

For those who have died, that they may carry with them the treasure of a life well lived, and that those who still undergo purification may soon find themselves rejoicing with Jesus forever

## Week 24, Saturday

*1 Tim 6:13-16, Ps 100, Luke 8:4-15*

That Jesus, who made His noble profession before Pontius Pilate, may enable our holy shepherds to be strong in their witness to the entire truth of the Gospel

That Jesus, King of Kings and Lord of Lords, who dwells in unapproachable light, may under gird with His divine authority all our efforts to uphold life, morality, and justice on the earth

That the Word of God, scattered among us with such divine bounty, may find in us a good and receptive soil, and that we may bear fruit through perseverance

For those who are encountering rocks and thorns upon their way, who suffer from illness, poverty, addiction, or grief, that our Blessed Mother of mercy may obtain for them the blessing of new life and joy

For those who have gone before us marked with faith and love, that they may enter God's gates with thanksgiving and His courts of heaven with praise

### Week 25, Monday

*Ezra 1:1-6, Ps 126, Luke 8:16-18*

For the church, experiencing her exile from the heavenly kingdom here on earth, that she may look forward in hope to the Lord's promised restoration

That leaders of nations may follow the example of King Cyrus of Persia, reverencing God and assisting those who believe in Him to construct a house in His honor, built of justice and peace

That we may listen to Jesus with hearts ready to shine like lamps in the darkness, accomplishing the deeds He asks so that even more grace may be given to us

For all who are sowing with tears in a time of sickness, poverty, or grief, that the Lord may grant what they reap with rejoicing

For all the souls who have gone before us, that they may be quickly purified, and that the works they bring into heaven may shine with light and love

### Week 25, Tuesday

*Ezra 6:7-8, 12b, 14-20, Ps 122, Luke 8:19-21*

That the elders of God's people today may make progress on the steady building of the house of the Lord, which is made of living stones, the souls of the faithful

That the prophets who support God's work by their messages may again be heard in our world, as they cry out for a culture of life and a society built on justice

That we may stand with Mary among those who hear the Word of God and act on it, becoming the mothers, brothers, and sisters of our Lord Jesus Christ

For all who are passing through trials or sickness at this time, that the Lord may bring them as permanent dwellers into His city of peace

For our departed loved ones that with purified souls they may go up to the house of the Lord and be welcomed into God's kingdom of light and joy

## Week 25, Wednesday

*Ezra 9:5-9, Tob 13, Luke 9:1-6*

That the church may always be aware of its sinfulness before God, and acknowledge God's undeserved merciful love in freeing her from the consequences of sin in Jesus Christ

That the good will of the rulers of the earth may be turned toward the poor, the hungry, and the oppressed, to relieve their distress and build up a culture of peace

For the grace of vocations, that Jesus may have close followers, given entirely to His will, whom He can send with authority over demons to proclaim the good news everywhere

That Jesus, who reached out through His apostles to cure diseases everywhere, may lay His healing hands upon the sick whom we recommend to His loving kindness

For all who have gone before us in death, that they may be brought into the house of God, restored, redeemed, and rejoicing

## Week 25, Thursday

*Hag 1:1-8, Ps 149, Luke 9:7-9*

That the prophetic voices in the church may always urge us to put God first in our lives and in all our works, so that everything else may prosper in His love

That the King Herods of our own day may come to an encounter with Jesus Christ, and as a result change their policies to a pursuit of the good of their people

That we who know who Jesus is may welcome Him into our hearts today as into His own temple, that He may take pleasure in us and receive His glory

That the Lord, who loves His people and adorns the lowly with victory, may raise up those who have asked our prayers and give them hope and healing

For the souls of all who have died, that they may soon be purified to sing in heaven the high praises of the Lord our God

## Week 25, Friday

*Hag 2:1-9, Ps 43, Luke 9:18-22*

That we may take courage and do our part to build up the house of the Lord on earth today, no matter how small and feeble it seems to look in our eyes, knowing that God's Spirit continues in our midst

That God may shake all the nations and bring their treasures of power and wealth to the service of the poorest and weakest among them

That we may have the courage to proclaim Jesus as the anointed One of God, and accept His road of death and resurrection as the way we ourselves must walk

For those who are in a season of trial and pain, who are lonely or grieving, that the Lord may visit His temple within their hearts, filling them with glory and giving them peace

For our beloved dead, that God's light and fidelity may bring them to His holy mountain, and to the dwelling place of gladness and joy

## Week 25, Saturday

*Zech 2:5-9, 14-15a, Jer 31, Luke 9:43b-45*

That the Lord may be for the church an encircling wall of fire to protect and defend her, and the glory in her midst

That many nations may join themselves to the Lord, obeying His commandments of life and justice, that He may dwell with them and bless them again

For all who are afraid to choose the way of the cross or even to ask the Lord about this saying, that they may come to understand that the cross is the only way to their own happiness and glory

That our Blessed Mother may see to the needs of those who have asked for our prayers because they are sick, poor, imprisoned, or addicted, helping and consoling them

That God may console and gladden the souls of our beloved dead after their sorrows, giving them light and eternal rest in heaven

## Week 26, Monday

*Zech 8:1-8, Ps 102, Luke 9:46-50*

For the church, the new Jerusalem, that she may earn the name of the faithful city of God, holy and united in faith and love

That what is impossible in our eyes may be made possible by the Lord: that nations may promote faithfulness and justice upon the earth

For those who want to be great in the kingdom of God, that they may be converted to the divine values of Jesus, choosing to be last and the servant of all

That God may gather the sick, the poor, the imprisoned, and all who need our prayers, into His embrace of healing love

For those who have died, that the Lord may rescue them and bring them back to dwell with Him in the heavenly Jerusalem

## Week 26, Tuesday

*Zech 8:20-23, Ps 87, Luke 9:51-56*

For the church, the New Jerusalem, that through the ministry of our Holy Father, our bishops and priests, many nations may be attracted to seek the Lord in her

That Jesus, who would not punish the towns who refused Him, may find a way into hardened hearts and turn the minds of national leaders to thoughts of morality and justice again

For all who feel a time of suffering approach, as Jesus did when He began His journey to Jerusalem, that like Him they may resolve to go forward, trusting in the love of the Father

That we may implore the favor of the Lord upon all who suffer and for all those who need to seek the Lord and return to the practice of their faith

For our loved ones who have gone before us, that the Lord may bring them into His holy city and upon His holy mountain of joy and eternal rest

### Week 26, Wednesday

*Neh 2:1-8, Ps 137, Luke 9:57-62*

For the builders of the church who are sad at heart because they see their work in ruins, that through the favoring hand of God, they may be given the chance to make a new start

That rulers and national leaders may show the same concern and compassion for the dignity and happiness of their people as the king showed toward Nehemiah in today's reading

For all who are called to follow Jesus in a vocation of complete consecration to His mission, that they may not offend Him by hesitation but be willing to share the uncertain circumstances of His journey

For all who feel exiled from happiness in life, for the sick and those who are in emotional or spiritual pain, that the Lord may lead them back into hope and gladness

For all those who have died, and for the souls who still undergo purification, that our prayers and love may move our Savior to free them from sin and bring them into heaven

### Week 26, Thursday

*Neh 8:1-4, 5-6, 7-12, Ps 19, Luke 10:1-12*

For our holy ministers who read and interpret the law of God to us, that they may have the joy of our full respect and response to God's holy word

That the Lord may create in the hearts of those who govern in the world a capacity for peace and justice and reverence for life, that the peace of God may rest upon us all

For vocations; that God may raise up in the church many young and generous souls who will catch the fire of the urgency to proclaim the Gospel and to teach and heal in the name of Jesus

For those who are sad at heart, who have lost hope amid the trials and difficulties of life, that through this Holy Sacrifice, their lot may be changed, and rejoicing in the Lord may become their strength

For our beloved dead, who did their best to keep the law of the Lord during their earthly pilgrimage, that they may now celebrate with great joy in His heavenly kingdom

## Week 26, Friday

*Bar 1:15-22, Ps 79, Luke 10:13-16*

For our Holy Father, our bishops and priests, that their words may be received with reverence, as we would wish to receive Jesus and His heavenly Father in whose name they speak

For the oppressed and the marginalized, the refugees and the poor, the unborn and the elderly, that their human dignity may be respected and that the powerful may come to their aid

For the church, that we may never lose sight of our failures to observe the law of the Lord and listen to His prophets, so that our hearts may always be soft with repentance and ready to begin again

For all who need Jesus to work His miracles of healing and hope in their lives in a time of illness or discouragement, that He may come quickly to their side

That our dear ones who have died may pass through the gates of final repentance in the presence of the divine judge, and soon find His mercy reaching out to enfold them

## Week 26, Saturday

*Bar 4:5-12, 27-29, Ps 69, Luke 10:17-24*

For our modern day apostles who work to spread the Gospel, that all power of evil may be subject to them in Jesus' name, and that nothing may harm them

For all who work in the cause of life, who prevent the sacrifice of the little ones to the demons of greed and pleasure, that God may prosper their work and make them strong in their witness

That we may be among the childlike to whom the mysteries of heaven and the treasures hidden in Jesus are revealed

That Jesus, to whom all things have been handed over, may use His power to come to the aid of all the distressed and ailing who call out to Him with confidence

For our brothers and sisters who have gone before us marked with the sign of faith, that our Blessed Mother may intercede for them and bring them into the heavenly kingdom

### Week 27, Monday

*Jonah 1:1–2:1-2, Jonah 2, Luke 10:25-37*

For the reluctant prophets, who hesitate to speak the truth for fear of others, that God may mercifully pursue them as He did Jonah for the sake of the church

For our nation, that it may continue to exercise its role of compassion towards those who have fallen victim to the robbers of our own day, who are oppressed by war, terrorism, hunger, and disease

For men and women of good will, who, though they do not know the Lord, can recognize His prophets and respect His ways, that God may build on their goodness with the gift of faith

For all who have asked our prayers in a time of sickness or pain, that we may fulfill God's law to love them as ourselves through our earnest intercession for their needs

That Jesus, who taught the scholar of the law how to inherit eternal life, may bestow that life upon our dear departed loved ones

### Week 27, Tuesday

*Jonah 3:1-10, Ps 130, Luke 10:38-42*

For the church, finding her way between activity and prayer, that the presence of her contemplatives may be a reminder of the value of silent attention to the person of Christ

That the prophets who walk our city streets may not be discouraged by the enormous problems they face, but remember always that they have God's mandate, and therefore God's help, in all they do

For vocations to the priestly and religious life, and especially for those who feel they have somehow missed the call, that the word of the Lord may come to them a second time

For all of us sharing this Eucharist, who bring the needs of those dear to us into the embrace of our Communion with Jesus, that His mercy may radiate into their hearts in grace and healing

That the "better part" of pure and blissful contemplation of God may be granted to our beloved dead in His heavenly kingdom

## Week 27, Wednesday

*Jonah 4:1-11, Ps 86, Luke 11:1-4*

For our Holy Father, our bishops and priests, and all who are called to lead the prayer of God's people, that the prayer of Jesus may form their own attitude before the Father

For the nations filled with people who cannot tell their right hand from their left in knowing the ways of God's peace, that the example of Christians may shine out in their midst as a prophetic influence

For all who are angry at God for the things that are painful in their lives, that God's patient teaching may bring them to a new understanding, as it did for Jonah

For all who suffer and are in need of prayer, that God may be good and forgiving to them, abounding in kindness and grace

For those who have left this world in peace, who longed for God's kingdom on earth and forgave those in debt to them, that they may have the vision of the Father who is in heaven

## Week 27, Thursday

*Mal 3:13-20, Ps 1, Luke 11:5-13*

For the church, possessing the bread of truth and grace so needed by strangers on the road today, that she may willingly rise and give to all who come knocking in the night

For the United Nations, that justice and compassion may be the stream towards which this tree continues to stretch its roots, that even in hard years it may bear the fruit of peace

That those who fear the Lord may speak with one another, encouraging each other and giving voice to the convictions that earn the divine approval

That on behalf of all who do not know their need for God, and those who are sick in soul or body, we may ask, seek, and knock, begging for the gift of God's Holy Spirit to heal and comfort them

For our beloved departed, that God may take compassion on them, and that the sun of justice may arise for them in His kingdom of peace and love

### Week 27, Friday

*Joel 1:13-15, 2:1-2, Ps 9, Luke 11:15-26*

For our Holy Father and all the religious leaders and teachers in the church, that with Jesus they may stand fully armed, guarding the people of God in safety and truth

For peace; for courage to take the arduous ways of justice that lead to peace, so that we may not be sunk in the pit of selfishness or caught in the snares of a culture of death, but follow God's way in truth

That God's people may not be afraid to do penance when penance is needed, to gather the assembly into the house of the Lord and take advantage of the sacrament of reconciliation

For all who are tormented by the demons of addiction, violence, or emotional illness, that they may know that the kingdom of God is in their midst as Jesus casts out the evil from their hearts by the finger of God

That those who have passed through the darkness and gloom of death may be soon purified to see God face to face

### Week 27, Saturday

*Joel 4:12-21, Ps 97, Luke 11:27-28*

For the whole church facing the purifications that come when the Lord rises for judgment, that she may also know the living waters of His mercy

That Our Lady, Queen of Peace, may teach us to establish our hearts, our homes, and our world on the values of life, of prayer, of moral integrity, and justice for all

For all of God's holy people, that with Mary we may be counted among the blessed who hear God's Word and observe it

For those who are suffering from sickness, poverty, addiction, or grief, that they may be granted a season of new wine and milk from the mercy of the Lord

For our dear ones who have passed through the Valley of Decision in their own death, that the Lord may now be a refuge to them and bring them into His heavenly Jerusalem

## Week 28, Monday

*Rom 1:1-17, Ps 98, Luke 11:29-32*

For all the beloved of God in the church, who are called to be holy and set apart for the Gospel of God, that we may be brought to the obedience of faith

That Jesus, who was established as the Son of God in power, may master the hearts of the powerful and turn their thoughts to concern for the poorest and weakest

That we may take seriously the message of Jesus, as the people of Nineveh did with the preaching of Jonah, and open our hearts to repentance and change

That the Lord may remember His kindness and His faithfulness toward the sick and the distressed who rely on our prayers

For our beloved dead, that Jesus may share with them the power of His resurrection, freeing them from sin and making them worthy of His heavenly kingdom

## Week 28, Tuesday

*Rom 1:16-25, Ps 19, Luke 11:37-41*

That our leaders in the church may never be ashamed of the Gospel, but preach it boldly for the salvation of everyone who believes

That those who rule in the world may not risk blindness in their reasoning by being forgetful of God, but make their decisions in justice and truth

That the vessels we offer to the Lord may be clean inside and out through our works of mercy and our humility in His presence

For all who are in need of loving intercession; especially those who are ill, imprisoned, unemployed, or grieving, that the power of this Holy Sacrifice may bring them relief and strength

For those who have gone before us in death, that Jesus may bring them in to recline at the banquet of eternal joy

### Week 28, Wednesday

*Rom 2:1-11, Ps 62, Luke 11:42-46*

For the church, that we may pay close attention to judgment and the love of God as our first priorities, and to helping one another carry our burdens in humility and obedience

For the prophets of our day, who like St. Paul thunder against the immorality of our age, that they may be heard and heeded by all but especially by the powerful and influential

That we may hold in reverence the priceless kindness, forbearance, and patience of God, responding to His silent invitation to repentance and to a change of heart

For all who have asked our prayers in a difficult time in their lives, that God may be their stronghold, giving them rest and salvation

For our dear departed loved ones, that they may be at rest, receiving glory, honor, and peace from the just Judge

### Week 28, Thursday

*Rom 3:21-29, Ps 130, Luke 11:47-54*

That the justification wrought by grace and God's mercy may be proclaimed in the church, and that our gratitude for this great gift may overflow in our outreach to bring it to others

That world leaders may listen to the prophetic voices when they urge justice and speak for the poorest and the most forgotten in the world, that there may be peace

For all of us receiving the Body and Blood of the One who is our expiation and our glory, that we may witness with joy and conviction to our faith in Him

For all who have asked for our prayers, who are crying out to God from the depths of their sickness, unemployment, or grief, that their trust in the Lord may be met by the generous response of His mercy

For our beloved dead, that they may be received into the company of the faithful prophets and martyrs of God through the redemption wrought in Christ Jesus

## Week 28, Friday

*Rom 4:1-8, Ps 32, Luke 12:1-7*

For our preachers and teachers in the church, that they may proclaim from the housetops the Good News of the Gospel with courage and joy

That the Lord may raise up in the world leaders after His own heart, who will rebuild a culture of life and a society based on justice for all

That we may have the confidence of those who know they are of great value to God, and that He may give us strength to have no fear of persecution for His name's sake

For those who are laboring under a burden of guilt, that they may come back to God's grace and love through the sacrament of reconciliation

That our brothers and sisters who have died may be among those whose iniquities are forgiven, whose sins are covered, that by God's mercy they may know eternal rest

## Week 28, Saturday

*Rom 4:13, 16-18, Ps 105, Luke 12:8-12*

For our holy ministers in the church, that the Holy Spirit may guide them at every moment with what they are to say to God's people in their work of preaching His Word

That our Blessed Mother, Queen of Peace, may move our hearts to prayer and sacrifice for this precious gift in our hearts, our homes, and our world

That as Christians we may be strong in our witness to Jesus Christ and to the values of His holy Gospel, so that He may acknowledge us before the angels of God as His true followers

For those who are counting on our prayers in a time of physical, mental, or financial distress, that their faith may be strong so as to be able to receive God's gifts of relief and peace of heart

For our beloved departed ones, that God who gives life to the dead may shorten the time of purification and raise them up to the heavenly places

### Week 29, Monday

*Rom 4:20-25, Luke 1, Luke 12:13-21*

For the faith of the church, that it may ever grow stronger and be a light in the darkness for all men and women of good will, leading the way to righteousness

That world leaders may not store up treasure for themselves, but become rich in what matters to God: respect for life, moral integrity, justice, and peace

That we who believe in Jesus may guard ourselves against all greed, taking care to place our riches in the heavenly kingdom by our generosity with the goods of this earth

For all those who are passing through a season of weakness and pain, that they may put their faith in God who raised up Jesus and has power to heal every wound

For those whose lives have been demanded of them in death, that the faith and love which they demonstrated on earth may be rewarded with eternal life

### Week 29, Tuesday

*Rom 5:12, 15b, 17-19, 20b-21, Ps 40,*
*Luke 12:35-38*

That even though sin increases, the church may proclaim with joy the abundance of grace, acquittal, and life that we have in Jesus

For the prophets of our own day who have ears open to obedience and whose delight is the will of the Lord, that they may be heard and heeded by those in authority in the world

That we may stand ready with our lamps alight as we wait for the return of the good Master

For all who have asked our prayers in their time of need, for the poor, the sick, the addicted and imprisoned, and those who have no one to pray for them

That our beloved dead may come to reign in life through the gift of justification in Jesus Christ our Lord

## Week 29, Wednesday

*Rom 6:12-18, Ps 124, Luke 12:39-48*

For our leaders in the church to whom much is given and much is expected, that they may be faithful and farsighted stewards in God's household

That our leaders in the temporal order may be sincere and trustworthy toward those who are going without their fair ration of grain, of dignity, of justice, and of peace

For all who are allowing sin to rule in their bodies and minds, that they may become vividly aware of where this is leading them, and submit instead to the gentle yoke of Christ

For all who feel overwhelmed by the torrents of affliction or caught in the trap of helplessness, that through the grace of this Holy Sacrifice the snare may be broken and they may be freed

For our loved ones who have passed from this world, who came under the law of grace by their obedience to God, that they may now pass from death to life in His glorious kingdom

## Week 29, Thursday

*Rom 6:19-23, Ps 1, Luke 12:49-53*

For our shepherds in the church, that by their holiness and preaching they may help our Lord Jesus Christ set fire to the earth

That world leaders may not follow the counsel of the wicked but delight in the law of the Lord, that their decisions may respect human dignity and build up peace

That the division Christ has initiated and the conflicts of loyalty that result from His presence may prove the worth of His saints

For all who have asked for our prayers, and for those who have no one to pray for them, especially the victims of natural disasters, terrorism, and war

For all who have died, that they may know the gift of God which is eternal life in Christ Jesus our Lord

## Week 29, Friday

*Rom 7:18-25, Ps 119, Luke 12:54-59*

That in the church the law of God may be our delight, and that the Lord may give us strength to carry out what we see is right

That God may raise up in our own day leaders who will base their decisions on the law of justice and moral integrity that He has planted in every human heart

That we may learn to judge for ourselves what is right, to know how to interpret the present time, and to achieve reconciliation before the hour of judgment

That the compassion of God may come upon the sick and the lonely, the poor and the oppressed, as we support them by our loving prayer

For those who have been released from this mortal body in death, that they may be brought rejoicing into the kingdom of heaven

## Week 29, Saturday

*Rom 8:1-11, Ps 24, Luke 13:1-9*

For those who tend the barren fig tree in the church, our leaders and teachers, that they may be diligent in their cultivation, and that their work may bear fruit for God's glory

That our Blessed Mother, Queen of Peace, may bring the hearts of the powerful to live in accord with the spirit of God, concerned with matters of life and peace

For all of us who belong to Christ and have the Spirit of God dwelling in us, that we may be faithful to such a lofty calling that brings the gift of eternal life

For all who are in need of loving intercession in their hour of illness, grief, imprisonment, addiction, or poverty, that through the power of this Holy Sacrifice they may be eased and blessed

That the law of the spirit of life in Christ Jesus may free our dear departed ones from the law of death and bring them into the joys of heaven

## Week 30, Monday

*Rom 8:12-17, Ps 68, Luke 13:10-17*

For the church, that her sons and daughters may always allow themselves to be led by the Spirit of God which cries out to the Father from each baptized soul

For world leaders, that God who defends the widow and the orphan may open their hearts to the rights of the poor, so that there may be true peace

That we may take hold of our divine adoption with gratitude, willing to suffer with Jesus so as to be glorified with Him

For all who are bowed down with heavy burdens of body, mind, or spirit, that Jesus, who reached out to cure the woman in today's gospel reading, may grant them His divine touch

That the dead who are still bound by sin may be freed from their shackles by the power of this holy sacrifice

## Week 30, Tuesday

*Rom 8:18-25, Ps 126, Luke 13:18-21*

For the church, that she may be the sacrament and the catalyst of the kingdom of God on earth until it is fully grown, giving shelter to many hearts

That creation may come to share in the glorious freedom of the children of God through leaders who respect life and foster moral values in the world

That we may take hold of our great hope in the revelation of our glory as the children of God, waiting for the fulfillment of the Lord's promise with faithful endurance

For all who are heavily burdened with the miseries and afflictions of life, that they may be surprised by the presence of God's kingdom growing quietly in their hearts, leavening everything with joy

For those who have died, that they be brought into the kingdom of heaven rejoicing, carrying their sheaves

### Week 30, Wednesday

*Rom 8:26-30, Ps 13, Luke 13:22-30*

That our holy shepherds and teachers may unfailingly point out for us the narrow way of obedience that obtains for us the Lord's recognition and admission into His house forever

That Christians may have the courage to stand up and be counted for the values of moral integrity and respect for human dignity, so that they may exert their proper influence on lawmakers and politicians

That the Holy Spirit may help us in our weakness when we pray, making our petitions pleasing and effective before the divine majesty

That God may make all things work together for the good of those who have asked for our prayers in their needs of soul and body, giving them healing and peace

For the souls of our loved ones who have gone before us in death, that they may be justified and glorified by the One who called them

### Week 30, Thursday

*Rom 8:31-39, Ps 109, Luke 13:31-35*

For our leaders in the church, that they may with Christ accomplish their purpose, gathering His children under the wings of their teaching and their holiness

For those who govern us in the temporal order, that with the Lord they may have regard for the wretched and the poor, that there may be peace

That we may believe that we cannot be separated from the love of Christ by anything, but conquer overwhelmingly in His power and desire to help us

For all who are in a season of suffering, that they may have the grace of unshakeable confidence in the power of Him who loved us

For our beloved dead, that Jesus who died and was raised may intercede for them at the right hand of God

## Week 30, Friday

*Rom 9:1-5, Ps 147, Luke 14:1-6*

That the church may reach out to the children of Israel, who have from God the adoption, the covenants, and the patriarchs, showing forth to them the love of their own brother in the flesh— Jesus Christ

That those to whom the Lord has made known His ordinances may put His word into practice in the sight of the nations, showing the way that leads to peace

That no consideration may prevent us from helping our brothers and sisters in their distress, as we imitate the divine charity of Jesus

That the healing power of our Lord may be upon the sick and the poor, raising them up from the cistern of their pain and oppression

For our loved ones who have gone before us in death, that they may not be cut off from Christ, but experience His merciful goodness bringing them into light and rest

## Week 30, Saturday

*Rom 11, Ps 94, Luke 14:1, 7-11*

For the gift of faith for the children of Israel, that the church and her ministers may repair the damage of centuries and make it possible for them to come to the truth of the Messiah

That world leaders may not become wise in their own estimation but serve the needs of each human being under their care

That we may willingly sit in the lowest place at the wedding banquet, and even be willing to join our Savior as the servant of all

For those who have been deeply humbled by suffering, sickness, oppression, or grief, that the divine law of compensation may raise them up in joy and newness of hope

That our deceased loved ones may experience that the gifts and the call of God are irrevocable, as He leads them through all purification into His kingdom of joy

## Week 31, Monday

*Rom 11:29-36, Ps 69, Luke 14:12-14*

For the shepherds of the church, that they may have a vivid understanding of how deep the riches and wisdom of God really are, and lead God's people in submission and reverence

That wealthy nations may show justice to the young and developing nations by helping them take their place in the world economy on a footing of equity and fairness

That all who have the means may make the poor and the disabled their guests in a feast of compassion, looking forward to God's repayment in the resurrection of the just

For all who are afflicted and in pain, that through the power of loving intercession they may know God's gifts and His mercy flowing into their hearts

That God's saving help may protect our loved ones who have gone before us into the shadow of death, bringing them into the realm of light and peace

## Week 31, Tuesday

*Rom 12:5-16, Ps 131, Luke 14:15-24*

For the church, filled with different gifts according to God's grace that the faithful exercise of ministry, teaching, exhortation, generosity, and mercy may build up the Body of Christ

That national leaders and those with power may see clearly what is true and what is false, so that they may hate the evil and hold on to the good, promoting justice in our day

That we who are invited to the banquet of the Eucharist may never prefer other occupations and interests to this divine food, but show God our gratitude and our joy

For those who must endure in affliction, undergo persecution, or weep in life's misfortunes and losses, that the solidarity of our prayer may support them in their hour of need

For our dear departed loved ones and all those who have died, that they may be in God's arms, stilled and quieted in the fullness of heavenly joy

## Week 31, Wednesday

*Rom 13:8-10, Ps 112, Luke 14:25-33*

For our Holy Father, our bishops and priests, that they may be a light for the upright, gracious and merciful and just

That national leaders may fulfill the law of love which does no evil to the neighbor and thus paves the way to peace

For the grace to truly follow Jesus, gladly paying the cost of renouncing all our possessions in order to possess Him as our one treasure

For all the needs and intentions entrusted to our prayers, that the power of this Holy Sacrifice may touch and transform every distress and trouble

For all the dead who feared the Lord and delighted in His commands, that this upright generation may be blessed with the rewards of heaven

## Week 31, Thursday

*Rom 14:7-12, Ps 27, Luke 15:1-10*

For our pastors in the church, that with Christ they may welcome the return of sinners and even go in search of them, in order to give joy to the heart of God and His angels

For political leaders, that they may not live for themselves, but for the Lord and for His people, especially for the smallest and most vulnerable

That no judgment of our brothers and sisters may come between us and the One to whom we must give an account of our lives, and who desires only the return of His children

For all who have lost their way in the sicknesses, troubles, and griefs of life, who need the Divine Shepherd to place them on His shoulders and return them to joy and peace

For our beloved dead, that by our prayer and the power of this Holy sacrifice they may be released to see the good things of the Lord in the land of the living

## Week 31, Friday

*Rom 15:14-21, Ps 98, Luke 16:1-8*

For all the ministers of Christ Jesus, that the grace given to them by God for the priestly service of the Gospel may bear fruit in many faithful followers of the Lord

That the leaders of this age may become willing to listen to the children of light when they speak of God's imperatives in relation to issues of justice and moral integrity

That we may know how to use the goods of this world in such a way that we are acting prudently to build up our treasure in heaven

That the power of signs and wonders and the Spirit of God may be at work in the lives of all who have asked our prayers in their time of need, healing and saving them

That those who have gone before us through the gates of death may now see the salvation of our God, as He purifies them and makes them capable of enjoying the bliss of heaven

## Week 31, Saturday

*Rom 16, Ps 145, Luke 16:9-15*

For all who are co-workers in Christ Jesus and give their lives to the proclamation of the Gospel, that their labors may be blessed, and that new ministers may come to join and support them

For all who work, pray, and suffer for the right to life, that their prophetic witness of love and truth may change hearts and begin a return to the culture of life

That we may have the light and grace to be wholly devoted to God, using earthly wealth for His service and for compassion towards His children

That God may strengthen the sick and the lonely, the poor and the oppressed, the imprisoned and the addicted, and bring them to the obedience of faith in His loving providence

For all who have died and especially for the souls who have no one to pray for them, that through the power of this Mass they may be welcomed into eternal dwellings

## Week 32, Monday

*Wis 1:1-7, Ps 139, Luke 17:1-6*

That wisdom and the holy spirit of discipline may awaken once more in the church, leading us in kindly ways towards union with God

That the rulers of the earth may love justice, seeking the common good in integrity of heart, winning the approval of the Lord of us all

That we may lovingly and honestly correct our brothers and sisters who do wrong, forgiving the ones who repent and standing fast in the truth for all

That our faith may be strong as we plead for those who have asked for the help of our prayers, that they may be relieved and helped by the Lord

For our loved ones who have died, that the Lord, who has probed them and knows them intimately, may repair whatever is keeping them from full joy in His kingdom

## Week 32, Tuesday

*Wis 2:23–3:9, Ps 34, Luke 17:7-10*

That grace and mercy may be with the holy ones who lead and guide God's people in the understanding of truth and the practice of love

For the just who face persecution for their stand on moral issues, that they may be held safe in the hand of God, knowing that in the end He shall judge the nations

That we who have done all that the Lord has commanded us may preserve our humility as His servants who have merely done our duty

For the brokenhearted and those who are crushed in spirit, that the Lord may be close to them and save them in His compassion

For those who have gone before us in death, that the Lord may find them worthy of Himself, proved like gold in the furnace and accepted as a sacrificial offering

### Week 32, Wednesday

*Wis 6:1-11, Ps 82, Luke 17:11-19*

For the ministers of God's kingdom, whose authority was given by the Lord, that they may hallow His precepts and teach others to do the same

For those who are in power over the multitude, that they may understand that the Lord will probe their works and scrutinize their counsels, and walk in obedience to His ways

That our gratitude for all the ways in which God heals and blesses us may bring us to the feet of Jesus, glorifying Him for His goodness and love

For all who need the pity of the Master, that we may cry out with them in prayer for His healing love

For all our dear departed ones, and for all the holy souls in purgatory during this month dedicated to prayer for them, that this Holy Sacrifice may release them into heavenly glory

### Week 32, Thursday

*Wis 7:22b-8:1, Ps 119, Luke 17:20-25*

For our leaders in the church, that they may be holy souls filled with wisdom, that will make them friends of God and prophets for our time

For world leaders, that wisdom, who is intelligent, clear, certain, firm, and all powerful, may be at their side, and inspire them with decisions that will lead to justice in God's sight

That we who know the kingdom of God in our midst as we receive this Holy Eucharist may sanctify ourselves by constant companionship with Jesus, even in His sufferings

That holy wisdom may penetrate and pervade all situations of sickness and distress and renew everything with firm and tranquil motion

For our beloved dead, that God's countenance may shine upon them, and they may live to praise Him in the kingdom of heaven

## Week 32, Friday

*Wis 13:1-9, Ps 19, Luke 17:26-37*

For the church, that she may always show her children and all who seek the truth how God is to be known from His beautiful and powerful work in creation

That those who govern may not be in ignorance of God, but honor Him by obedience to the natural law He has placed in their hearts

That we may be ready for the day on which the Lord is revealed, conducting the business of our everyday lives with the will to leave everything and join Him at any moment

For those who seem to be losing their lives to sickness or misfortune, that God may save them and raise them up through the offering of this Holy Sacrifice

For those who have gone before us to meet the Lord, that they may be gathered with Him into His kingdom of joy and peace

## Week 32, Saturday

*Wis 18:14-16, 19:6-9, Ps 105, Luke 18:1-8*

That the Son of Man may always find faith on earth in the hearts of those who love Him in His holy Church

That those who judge the earth may deliver just decisions for the needy and the helpless, especially those who need the right to life

That we may never become weary in our prayer but persevere with confidence, knowing that our Father will do us justice and show us mercy

That the wonders worked by God's all-powerful Word for the sake of His Israelite children may be repeated for those who are now crying out to Him in their need

That God may lead forth the souls of those who have died with joy, and His chosen ones may enter His gates singing their praise

### Week 33, Monday

*1 Macc 1:10-15, 41-43, 54-57, 62-63,*
*Ps 119, Luke 18:35-43*

For the members of the church, that we may be determined and resolved in our hearts never to profane the holy covenant we have with God in Christ Jesus

That the prayer and prophetic witness of committed Christians may inspire our national leaders to pursue justice and promote life and peace

That we may cry out to Jesus from all our areas of spiritual blindness with the profound faith and persevering conviction that pleases Him and awakens His healing power

For those who are living under terrible affliction, who are in the throes of persecution, poverty, illness, or grief, that our fervent prayer may uphold and support them through the grace of Jesus

For our beloved dead, that they may have sight of God in the eternal dwelling places, giving Him praise and glory

### Week 33, Tuesday

*2 Macc 6:18-31, Ps 3, Luke 19:1-10*

For the church, especially where her members are undergoing persecution, that they may be loyal to the holy laws given by God, suffering with joy in their souls because of their devotion to Him

For world leaders, that they may respect the dignity and the religious convictions of those under their jurisdiction

For the conversion of those who have fallen away from their faith, that like Zacchaeus they may be surprised by the mercy of Jesus as He invites Himself into their lives again

That Jesus, who came to seek out and save what was lost, may come to the aid of those who have lost their bearings in the midst of illness or affliction, restoring their health and their joy

For those who have lain down in the sleep of death, that they may wake to new life, upheld by the merciful power of the Lord

## Week 33, Wednesday

*2 Macc 7:20-31, Ps 17, Luke 19:11-28*

That our holy shepherds in the church may be God's good servants, working with the wealth of grace entrusted to them to bring to the Lord a great profit in souls

That the Creator of the universe who shapes each person's beginnings may direct the hearts of the powerful in the ways of His holy laws

That we may be among those servants approved by the king for our diligence and imagination in using the resources He has given us

That God may take under the shadow of His wings all those who have asked our prayers, filling them with mercy and peace

For those who have accepted death and passed into eternity, that they may behold God's face, and awakening, be content in His presence

## Week 33, Thursday

*1 Macc 2:15-29, Ps 50, Luke 19:41-44*

For the church, that zeal for God's commandments and His holy covenant may be the driving force behind her actions in every situation of apostasy and moral decadence

That our leaders may have God's holy laws in their hearts, upholding human dignity in their decisions

That we may not miss the time of our visitation or ignore what makes for our peace, but accept the salvation of Jesus as loyal and zealous followers

For those in whose lives not one stone is left upon another because of the ravages of oppression, natural disaster, violence, illness, or grief, that our loving prayer may help them

For our loved ones who have died, and for all those forgotten souls who are still undergoing purification, that through the power of this Holy Mass they may be released into heavenly joy

### Week 33, Friday

*1 Macc 4:36-37, 52-59, 1 Chron 29,
Luke 19:45-48*

For our Holy Father, our bishops and priests, that they may be totally dedicated to God, along with the altars on which they celebrate the Holy Sacrifice of the Mass

For world leaders, that God who has dominion over all may give them strength and wisdom in the difficult challenges they face

That we who become God's temple in our Holy Communion may allow Jesus to cleanse us of all that prevents us from being a house of prayer today

For all who are in a season of distress, facing surgery, or the loss of a loved one, those who are homeless in the winter weather, and all who have asked us to pray for them

For our beloved dead, dedicated now entirely to God after being freed from the bonds of this earthly life, that they may be purified quickly and taken home forever

### Week 33, Saturday

*1 Macc 6:1-13, Ps 9, Luke 20:27-40*

For our holy shepherds in the church, that like the armies of Israel they may be in the forefront of every battle against evil, and prevail in the struggle

That world leaders may learn from the fate of King Antiochus that the seeds of a nation's downfall are planted when they desert the ways of the living God

That our dynamic hope in the future resurrection may help us to be strong followers of Jesus in all the disturbances and persecutions of this present age

For all who have asked for our intercession in their need and affliction of any kind, that they may have reason to exult and praise God for the answer to their prayers

That those who have gone before us may be worthy of a place in heaven and be made sons and daughters of the resurrection through the mercy of our Savior

## Week 34, Monday

*Dan 1:1-6, 8-20, Canticle of Three Youths, Luke 21:1-4*

For our leaders in the church, that like the noble young men of Israel they may keep themselves undefiled by attachment to anything in this world of exile

That those who lead the nations may be sensitive to God's voice in every question of wisdom and prudence with which they are faced

That the poor widows whose generosity still supports so many good causes in the church may inspire those who have surplus wealth to be open-handed in what they share with those in need

For all who need healing, strength, and comfort, those who have asked for our prayers and those who are most forgotten, that they may be answered in their time of need

For our faithful departed who are still undergoing purification, that the One who looks into their depths from His throne upon the cherubim may bring them soon into His kingdom of light and peace

## Week 34, Tuesday

*Dan 2:31-45, Dan 3, Luke 21:5-11*

That the sober consideration of the final realities of life and how quickly everything earthly passes away may help the church focus on the kingdom of God and shine in her witness before the world

That the rulers of the earth may come to understand that the only everlasting kingdom is the one that God will set up in Christ Jesus, and channel their decisions so that they may be acceptable to the King of kings

That we may hold fast to the anchor of our hope in Jesus and remain calm in the upheavals that will precede His coming, keeping our eyes fixed on Him

For young people and students, that they may learn the truth about what is temporary and what lasts, and cast their lot in life with Jesus and His kingdom of love

For our dear departed ones, that the angels and hosts of the Lord may bring them into heaven, where it will be their bliss to praise and exalt God above all forever

### Week 34, Wednesday

*Dan 5:1-6, 13-14, 16-17, 23-28, Dan 3, Luke 21:12-19*

For the persecuted church, that her martyrs may give their testimony fearlessly and persevere to the end, firm in their faith and their love

That sovereigns of nations and all the powerful may realize that their life-breath is in the hand of God, and glorify Him by their work to uphold the life and dignity of all His children

That we may not be weighed on the scales and found wanting, but sincere in our loyalty to Jesus, knowing that by our perseverance we will secure our lives

That God, who watches over and saves His children, may care for the sick, the poor, the imprisoned, and the grieving little ones who call upon His name

For all who have gone before us marked with the sign of faith, that our loving prayers for them may bring them rejoicing into the presence of Jesus

### Week 34, Thursday

*Dan 6:12-28, Dan 3, Luke 21:20-28*

That the example of Daniel may be an inspiration for the church and her holy shepherds, and that we may all be found faithful in our prayer and in our innocence before God

That the rulers of the earth may come to reverence God as did King Darius, recognizing His power to save and the holiness of His prophets

That we may stand straight and raise our heads when we encounter tribulation, putting our trust in Jesus and knowing that His salvation is near at hand

For the poor and the homeless as winter draws near, that those who are thankful to God for warm homes and good food may reach out to them with compassionate hearts

That God, whose kingdom shall not be destroyed and whose dominion is without end, may raise up our dear departed ones to light and peace

## Week 34, Friday

*Dan 7:2-14, Dan 3, Luke 21:29-33*

For the fortitude of Christ's church, that she may stand fast through political upheavals and the rise and fall of kingdoms, knowing that in the end her Lord will triumph forever

That world leaders may realize they have been given power only for a time and a season, and use it wisely to promote justice and peace

That Jesus, the Son of Man, who will come on the clouds of heaven to receive from His Father an everlasting kingdom, may find us eager and ready for His coming as loyal disciples and friends

For all who are in need of our loving intercession, especially the sick and the poor, the imprisoned and the grieving, that this Holy Sacrifice may bring them relief and joy

For all our beloved dead, that they may soon be purified to take their place before the Ancient One on His throne of glory, welcomed by Jesus as the fruit of His victory over sin and death

## Week 34, Saturday

*Dan 7:15-27, Daniel 3, Luke 21:34-36*

For the church as this liturgical year ends, that she may always support her people in their labors and tribulations, while pointing with hope to the coming of the Lord

For the nations and kingdoms of the world, that God who holds their destinies in His powerful hands may move them into the ways of His holy laws

That we as God's people may be vigilant at all times, resisting drowsiness and anxiety, awake and prepared for the return of the Bridegroom

For all who have asked for our prayers or have need of loving intercession at this time, that Mary, our Mother, may cover them with her protective veil and obtain for them the relief of their sufferings

For our beloved dead who served God, holy and humble of heart, while they lived in this passing life, that they may be given to drink of life eternal

# PROPER OF TIME

## WEEKDAYS OF ORDINARY TIME
### YEAR II

## Week 1, Monday

*1 Sam 1:1-8, Ps 116, Mark 1:14-20*

For our ministers in the church, who imitate Jesus in His mission of proclaiming the Good News, that they may be strong and faithful messengers of the reign of God

That new prophets of life, justice, and peace may replace those who have been arrested and silenced, as once Jesus replaced John the Baptist

For vocations; that our young men and women may freely and gladly abandon their projects and profits to follow the inner call of the Lord and spend their lives in His company

For all who are suffering, especially those who, like Hannah, must endure the reproaches of others, that their affliction may be relieved

For our beloved dead, that the Lord may loose their bonds and bring them into His presence to offer their joyful sacrifice of thanksgiving

## Week 1, Tuesday

*1 Sam 1:9-20, Sam 2, Mark 1:21-28*

For our priests, who like Eli guard the doorpost of the Lord's temple, that they may be holy, and compassionate toward those who suffer

For all who hold positions of power and influence, that their borrowed authority may be subject to the divine spirit of authority with which Jesus taught us the ways of love and justice

For barren mothers who long for a child, for confused young mothers who are tempted to abort their children, that adoption may be the link of life between them

That the weak may gird on strength and the hungry and homeless find shelter and care, and that Jesus may again cast out every unclean spirit that troubles us

For those who have gone before us in death, that they may rejoice in the victory of the Lord who gives life and raises His own from the nether world

## Week 1, Wednesday

*1 Sam 3;1-10, 19-20, Ps 40, Mark 1:29-30*

For our leaders in the church, that the Lord may be with them as He was with Samuel, not permitting any word or deed of theirs to be without effect

For those who oppose oppression wherever they find it, announcing God's justice in the vast assembly, that the fruit of their courage may be peace

For all who are being awakened by a mysterious call for the first time, who are not yet familiar with the Lord, that they may find someone who understands who is calling them, and help them to respond

For those who are suffering, who are bound by any kind of evil, that Jesus, who came to proclaim good news by word and deed, may bring them healing and liberation

For our dear departed ones who are still waiting for the Lord, that He may stoop toward them and hear their cry, and take them home to His heavenly kingdom

## Week 1, Thursday

*1 Sam 4:1-11, Ps 44, Mark 1:40-45*

For the priests of the church who bear the ark of God through the battles of human history, that they may be worthy of their sacred charge for the sake of God's people

For the areas of our world where war threatens or rages and each faction imagines God to be on its side, that both may be given the grace to see that God is on the side of justice, arbitration, and peace

For teachers and students at all levels of education, especially those in Catholic schools, that God may be honored among them and His moral values held in respect again

For those afflicted with AIDS, for the imprisoned, the addicted, and the forgotten poor, that there may be someone to be moved with pity for them who will reach out hands of healing

For all who have died on the battlefield or as victims of violence, and for all the dead, that Jesus may show His face to them and heal them with heaven's pure joy

## Week 1, Friday

*1 Sam 24:3-21, Ps 57, Mark 3:13-19*

For our Holy Father and our bishops and priests, successors to the first apostles and personally chosen by Jesus, that they may be faithful to the mission He has entrusted to them

For the oppressed, for the helpless unborn, for all who are pursued and hunted down by the mighty, that God may grant them justice beyond the reach of the powerful ones

That we may treat our enemies with the high mindedness and generosity that David showed to Saul, that the Lord may take our part and keep us from harming our own souls with revenge and hatred

For the poor, the sick, and victims of natural disasters and conflicts, that God may send them His mercy and faithfulness and give them refuge under the shadow of His wings

For all who have gone before us, that they may come to know God's mercy personally as He purifies them and welcomes them into heaven

## Week 1, Saturday

*1 Sam 9:1-4, 17-19, 10:1, Ps 21, Mark 2:13-17*

For our priests, anointed by God in the sacrament of ordination to guide and govern His holy people, that this anointing may come to full awakening in their lives and ministry

For world leaders, who have been given authority to govern the nations, that their fidelity to God's inner guidance may make their efforts fruitful in justice and peace

For the conversion of the self righteous, for the humility to see that we all need Jesus to take the initiative and call us forth to be His true followers

For the tax collectors and sinners of our own day, those who are avoided because of addiction, violence, or dangerous disease, that in Jesus' name there may be doctors of body and soul who reach out to heal them

For those who have gone before us, that God may grant their heart's desire and welcome them to heaven with goodly blessings, giving them length of days forever

### Week 1, Friday
*1 Sam 8:4-7, 10-22, Ps 89,*
*Mark 1:1-12*

That the church may always hold in honor the spiritual and prophetic authority of our Holy Father, so that God may truly be the king and shepherd of our souls

For our nation, which inscribes on its coins "In God We Trust," that we may make our decisions according to His laws, acknowledging Him as our true interior King

For those who are constrained and bound by their sins, that they may have the grace to return to Jesus and hear Him say: Child, your sins are forgiven

For those paralyzed in body, mind, emotions, or spirit, that the fervent prayer of our faith may carry them through all obstacles to the feet of Jesus

For our loved ones who have died, for all who grieve their loss, that the radiance of Jesus may soften the parting and bring the departed ones into His Father's dwelling places

### Week 1, Saturday
*1 Sam 9:1-4, 17-19, 10:1, Ps 21,*
*Mark 2:13-17*

For our priests, anointed by God in the sacrament of ordination to guide and govern His holy people, that this anointing may come to full awakening in their lives and ministry

For world leaders, who have been given authority to govern the nations, that their fidelity to God's inner guidance may make their efforts fruitful in justice and peace

For the conversion of the self righteous, for the humility to see that we all need Jesus to take the initiative and call us forth to be His true followers

For the tax collectors and sinners of our own day, those who are avoided because of addiction, violence, or dangerous disease, that in Jesus' name there may be doctors of body and soul who reach out to heal them

For those who have gone before us, that God may grant their heart's desire and welcome them to heaven with goodly blessings, giving them length of days forever

## Week 2, Monday

*1 Sam 15:16-23, Ps 50, Mark 2:18-22*

For the church in all her members, that each baptized soul may be a new wineskin, capable of receiving all the truth and grace that the Lord wishes to pour in

For the powerful, who like Saul are tempted to take for themselves the resources that God has put at the service of all, that they may be converted to obedience and generosity

For all who twist and interpret God's commands to fit their own will, that those who see more clearly may have Samuel's courage to speak up and lead them back to humble submission

For those whose lives are a long fast, afflicted with sickness, poverty, pain, addiction, or grief, that the Bridegroom may return and bring the joy of the wedding feast again

For our dear ones who have passed away, who went along the right way of obedience in this life, that they may now see the salvation of God in His divine light and glory

## Week 2, Tuesday

*1 Sam 16:1-13, Ps 89, Mark 2:23-28*

That the Spirit of the Lord may rush upon the anointed ministers of Christ, stirring up the grace of their ordination for the salvation of all

That the Lord who looks into the heart may choose and anoint rulers of nations who will do His will, pursuing justice, protecting life, upholding morality, and fostering peace

That Jesus, who defended His disciples from the attacks of the Pharisees, may uphold and defend believers who are attacked for their faith

That God, Father, Rock, and Savior of His suffering little ones, may assist all who have asked our prayers in their need

That our loved ones who have gone before us may soon be seated at the sacrificial banquet in God's presence and with His saints

### Week 2, Wednesday

*1 Sam 17:32-33, 37, 40-51, Ps 144, Mark 3:1-6*

That the Church may take the part of David, relying completely on the Lord in every conflict with the powers of evil

That Christians may do all they can to exert their influence for the cause of Gospel morality, justice, concern for the poor and for the planet, and peace

That we may never remain silent when there is a question of preserving life or destroying it, but always let our voice be heard bravely on the side of the God of the living

That God may be a refuge and a fortress, a stronghold and a deliverer to those who call upon His name in their sickness, poverty, and grief

That our beloved dead may soon be singing a new song of deliverance and victory in the presence of the Lord in His heavenly kingdom

### Week 2, Thursday

*1 Sam 18:6-9, 19:1-7, Ps 56, Mark 3:7-12*

For our leaders and teachers in the church, for those who heal and nourish God's people, for our priests, that they show Christ's love in word and deed

For leaders of nations, that they may not act out of anger or jealousy, but let themselves be persuaded into honorable and peace keeping actions

That Christ may be powerful in us, the members of His body, to drive out evil in all its forms, and to bring healing to those who are oppressed by dark forces of mind and soul

For those who are in distress, whose tears are stored in God's flask, that they may know that God is with them through the loving actions of those who help and console them

For our beloved dead, that they may be purified quickly through this Holy Sacrifice, to walk before God in the light of the living

## Week 2, Friday

*1 Sam 24:3-21, Ps 57, Mark 3:13-19*

For our Holy Father, our bishops and priests, successors to the first apostles and personally chosen by Jesus, that they may be faithful to the mission He has entrusted to them

For the oppressed, for the helpless unborn, for all who are pursued and hunted down by the mighty, that God may grant them justice beyond the reach of the powerful ones

That we may treat our enemies with the high mindedness and generosity that David showed to Saul, that the Lord may take our part and keep us from harming our own souls with revenge and hatred

For the poor, the sick, and victims of natural disasters and conflicts, that God may send them His mercy and faithfulness and give them refuge under the shadow of His wings

For all who have gone before us, that they may come to know God's mercy personally as He purifies them and welcomes them into heaven

## Week 2, Saturday

*2 Sam 1:1-4, 11-12, 19, 23-27, Ps 80, Mark 3:20-21*

For the church, that Mary, her model and Mother, may assist each baptized soul to be faithful to Jesus through all the changes of life

For nations who try to seek the solution of their issues in war and violence, that the international community may give an example of negotiation and peaceful means to resolve issues

For those who are dear friends to one another, as Jonathan was for David, that their unity and loyalty may remain unshaken

For all who have asked our prayers and for those most in need of prayer today, that their distress may be relieved by the power of love in this Holy Sacrifice

For the dead and those who mourn for them, as David did for Saul and Jonathan, that the souls of the deceased may find rest, and those who are left behind may find comfort

## Week 3, Monday

*2 Sam 5:1-7, 10, Ps 89, Mark 3:22-30*

That the church may never become a house divided against itself, but that all parties may put their faith in Jesus to work as they labor to remain strong and united in love

That those who lead the peoples out and bring them back may be anointed by the Lord as He once anointed David, with power to govern wisely and well

For the gift of discernment of spirits, that the Holy Spirit may guide and direct us in our assessment of what is good and what is evil

That God's faithfulness and mercy may be with the sick, the poor, those suffering from war and natural disasters, and all who need His help today

That our dear departed ones may be brought into the New Jerusalem, the stronghold of the Lord, with splendor and rejoicing

## Week 3, Tuesday

*2 Sam 6:12-15, 17-19, Ps 24, Mark 3:31-35*

That the King of Glory, throned upon the cherubim, may find a permanent resting place in the church, honored and exalted with joy by her members

That our world leaders may be as devoted to God as David was, so that they too may be able to bless their people with life, justice, and peace

That we may take our place with Mary as loyal disciples of Jesus, earning the right to be in His intimate family circle by our faithful obedience and love

For all who are suffering, lonely, depressed, imprisoned, or ill at this time, that this Holy Sacrifice may have the power to bring them healing and grace

That the ancient portals of heaven may open to allow our beloved dead to enter, crowned with everlasting joy

## Week 3, Wednesday

*2 Sam 7:4-17, Ps 89, Mark 4:1-20*

For the church, the house of the Lord, built of living stones, that each of us may be dedicated to His honor and to the building of His kingdom upon the earth

That world leaders may make it their first priority to build up their nations in justice, truth, and peace, so that God will make each country and dynasty stand fast in His favor

That we may receive the seed of God's Word on good soil, not allowing persecution, the lure of riches, or the wiles of Satan to choke it off, so that we may bear good fruit in joy and praise

For those who are struggling to grow amid the thorns of illness or tribulation, that our love and prayers and the gracious power of Jesus may help them to thrive again

For our dear ones who have gone before us, that God will establish His covenant of love with them in the heavenly kingdom that will stand firm forever

## Week 3, Thursday

*2 Sam 7:18-19, 24-29, Ps 132, Mark 4:21-25*

For our Holy Father, our bishops and priests, keepers of the house built for the Lord by His Son Jesus Christ, that they may be its strong guardians worthy of the Lord's blessing

That world leaders may keep God's covenant and decrees, which He teaches them through an upright conscience, so that God may establish and prosper their authority upon the earth

For all of us who are entrusted with the lamp of faith, that we may reveal the One who lies hidden in our hearts through the radiance of our words and actions

For those who have asked our prayers in a time of struggle, grief, and distress in their lives, that God may grant them His blessing of health and grace and hidden joy

For all the dead whose faith is known to God alone, that they may be purified to become shining lights in the kingdom of light and beauty which is heaven

## Week 3, Friday

*2 Sam 11:1-4a, 5-10a, 13-17, Ps 51, Mark 4:26-34*

For the church, that she may stand firm in her teaching about purity of life and conduct, becoming a beacon of light in a world darkened by lust

That rulers may be upright and honest, respecting the laws of God and working for life, truth, morality, justice, and peace

For patience with the slow growth of the Kingdom of God in our lives, for hope in the harvest coming to birth in each one of us, as God keeps planting the tiny mustard seeds of His grace in our hearts

For those whose bones seem crushed under a weight of tribulation and worry and grief, that through this Holy Sacrifice, they may know songs of joy and gladness again

For our dear departed ones, that our Blessed Lord, who is the Divine Grain of wheat that fell into the ground and died for us, may bring them as His beloved harvest, safely into His kingdom

## Week 3, Saturday

*2 Sam 12:1-7, 10-17, Ps 51, Mark 4:35-41*

For the priests of the church, that they may bravely and compassionately confront those who have sinned, giving them the chance to repent and be forgiven

That the rich and powerful of this world may cease to take the ewe lambs of those who are poor and struggling, but instead share with them their wealth in a brotherhood of cooperation and trust

For those who have fallen into sin or careless neglect of God's grace and His sacraments, that through the intercession of Mary, our loving Mother, they may have the grace to repent and return to His embrace

For those caught in violent squalls of sickness and distress, in whose boats the Lord seems to be sleeping, that their confidence and ours may awaken His power to create for them a great calm

That Jesus, whom winds and seas obey, may use His divine power to establish and purify our dear ones who have died and bring them safely to the other shore of His heavenly kingdom

## Week 4, Monday

*2 Sam 15:13-14, 30, 16:5-13, Ps 3,*
*Mark 5:1-20*

For the church, that like the man freed from the evil spirits, she may proclaim with joy all that the Lord has done for her, attracting others to experience His saving power

That the humility and truth of King David may live in all rulers and heads of state, that they may see clearly that there are personal and national consequences of disobedience

That Jesus, who freed the demoniac with authority, may again cast out from our families and our nation all dark forces which seek to wound and destroy, restoring all to grace and light

That the sick may be healed, the grieving consoled, the oppressed set free, and the sinners converted, through the power of this Holy Sacrifice

For all who have laid down in the sleep of death, that they may wake again in the sustaining power of the Lord, fully alive in His heavenly kingdom

## Week 4, Tuesday

*2 Sam 18, Ps 86, Mark 5:21-43*

For the church, that her ministers may be as devoted to her wayward sons as David was to Absalom, grieving over their destruction and always reaching out to save them

For nations that are weakened by loss of blood from violence or tyrannical governments, that they may reach out to touch the robe of Jesus who has the answer to their affliction

That we may refuse to give the useless emotion of fear room to grow in our lives, but instead practice the trust that taps the saving power of Jesus

For those who are afflicted and poor, that God may attend to the sound of their pleading and gladden their souls with hope and help in their troubles

For our loved ones who have gone before us, that the Lord, who is good and forgiving, may show them His abounding kindness in the land of the living

### Week 4, Wednesday

*2 Sam 24:2, 9-17, Ps 32, Mark 6:1-6*

For the prophets and leaders of the church, that their power to perform mighty deeds and give powerful witness may never be hampered by lack of faith among the people of God

For the shepherds of the nations, that they may never be the cause of evil for their people as David once was, but may be humble and loyal before the face of God

That Jesus may never be without honor among those who know Him intimately, but that we may always acknowledge Him as our Lord and our God

For all who are in a time of stress, for whom the deep waters of affliction overflow, that God may be their shelter and ring them round with glad cries of freedom

For our deceased loved ones, that their faults may be taken away and the Lord impute to them no guilt, but welcome them into the heavenly mansions He has prepared for them

### Week 4, Thursday

*1 Kgs 2:1-4, 10-12, 1 Chr 29, Mark 6:7-13*

For today's apostles, called and commissioned by Jesus, who still preach repentance in His name, that their ministry may be effective and their authority over unclean spirits secure

That the Lord, to whom belongs all sovereignty, majesty, splendor, and glory, may raise up government leaders who will uphold His laws and decrees

That the Lord may call new missionaries, generous souls willing to preach and heal in His name without any support but His commissioning word

For the sick and those who are sorely afflicted, that the anointing of the Lord may be upon them for restoration to health and joy

For those who have gone the way of all flesh, that they may be at rest with their ancestors in the heavenly kingdom of love and peace

## Week 4, Friday

*Sir 47:2-11, Ps 18, Mark 6:14-29*

For our leaders in the church, that God's people may feel the attraction of their words, and even more of the witness of their lives

For leaders of nations, that like King David they may live powerful and sincere lives before God, drawing on His power and wisdom to establish peace

For musicians who add beauty to the feasts and solemnity to the seasons of the church year, providing sweet melody for the praise of God, that their own hearts may share in the joy they give to others

For the persecuted prophets of our own day, that they may persevere in their witness to the end

For the homebound and the homeless, for those imprisoned or held captive in the chains of addiction, for the souls who long to be released from purgatory, for all who need our prayers today

## Week 4, Saturday

*1 Kgs 3:4-13, Ps 119, Mark 6:30-34*

For the church, which still offers the most renowned place of sacrifice to the great and the small, that God may favor His people there as He once favored Solomon with the answer to His prayer

That heads of nations and kingdoms may seek from the Lord the gift of wisdom and an upright heart to govern their people with justice and integrity

That those who serve Jesus and His people may heed His invitation to come away by themselves and rest awhile, taking time for prayer and personal renewal as they need it

That Jesus, whose heart was moved with pity for the sheep without a shepherd may again come to the poor, the sick, the ignorant, and the grieving with His comfort and light

That Mary, Gate of Heaven, may receive our dear departed ones at their passing and present them to her Son, purified and pleasing in His sight

### Week 5, Monday

*1 Kgs 8:1-7, 9-13, Ps 132, Mark 6:53-56*

For the church, that there may be nothing within the ark of the covenant she has made with God but His commandments, that are treasured and obeyed by all the faithful

That the rulers of the earth may build a dwelling place for God in their hearts, honoring Him with decisions that uphold a culture of life and a civilization of love

For our priests, especially those who are struggling to be faithful to their vocation, that they may be clothed with justice and filled with strength from on high

That the tassel on the cloak of Jesus and the gentle touch of His hand may cure the sick, the distressed and the grieving, the anxious and the afraid who have need of loving intercession today

That the cloud of the Lord's living presence, which has taken our departed loved ones beyond the limits of our sight, may envelop them in mercy and lead them home to heaven

### Week 5, Tuesday

*1 Kgs 8:22-23, 27-30, Ps 84, Mark 7:1-13*

That the eyes of God may watch day and night over the holy church, where He has decreed He shall be honored upon the earth

That the powerful may come to be faithful to God with their whole heart according to the dictates of their consciences, so that God's covenant of mercy and peace may stand fast

That honor may be paid to fathers and mothers by their children, and that their role as architects of the family may be held in respect by society again

For those who are called to dwell in the house of the Lord by a special vocation, that they may fly like swallows in His holy courts, irresistibly attracted by His love

For all who have asked our prayers in their suffering, and for our faithful departed, that God's mercy may be granted to each of them in overflowing measure

## Week 5, Wednesday

*1 Kgs 10:1-10, Ps 37, Mark 7:14-23*

For the ministers of the Lord, that they may be endowed with a spirit of wisdom, so that there may remain nothing hidden from them which they cannot explain for the building up of the faithful

For those who have been placed on the thrones of power over nations and peoples, that they may carry out judgment and justice and foster peace

That we may never be defiled by evil thoughts, unchastity, arrogance, or folly, but produce the fruits of pure and grace-filled hearts before the Lord

For those who have suffered from the evil coming out of the hearts of others, for the oppressed, the sick, and the hungry, that our loving prayers may lift their spirits and bring them help in their need

For those who sleep in death, that by God's mercy their purification may be swiftly accomplished, and they may be admitted to the kingly banquet in the house of the Lord

## Week 5, Thursday

*1 Kgs 11:4-13, Ps 106, Mark 7:24-30*

For the children of the kingdom and their holy leaders, that they may reach out to those who do not know the power and love of Jesus Christ, healing and witnessing in His name

For leaders of nations whose hearts have turned to the gods of power and greed, that they may be converted to the God of life and truth

That the faith and humility of the Syro-Phoenician woman may be manifested in all those who wish to obtain the merciful energy of the Savior to drive out the evils of our own day

That Jesus, who cured and comforted the people of His own time, may come to the aid of the sick, the poor, the grieving, the imprisoned and addicted, and all who need our prayers today

For our faithful departed ones, that this Holy Sacrifice may release them into the joy of heaven

## Week 5, Friday

*1 Kgs 11:29-32, 12:19, Ps 81,*
*Mark 7:31-37*

For the prophetic voices that speak in the name of the Lord in the church, that they may be heard and heeded by God's holy people

That leaders of nations may not walk according to the counsels of hearts that are hard, but instead make just and wise decisions that promote peace

That our ears may be opened to hear God's word, and our tongues loosed to speak plainly in His name

That Jesus may take apart by themselves those whom we recommend to His mercy and work for them the secret marvels of His powerful love

For our loved ones who have died, who walked in the ways of the Lord while on earth, that God may humble all the enemies of their souls and bring them into His holy Kingdom

## Week 5, Saturday

*1 Kgs 12:26-32, 13:33-34, Ps 106,*
*Mark 8:1-10*

For our consecrated priests, set apart for the preaching of the Gospel and the offering of sacrifice to the True God, that they may be strong and faithful in their holy ministry

That world leaders may not cause their people to sin, setting up the false gods of power and greed, but that they may turn and be faithful to the Living God whose law is in their hearts

That the blessing of Jesus over the broken bread of our gifts to Him for the poor and the hungry may multiply our resources and satisfy their needs

That the heart of Jesus may again be moved with pity for the sufferings of all those we bring before Him in their sickness and pain

For those who have gone before us, that the motherly heart of Mary may speed their purification and bring them soon into God's kingdom of peace and joy

## Week 6, Monday

*Jas 1:1-11, Ps 119, Mark 8:11-13*

For the church, that God's gift of wisdom may dwell in her midst, desired firmly and without doubt by all her members

That the rich and powerful may realize how quickly their wealth will vanish and how important it is to pursue kindness to the poor and justice for the oppressed

That we may not grieve Jesus by demanding signs and reassurances, but live our faith fully and generously in order to give Him pleasure

For those who are passing through trials, whose perseverance is being tested, that our prayers may support them until God's work in them is perfected

For our dear departed loved ones, that God's kindness and faithfulness may comfort them and deliver them from all afflicting purification into the joy and peace of heaven

## Week 6, Tuesday

*Jas 1:12-18, Ps 94, Mark 8:14-21*

For our Holy Father, our bishops and priests, that they may have eyes to see and hearts to understand how great is God's power at work when their own powers fail

That world leaders may be men and women whom God instructs and teaches by means of His law, so that they may lead us into the ways of peace

For those who are being enticed and lured by their desires into the realms of sin and death, that the Father of Light may help them to see their peril and pull them back from danger

For all who have asked our prayers in a season of weakness or suffering, whose cares abound within them, that they may know the presence of God's comfort gladdening their souls

For our beloved dead, that God who does not cast off His people or abandon His inheritance, may lead them into the shining realms of His kingdom

## Week 6, Wednesday

*Jas 1:19-27, Ps 15, Mark 8:22-26*

For the church, that we may humbly welcome God's word that has taken root in us, with its power to save

That leaders of nations may remember the lowly ones, the widows and orphans, and look after them in their decisions and policies

That we may act on freedom's ideal law, studying it and abiding by it, controlling our speech in kindness and compassion, so that we may be blessed in whatever we do

That Jesus, who restored the blind man's sight slowly and completely, may come to the aid of those who are sick, depressed, or grieving, restoring them carefully and securely to the fullness of life

For those who have gone before us marked with the sign of faith, that through this Holy Sacrifice, they may be soon made pure and worthy of a place in heaven

## Week 6, Thursday

*Jas 2:1-9, Ps 34, Mark 8:27-33*

For our holy shepherds in the church, that they may continue to proclaim with Peter's faith that Jesus is the one Savior, and accept the way in which He chooses to save us

For our leaders in the world, that they may show no favoritism but treat all with fairness and compassion

For a renewal in all of our lives of the basic law of the Kingdom, to respect and love one another, judging everything by God's standards

For all who suffer and who experience rejection, poverty, weakness, or disability, that they may also be rich in faith and experience their nobility as the aristocracy of God's kingdom

For our dear departed ones, that through our loving prayer they may be radiant with joy and find their glory in the presence of the living God

## Week 6, Friday

*Jas 2:14-24, 26, Ps 112, Mark 8:34–9:1*

For the church, that faith may be the root and foundation of our lives, and good works the proof that faith undergirds our actions

That those in a position of power and influence may move to meet the bodily needs of those who are hungry and cold, thus establishing a bond of justice and compassion

That we may willingly lose our life for the sake of Jesus and His doctrine, taking up our cross resolutely and following in His steps

For those who are heavily laden, who are collapsing under their burdens, for whom the cross is very heavy at this time, that our prayers and this Holy Sacrifice may give them strength and grace

For those who have died, that God may be for them a light breaking through the darkness, inviting them into the realms of joy and peace

## Week 6, Saturday

*Jas 3:1-10, Ps 12, Mark 9:2-13*

For the apostles of our own day, that they may be granted a glimpse of the Lord's splendor, and understand that it is by joining in His suffering and death that we share in His glory

That Mary, Queen of Peace and Mother of Life, may guide the rulers of nations, so that their decisions may respect the unborn and the disabled, the oppressed and the poor

For the grace to watch carefully how we use our tongues; that our speech may be modest and pleasing, and what we say about one another may be loving and respectful

For those who are weighed down by suffering, sickness, unemployment, homelessness, or grief, that Jesus may transfigure their pain into joy and praise

For those who have gone before us marked with the sign of faith, that Jesus may be with them, making them pure and bringing them into eternal rest

## Week 7, Monday

*Jas 3:13-18, Ps 19, Mark 9:14-29*

For the gift of wisdom for our leaders in the church, that they may be pure, gentle, compliant, full of mercy and the good fruits of holiness

That our statesmen and political leaders may turn from all jealously and selfish ambition to the ways of justice, truth, and peace

That the Lord may help our unbelief, strengthening the kernel of faith that He has planted within us, especially faith in His merciful love

That by God's help, our prayer may be deep and heartfelt enough to drive out demons and keep the forces of evil from harming those whom we love in His name

For all who are suffering at this time, for the sick and the lonely, the unemployed and the grieving, and for our beloved dead, that Jesus may receive them all into the embrace of His compassion

## Week 7, Tuesday

*Jas 4:1-10, Ps 55, Mark 9:30-37*

For our servant leaders in the church, and for all of us who follow Jesus, that we may resist ambition and be content to become like little children, held fast in His arms

For an end to wars and conflicts in the world, for the grace to see their roots in covetousness and envy and to turn from these motivations to the ways of justice and peace

That God who resists the proud but gives grace to the humble may help us to submit humbly to Him, allowing Him to be the One who will exalt us

For those in violent storm and tempest, who long to fly away and be at rest, that they may have the light to throw their cares upon the Lord, and feel His loving support

For those who have gone before us, that their hands may be cleansed and their hearts purified for the divine vision of God that will be their eternal joy

## Week 7, Wednesday

*Jas 4:13-17, Ps 49, Mark 9:38-40*

For the church, that we who know the right things to do may be the first to do them, avoiding all sin

For those who make plans for nations and kingdoms, that they not boast in their arrogance but understand that they are a puff of smoke and that only the Lord sustains their works

For those who work wonders in the name of Jesus, even without the fullness of faith, that their work may prosper and grow for the glory of His name

For all who have asked our prayers in a time of distress, sickness, poverty, or grief, and for all who have no one to pray for them

For our dear ones who have died, that this Holy Sacrifice may be efficacious for them, purifying them and releasing them into the joys of heaven

## Week 7, Thursday

*Jas 5:1-6, Ps 49, Mark 9:41-50*

For our shepherds in the church, that they may keep guard over the lambs of Christ's flock, so that these little ones will not be led into sin

For our nation, that the impending miseries of the rich may not be our portion, but that we may reach out ever more generously to restore the balance of justice with the developing nations

That we may be willing to cut out of our lives all that we perceive to be a hindrance to the full following of Jesus, so that we may be the salt of the earth in His name

For those who are oppressed under the injustice of others, for the sick and the poor, for the righteous who suffer persecution, that God may vindicate them and restore them

That God may redeem our beloved dead by receiving them into the kingdom of His light and joy forever

### Week 7, Friday

*Jas 5:9-12, Ps 103, Mark 10:1-12*

For the church, that her members may be the first to be honest and plain in their speech and the last to complain about one another

That the prophets who speak in the name of the Lord may be heard and heeded by those in authority, as they urge them to promote the dignity of human life and the justice due to all

That the clear and direct teaching of Jesus on the sanctity of marriage may be restored to the mainstream of our culture, and that families may be stable and loving in our day

That the Lord may be compassionate and merciful to those who are giving us an example of hardship and patience in their time of trial

For our deceased relatives and friends, that the Lord may pardon their iniquities, redeem their lives from destruction, and crown them with kindness and compassion in His heavenly kingdom

### Week 7, Saturday

*Jas 5:13-20, Ps 141, Mark 10:13-16*

For the leaders in the church, that they may have the courage and compassion to reach out to those who need to be brought back to the way of truth

For peace, that through the fervent prayers of many righteous people we may obtain peace for all the war-torn areas of our world

For the children, so loved by Jesus, especially children who are in grave danger or at risk in a hostile environment

For the sick in body and spirit, that our prayers and the sacraments of anointing and reconciliation may bring them to renewed health and vigor

For the souls of all who have died, that Mary, our compassionate Mother, may speed their purification and bring them into the wedding banquet of heavenly joy

## Week 8, Monday

*1 Pet 1:3-9, Ps 111, Mark 10:17-27*

For the church, that she may always proclaim with joy her faith in the salvation won by Christ, and love Him even without seeing Him, as she works out the salvation of all her members

For the rich who encounter difficulty in their attempts to be saved in proportion to their attachment to their wealth, that the change that is impossible for them may be made possible by God

For all those on whom Jesus looks with special love and calls to follow Him in poverty and freedom, that they may not go away sad, but joyfully sell all for His sake

For those who are suffering through various trials, whose faith is being tested and purified like gold in the fire, that our loving prayers may draw down upon them the Lord's support and deliverance

For our dear departed ones, that through the resurrection of Jesus Christ from the dead, they may receive the inheritance that is imperishable, undefiled, and unfading kept in heaven for them

## Week 8, Tuesday

*1 Pet 1:10-16, Ps 98, Mark 10:28-31*

For our leaders and teachers in the church, that they may be people who serve not themselves but others, spreading the fragrance of Christ's charity to all

That the Lord may make His salvation known in the sight of the nations through those who are willing to work for justice and peace

For all who have given up everything to follow Jesus, that they may have joy in the hundredfold promised to them and courage for the persecutions that must be present in their earthly journey

For all who have asked our prayers in a time of illness or distress, that we may set our hopes completely on the grace of Jesus Christ, obtaining for them healing and relief

For our beloved dead, that they may inherit the promise of eternal life offered by Jesus to all His faithful

## Week 8, Wednesday

*1 Pet 1:18-20, Ps 147, Mark 10:32-45*

For our holy shepherds in the church, that as they pour out their lives in service for the many, the Lord Jesus may pour out His grace and blessing on their work

For our leaders in the world, that their authority may be felt in ways that truly benefit the people they serve and be used to build up justice, life, and peace

That we who have purified ourselves by obedience to the truth, and have been ransomed by the precious blood of Jesus Christ, may love one another intensely from a pure heart

For those who are undergoing a baptism of pain and drinking the cup of suffering with Jesus, that our constant love and prayer may support them

That Jesus, who has come at last into His glory, may share that glory with our dear ones who have died in faith and trust

## Week 8, Thursday

*1 Pet 2:2-5, 9-12, Ps 100, Mark 10:46-52*

For the church, a chosen race, a royal priesthood, a holy nation, that we may offer spiritual sacrifices acceptable to God through Jesus Christ

That the powerful and influential may observe the good works of the followers of Christ and glorify God by their own decisions to create a culture of life and a civilization of love

That we may seize the opportunity to call out to Jesus in our needs like Bartimaeus, asking Him for the grace to see and to follow Him on the way

That Jesus, who responded in compassion to the blind man, may come to the aid of all those for whom we have promised to pray

For those who have gone before us, that they may enter the gates of God's kingdom with thanksgiving, and His courts with praise

## Week 8, Friday

*1 Pet 4:7-13, Ps 96, Mark 11:11-26*

For the church, that it may truly be a house of prayer for all the nations, free from buying and selling, envy and ambition, a shelter of peace and love

That God who governs the peoples with equity and rules the earth with justice may direct the decisions of world leaders into the ways of justice and life and truth

That we may gladly place our gifts at the service of one another, speaking, serving, and being hospitable to the glory of God

For those who are sharing Christ's sufferings, who are passing through a time of trial, that their faith may help them to remain calm until the hour of deliverance and exultation

For those who have died, who put their trust in God while on earth, that mountains may be moved to give them a place of rejoicing and rest in heaven

## Week 8, Saturday

*Jude 17:20-25, Ps 63, Mark 11:27-33*

For our holy shepherds in the church, that they may persevere in God's love, correcting the confused, and rescuing those who are becoming lost

That Mary, Queen of Peace, may hear the prayers and receive the sacrifices of her children, and turn the hearts of world leaders to the ways of justice, life, and peace

That the power and authority of Jesus may be at work in each of us, healing and strengthening us to follow Him with all our hearts

For all those who have asked our prayers, who are laboring under a heavy burden of suffering, that by the power of this Holy Sacrifice Jesus may comfort and uphold them

For those who have gone before us marked with the sign of faith, that they may now stand, unblemished and exultant, in the presence of God's glory

## Week 9, Monday

*2 Pet 1:2-7, Ps 91, Mark 12:1-12*

For the ministers of the church, to whom the care of God's vineyard has been entrusted, that they may give the Lord His harvest of holy souls by their diligent labor

That the faith and discernment of modern day prophets may have an influence upon politicians and statesmen, urging them to work for justice, life, and peace

That we who have been invited through grace to become sharers of the divine nature may respond with a life of virtue and joyful perseverance

For all who are in need of prayer today in their suffering, that God may deliver them and glorify them, showing them His salvation

For our dear ones who have died, that they may now be safe in the shelter of the Most High, gratified with length of days in heaven

## Week 9, Tuesday

*2 Pet 3:12-15a, Ps 90, Mark 12:13-17*

For our leaders in the church, that they may help God's people by word and example to grow in grace and in the knowledge of our Lord Jesus Christ

For world leaders. May they understand what belongs to Caesar and what belongs to God, so that their decisions may lead to justice and peace

For our elderly, especially those who are rounding out the sum of their years in emptiness and pain, that they may be filled with God's kindness and the love of their families as the eternal daybreak draws near

For those who are in special need at this time: the sick, the homeless, the poor, prisoners, and all who have asked for our prayers

For our beloved dead, that they may be found without spot or blemish in God's sight and enjoy the bliss of His heaven

## Week 9, Wednesday

*1 Tim 1:1-3, 6-12, Ps 123, Mark 12:18-27*

For our Holy Father, our bishops, priests, and deacons, that they may stir into flame the gift they have received by the laying on of hands for the good of the church

That world leaders may have the light and grace needed to make wise and compassionate decisions that will promote justice for every human being, especially the most helpless and vulnerable

For all of us sharing in this Holy Sacrifice, that through our communion today we may come to know better the One in whom we have believed, and that our confidence in Him may grow stronger

For all who are bearing hardship for the sake of the Gospel, that the Spirit of power and love and self control given to them by God may be their strength and guide

For our beloved departed ones, that God who is God of the living and not the dead, may receive them into His presence

## Week 9, Thursday

*2 Tim 2:8-15, Ps 25, Mark 12:28-34*

For our holy shepherds, that they may make themselves worthy of God's approval, following a straight course in preaching the truth to His people

That God may make known to the powerful and the influential His ways, teaching them to be good and upright, and holding them in kindness and constancy

For all who hear the Great Commandment proclaimed in today's liturgy, that the Holy Spirit may support with strength our attempts to give God our undivided love

For all who suffer for their faith, who are persecuted like criminals for their moral stands, that they may hold out to the end for the truth

For those who have died in Christ, that they may now live with Him, reigning forever in the kingdom of heaven

### Week 9, Friday

*2 Tim 3:10-17, Ps 119, Mark 12:35-37*

For the church and her holy leaders, that they may use the Word of God for teaching, reproof, correction, and training in holiness, as God intended

That Jesus, who sits at God's right hand until His enemies are made His footstool, may trample all evil underfoot and convert us to His laws of justice and morality

That we may remain faithful to what we have learned and believed, drawing from the source of wisdom in the Scriptures for light upon our journey

For those who are suffering in any way, though sickness, poverty, or persecution, that God may grant them patience, love, and endurance until He delivers them from all evil

For our deceased loved ones, friends, and benefactors, that their purification may be swift and their time for rejoicing in heaven very soon

### Week 9, Saturday

*2 Tim 4:1-8, Ps 71, Mark 12:38-44*

For all who preach the Gospel, that they may have the courage to perform the work of an evangelist whether it is convenient or inconvenient, with all patience and teaching

For world leaders who must maintain a delicate balance of power to ensure peace, that they may be men and women of integrity and moral courage

For God's faithful little ones, who like Mary are true to Jesus and His church and generous down to all they have to live on, that they may be aware of the dignity that is theirs in God's kingdom

For all the intentions recommended to our prayers, for all who are in special need of prayer at this time, that they may have reason to sing of God's faithfulness in their lives today

For all who have gone before us and have stood before the judgment of Jesus Christ, that this Holy Sacrifice may make up whatever is lacking for them

## Week 10, Monday

*1 Kgs 17:1-6, Ps 121, Matt 5:1-12*

For the church, that we may be among the clean of heart who see God in the events of every day and respond with faith and love to every indication of His will for us

For those who hunger and thirst for righteousness in the world, for the peacemakers, that their efforts may change the course of our culture back to life and justice

For the prophets, that they may be protected and nourished by the hand of God as Elijah was, until their holy ministry is fulfilled in His name

For the poor, for those who mourn, for all the suffering, for all who have asked for our prayers, that they may be comforted with healing and grace

For our beloved departed ones, that the Lord may guard them from all evil until they are pure and ready for entry into His glorious kingdom

## Week 10, Tuesday

*1 Kgs 17:7-16, Ps 4, Matt 5:13-16*

For the church and her holy leaders, that our good deeds may shine so brightly that we may give light to all in the house, glorifying our heavenly Father

For the men and women of rank in our own day, that they may not be dull of heart but reflect on God's ways in the silence of their souls, and put God's commands into practice

That like the widow of Zarephath we may believe the word of God, so that our jar of flour will not go empty nor our jug of oil run dry when we reach out to help those God sends to us

For all who are desperate, who are at the end of their resources, who are unemployed, depleted through illness, or close to death, that God may send them a prophet of hope and comfort

For our dear ones who have died, that as they once seasoned this life with the salt of their witness to Christ, He may now receive them into the eternal city which shines on the mountain of heaven

### Week 10, Wednesday

*1 Kgs 18:20-39, Ps 16, Matt 5:17-19*

For our leaders in the church, that like Elijah they may faithfully do everything at God's command, rebuilding His altars and bringing His people back to Him by their powerful witness

That we may no longer straddle the moral issues of our day, but acknowledge the Lord as our God and stand up for His commandments

That as we offer ourselves upon this altar and take part in this Holy Sacrifice, God's merciful fire may consume our gifts as an acceptable holocaust for His glory

For those who are passing through a time of sickness, financial difficulty, and distress of heart or mind, that God may answer our fervent prayers on their behalf as He once responded to His holy prophet

For our dear ones who have gone before us, that the Lord may show them the path to life and the delights at His right hand forever

### Week 10, Thursday

*1 Kgs 18:41-46, Ps 65, Matt 5:20-26*

For our Holy Father, our bishops, and priests, that they may preach and teach the Gospel with the same clarity as the Lord Jesus did when He walked among us

For healing of the anger and tendency to judge that sets religions and nations against each other, for an anointing of forgiveness so that there may be peace

For a spirit of confident and powerful prayer, such as Elijah offered, so that the blessing of new growth may be given to lives that are parched and weary

For those who are sick, bereaved, or suffering from war and natural disasters, that an abundant rainfall of grace, healing, and mercy may fall upon them

For our beloved dead, that Our Lady may be for them the merciful sign of a little cloud, an open invitation into the kingdom that is drenched with God's loving welcome

## Week 10, Friday

*1 Kgs 19:9, 11-16, Ps 27, Matt 5:27-32*

That the sacred covenant of marriage may be honored in the church, and adultery condemned for the evil that it is

That the Lord, who directed Elijah to anoint the kings of His choice, may raise up leaders among the nations who will do what is acceptable in His sight

That we may recognize God in the tiny whispering sound of His coming, and obey what we hear in the murmur of that gentle voice

For all who feel forsaken as Elijah did, pursued by sickness, misfortune, disaster, or persecution, that God may give them a new direction and strength for the journey

For all who have gone before us marked with the sign of faith, that they may see the bounty of the Lord in the land of the living

## Week 10, Saturday

*1 Kgs 19:19-21; Ps 16; Matt 5:33-37*

For our Holy Father, our bishops, and priests, who have inherited the cloak of leadership in the church, that they may be prompt and faithful to their divine calling

For peace, that our Lady, Queen of Peace, may shine brightly in our troubled world, called forth by the loving prayers and sacrifices of her faithful children

For the grace of complete honesty in our relations with God and each other, and especially that our Yes may be Yes when it comes to serving our neighbor in love

For all who are being called to a prophetic and religious vocation, that like Elisha they may respond with promptness and generosity

For our beloved departed ones, that God may be their allotted portion and their cup, keeping them safe from the netherworld and holding fast their lot in His heavenly kingdom

## Week 11, Monday

*1 Kgs 21:1-16, Ps 5, Matt 5:38-42*

For the church and her holy leaders, who are often pressed into service and asked to turn the other cheek, that they may have the grace to respond as the Lord desires

For rulers who use extortion and violence to acquire land and goods, that they may come to realize the seriousness of their offenses against justice, and repent of their ways

That we may be willing to give to those who need our help, and offer no resistance to those who are evil, as the Lord teaches us

For all who are suffering injustice as Naboth once did, for all who are oppressed and forgotten and poor, for the sick and lonely, for all who need our prayers

That the Lord who urges us to forgive may have mercy on our dear departed ones, purifying them quickly to welcome them into His heavenly kingdom

## Week 11, Tuesday

*1 Kgs 21:17-29, Ps 51, Matt 5:43-48*

That the church may make every effort to be perfect even as the Heavenly Father is perfect, according to the way given us by the Father's only Son

For those who murder and then take possession, that they may meet a prophet upon their way, who will speak the truth about their sins and offer them a chance to make amends

That we may learn to obey the difficult command of Jesus to love our enemies and to pray for those who persecute us, putting our trust in His all-powerful grace

For all who have asked for our prayers in a time of suffering and pain, sickness and grief, that God may cause His rain of compassion and mercy to fall abundantly upon them

For all who have died, that they may be thoroughly washed of any guilt through God's merciful purification and brought before His face to rejoice in His goodness

## Week 11, Wednesday

*2 Kgs 2:1, 6-14, Ps 31, Matt 6:1-6, 16-18*

For the disciples of Jesus, that our works of mercy may be done in secret and not for all to see, so that the Father who is hidden may be the one to give us our reward

That Elijah may let the mantle of His fiery spirit fall upon all those who must witness to the supremacy of God, especially those who must undergo persecution

That our prayers may be earnest but very hidden, our fasting be offered with an anointing of gladness, and everything we do be seasoned with the love that comes from the invisible God

For all the intentions recommended to our prayers, for those who suffer in loneliness and poverty, that their hearts may take comfort, hoping in the Lord

For our beloved dead, that with Elijah they may be welcomed into heaven in a whirlwind of God's mercy and love

## Week 11, Thursday

*Sir 48:1-14, Ps 97, Matt 6:7-15*

For our Holy Father, our bishops and priests, that their ministry may be filled with fiery zeal for God as was the prophet Elijah

That the prophetic power of Elijah that once sent kings down to destruction and broke the power of wickedness may battle against the entrenched evils of our own society

For all of us sharing this Eucharist, given our holy daily bread by the best of Fathers, that our gratitude may show itself in forgiveness and zeal for the coming of His kingdom

For all the intentions recommended to our prayers, that the Father, who knows what we need before we ask, may in mercy grant the desires of all who seek His help

For our beloved departed ones, that their trespasses may be forgiven, and for their peace and joy in God's Kingdom

### Week 11, Friday

*2 Kgs 11:1-4, 9-20, Ps 132, Matt 6:19-23*

For the priests of the Lord, that like Jehoida they may act prudently and bravely to safeguard the covenant between God and His people, renewing the bond whenever it comes under attack

That the nations of the world may rejoice and their lands may be quiet and at peace with one another under rulers who fear the Lord

That our eyes may be sound to see the truth of every situation, and that the radiance of the Holy Spirit may fill us with light and counsel to guide our actions

For those who are in need of prayer today: the sick, the unemployed, the imprisoned and abused and addicted, that the power of this Holy Sacrifice may shatter the chains that bind them

For our dear ones who have died, that they may find a treasure waiting for them in heaven, where their good works commend them to a merciful Father

### Week 11, Saturday

*2 Chr 24:17-25, Ps 89, Matt 6:24-34*

For our leaders in the church, that the Spirit of God may possess them and they may speak out prophetically against the evils of our day

That leaders of nations may make decisions based on justice and compassion, so that God will establish their power on a firm foundation and give us peace

For all of us in these times when anxiety about material necessities reigns in so many hearts, that we may seek first the kingdom of God and allow Him to faithfully provide for what we need

For the sick, the poor, those who are suffering from natural disasters, all who have asked our prayers, that Our Blessed Mother may come to their side today with all her tender power

For our beloved departed ones, that God may remember His faithful love and His mercy toward them, and lead them into life everlasting

## Week 12, Monday

*2 Kgs 17:5-18, Ps 60, Matt 7:1-5*

For the church, that we may be the first to cleanse and reform our ways under the continual urging of conscience, giving an example to all nations of a people faithful to the Lord

That the world community may listen to the warnings of the Lord through rising prophetic voices of our day who rightly cry out against serious objective moral evil in each society

For grace to perceive and remove the significant obstacles that obstruct our vision, to attend to our own faults rather than point out and condemn the faults of others

For all who are feeling hardships, whose lives are cracked and tottering, whose defenses are broken, that through earnest and loving intercession, God may return to them with compassion

For those who have gone before us, that the measure of their goodness may be measured back to them with an overflow of divine clemency

## Week 12, Tuesday

*2 Kgs 19, Ps 48, Matt 7:6, 12-14*

For our shepherds in the church, that they may be given light to see who is ready to receive the holy message they preach and the pearls of wisdom they have to share

That the arrogance of nations and governments that insult and oppose God may be checked by the work of God's holy angels

That we may be among those who find the narrow gate and the constricted way that leads to eternal life, keeping closely to all God's commandments, especially in regard to the way we treat others

For all who are under mortal threat through poverty, oppression, or persecution, that the zeal of the Lord of Hosts may save them as the remnant on whom He has set His favor

For our beloved dead, that they may now be with God on His holy mountain, in the stronghold of His mercy, pondering His love forever in His holy temple

### Week 12, Wednesday

*2 Kgs 22:8-13, 23:1-3, Ps 119, Matt 7:15-20*

For our Holy Father, our bishops and priests, that their fidelity to the covenant may be an example to God's people

For world leaders, that the law of God may be uppermost in their thoughts and decisions, so that they may walk in the pathways of peace

That we who receive the most beautiful fruit of Jesus' self gift in this Holy Eucharist may be good trees that bring forth our own good fruit in His honor today

For all the intentions that have been entrusted to us for prayer, for all who have no one to pray for them, especially prisoners, drug addicts, and those suffering from war and natural disasters

For our dear departed ones, that as they were faithful to God's covenant when they were with us, God may show His magnificent fidelity by welcoming them into His rest

### Week 12, Thursday

*2 Kgs 24:8-17, Ps 79, Matt 7:21-29*

That those who work and exercise ministry and invoke the name of the Lord Jesus may be the first to do the will of His Father

That nations may cease to do evil in the sight of the Lord, but turn back to the ways of sound morality and justice, thus strengthening their national defenses and promoting world peace

That we may build our spiritual homes on a rock foundation, putting into practice all that we hear from the Lord, ready to stand firm against the storms and floods that will test our fidelity

For those who are brought very low through trial and distress of mind, body, and spirit, that God's compassion may quickly come to them in their hour of need

For our loved ones who have died, that the power of this Mass and our fervent prayer for them may speed their entrance into God's heavenly kingdom

## Week 12, Friday

*2 Kgs 25:1-12, Ps 137, Matt 8:1-4*

For the church, that she may keep the celestial songs of the heavenly Jerusalem in her heart as she endures her times of persecution and despoilment on earth

That the fall of the city of Jerusalem and the fate of her king may be a sober warning to any nation that abandons the law of God for immorality and wickedness

That we may confidently approach Jesus in our uncleanness of soul and our infirmity of body, appealing to His power and goodness for help in our need

That Jesus, who promptly stretched out His hand to touch and cure the leper, may heal and console all those who have asked us to pray for them in their time of sickness or destitution

For our dear departed ones, that they may be purified to joyfully sing the songs of Zion in the gracious presence of God and all His saints

## Week 12, Saturday

*Lam 2, Ps 74, Matt 8:5-17*

That the prophets and leaders of the church may shun all false visions and misleading portents, honestly laying bare the guilt of God's people for correction and healing

That our hearts may be poured out like water and our hands lifted up to heaven for the lives of God's little ones whose rights to life and justice are trampled upon in our world

That the honest humility and absolute trust of the centurion may be in our hearts as we repeat His words while approaching Jesus in every Holy Communion

That the diseases and the troubles of those who have asked us to pray for them may be subject to the divine authority of Jesus and His healing power

For our deceased loved ones and those who lament their passing, that our Blessed Mother may obtain swift entrance into heaven and comfort for all her children

### Week 13, Monday

*Amos 2:6-10, 13-16, Ps 50, Matt 8:18-22*

For our leaders and priests in the church, that as they glorify our heavenly Father with their sacrifices of praise, they may show others the right way to the salvation of God

For world leaders, that they may follow the dictates of the natural law planted in their hearts, respecting the weak and the lowly in their decisions, and reverencing all life

For vocations, that more generous hearts may be willing to follow Jesus wherever He goes, courageously leaving behind all that is dear to them

For all who have asked our prayers in a time of distress or sickness, and for all who are in special need of prayer at this time, that our fervent intercession may bring them healing and grace

For our beloved dead, who have crossed to the other shore with Jesus, that His Holy Sacrifice may supply their purification, so that they may enter with Him into His heavenly kingdom

### Week 13, Tuesday

*Amos 3:1-8, 4:11-12, Ps 5, Matt 8:23-27*

That prophetic voices may be raised in the church, preparing the people to meet their God in holiness and justice

That the Lord, who destroys all who speak falsehood, who hates deceit, may bring the nations back to obedience under His omnipotence and His mercy

That our courage and our faith may not fail us as the storm waves rise up and the winds begin to blow, knowing that the One who has power over the storm is inside our boat

That those who have appealed to our prayers in their illness, poverty, oppression, or persecution may know the complete calm that comes when Jesus wakes up to exercise His divine power in their lives

For those who have gone before us, that they may enter God's house because of His abundant kindness, worshiping in the temple of heavenly joy

## Week 13, Wednesday

*Amos 5:14-15, 21-24, Ps 50, Matt 8:28-34*

For the church, that her feasts may be acceptable to the Lord and that He may take pleasure in her solemnities, because His own goodness is flowing in her like an unfailing stream

For the nations, that justice may prevail at the gates of all peoples, and that their leaders may hate evil and love life, truth, and integrity

That Jesus, the Son of God, may take up His power against the demons that plague our society, casting them out for the sake of the innocent who cry out to Him for help

For the sick, those who are suffering financially, for the abused and imprisoned and addicted, for all who are in need of healing and hope from the Lord

For our dear ones who have died, that no demons may have power to touch them, and that the merciful purification of the Lord may soon release them into heaven's perfect joy

## Week 13, Thursday

*Amos 7:10-17, Ps 19, Matt 9:1-8*

That the messages of the prophets who have been taken from their ordinary occupations and sent to speak out for justice and truth may be heard and heeded in the church

That the perfect, trustworthy law of the Lord may give wisdom to the powerful, enlightening their eyes and changing the course of the world

For all who are paralyzed by their sins, who lie helpless and unable to rise again by their own power, that loving hearts and hands may reach out to them and bring them with faith to Jesus

For all who are paralyzed by the sufferings of life, illness, poverty, oppression and grief, that the authority given to Jesus may once again be extended over them for healing and vigor

For those who have died and come before the true and just judgments of the Lord, that His mercy may envelop them in purification and eternal peace

## Week 13, Friday

*Amos 8:4-6, 9-12, Ps 119, Matt 9:9-13*

That the Word of the Lord may be heard loud and strong within the church, proclaimed by her priests and deacons and shining in the lives and example of her people

For those who trample on the needy and destroy the poor, who cheat and lie to make a profit at the expense of the lowly, that God's just judgment may bring them to repentance

For the sinners, for the tax collectors, for all who need the divine physician, who are sick in their souls, that they may encounter the call of mercy in their lives

For the unlikely vocations, for those who would never expect Jesus to pass by and call them, that they may be shaken by His compassion and, like Matthew, get up to follow Him

For all the intentions recommended to our prayers, and especially for our departed loved ones, that God, who desires mercy and not sacrifice, may now welcome them into His kingdom

## Week 13, Saturday

*Amos 9:11-15, Ps 85, Matt 9:14-17*

For the church, fasting and praying as she awaits the return of the Groom, that she may be found clothed in her wedding finery, wrapped in a new cloak of justice and truth

For the restoration of ravaged nations, for abundance of vintage and harvest for the hungry, for the solid planting of lives that have been breached, for the blessing of peace upon all

That the new wine of Christ's doctrine and His powerful salvation may be poured into hearts ready to expand with the glorious effervescence of the divine gift

For all the little ones of our society, the fallen huts of hopes and lives, that through the loving efforts and prayers of committed Christians, their hearts may be rebuilt in joy

For those who have gone before us marked with the sign of faith, that the Bridegroom may soon admit them into the wedding banquet that is heaven

## Week 14, Monday

*Hos 2:16-22, Ps 145, Matt 9:18-26*

For our Holy Father, our bishops, and priests, that like the synagogue official they may approach Jesus with the confidence that draws His healing power down upon His beloved church

For peace, that the Lord who espouses His people in right and justice, in love and mercy, may enable nations to forge bonds of justice and compassion with one another

For all of us who meet in this Eucharist the Divine Bridegroom of our souls, that we may allow Him to lead us into the desert and speak to our hearts, awakening our first love for Him again

For all the intentions we bring to this Mass, for the little daughter who needs Jesus to take her by the hand, for those whose inner strength is draining away, whose hope is reaching out to touch the Lord

For our beloved dead, that they may be lifted up by the compassion of the Lord to new life in His presence

## Week 14, Tuesday

*Hos 8:4-7, 11-13, Ps 115, Matt 9:32-38*

For God's blessing on the preachers who continue in the footsteps of Jesus: teaching, proclaiming the Gospel of the Kingdom, and allowing their hearts to be moved with pity for the sufferings of the people

That our political leaders may not sow the wind and reap the whirlwind, but in their decisions and policies return to the moral guidelines handed down by the God-fearing founders of our nation

That God may call more laborers into the harvest field of souls who are waiting, exhausted, like sheep without a shepherd, for the divine word that will raise them up and give them direction and strength

That the golden calves and idols of money and power that have been set up in many lives may be shown for what they are: dead things destined for destruction

For our dear ones who have gone before us in death, that Jesus, who reached out to cure every disease and illness, may free them from all evil and establish them in His heavenly kingdom

## Week 14, Wednesday

*Hos 10:1-12, Ps 105, Matt 10:1-7*

For the modern day apostles who minister in the church, that like the twelve, they may be given authority over unclean spirits and the power of healing for every spiritual disease

That world leaders may break up for us a new field, sowing justice and a culture of life, so that we may reap God's blessing and the fruit of peace

That the kingdom of heaven may be at hand for our dear ones who have wandered far from their faith, through the love and prayer and outreach of the faithful

For all those who are in a season of suffering and pain in body or soul; those in grief or illness, the imprisoned, the abused, the addicted, all who need our special prayer

For our beloved dead, that their purification may be shortened as the mercy of God rains down upon them and releases them for eternal rest

## Week 14, Thursday

*Hos 11:1-4, 8-9, Ps 80, Matt 10:7-15*

For the new apostles of Jesus in our own day; that they may be the first to call down the gift of peace upon the church, giving themselves without counting the cost

That lay Christians may be in the forefront of the battle to reestablish moral values in our world today

That all the children of God may come to know their healer and the One who feeds them and draws them with human cords, with bands of love

For all who are suffering and struggling along life's way, bowed down with weariness and grief, that God's pity may be stirred, not allowing their pain to consume them

For those who have gone before us marked with the sign of faith, that God may take them in His arms, fulfilling their every desire for blessedness in His embrace

## Week 14, Friday

*Hos 14:2-10, Ps 51, Matt 10:16-23*

For our holy shepherds and apostles in the church, that they may be as shrewd as serpents and as simple as doves, able to deal with the wolves in the midst of whom they find themselves

For governors and kings and leaders of nations, that the example and courage of committed Christians may help them focus their decisions on life, morality, and justice

For those who have collapsed through their guilt, that they may have the grace to return to the Lord to be healed and loved freely, so that they may strike root and give forth the beautiful fragrance of redemption

For those who are persecuted for their faith, that they may be given what they need to say by the Spirit in order to bear witness to Jesus, and His courage to endure whatever may come as a consequence of their testimony

For those who have endured to the end, who have died in the peace of Christ, that they may be brought rejoicing into the House of the Father

## Week 14, Saturday

*Isa 6:1-8, Ps 93, Matt 10:24-33*

For the church, that the angel of the Lord may change her and purify her lips so that she may become an effective and united witness, ready to be sent wherever He wills

That Christians may not be afraid of any temporal power, but speak in the light what they have heard, and proclaim from the housetops the witness of their good example

For the calming of our fear, for confidence in Our Father who has numbered the hairs of our heads and who cares for us more attentively than many of His beloved sparrows

For all who are suffering and struggling along life's way, that Our Blessed Mother may meet them on the road with all her maternal power and tenderness

For all who have died, that their sins may be purged to come before the awesome holiness of God in His heavenly kingdom

### Week 15, Monday

*Isa 1:10-17, Ps 50, Matt 10:34–11:1*

For the church, that the Holy Sacrifice offered daily in her churches may be united to good deeds of every sort, making a pleasing offering to the Father

For world leaders, that they may make justice their aim, redressing the wronged, hearing the plea of the orphan, upholding the dignity of every human being

That our Lord Jesus Christ, whose life and doctrine compel us to choose Him at the expense of good relations with those who oppose Him, may give us the grace to put Him first in our lives

For all who are sinking under their crosses, who need a helping hand along the way, a word of encouragement and cheer, that we may be their consolers until the trial is over

For those who have come to the complete loss of their life in death, that they may soon be purified to gain eternal and abundant life in heaven

### Week 15, Tuesday

*Isa 7:1-9, Ps 48, Matt 11:20-24*

For the church and her leaders, especially those who are under attack in any way, that their faith may hold firm and their teaching be consistent

That world leaders may remember and come to the aid of those who have been torn asunder by war, famine, poverty, and oppression

That we may never get used to God's wonderful deeds in our midst, but keep our hearts grateful and humble as we experience His faithfulness and hidden power

For all who feel their hearts trembling under the weight of life's challenges, that they may take courage from God who never deserts His faithful ones, and remain tranquil in the midst of the storm

For our dear ones who have gone before us in death, that the power of this Holy Sacrifice may cleanse them for a speedy entrance into the kingdom of heaven

## Week 15, Wednesday

*Isa 10:5-16, Ps 94, Matt 11:25-27*

For the church, to whom Jesus has chosen to reveal the knowledge of His heavenly Father, that we may be grateful and responsive to this surpassing gift

That powerful nations may understand that they are only instruments in the hand of God, that their strength and wisdom are His gifts, and that they will use them according to His will

That all who are wise and learned in the ways of the world may change and become like little children in their hearts, so that the secrets of God's heavenly kingdom may be revealed to them

That Jesus, who has received all things from the hand of His Father, may come with His riches of grace and healing to all who are in need of these blessings

For our beloved dead, that our Blessed Mother may be their guide and light across the waters of purification until they reach the promised shores of heavenly bliss

## Week 15, Thursday

*Isa 26:7-19, Ps 102, Matt 11:28-30*

For the church, that she may yearn for God throughout the night of her trials in this world, and that His name and His title may be the desire of our souls

That the world's inhabitants may learn justice as God's judgment dawns upon the earth, turning our thoughts to His abiding and compassionate law for our lives

That we may come to the heart of Jesus to learn the ways of gentleness and humility, taking His easy and light yoke upon our shoulders with a willing spirit

For all who labor and are burdened by the trials and sorrows and anxieties of life, that Jesus may give them rest as we hold them up in loving intercession

For our dear departed ones, that those who lie in the dust may awake and sing of God's salvation, as He leads them into the realms of light and glory

## Week 15, Friday

*Isa 38:1-6, 21-22, 7-8, Isa 38, Matt 12:1-8*

That Jesus may continue to come to the defense of His disciples before all who would constrict them with oppressive legalistic demands, and give His church the freedom of the sons and daughters of God

That the legitimate right of the poor to have their share of grain to sustain life may be honored and that the world's resources may be distributed fairly among all her people

That we, like Hezekiah, may conduct ourselves faithfully and wholeheartedly in the Lord's presence, doing what is pleasing to Him

That God may be a shield and a rescuer to all who are in desperate need of His help, especially the sick and the oppressed who cry out to Him in their need

For those whose dwelling has been struck down and borne away from them in death, that God may grant them newness of life and length of days in His heavenly kingdom

## Week 15, Saturday

*Mic 2:1-5, Ps 10, Matt 12:14-21*

For our chosen servant leaders in the church, that God may place His spirit upon them, and they may be men and women in whom the Lord takes delight

For those who take counsel against the helpless and the vulnerable to put them to death, that the little ones may be saved from their power

That those who plan iniquity and work out evil in their hearts, accomplishing it when it lies in their power, that they may be converted to the ways of justice and honor

For the bruised reeds and smoldering wicks, those who have almost given up hope under the duress of their trials, that Jesus may restore them in His divine mercy

For our dear ones who have passed away, that Mary, Mother of fair love and holy hope, may intercede for them and bring them soon to the joys of heaven

## Week 16, Monday

*Mic 6:1-4, 6-8, Ps 50, Matt 12:38-42*

That the church and her holy leaders may always be attentive and responsive to the Lord Jesus, realizing His greatness and dignity as well as His loving kindness

That our generation may not be an evil and unfaithful one, but that we may repent like the men of Nineveh and return to the ways of life, love, and justice upon the earth

That we who follow Jesus may accomplish what the Lord requires of us, doing right, loving goodness, and walking humbly with our God

That God, who brought His people out of slavery, may hear the cries of all those who are bound by disease, oppression, grief, and addiction, and come swiftly to their aid

For those who have passed through their own death and judgment, that Jesus, who was in the belly of the earth till the third day, may raise them up to life and glory in heaven

## Week 16, Tuesday

*Mic 7:14-15, 18-20, Ps 85, Matt 12:46-50*

That the church may be the true family of Jesus, seeking to do the will of His Heavenly Father at all times, following the example of His Blessed Mother Mary

That God may show wonderful signs among the peoples of the world, establishing justice and raising up the lowly

That God may continue to call souls to swell apart, dedicated to Him as a sacrificial offering in the cloisters of His Church

That Jesus, who delights in clemency, may have compassion on all who are crying out to Him in their distress of mind or body, granting them grace and faithfulness in their time of trial

For those who have gone before us through the gates of death, that the Father may remove their guilt and pardon all sin, bringing them, pure and clean, into His heavenly kingdom

## Week 16, Wednesday

*Jer 1:1, 4-10, Ps 71, Matt 13:1-9*

For the priestly prophets of the church, who like Jeremiah have been called and dedicated to proclaim the word of the Lord, that they may fulfill their task with courage

For those who have been sent to witness to God and His law of life and love among the nations, that they may have no fear, knowing that God is with them to deliver them

That Jesus, who passes by sowing the seeds of eternal life, may find in our hearts a rich and abundant soil for His gracious gift, and ears that are open to His message

For all who labor under a weight of misery and pain, that through this Holy Sacrifice God may incline His ear to them and save them

For our dear ones who have died, who once accepted the teachings of Jesus as the earth accepts the seed, that they may now reap a harvest of joy and peace in heaven

## Week 16, Thursday

*Jer 2:1-3, 7-8, 12-13, Ps 36, Matt 13:10-47*

For our leaders in the church, that they may find refuge under the shadow of God's wings and drink from the streams of His delights, even as they channel these streams to others

For peace, for the courage to take the steps needed to create peace; that world leaders may see the light to go forward from the law God has implanted in every human heart

For the grace to truly hear what Jesus is trying to tell us, and for eyes to see His action in our lives today, so that His blessing may rest upon us

For all who have forsaken the Lord and dug for themselves broken cisterns of power and pleasure that can never serve to quench their thirst, that they may come back to the source of living waters

For our beloved departed ones, that they may be given complete knowledge of the kingdom of God in heaven

## Week 16, Friday

*Jer 3:14-17, Jer 31, Matt 13:18-23*

For our Holy Father, our bishops and priests, that they may be shepherds after God's own heart

For peace, that violence may be replaced by negotiation and that the hardness of hearts at enmity with each other may be softened

For the grace to be good soil for God's holy word, accepting it, understanding it, and bearing good fruit

For all who are suffering, especially those who have asked for our prayers, that God will turn their mourning into joy and gladden them after their sorrows

For our dear ones who have gone before us through the gates of death, that they may come streaming to the Lord's blessings in the heavenly Jerusalem

## Week 16, Saturday

*Jer 7:1-11, Ps 84, Matt 13:24-30*

That God may remain with us in His dwelling place, our holy church, because we have reformed our ways and our deeds are pleasing in His sight

That there may be no more oppression of widows and orphans, that innocent blood may no longer be shed, that all human life may be upheld and protected

For patience to wait till harvest time for the weeds in our midst to be collected and burned, for the strength to persevere in bearing good fruit in the midst of opposition and difficulty

That our prayers and the power of this Holy Mass may uphold and heal all who are in distress, giving them grace and light on their way

For our deceased loved ones, that our Blessed Mother may find them a home and a nest among the altars of the Lord of Hosts in His heavenly kingdom

### Week 17, Monday

*Jer 13:1-11, Deut 32, Matt 13:31-35*

For our holy and prophetic leaders in the church, that they may be obedient to the Lord's commands like Jeremiah, teaching and exhorting God's people according to His desires

That the world may no longer be forgetful of the God who gave us all birth and who holds us in being, so that we will not have to endure having Him hide His face from us

That we may faithfully plant our mustard seeds and mix the yeast into our flour, allowing the kingdom of God to work its miracle of abundant growth in our midst

For those whose lives have been buried away like Jeremiah's loincloth, who feel rotted and good for nothing through poverty, illness, or grief, that God may restore them to His grace and favor

For those who have gone before us in death, that they may know the complete fulfillment of growth and expansion of God's kingdom in their heavenly home

### Week 17, Tuesday

*Jer 14:17-22, Ps 79, Matt 13:36-43*

For the leaders and prophets of the church, that like Jeremiah they may feel the sorrows of their people and cry out to God on their behalf, drawing down His mercy by their purity and fervor

For people who are waiting for peace to no avail, and for a time of healing, but terror comes instead, that the balance of justice may be restored for them in our world

For the children of the kingdom, who struggle to grow among weeds which are the children of the Evil One, that they may persevere with courage till the harvest

For those who feel overwhelmed with great destruction, whose wound seems incurable, that the God of all compassion may quickly move into their lives with healing and hope

For our beloved dead, that they may be shining like the sun with all the righteous in the kingdom of their Father in heaven

## Week 17, Wednesday

*Jer 15:10, 16-21, Ps 59, Matt 13:44-46*

For our leaders in the church, who bear God's name, that His word may be the joy and happiness of their hearts and that God may be with them to deliver and rescue them

For the leaders of our nation and of the world, that they may bring forth the precious gift of life and justice for all peoples

That each of us may find with joy the treasure that is worth selling everything to possess, our Lord Jesus Christ and His holy kingdom

For the sick, the elderly, the lonely and depressed, the poor and unemployed, that they may discover the stronghold and refuge they have in God

For our departed loved ones, that they may find that the pearl of great price, the kingdom of heaven, is now their blissful home forever

## Week 17, Thursday

*Jer 18:1-6, Ps 146, Matt 13:47-53*

For the leaders of the church, who bring from her storeroom both the new and the old for our instruction and help, that they may understand and live all that they have learned from God

That no trust may be put in princes, or in the sons of men whose plans of power perish in death, but that all nations may return their trust to God and renew their obedience to His holy laws of love and life

For our patience with ourselves and with one another, that we may continue in love even when things turn out badly in our hands, and try again in hope

For all who feel themselves thrown on a potter's wheel of events and sufferings beyond their control, that they may trust the Divine hands that support their shaping into beauty and strength of soul

For our loved ones who have died, that they may be among those God chooses from the catch as worthy of eternal life

## Week 17, Friday

*Jer 26:1-9, Ps 69, Matt 13:54-58*

For our Holy Father, our bishops and priests, that they may be consumed with zeal for the house of God and speak the truth about everything He commands them to say

For all the places that are desolate and deserted because of war, hatred, oppression, genocide, and famine, that the hearts of those who can help may be moved to do so

For the prophets of our own day, that they may be recognized and their message honored even among those most familiar with them

For all the intentions we carry in our hearts, especially for the sick and troubled who have been recommended to our prayers, that the wisdom and mighty deeds of Jesus will be active in their lives

For those who have gone before us, that our prayers and the grace of this Holy Sacrifice may bring them, purified and exulting, into God's heavenly kingdom

## Week 17, Saturday

*Jer 26:11-16, 24, Ps 69, Matt 14:1-12*

For our leaders in the church, that they may have the courage to speak out for the truth as did John the Baptist

That world leaders may give a hearing to the prophets of our day and accept the guidance of the Lord in their decisions, so that there may be protection for life, justice, and peace

That we may be like the people of Jeremiah's day, defending those who speak in God's name and not allowing them to come to harm

For all the intentions recommended to our prayers, and for those who have no one to pray for them, that mercy and healing may come through this Holy Sacrifice

For our beloved departed ones, that our Blessed Mother may take them under her protection and unite them with all the saints

## Week 18, Monday

*Jer 28:1-17, Ps 119, Matt 14:13-21*

For our Holy Father, our bishops and priests, that like Jesus they may take time for prayer as the foundation of their ministry in the church

That world leaders may walk in the way of the law God has written on every human heart, keeping His ordinances and paying heed to His decrees

That we may bring our small loaves and fishes to Jesus with confidence, allowing His power to multiply our resources on behalf of those who hunger for our compassion and generosity

For all who are sick, lonely, or anxious, that the heart of Jesus may be moved with pity for them, and they may feel His healing touch upon all their afflictions

For our beloved departed ones, that every yoke of sin may be broken from their necks, and they may enjoy the perfect freedom of the heavenly kingdom

## Week 18, Tuesday

*Jer 30:1-22, Ps 102, Matt 14:22-36*

For the church, tossed about in the night on a stormy sea, that Jesus may come to us and to our apostolic leaders and build up our courage with His divine presence

That God may restore the tents of the oppressed and pity their dwellings, rebuilding destroyed cities and making their assemblies stand firm before Him

That we may not be of little faith, but may respond to the invitation of Jesus even if it means walking on the water against the wind and the waves

For all who have appealed to our prayers in a time of need or turbulence in their lives, that Jesus may get into their boats and make the winds die down

For our dear ones who have died, that God may summon them to approach close to Him in the heavenly Jerusalem, choosing them as His own beloved sons and daughters

## Week 18, Wednesday

*Jer 31:1-7, Jer 31:10-13, Matt 15:21-28*

For the church, loved with an age-old love by her God, that He may again gather and restore her as the virgin bride that dances before Him in celebration of His mercy

For our leaders who preside at the head of the nations, that they may allow the Lord to be the watchman of their ways, pointing out the paths that lead to compassion, justice, and peace

That we who approach the Lord in the intimacy of the Eucharist, who eat the holy bread reserved for the children of God, may welcome Him with the vibrant faith that is so pleasing in His sight

For all who are in a season of special trial like the Canaanite woman, for all who suffer over the power of evil in the lives of those they love, that they may obtain mercy and healing

For those who have gone before us in death, that they may be mounting the heights of Zion, streaming to the Lord's blessings in heaven

## Week 18, Thursday

*Jer 31:31-34, Ps 51, Matt 16:13-23*

For our leaders in the church, entrusted with the faith of St. Peter and His power to bind and loose upon earth, that they may use these keys wisely

That God's people may attend to the law He has written on our hearts through the redemption of Jesus, and that all may come to know this law through our radiant culture of love

That we may steadfastly accompany our Master along His road of suffering, learning to think as God does

For all who are experiencing sickness, trial, diminishment, unemployment, or any kind of distress in their lives, that they may know the joy of God's salvation through our earnest prayer for them

For our beloved dead, that God may make a new covenant of everlasting love and fidelity with them, giving them rest and peace in His holy kingdom

## Week 18, Friday

*Nah 2:1, 3, 3:1-3, 6-7, Deut 32,
Matt 16:24-28*

For the church, the luxuriant vine growing from Jesus Christ and tended by the Father, that she may celebrate her feasts and fulfill her vows in holiness and purity of heart

For all the war ravaged lands of the world, for the struggling and oppressed peoples, that they may soon see upon the mountains bearers of good news, announcing peace

That we may begin to follow in the footsteps of Jesus, shouldering our cross and becoming willing to lose our lives for the sake of the Master who gave His life for us

For the intentions of our loved ones and all who have asked our prayers, that their needs of body, mind, and spirit may be met by the restoration of God

For those who have passed through death and the judgment of Jesus upon their conduct, that they may be purified to find everlasting life now with Him in His Father's glory

## Week 18, Saturday

*Hab 1:12-2:4, Ps 9, Matt 17:14-20*

For our leaders in the church, that they may firmly take their stand at the guard post to hear what the Lord God is saying, and faithfully transmit the message to His people

For peace, that the eyes of the Lord which are too pure to look upon evil and misery, may impel world leaders to make decisions that are compassionate and just

For the gift of faith that can move mountains, the mustard seed of confidence that can work miracles in the name of Jesus

That Jesus, who reached out in compassion and mercy to heal diseases and drive out demons, may come to the aid of all who are troubled and afflicted today

For our beloved dead, that the vision which presses on to fulfillment and will not disappoint may be theirs, and they may enjoy the sight of God forever

## Week 19, Monday

*Ezek 1:2-5, 24-28, Ps 148, Matt 17:22-27*

That the glory of the Lord may always be above His holy church, and the voice of the Almighty may be her guidance and command

That the Lord may sit enthroned above the kingdoms and nations of the earth, directing the decisions of world leaders in obedience to His decrees

That we may carry the passion and death of the Lord in our thoughts and in our hearts, remembering His love for us, so that we may also be part of His glorious resurrection

For those who are suffering: the sick, the oppressed poor, the unemployed, the grieving, the imprisoned, and the addicted, that our earnest prayers before God's throne of glory may bring them relief

For our dear departed ones, that they may be soon purified to praise God with His angels and all His hosts in the kingdom of His peace and joy

## Week 19, Tuesday

*Ezek 2:8-3:4, Ps 119, Matt 18:1-5, 10, 12-14*

For our shepherds in the church; our bishops, priests, and deacons, that they may be faithful and persevere in seeking out the lost and straying sheep of God's flock

That world leaders may heed the prophetic voices that speak out for justice and compassion, so that there may be peace

For the grace to turn and become like little children, humble and obedient in God's sight

For all the special intentions that have been recommended to our prayers, for the little ones who suffer in body and soul, that their angels may mediate God's healing and grace to them

For our beloved departed ones, who were faithful to God in this life, that He may be their sweetness and joy now in heaven

## Week 19, Wednesday

*Ezek 9:1-7, 10:18-22, Ps 113,*
*Matt 18:15-20*

For the church, that her children may always be marked with the sign of the cross of Jesus, closely united with Him in His values and priorities

That the abominations of the emerging culture of death in our country may be overcome by the prayer and witness of those united in the name of Jesus

For all who must point out the faults of those they love, that the correction may show a patient and loving concern and bear the fruit of conversion

For all who have asked for our prayers in a time of need, that with Jesus in our midst we may unite in our charity to effectively obtain our heavenly Father's favor

For our loved ones who have died, that the glory of the Lord may never depart from their baptized souls, but that they may enter into His joy in the kingdom of heaven

## Week 19, Thursday

*Ezek 12:1-12, Ps 78, Matt 18:21–19:1*

For our leaders in the church, that they may also be prophets who shoulder the burdens of their people

For the princes and leaders in the world today, that they may not set out in darkness, but invoke the light of God's will in all their decisions

That we may all realize how deeply we are in debt to God and how dangerous it is not to forgive from the heart

For all who are suffering in mind, emotions, body, or soul, especially the seriously ill, the unemployed, and those with critical family problems

That our beloved dead may know the forgiveness of their debts and the welcome of a merciful Father

### Week 19, Friday

*Ezek 16:1-15, Isa 12, Matt 19:3-12*

That the church may be strong in her doctrine on the sanctity of marriage, helping her children to work through the problems of close relationships without recourse to the escape of easy divorce

That modern society may rediscover the value of strong families, may build up a culture that respects life in all its stages, and may support traditional marriage

That we may come to appreciate all that God has done for each soul as His dearly beloved bride, giving Him our complete faithfulness and grateful devotion

For those who labor under a burden of sorrow or pain, that through the power of loving intercession they may draw water with joy at the fountain of salvation and healing

For those who have gone before us marked with the sign of faith, that God may set up with them an everlasting covenant, pardoning and purifying them to be welcomed into His kingdom

### Week 19, Saturday

*Ezek 18:1-10, 13b, 30-32, Ps 51,*
*Matt 19:13-15*

For the grace of continual conversion in the church, that she may be the first to give an example of a renovation of heart and a willing spirit before God

That virtuous men and women may be raised up to become leaders among the nations, who will promote justice, defend life, and create peace

For the children, so loved by Jesus, who placed His hands on them and prayed for them, that no one may snatch the kingdom of heaven from their innocent hearts

That our Blessed Mother may come to the aid of her children who are suffering, obtaining for them grace and mercy, healing and strength

For all who have died and have been judged according to their ways, that through this Holy Sacrifice they may be forgiven, purified, and at rest in the joys of heaven

## Week 20, Monday

*Ezek 24:15-23, Deut 32, Matt 19:16-22*

That the church may be always ready to proclaim the commandments which must be kept to do what is good and to obtain eternal life

That God may not be obliged to hide His face from our nation because we have been willfully unmindful of Him in our culture and our policies

For those who seek to be perfect, that they may freely and willingly sell what they have for the sake of treasure in heaven, and then come to follow Jesus in close discipleship

For those who have had to endure sudden blows in their lives, who have been plunged into grief, sickness, or financial straits

For our dear ones who have died, that God's sanctuary in heaven may be the delight of their eyes forever

## Week 20, Tuesday

*Ezek 28:1-10, Deut 32, Matt 19:23-30*

For our leaders in the church, that they may be the first to proclaim the blessedness of the poor in spirit and to model this virtue in their own lives

That the princes and rulers of the earth may not be haughty of heart because of their wisdom and their power, but serve their people humbly in God's sight

For vocations; that more young people may be willing to leave behind home and family, lands and possessions for the sake of the name of Jesus Christ

For those who are trapped in impossible situations of illness, abuse, addiction, or imprisonment, that God, for whom all things are possible, may come to their rescue with power and mercy

For those who have gone before us, that they may soon be made pure to enter the kingdom of heaven

## Week 20, Wednesday

*Ezek 34:1-11, Ps 23, Matt 20:1-16*

For our Holy Father, our bishops, priests, and deacons, that they may be shepherds after God's own heart, tending and looking after His sheep with patience and care

For world leaders, that they may be mindful of the weak and the injured in their efforts at diplomacy

For all who labor in God's vineyard, that they may work with joyful hearts, sure of a generous recompense, and that God may send new laborers into His vineyard to help them

For all who are traveling through a dark valley of distress and constraint at this time, that they may feel the press of the Good Shepherd's staff guiding their footsteps

For all our beloved dead, that they may be given repose in the verdant pastures of heaven, where God spreads His holy table and makes their cup of blessings overflow

## Week 20, Thursday

*Ezek 36:23-28, Ps 51, Matt 22:1-14*

For all of us in the church, called to this wedding banquet of the Eucharist, robed in God's grace and honored at His table, that we may always remember how unworthy we are and come with grateful hearts

For our leaders in the world, that they may live by God's statutes, careful to observe His decrees, building up a civilization of moral decency and loving kindness

For all who are in need of conversion, especially those who are not aware of it, that God may sprinkle clean water on us all and give us a new heart and a new spirit for the glory of His name

For the sick, the unemployed, those suffering from natural disasters, displacement, war, and famine, that God may give them the joy of His salvation and God's people may come quickly to their aid

For our dear departed ones, that God may cleanse them by giving them a new heart and a new spirit, worthy of a place in His heavenly kingdom

## Week 20, Friday

*Ezek 37:1-14, Ps 107, Matt 22:34-40*

For our preachers and prophets in the church, that they may not hesitate to prophesy over the dry bones at God's command, bringing dead souls back to life by the power of the Spirit

For the oppressed, for the displaced, for those who long to be resettled in their own lands again, that their spirits may be lifted by the help of good national leaders who care about their fate

That we may concentrate on the two pivotal commandments of the law, love of God and love of neighbor, gathering all our resources of body and mind and spirit into their observance

For all who feel that their bones are dried up, their hope is lost, and they are cut off from God, that the Spirit's breath may bring them life and joy again

For those who have gone before us marked with the sign of faith, that God, who has power to raise the dead, may give them abundant life in His kingdom of happiness and peace

## Week 20, Saturday

*Ezek 43:1-7, Ps 85, Matt 23:1-12*

For the church, the place upon earth where God sets the soles of His feet and dwells forever, that she may be filled with the glory of the Lord and shine for all to see as a beacon of hope and comfort

For the rich and the powerful, that they may set aside their desire for places of honor and turn to serve the lowliest upon the earth

That we may be content to be servants, humbling ourselves in deference to others and letting God exalt us as He will

For those who are dragging heavy burdens on their journey through life, that they may know the help of God and the loving assistance of their fellow travelers

For those who have died, that they may soon be purified through the intercession of our Blessed Mother to be admitted to the heavenly banquet

## Week 21, Monday

*Thess 1:1-5, 11-12, Ps 96, Matt 23:13-22*

For our Holy Father, our bishops and priests, for their perseverance and faith in all the hardships they endure to be faithful to their ministry in the church

That the blessing of God who is glorified among the nations may bring world leaders together to work for peace

That God may make us worthy of His calling and powerfully bring to fulfillment every good purpose He inspires in us

For all who are undergoing hardship and suffering at this time, that through the power of prayer they may yet have reason to sing a new song of thanksgiving to the Lord for His merciful intervention

For our faithful departed, that by the sacrifice of this altar and its sacred gifts the name of the Lord Jesus may be glorified in them, and they may know the joys of eternal life

## Week 21, Tuesday

*2 Thess 2:1-3, 14-16, Ps 96,*
*Matt 23:23-26*

For the church, that we may stand fast and hold to the traditions we have received from the apostles, so that the good news may continue to be effective in our own day

That leaders of nations may be sure that the inside of their cup is clean, free of oppression, as they present polished appearances to the view of all

That we may never deserve the rebuke that Jesus addressed to the Pharisees, but cast aside all stubborn blindness and walk in the radiance of His truth

That God, who loved us and gave us eternal consolation, may in His mercy console the hearts of those in pain and sorrow, and strengthen them with grace and hope

For our deceased brothers and sisters, that through the power of this Holy Sacrifice, they may achieve the glory of our Lord Jesus Christ in His heavenly kingdom

## Week 21, Wednesday

*2 Thess 3:6-10, 16-18, Ps 128,*
*Matt 23:27-32*

For our leaders in the church, that like St. Paul they may conduct themselves in such a way as to be an example of holiness for the imitation of God's people

That the Lord of peace may give to our hearts, our homes, and our world, peace at all times and in every way

For all who are infected with the disease of hypocrisy, whose hearts do not match the role they play before others, that they may receive the great grace of insight and conversion

For those who are forced to labor in toil and drudgery under the trials and burdens of life, that they may find loving hearts and willing hands to help them

For all who have gone before us marked with the sign of faith, that the grace of the Lord Jesus may be with them, purifying them and leading them to their heavenly home

## Week 21, Thursday

*1 Cor 1:1-9, Ps 145, Matt 24:42-51*

That grace and peace may come from God our Father and the Lord Jesus Christ upon the church of God, sanctified in Christ Jesus and called to be holy

That through the prayers of many, world leaders may be enriched with all discourse and all knowledge, respecting life and upholding justice in our world today

That we may be good servants of our Divine Master, staying awake to greet Him when He comes, blessed for our faithful and prudent service

For all who have asked our prayers in a time of trouble, pain, or grief, that God who is faithful and filled with abundant goodness may see to their healing and restore their joy

For those who have died, who have met the Master in their own personal encounter and come under His judgment, that His mercy may lead them to a place of refreshment, light, and peace

### Week 21, Friday

*1 Cor 1:17-25, Ps 33, Matt 25:1-13*

That the cross of Christ may never be emptied of its meaning in the mouths of our holy preachers, but that like St. Paul, our preachers may prefer Christ crucified to the wisdom of human eloquence

For the statesmen of this age and those who are wise in the ways of the world, that God's wisdom may begin to alter their views and influence their decisions

That the prudence of the wise virgins may be ours, and that the Bridegroom may find us with our lamps filled with oil, shining and glowing with joy before Him

For all who need prayer today, who are sick, troubled, or restless, that the designs of God's heart for them may be mercy, light, health, and peace

For our beloved departed ones, who have passed through the mystery of the cross of Jesus, that the power and wisdom of God may now bring them into the heavenly realms of light and peace

### Week 21, Saturday

*1 Cor 1:26-31, Ps 33, Matt 25:14-30*

For our Holy Father, our bishops and priests, who have been given charge of the master's riches for the building up of His kingdom, that they will be faithful in their holy ministry

For the powerful, those of noble birth and great wealth, who guide the direction of world events, that they may be converted to the prudence that comes from God

That we may never bury our gifts and talents out of fear or laziness, but diligently put them to use for the good of all and the approval of the Master

For all of us partaking in this Eucharist, receiving the One who is our wisdom, our justice, our sanctification, that we may allow Him to work freely in our hearts this day

That our Blessed Mother may take into her care all the intentions of those who have asked our prayers, and bring to heaven our loved ones who have died

## Week 22, Monday

*1 Cor 2:1-5, Ps 119, Luke 4:16-30*

For all of us in the church of Jesus Christ, that through the ministry of true preaching our faith may rest not on human wisdom, but on the power of God

That world leaders may have the understanding and discernment that comes from putting God's laws first in their deliberations and decisions

That Jesus, whose preaching was met with violence and disbelief in His hometown, may find in us a resting place for the gracious words that come from His lips

For the poor, for captives of illness and trial, for the blind and the oppressed, that Jesus, who was anointed to bring them glad tidings, may lift their hearts and answer their hopes

For those who have kept company with Jesus crucified in the pains of death, that the Lord may now demonstrate His spirit and power in raising them to the life of heavenly joy

## Week 22, Tuesday

*1 Cor 2:10-16, Ps 145, Luke 4:31-37*

For our leaders and teachers in the church, that they may understand the things of God by the light of His Spirit, and speak of them in words taught by the Spirit

That the powerful and the influential of the world may no longer be natural men and women, refusing to accept God's wisdom, but instead put on the mind of Christ and make their decisions under His direction

That the authority and power of Jesus may be invoked over all unclean spirits and all forces of darkness, removing them from harming human souls and bodies

That the Lord may triumph in every unhappy human situation, faithful and holy in His works, lifting up all who are falling and raising up all who are bowed down

For our beloved departed ones, that the merciful and gracious Lord may be good and compassionate to them, bringing them to a place of light and peace

## Week 22, Wednesday

*1 Cor 3:1-9, Ps 33, Luke 4:38-44*

For our holy preachers and ministers in the church, who plant and water the seed of God's word in our lives, that the wages due their labors may begin with the joy of seeing us respond and grow in the spirit

That God, who fashions our hearts and knows all our works, may redirect the hearts of world leaders to put aside jealousy and rivalry, and to work together for the good of all

That we may imitate our Lord in His silent prayer, so that our efforts may be focused and united in the accomplishment of the Father's will

For all the sick entrusted to our prayers, and for those constrained under the influence of evil, that Jesus may stand over them in the fullness of His power and cast out everything that binds and oppresses them

For our dear ones who have died, and for all the holy souls in purgatory who wait patiently for the Lord, that in Him they may rejoice as He leads them out into the joys of heaven

## Week 22, Thursday

*1 Cor 3:18-23, Ps 24, Luke 5:1-11*

For all Christians, called to become fools for Christ because they believe in the wisdom of God, that they may be faithful to the Spirit who guides them

For those who are wise in the ways of the world, that they may realize that the wisdom of this world is foolishness in the eyes of God, and obtain grace to see everything as the Lord does

For vocations to the priesthood and religious life, that many more generous souls may have the courage to leave everything and follow Jesus

For all who seem to work hard through the long night of suffering and find nothing, that in obeying Jesus they may be gladdened by a great catch of healing and grace

For our beloved dead, that they may belong to Christ, as Christ belongs to God, in the joys of eternal happiness

## Week 22, Friday

*1 Cor 4:1-5, Ps 37, Luke 5:33-39*

For our Holy Father, our bishops and priests, servants of Christ and stewards of the mysteries of God, that they may always be trustworthy in God's eyes

That those in power in the world may commit their way to the Lord, so that He may make justice dawn among the nations and peace among the peoples

That we may be fresh wineskins for the effervescence and joy of the Gospel, expanding with the Word of God and allowing Jesus to stretch our capacity for His grace

For those who are fasting in the absence of the divine bridegroom, who are mourning and groaning under burdens of pain and misfortune, that Jesus my return and bring them joy and feasting again

For those who have died, for whom the Lord has brought to light what was hidden in their hearts in the hour of judgment, that they may soon be purified to sing His praise in heaven's glory

## Week 22, Saturday

*1 Cor 4:6-15, Ps 145, Luke 6:1-5*

That the apostles of our own day may become a spectacle to the world, consenting to be fools on Christ's account and showing forth His holiness and glory

For those who are strong, who are held in honor, who are wise and powerful, that they may use their influence in the service of justice, life, and peace

That we who enter into the house of God and eat the bread of offering may allow Jesus to be Lord of our hearts even as He is Lord of the Sabbath

For those who are hungry and thirsty, homeless, poorly clad, and roughly treated, that the followers of Jesus may see Him in them and reach out with love and care to help them

For our deceased loved ones, that our Blessed Mother may be their comfort in their time of purification, leading them soon to the joys of heaven

## Week 23, Monday

*1 Cor 5:1-8, Ps 8, Luke 6:6-11*

For our leaders in the church, that they may have the courage of St. Paul to name evil in her members, and the wisdom to apply a remedy

For the bloodthirsty and the deceitful among the powerful of the world, that their arrogance may be changed into humility and their deeds to justice

For all of us sharing this Eucharistic Banquet, that we may celebrate the feast of the Paschal Lamb with the unleavened bread of sincerity and truth

That Jesus, who had the compassion to reach out and cure in spite of the consequences to Himself, may restore all those we entrust with confidence to His healing power

For our dear ones who have died, that their purification may be accomplished swiftly, and that they may be glad and exult forever in the joy of God's holy name

## Week 23, Tuesday

*1 Cor 6:1-11, Ps 149, Luke 6:12-19*

That Jesus, who prayed all night before choosing His first apostles, may be the example for how our apostolic leaders today must prepare for their important decisions

That the leaders of Christian nations may be among the holy ones who have the wisdom to judge the world, governing their people with justice and morality

That Jesus may again call many disciples to Himself from the ranks of our young people, and choose from them His close followers who are willing to imitate His poverty, chastity, and obedience

For all those in need of restoration and grace, that power may come forth from Jesus to heal them all

For those who have gone before us marked with the sign of faith, who have been washed and sanctified in the name of Jesus, that they may now be rejoicing with Him in heaven

## Week 23, Wednesday

*1 Cor 7:25-31, Ps 45, Luke 6:20-26*

That the virgins of the church may be a shining example to us who have our eyes fixed on the return of the Bridegroom, showing the detachment necessary to live in a world that is quickly passing away

That world leaders may not be those who are rich, full, and well spoken of, but men and women of integrity, justice, and truth, upholding human dignity in all they do

That the reversal of human values proclaimed by Jesus in His beatitudes may channel our choices into the divine sphere that defines the kingdom of heaven

For all who are weeping and poor and persecuted, that they may have a deep sense of their blessedness in the eyes of God, and the joy of the help and love of Jesus' followers

For our deceased loved ones, for whom the world as we know it has passed away, that they may be at peace in God's presence and may help us to keep our eyes fixed on our ultimate resting place

## Week 23, Thursday

*1 Cor 8:1b-7, 11-13, Ps 139, Luke 6:27-38*

For our Holy Father, our bishops and priests, that they may build up the spirits of those who are weak in faith by their teaching and example

That our world leaders may be among those who hear the divine wisdom of Jesus when He speaks of engaging rather than punishing our enemies, thus building up the ways of peace

That we may joyfully take advantage of the opportunity to escape God's judgment by refusing to judge others, and forgive in order that we ourselves may be forgiven

For those who are hated, cursed, mistreated, and persecuted, that they may have the grace to return good for evil, imitating the kindness and mercy of our God

For our dear ones who have passed through the doors of death, that they may experience in heaven the gifts Jesus speaks of, gifts given in good measure, packed together, shaken down, and overflowing

### Week 23, Friday

*1 Cor 9:16-19, 22-27, Ps 84, Luke 6:39-42*

For the preachers of the Gospel, that they may carry their obligation willingly, deserving the divine recompense for their stewardship

That the powerful and the influential may not run aimlessly, but train themselves to pursue justice and morality in the world today

That we may remove all obstacles to our own sight before trying to correct the lives of others, keeping our gaze on what needs the remedy of God's merciful grace in ourselves

For the gift of good vocations, that many more young souls may find a home and a nest among the altars of the Lord of Hosts, setting their hearts on the pilgrimage of consecration

For all the intentions recommended to our prayers, and especially for our beloved dead, that the Lord may withhold no good thing from those for whom we pray

### Week 23, Saturday

*1 Cor 10:14-22, Ps 116, Luke 6:43-49*

For our holy priests, who offer the cup of blessing that is the Blood of Christ, and the bread that is the Body of Christ, that they may help us to be one Body as we partake in this Eucharistic Banquet

For our political leaders, that they may be good trees, bearing the fruit of decisions for the building up of a moral society

That our spiritual homes may be built upon the rock foundation of obedience to the words of Jesus, so that the floods and rising rivers of life may not be able to destroy us

That Our Lady may take under the mantle of her protection all who are in need of our loving intercession, comforting them with her maternal care

For those who have died and whose works have been tested on the day of judgment, that their good fruit may accompany them to the celestial dwelling places

## Week 24, Monday

*1 Cor 11:17-26, 33, Ps 40, Luke 7:1-10*

That our celebrations of the Holy Eucharist may be feasts of charity among ourselves as well as humble worship before the Father of us all

That Jesus may find faith among the leaders of the nations, and the will to put that faith into practice through just and morally upright decisions and policies

That the centurion's humble trust may be our own attitude toward Jesus, especially as we prepare to receive Him under our roof in Holy Communion

That Jesus, who willingly healed the centurion's slave, may say the word of power and compassion over all the sick and distressed who have asked our prayers

For those who have died in Christ after having partaken of the new covenant in the blood of the Lord, that they may now be joined to the One Body of Christ in the joys of Heaven

## Week 24 Tuesday

*1 Cor 12:12-14, 27-31a, Ps 100, Luke 7:11-17*

For the apostles and teachers of the church, first in rank among the Spirit's gifted ones, that their words may be respected and their deeds be worthy of their office

That great prophets may arise in the world today, gifted with power to raise hopes to life and find ways to defend human dignity and uphold God's justice

For all of us in the church, baptized in one Spirit into one Body, members of one another under Jesus our Head, that all may work to build her up in harmony and in beauty

For widows, for those who have been bereaved, for the families of those with terminal illness, that the Savior may be moved to pity for them, and dry up their tears with His peace

For our dear departed ones, that Jesus may raise them up to new life with the same power He showed the young man who had died in today's Gospel

## Week 24, Wednesday

*1 Cor 12:31–13:13, Ps 33, Luke 7:31-35*

For our Holy Father, our bishops and priests, that the gifts they have been given for leadership may be perfected by the greatest gift of love

For world leaders, that they may not be pompous, seeking their own interests and brooding over injuries, but act in a loving way, looking always to the common good

That all followers of Christ may respect the gifts of tongues and knowledge and prophesying, but strive eagerly for the faith, hope, and love which are greater than all other spiritual gifts

For those laboring under the dirge of sickness, poverty, addiction, or grief, that Jesus may be for them a new song of gladness and grace, helping them to resume the dance of life

For our loved ones who have died, that as the reward for their patience and kindness, all the fruits of love may be theirs in the perfect adulthood of the heavenly kingdom

## Week 24, Thursday

*1 Cor 15:1-11, Ps 118, Luke 7:36-50*

For the apostles of our own day, that they may continue to preach the word they have received from Scripture and from the church's tradition without deviation for the sake of our salvation

For God-fearing statesmen and peace-makers, that grace may be effective in them, supporting their toil in their negotiations and decisions

That those who have sought love in affairs and entanglements may discover Jesus, and bring Him their alabaster flask of ointment in pure repentance and gratitude

For those in need of mercy, healing, and forgiveness, that as they come to Jesus with their tears they may hear His loving words restoring them to grace and wholeness

For our beloved dead, that they might be alive and joyous in the heavenly kingdom, declaring the works of the Lord, loving and extolling Him for His power and tenderness

## Week 24, Friday

*1 Cor 15:12-20, Ps 17, Luke 8:1-3*

For the church, that within her walls Christ may always be preached as raised from the dead, so that preaching may not be empty and our faith may not be in vain

That those who have faith in Christ's ultimate victory of life may stand up and be counted for their convictions, turning the tide of public policy to a culture of life and a civilization of love

That the help of holy women may always be welcome in the church as they were with Jesus and His apostles, and that their gifts and special graces may be valued and honored

For all the intentions we bring to this Holy Sacrifice, especially for those in special need who have asked for our prayers, that they may be hidden in the shadow of God's wings and filled with His love

For those who have gone before us in faith, believing in the resurrection, that Christ, who is the first fruits of those who have fallen asleep, may bring them with joy into the presence of the Father

## Week 24, Saturday

*1 Cor 15:35-37, 42-49, Ps 56, Luke 8:4-15*

For the pastors and teachers of the church who work so hard at sowing the good seed, that they may not be discouraged over lack of results, but have the joy of seeing many bear fruit

For those whose progress in love has been stifled by the cares and riches and pleasures of life, and for those prophets who try to awaken their consciences

For all who are tempted and are falling away from the Word of God, that they may encounter someone willing to spread new seeds of forgiveness and hope in their hearts

For all who suffer from terminal illnesses, that with the help of faith they may become willing to be sown in weakness so as to be raised up in the likeness of the Risen Christ

For all who have died, that Jesus may be for them the life-giving spirit that lifts them up to new life in heaven's glory

## Week 25, Monday

*Prov 3:27-34, Ps 15, Luke 8:16-18*

For our teachers in the church, that their lives may radiate the effects of truly hearing God's word, so as to reinforce their preaching and help us put it into practice

For world leaders, that they may withdraw from arrogance and treat other nations with justice, plotting no evil against peace

For all of us who have so much of God's grace and are given even more in this Eucharist, that the living presence of Jesus may come to life in our words and actions

For all who are in a season of suffering, that those who can comfort and help them will do so at once and not make them wait until tomorrow

For all who have been humbled by passing through the experience of death, that God, who shows kindness to the little ones, may free them from sin and bring them into the realms of light and peace

## Week 25, Tuesday

*Prov 21:1-6, Ps 119, Luke 8:19-21*

For our holy priests and ministers in the church, that they may have the discernment to guide us in the paths of the Lord's commandments by both word and example

For peace, that the hearts of world leaders may truly be streams that the Lord can direct as He pleases

That we may be counted with Mary among the brothers and sisters of the Lord, who hear His word and act upon it

That we may not be among those who shut our ears to the cry of the poor, the sick, the helpless unborn, but champion their cause so that we ourselves may be heard in our time of need

For our beloved departed ones, who set the ordinances of the Lord before them and chose the way of truth, that they may now receive their reward in the kingdom of heaven

## Week 25, Wednesday

*Prov 30:5-9, Ps 119, Luke 9:1-6*

That those who proclaim God's word may add nothing to it in their preaching but practice it as it stands, thus winning divine approval for their faithfulness

That falsehood and lying may be far from the minds of the powerful and the influential, and that integrity and justice may be their goals

For the grace of good vocations, that Jesus may be able to summon new apostles to proclaim the kingdom of God

That Jesus, who sent the Twelve to heal the sick and cure diseases, may now exert His merciful power to restore all those we bring before Him in prayer today

For those who have entered into the despoilment of death, that Jesus may raise them up to life and glory in His heavenly kingdom

## Week 25, Thursday

*Eccl 1:2-11, Ps 90, Luke 9:7-9*

That the spirit of John the Baptist and Elijah and all the prophets may be at work in the church, pointing unfailingly to the One who surpasses and completes them all: Jesus Christ

For political candidates and leaders of nations, that they may have the biblical perspective to see through illusions of power and fame to the lasting reality of service to the cause of human dignity and world peace

That God may return to us and help us to number our days aright, that we may gain wisdom of heart in the science of divine love

For all the intentions confided to our prayers, that the Lord may have pity on His servants, filling them at daybreak with His kindness and giving them joy and gladness again

For our beloved dead, whose remembrance we hold in our hearts, that our prayer for them may speed their entry into the kingdom where God will make all things new

### Week 25, Friday

*Eccl 3:1-11, Ps 144, Luke 9:18-22*

For our Holy Father, our bishops and priests, that they may proclaim Jesus as the Christ of God and His way of the cross as the way to God

That the Lord, our rock, our stronghold, our deliverer, may uphold every work that is done in the world today for life, for justice, and for peace

That as we pass through the changing seasons of our lives, we may allow God to keep our eyes fixed on the goal of eternal salvation

For all who are experiencing a time of weeping, loss, rending asunder, that our prayers may uphold them until healing resumes its work in their lives

For those who have gone through their time of uprooting and death, that in Christ Jesus and through His passion, new life may be poured out upon them

### Week 25, Saturday

*Eccl 11:9–12:8, Psalm 90, Luke 9:43b-45*

For our beloved priests and all our leaders in the church, that they may understand and preach the hidden wisdom of the cross and the dynamics of redemption

For all who work for human rights and human dignity, especially the basic right to life, that the Lord may prosper the work of their hands and hearts, so that He can freely grant us peace

For the young, that the ways of their hearts and the vision of their eyes may be acceptable to God, and that they may remember their Creator in the days of their joy

For the elderly and the sick, for those who are approaching death, that before the pitcher is shattered at the spring, they may make their peace with God and close their eyes rich in His grace

For all our loved ones whose life breath has returned to the God who gave it, that they may be with Him in His kingdom of light and love

## Week 26, Monday

*Job 1:6-22, Ps 17, Luke 9:46-50*

That the members of the church may always be respectful of the good work done by non-members, remembering Jesus' words: "Whoever is not against you is for you"

For the nations whom God has surrounded with His protection, who prosper in all directions like Job, that they may reverence God in the time of their prosperity and do His will

That we may never be concerned about being the greatest among the followers of Jesus, but be content to be the least, ever learning and depending wholly upon the Lord

For those who have been visited with disasters in their family and their possessions, that they may realize that nothing is ours permanently on earth, so that they may pass through the trial with reverence and serenity

For our dear departed ones, that they soon may be purified to take their place among the angels who come to present themselves before the Lord

## Week 26, Tuesday

*Job 3:1-3, 11-17, 2-23, Ps 88, Luke 9:51-56*

That Jesus, who resolutely determined to journey to Jerusalem and His painful sacrifice, may help the church to face persecutions and difficulties with confidence in God's power to uphold her

For the kings and counselors of the earth, for the rulers of nations, that they may build their destinies on God's laws so that they may enjoy His blessing

That we may never earn Jesus' rebuke for desiring vengeance on those who cause us harm, but forgive and endure like the Master

For the toilers, for the bitter in spirit, for those whom God has hemmed in with suffering, that they may persevere in faith and trust until the moment of divine deliverance

For those who have died, that this Holy Sacrifice may help in their purification so that they can be tranquil and at rest in the kingdom of heaven

### Week 26, Wednesday

*Job 9:1-12, 14-16, Ps 88, Luke 9:57-62*

For our Holy Father, our bishops and priests, who have left all to follow Jesus and proclaim the kingdom of God, that they may never look back

That world leaders may be just before God in their decisions and policies, upholding human dignity and working for justice and peace

That the transcendent and all powerful God, so reverenced by Job, may do marvelous things beyond reckoning for all of us who approach Him humbly in this Eucharist

For the poor and the displaced, for refugees and immigrants, that Jesus, who in His life also had nowhere to lay His head, may uphold them in their wanderings and help them to find a home

For our beloved dead, that God, who is wise in heart and mighty in strength, may purify them quickly in His wisdom and love and bring them rejoicing into His divine presence

### Week 26, Thursday

*Job 19:21-27, Ps 27, Luke 10:1-12*

For the laborers in the harvest, that they may not be overwhelmed by the magnitude of the task, and that the Master of the harvest may hear our prayer to send out new laborers to help them

For all the nations who have heard the proclamation of the Good News, that they may not be among those who refuse to act according to the laws of the kingdom of God

For all of us sharing in this Holy Sacrifice, that Christ's peace may rest upon us and that we may carry peace as our gift wherever we go

For all the intentions we bring to this altar, for our loved ones, for all who have asked our prayers, and for those most in need of loving intercession

For those who have gone before us, that they may now know that their Vindicator lives, and that they may see Him in the glory of heaven's face-to-face vision

## Week 26, Friday

*Job 38:1, 12-21, 40:3-5, Ps 139,*
*Luke 10:13-16*

That the mighty deeds of Jesus may have a profound effect on the faith of the church and her holy ministers, for repentance and renewal

For the re-evangelization of the nations who are beginning to lose hold of the faith, and that the Gospel may change the outlook and decisions of those who lead them

That Job's encounter with the living God may help us to be more reverent in our prayer and more patient in the mysterious trials God sends us

For those who have walked in the depths of the abyss of sickness, poverty, depression, and pain, that God may show them the way to the dwelling place of light and peace again

For our dear departed ones who have come face to face with God in all His majesty, that they may know the power of His might and the tenderness of His mercy

## Week 26, Saturday

*Job 42:1-3, 5-6, 12-17, Ps 119,*
*Luke 10:17-24*

For our Holy Father, our bishops and priests, our missionaries and apostles, that they may experience the power of the name of Jesus in overcoming all evil resistance to His saving work in the world

For the gift of peace, that we may be made worthy of this gift by our work for justice, for life, and for the dignity of all

That the humility practiced by Job and recommended by Jesus may be ours, so that we may take our place with Mary among the little ones favored by the Lord

For all who know afflictions, and have been humbled by adversity and by the dawning awareness of the sovereignty of God, that like Job, they may know the returning blessing of His healing and abundance

For all our faithful departed, that their eyes may be blessed with what they see in the face-to-face vision of Jesus and His beloved Father

## Week 27, Monday

*Gal 1:6-12, Ps 111, Luke 10:25-37*

For all who are entrusted with the Gospel of Jesus Christ, that they may preach it fully, faithfully, and with conviction, whatever the cost

For peace in every part of the world where war has robbed and stripped and injured the people, and that there may be good Samaritans willing to bind up and heal

For all who have been led astray from the Gospel of Christ, that the divine truth, sure in all its precepts, wrought in truth and equity, ratified forever, may by its very endurance win them back

That we may allow our hearts to be moved with compassion for those who lie, despoiled and discouraged, along our path, and hasten to help them, generously and at our own expense

For our beloved departed ones, that they may find their journey complete in God's kingdom of love, truth, and joy

## Week 27, Tuesday

*Gal 1:13-24, Ps 139, Luke 10:38-42*

For the church, that those who are persecuting and harassing her may, like St. Paul, come to the point of personal conversion

That those who are zealots for their ancestral traditions and their religious beliefs to the point of doing violence to others, may come to understand the necessity of tolerance and respect

That with Martha we may be eager to serve Jesus in others, but without anxiety or worry, taking time to be like Mary, listening silently and lovingly at the feet of the Lord

That the poor, the sick, the hungry, and grieving little ones may find a home of hospitality and a loving welcome in Christian hearts

For those who have died, that God, who has probed them and knows them well, may forgive their sins and purify them quickly to enter the joys of heaven

## Week 27, Wednesday

*Gal 2:1-2, 7-14, Ps 117, Luke 11:1-4*

For our Holy Father and all the leaders of the church, that in the tradition of the fearless St. Paul, they may continue to be straightforward about the truth of the Gospel

That world leaders may not lack for prophets who oppose them when they are clearly in the wrong, so that the work of life, justice, and peace may go forward

That we who approach the throne of mercy in the sacrament of reconciliation, may remember always that the Father desires us to forgive as we are forgiven

For all who need our prayers in a time of personal crisis, that Jesus who teaches us to pray, may also answer our petitions on their behalf

For our beloved departed ones, that they may be welcomed into the heavenly kingdom for which they prayed while they were on earth

## Week 27, Thursday

*Gal 3:1-5, Benedictus, Luke 11:5-13*

For the church, that she may raise up and fearlessly display before the eyes of all the Crucified One in whom she has placed all her faith

That all men and women who grope in the darkness toward the peace that alone can nourish the heart, may knock insistently at the door of the Divine Friend for this precious gift

For those who dedicate themselves to the apostolate of prayer, that today's Gospel may be encouragement to keep up their insistence, since they have the assurance that they will be heard in the end

For all who have asked for our prayers, who trust in the power of prayer, that together we may persevere in our asking and seeking, confident in the One who makes all things work for our good

For our departed loved ones, that our Father, who knows how to give all good things, will draw them into His loving embrace in heaven

## Week 27, Friday

*Gal 3:7-14, Ps 111, Luke 11:15-26*

For the church, that she may use her power to drive out demons by the finger of God, so that the kingdom of God may come upon all who hear her

That world leaders may learn to respect the dignity of all, that there may truly be justice and peace

That we may truly be the children of Abraham, living by faith even in hard times, giving glory to God by our trust and confidence

That Jesus, who is master of every force of evil, may be invoked and trusted by those who are bound in body, mind, and spirit, so that His power may cleanse and stand guard over them

For our dear ones who have gone before us, that the faith they had while on earth may be their salvation now in heaven

## Week 27, Saturday

*Gal 3:22-29, Ps 105, Luke 11:27-28*

For our Holy Father, our bishops and priests, that they make take the role of exemplars and make themselves guardians of our freedom and faith in Christ

For our leaders in the world, that their decisions may be influenced by attention to God and to His will for life, justice and peace

For all Christians who have not yet discovered the freedom of their faith, that they may let go of any legalism that prevents them from tasting the joy of being children and heirs of God

For all who are in a period of sickness, mourning, or financial distress, that Mary, who endured every sorrow with her Divine Son, may be their light and comfort

For our beloved dead, who clothed themselves with Christ in Baptism and are heirs according to the promise, that they may receive their inheritance in the heavenly kingdom

## Week 28, Monday

*Gal 4:22-27, Ps 113, Luke 11:29-32*

For the ministers of the church, that they may be a sign of holiness for the people of today as Jonah was a sign to the people of Nineveh

That this generation may not be an evil generation in the sight of God, but that our leaders may turn again to the paths of life, justice, and morality

That we may rejoice in the holy freedom for which Christ has set us free, and refuse to submit to the yoke of sin and error in our Christian lives

That God, who raises the lowly from the dust, may comfort and heal all those who have recommended themselves to our prayers

For those who have died and passed through the judgment, that the Savior may be their advocate before the Father, bringing them soon to light and peace

## Week 28, Tuesday

*Gal 5:1-6, Ps 119, Luke 11:37-41*

For our leaders and teachers in the church, that the word of truth may be found in their mouths and the commands of God be in their minds and hearts

For the conversion of those who are blinded to the evils of our day, that government leaders may respect the dignity of every human being, so that we may be blessed with peace

That we who have been set free by Christ may never submit to the slavery of sin, but continue to grow into the fullness of our inheritance in Christ Jesus

For all who have need of prayer in a season of physical, emotional, or financial difficulty, that they may receive help from those whose faith is working through love

For our beloved departed ones, who through the Spirit, by faith, awaited the hope of righteousness on earth, that they may now be receiving its fullness in heaven

### Week 28, Wednesday

*Gal 5:18-25, Ps 1, Luke 11:42-46*

For our holy priests and bishops, that they may be the first to lift the burdens laid on the people of God, replacing them with the light and easy yoke of Christ

That our world leaders may be among those who delight in the law of the Lord, planted near the running waters of justice and yielding the fruit of peace

That we who live in the Spirit may follow the Spirit's lead, bringing forth the fruits of love, patience, self control, and faithfulness

For those who are crucified by illness, depression, abuse, or grief, that they may know God's compassion and the kindness and gentleness of the followers of Jesus

For our dear ones who have gone before us in death, that the Lord may watch over their ways, leading them soon into His glorious kingdom

### Week 28, Thursday

*Eph 1:1-10, Ps 98, Luke 11:47-54*

For the church, all of us who partake of the Divine Blood in which we have our redemption, and receive in the Body of Christ every spiritual blessing in the heavens, that we may carry this treasure in faithful hearts

For world leaders, that they may be agents of the justice and diplomacy that lead to the blessing of peace

That we who are destined for adoption through Christ Jesus, to the praise of the glory of His grace, may live in accord with the dignity of our calling

For all who are in a season of suffering or special need at this time, that through our loving prayer, grace and peace may be their portion today

For our beloved departed ones, that they may have forgiveness in accord with the riches of Christ's grace, and come soon into the joys of heaven

## Week 28, Friday

*Eph 1:11-14, Ps 33, Luke 12:1-7*

For the church, the people the Lord has chosen to be His own, that her holy preachers may keep the truth of our divine inheritance always before us to strengthen our faith

For world leaders, that they may say and do nothing in the dark that will not stand up to the scrutiny of the light, but follow God's ways honestly in their policies and decisions

That all who have heard the Gospel of our salvation and been sealed with the Holy Spirit may live for the praise of God's glory as His own precious possession

For the sick and those in distress of any kind, that they may be consoled with the certainty that they do not escape God's compassionate notice, and are worth more than many sparrows

For those who have gone before us marked with the sign of faith, that they may soon come into their full inheritance in the kingdom of heaven

## Week 28, Saturday

*Eph 1:15-23, Ps 8, Luke 12:8-12*

For the zeal of the church and her leaders, that we may be unafraid to acknowledge Jesus before others, looking forward to the moment when He will acknowledge us before the angels of God

For those who work prophetically for justice and peace, that the Holy Spirit may teach them what to say before the authorities and rulers of this world

That the eyes of our hearts may be enlightened, that we may understand how well founded is our hope in the might of the Father and the glory of the Son, our Lord Jesus Christ

For all the intentions we carry to this Eucharist, that Jesus, who is the fullness of the One who fills all things with compassion and power, may help all those we bring to Him in faith

For those who have died, that Mary, mother of the one who is seated above every principality and power, may use her motherly influence on their behalf

### Week 29, Monday

*Eph 2:1-10, Ps 100, Luke 12:13-21*

For our leaders in the church, that they may joyfully show the way to practice the good works for which we were all created in Christ Jesus through His grace

For the prophetic voices that speak for the cause of justice and of respect for the dignity of each human being, that they may be heard and heeded in our world

That Christians may learn to become rich in what matters to God, sharing their resources with their less fortunate brothers and sisters

For all who have asked our prayers in a time of physical, emotional, or financial crisis, that God, who is rich in mercy, may show the great love He has for each of them in blessings of healing and restoration

For our beloved departed ones, that they may enter the gates of heaven with thanksgiving and God's courts with songs of praise

### Week 29, Tuesday

*Eph 2:12-22, Ps 85, Luke 12:35-38*

For the church, whose members are fellow citizens with the holy ones and members of the household of God, that Jesus may be the cornerstone of our faith, holding the whole structure together

That Jesus may be our peace, breaking down the dividing wall of enmity between peoples and nations, and reconciling all with God

That Jesus, our Master, who already serves us at the banquet of this Eucharist, may always find us awake and vigilant, with our lamps shining in our hands before His face

For those who feel they are without hope and without God in the world, caught in misfortune, illness, addiction, or grief, that Jesus may relieve them with divine compassion

For those who have heard the Master's knock at the hour of death, that He may forgive all sin, and reward their measure of vigilance with a share in His own joy in heaven

## Week 29, Wednesday

*Eph 3:2-12, Isa 12, Luke 12:39-48*

For our leaders in the church, that they may be faithful and prudent stewards of gifts of the Master's grace

For world leaders of Christian nations, that they who know the will of God may make preparations to act in accord with the demands of peace

That we may be servants on whom the Lord can depend, ready to welcome Him at any time, careful in our duties of love and care toward each other

For all who are in a season of distress and weakness and have asked our prayers, that they may know the strength and courage that come from God

For our beloved departed ones, that by the power of this Holy Sacrifice they may now share in the mysteries of God hidden from this age, the mysteries of light and joy

## Week 29, Thursday

*Eph 3:14-21, Ps 33, Luke 12:49-53*

For our leaders and teachers in the church, that they may be willing agents of the holy fire that Jesus came to cast upon the earth

That world leaders may act in accord with the designs of God's heart, loving justice and right, and upholding the cause of peace

For all of us, that we may be strengthened with power through the Holy Spirit, rooted and grounded in love, and filled with the fullness of God

For all who have special need of prayer at this time, that they may come to experience the breadth and length and height and depth of God's love in the mercy they experience today

For our beloved dead, that through the power of God, who is able to accomplish more than we ask or imagine, they may be freed from all sin and brought rejoicing into heaven

## Week 29, Friday

*Eph 4:1-6, Ps 24, Luke 12:54-59*

For our Holy Father, our bishops and priests, that they may form consciences in the teaching of the church, that we may be equipped to judge for ourselves what is right

That world leaders may come to heed the prophetic voices that speak out for life and justice, so that we may be united in the bond of peace

That as Christians aware of the dignity of our call we may live in humility and gentleness, bearing with one another through love, and promoting the unity of one faith

For all who need healing of body or soul, that our humble prayers and the power of this Holy Sacrifice may bring them the blessings they seek

For our dear departed ones, who longed to see God's face, that they may now ascend the mountain of the Lord and stand firm in His holy place

## Week 29, Saturday

*Eph 4:7-16, Ps 122, Luke 13:1-9*

For our pastors and teachers, that they may equip us for building up the Body of Christ to the full measure of His divine stature

That the church, joined and held together by every supporting ligament, may give united witness to our world leaders for the cause of life, truth, justice, and peace

That we may not be barren fig trees in God's garden, but respond to the cultivation of Christ for the harvest of good works

For the poor, the sick, the forgotten and lonely little ones of our world, that through the intercession of Mary, their gentle mother, they may know relief and consolation

That Jesus, who ascended far above all the heavens, may fill with good things our brothers and sisters who have died, and bring them in His triumphal train into the kingdom of heaven

## Week 30, Monday

*Eph 4:32-5:8, Ps 1, Luke 13:10-17*

For our teachers in the church, that they may be like trees planted firmly beside the running water of God's Word, drawing upon His living grace to produce all the fruits of their ministry

For peace; that all who are caught in the chains of their own violent behavior, may come to see their offenses against justice for the darkness they are, and turn to the light of holiness and love

That we may imitate God who has forgiven us in Christ, becoming kind, compassionate, and forgiving toward each other

For all who are bent down and drained of strength under a long burden of suffering, those crippled by physical, emotional or spiritual sickness, that Jesus may lay His hands on them and set them free

For all our dear departed ones, that they may encounter a Sabbath of liberation and joy at the hands of Christ in the Father's kingdom

## Week 30, Tuesday

*Eph 5:21-33, Ps 128, Luke 13:18-21*

That the great mystery of the spiritual union between Christ and His church may help us to realize how beautiful and holy she is, that we may be eager for her unity and growth

That the nations of the world may return to a concept of marriage as the union between one man and one woman, so that the home may again be a nurturing sanctuary of life

That the kingdom of God may take root within us and put forth large branches in which the poor and the little ones of the earth can find a nest of peace and joy

For those who feel the heaviness of unrelieved trial, that into their lives the leaven of the kingdom may be worked through the love of the followers of Christ, raising them up again in joy

For our loved ones who have died, that they might soon be purified to appear without spot or blemish before the heavenly Bridegroom in His glorious kingdom

### Week 30, Wednesday

*Eph 6:1-9, Ps 145, Luke 13:22-30*

For our leaders in the church, that like St. Paul they may call us to obedience with exhortations suited to the station of each one, that conform us to the Gospel

That the Gospel of life, upheld by the church and her faithful, may shed its light on the deliberations of our national and world leaders

That we may be among those who enter through the narrow gate, that we may not be locked out of the banquet by the Master, but be welcomed as companions and faithful followers

For the sick, the poor, and all who are suffering, that their experience of being the last and the least may be transformed into knowing that they are the aristocracy of God's kingdom

For our beloved departed ones, that the Lord, who lifts up all who are falling and raises those who are bowed down, will bring them rejoicing into the wedding feast of heaven

### Week 30, Thursday

*Eph 6:10-20, Ps 144, Luke 13:31-35*

For our holy ministers in the church, that like Jesus they may proceed on course until all of His purposes for them are accomplished

For peace, especially the peace of Jerusalem, and that the followers of Jesus will be able to remain and to thrive in this holy city, propagating the Gospel of peace

For all of us engaged in the hidden but fierce spiritual warfare with the forces of evil in our world, that truth, faith, justice, and zeal may protect us as we defend ourselves with the sword of the Spirit

That we may pray constantly and attentively for all in the holy company who are laboring under sickness, depression, grief, or poverty, that they may be consoled and helped

For our dear ones who have died, that Jesus may gather them under His wings, giving them light and rest in His holy shelter

## Week 30, Friday

*Phil 1:1-11, Ps 111, Luke 14:1-6*

For our Holy Father, our bishops and priests, who like Jesus are observed carefully by friend and foe alike, that they may always act with mercy and truth

That the defense and confirmation of the Gospel of life by all Christians may influence the political deliberations of every country

For all followers of Jesus, that their love may increase more and more in knowledge and perception, to discern what is of value in His service and do it

For all who are in a season of sickness, weakness, poverty, and pain, that the merciful and healing love of Jesus may be extended to them by His disciples

For our beloved departed ones, that God who began the good work of grace in them at their baptism, may complete it in the full glory of His kingdom

## Week 30, Saturday

*Phil 1:18b-26, Ps 42, Luke 14:1, 7-11*

For our holy priests and ministers in the church, that they may faithfully continue in the service of God's people for their progress and joy in the faith

For world leaders, that they may not try to take the places of honor and prestige, but rather let their lives of justice and integrity commend them before all

That we may imitate the example and follow the teaching of Jesus, letting humility be our companion and guide

For all who are experiencing sickness, weakness, or trouble in their lives, that our loving prayer may support them and lead them to a new place of joy and thanksgiving

For our beloved departed ones, that they may now be with Christ and see that their death has been a gain for them, as Our Lady gathers them into the joys of heaven

## Week 31, Monday

*Phil 2:1-4, Ps 131, Luke 14:12-14*

For the church, that we may make Christ's joy complete by our union in spirit and ideals, possessing the one love that is His gift to us

That world leaders may refrain from acting out of rivalry or conceit, but truly serve the interests of all, especially the poorest and most defenseless

That we may provide a feast of love to those who are left out of the mainstream of attractiveness and wealth, confident of the reward we will enjoy together with them in the banquet halls of heaven

For the beggars, the crippled, the lame, and the blind in our midst, for all who suffer, that we may offer them the hospitality of our time and attention and loving care

For our dear ones who have died, that they may be found pure and worthy of God at the resurrection of the just

## Week 3, Tuesday

*Phil 2:5-11, Ps 22, Luke 14:15-24*

For the church gathered around the table of the kingdom of God, that we may be grateful guests who will in turn prepare a feast of love and peace for others

That the powerful and the influential may not be so distracted by business and other occupations that they would ignore the invitation of God to justice and morality in their deeds

For the return of the spirit of humility and obedience and vulnerable love to the earth, that our age may be redeemed by the self-emptying of those whose attitude has become like that of Christ

For those who have been humbled by pain and distress, that they may unite themselves to Jesus in His willingness to accept even death, so that God may raise them up again in joy and hope

For all who have died and who sleep in the earth, that Jesus may be their life and purification, bringing them soon into the bliss of heaven's light

## Week 31, Wednesday

*Phil 2:12-18, Ps 27, Luke 14:25-33*

For our Holy Father, our bishops and priests, that in their care for us they may not labor in vain, but have the joy of seeing us shine like lights in the world

For our national leaders, that God may be in them, creating both the desire and the work to care for the life and dignity of each human being

For all of us, that we may consider carefully the cost of discipleship, and give up all that can hold us back from following Jesus as He carries His cross to show us the way

For all who have asked for our prayers in a time of special need or suffering, that through our loving prayer the Lord may be for them their light and their salvation

For our beloved dead, that they may be quickly purified and see the bounty of the Lord in the land of the living

## Week 31, Thursday

*Phil 3:3-8a, Ps 105, Luke 15:1-10*

For our shepherds in the church, that our prayer may help them in their humble and dedicated search for the lost ones who are so precious to God and to His angels

That God's judgments may prevail throughout all the earth in the hearts of those who have power and influence, so that they may work for life, for justice, and for peace

That we may reappraise all the gains of this world as loss compared to the supreme good of knowing Christ Jesus our Lord, and follow Him with a sincere and dedicated heart

That there may be new cause for rejoicing in the hearts of all those who have asked our prayers in a time of sorrow or pain

For our beloved departed ones, that Jesus may set them on His shoulders with great joy and bring them to their everlasting home

## Week 31, Friday

*Phil 3:1–4:1, Ps 122, Luke 16:1-8*

For our leaders in the church, that their exemplary lives may reveal Christ, and they may help us to stand firm in the Lord

For our leaders who occupy the judgement seats in the world, especially whose who are Christian, that they may remember that their true citizenship is in heaven and work to build up peace and justice on earth

For those who are skilled in taking initiative in the affairs of commerce, that they may apply their good business sense to investing in wealth that will last forever, by sharing their riches as Jesus recommends

For all the sick, the poor, the forgotten elderly, the prisoners, and all who need our prayers, that this Holy Sacrifice may lighten their burdens and bring them joy of heart

For our beloved dead, that they may go up with rejoicing to the house of the Lord and take their place forever in the heavenly Jerusalem

## Week 31, Saturday

*Phil 4:10-19, Ps 112, Luke 16:9-15*

For the members of the church, that our generosity towards the servants of God may be a fragrant aroma, an acceptable sacrifice, pleasing to our heavenly Father

For the wealthy and the powerful, that they may learn to handle dishonest wealth in a way that will foster the work of justice, life, and peace in the world

That we may make a strong choice for God as our sole master, and subordinate all other riches and resources to His will, so that He may entrust us with true wealth

For those in humble circumstances, who are hungry and in need, who are sick and lonely, that with St. Paul they may discover the secret of equanimity until their needs are supplied by loving hearts

For our dear ones who have gone before us, that through the intercession of our Blessed Mother, they may soon be received into eternal dwellings of light and joy

## Week 32, Monday

*Titus 1:1-9, Ps 24, Luke 17:1-6*

For our shepherds in the church, that they may be lovers of goodness, temperate, just, holy, self controlled, and holding fast to the true message of the Gospel

For leaders of Christian nations, that they may be people of faith and lovers of life in all its stages, promoting justice and peace in the world

For the courage to confront and correct what is wrong, and for the humility to be open to challenge and correction, that truth may do its work of healing in us

For all the sick and the suffering, the poor and those in prison, that our faith may grow like a mustard seed so that our prayers for them may be effective in healing and new hope

For our dear departed loved ones, that their sharing in our common faith may now bring them grace and peace before our Father and the Lord Jesus Christ

## Week 32, Tuesday

*Titus 2:1-8, 11-14, Ps 37, Luke 17:7-10*

For our shepherds in the church, that they may be models of good deeds in every respect, with dignity, integrity in their teaching, and sound speech

For world leaders, that they may live temperately and justly in this age, showing respect for life and working for peace

For all God's servants, that they may do their appointed work cheerfully and with patient submission, looking forward to the rewards of heaven

For all who need our prayers: the sick, the unemployed, and the poor, that the grace of God may appear in their lives with healing, hope, and guidance

For our dear ones who have died, that as they were wholehearted in doing the Lord's will on earth, their inheritance may now last forever in His kingdom

### Week 32, Wednesday

*Titus 3:1-7, Ps 23, Luke 17:11-19*

For our Holy Father, our bishops and priests, that they may be good shepherds, leading God's flock to the verdant pastures and restful waters of truth and goodness

For magistrates and authorities, that they may operate under the control of the natural law that God has implanted in every human heart, and render decisions that uphold life, justice, and peace

That we may be among the most grateful people, returning to thank Jesus from our hearts for all His favors, and especially for the great grace of our salvation

For all who stand in need of prayer today, especially the sick, the poor, exiles, the persecuted, that through this Holy Sacrifice their cup may overflow with goodness and kindness from the Lord

For all the faithful departed, who were justified by grace in this life, that they may be heirs of eternal life now in God's kingdom

### Week 32, Thursday

*Phlm 7-20, Ps 146, Luke 17:20-25*

That the hearts of our leaders in the church may be refreshed in the Lord by the love we show and the good deeds we do in Jesus' name

That the Lord, who secures justice for the oppressed and gives food to the hungry, may raise up world leaders who will be His instruments of compassion and mercy

That we may understand that the kingdom of God is already among us and within us, as we look forward in hope to the coming of Christ in His final glory

For those who are suffering greatly and for those who are persecuted and rejected by this generation, that Jesus may be with them for comfort and strength

For those who have gone before us, that they may be quickly purified to see the day of the Son of Man in the kingdom of heaven

## Week 32, Friday

*2 John 4-9, Ps 119, Luke 17:26-37*

For the church and her leaders, that we may remain in the teaching of the Christ who has come in the flesh, and walk in the truth He taught us

That our leaders in the world may be given a clear perception of the transience of human existence, and be motivated to work for God's law and the values that will endure in His eternal kingdom

That we who are united with Jesus in this eucharistic sacrifice may also walk with Him in His commandment of love for one another and for all

For all who are in special need of loving intercession at this time, especially for those who have recommended themselves to our prayers, for their relief and comfort

For the souls of those who have entered into the gates of death, that they may soon see the Son of Man revealed in the glory and joy of heaven

## Week 32, Saturday

*3 John 5-8, Ps 112, Luke 18:1-8*

For our leaders in the church and for missionaries, that they may receive the help of the faithful in a way worthy of God, in support and in prayer

For those in positions of power and influence in the world, that they may be just and honest and respectful of the rights and dignity of every human being

That Jesus may find faith in our hearts when He comes today in the sacrament of His love, and that we may always please Him by our trust

For all who are in need of our prayers today, that we may pray earnestly without becoming weary for their healing and peace, as Jesus desires

For our beloved departed relatives and friends, that through the intercession of our Blessed Mother, their purification may be completed, and they may be received into heaven with great joy

### Week 33, Monday

*Rev 1:1-4, 2:1-5, Ps 1, Luke 18:35-43*

For the angels of the churches, the bishops who oversee and administer the inheritance of the Lord, that their labor and their endurance may win favor before Him

That heads of nations and those who exercise influence on the world scene may be among the just, delighting in God's law of love and compassion for all

That those who are fervent in God's service may not lose the love they had at first, and that those who have fallen away from love may repent

For those who sit by the roadside in need and sickness, in grief and blindness, that Jesus may pass by and reward their faith with the gift of complete healing

For our dear departed loved ones, that grace and peace may come to them from Him who is and who was and who is to come as the joy of all His holy ones

### Week 33, Tuesday

*Rev 3:1-6, 14-22, Ps 15, Luke 19:1-10*

For our holy shepherds, that they may be fervent in God's service, repenting of any tepidity so that Jesus may enter in and eat with them and help their ministry

For world leaders, that they may walk blamelessly and do justice, never harming their fellow men and honoring those who fear the Lord

That Jesus may invite us down with Zacchaeus into the familiarity of intimacy with him, forgiving us all our sins and bringing salvation to our house

For all who are lost and far from God, that Jesus, who came to seek and save what was lost, may hear our fervent prayers on their behalf

For our beloved dead, that they may be among the victors who are dressed in white, and who are acknowledged by Jesus before the Father and the angels in heaven

## Week 33, Wednesday

*Rev 4:1-11, Ps 150, Luke 19:11-28*

For the church, whose goal is the vision of heaven described today, that the glimpse of the glorious life that awaits us may give us courage for our journey here below

For our political leaders and all those in a position of power and influence, that they may work faithfully for human dignity, for life, and for peace

For all Christ's followers who have received precious resources and gifts to be worked with until the Master's return, that they may deserve to hear His praise of them as good and faithful servants

For the poor, the sick, those in financial distress, and all who have asked for our prayers, that they may have cause to praise the Lord again for His mighty deeds of mercy and love

For our beloved dead who have come before the throne of God in the hour of their judgment, that they may join the chorus of those who give glory to God with joy and adoration in heaven

## Week 33, Thursday

*Rev 5:1-10, Ps 149, Luke 19:41-44*

For the whole church, the kingdom of priests set apart to serve God by the Blood of the Lamb, that her faith may teach her the new song of victorious praise even in the midst of present hardship

That world leaders may understand what makes for peace, and work for God's will to be done in their areas of influence

That we may not miss the time of our visitation, but welcome Jesus into our hearts as Master of our lives, so that He may accomplish His saving work in us

That the Lord who loves His people and adorns the lowly with victory, may hear our prayers for the poor, the sick, and all who are humbled by distress and suffering

For those who have gone before us, that this Holy Sacrifice may purify them so that they will be among those joyfully singing a new hymn to the Savior

### Week 33, Friday

*Rev 10:8-11, Ps 119, Luke 19:45-48*

For the whole church and especially her leaders, that the decrees of the Lord may be our delight and our counselors, the joy of our hearts

For government leaders and all who exercise influence on the affairs of state, that they may be attentive to the prophetic voices that are raised on behalf of life, justice, and peace

For each of us, that the temple of our baptized souls may be a place holy to the Lord, cleansed of all alien elements

For those who have no home as winter approaches, for the sick, the imprisoned, those who are left alone in their trials, that Christ's followers may reach out to them in their need, by prayer and loving action

For those who have gone before us in faith, that God's promises, which gave them sweetness on earth, may now blossom into glory in heaven

### Week 33, Saturday

*Rev 11:4-12, Ps 144, Luke 20:27-40*

For our leaders in the church, that their prophetic witness may effectively challenge the world and leaven it from within

For the gift of peace; that conflicts may be worked through in a way that will address the needs of all involved, especially the most vulnerable

That we may be faithful witnesses to the Lord, lamps who give light to all and stand shining and glowing before the Lord of all the earth

For all who have asked our prayers and all who are in a season of special need at this time: that our Blessed Lady, Mother of Mercy, may come to them with consolation and healing

For all our loved ones who have died, that the God for whom everyone is alive may purify them quickly and make them an angel of comfort to those they have left behind for a little while

## Week 34, Monday

*Rev 14:1-3, 4-5, Ps 24, Luke 21:1-4*

For the whole church, contemplating in this last week of the year the vision of the heavenly Jerusalem, that our hearts may be stirred to desire what we see now only in symbol and mystery

That world leaders may be men and women who long to see the face of the Lord, who keep their hands sinless and their hearts clean, that we may know God's peace

That we who partake in this Eucharist of the Lamb of God may be among the perfect number who follow Him wherever He goes

For all those who have only their poverty to share with God and with others, that they may look up to see Jesus watching them with approval and blessing in His eyes

For all our faithful departed ones, that they may ascend the mountain of the Lord and stand in His holy place, rejoicing before the Lamb who has redeemed them

## Week 34, Tuesday

*Rev 14:14-19, Ps 96, Luke 21:5-11*

For our church leaders, that the vision of the last judgment may keep their vision clear and their message of repentance strong

For our nation and our world, troubled by wars and insurrections, that Jesus, whose vision penetrates all upheavals, may keep us steady and help our efforts towards peace

For reverence in our hearts as we receive the Lord in the Eucharist, realizing that He who comes to us so humbly is the same Son of Man who will reap the earth's harvest at the end of time

For those in whose lives there is not left a stone upon a stone, devastated by sickness, financial disaster, and all the hard blows of life, that our prayers may bring them comfort and strength

For our faithful departed, whose lives have already been harvested by the Son of Man, that they may come to the perfect peace and joy of heaven

## Week 34, Wednesday

*Rev 15:1-4, Ps 98, Luke 21:12-19*

For the church, that by untiring evangelization, she may bring all the nations to come and worship before God and before the Lamb

For world leaders, that God who rules the world with justice and the peoples with equity may teach them the ways that lead to peace

For all who are being persecuted for their faith, who must give testimony to Jesus in the face of torture and death, for their courage and for their triumph

For all those who are undergoing the test of patient endurance, that God may give them the inner defenses and wisdom they need

For our beloved departed ones, that they may be among those who have won the victory and who are standing glorious and immortal before God's throne

## Week 34, Thursday

*Rev 18:1-2, 21-23, 19:1-3, 9, Ps 100, Luke 21:20-28*

For the church, that in all her sufferings and the disasters that come upon the world, she may stand up straight and raise her head, knowing that her ransom is at hand

For all the nations who are in anguish at this time, for whom the waves of death are roaring, that there will be many who will come to their aid in their time of need

For all of us who are invited to the wedding feast of the Lamb in this Holy Eucharist, that we may stand strong in every trial that we endure for our blessed Lord

For all who have asked our prayers, for those most forgotten and most in need of prayer, that this Holy Sacrifice may be for them a source of grace and healing

For our dear ones who have died, that they may enter God's gates with thanksgiving and His courts with praise, joining the great assembly of the just in heaven

## Week 34, Friday

*Rev 20:1-4, 11–21:2, Ps 84, Luke 21:29-33*

For all of us in the church as we prepare to meet the bridegroom Christ, that our hearts may yearn and pine for His courts during our earthly pilgrimage

That those who hold the destinies of nations in their hands may be given light to see that their actions will be judged before God, and so be moved to work for life, for justice, and for peace

For the little ones of our world, the poor sparrows who find a nest in God's house and whose only friends are Christ's disciples, that they may be cared for with loving faith and deep respect

For the unemployed as the holidays approach, for those who are sick and those who are near death, that they may receive signs of hope and new growth like buds bursting open in the spring

For our beloved dead who have come before the throne of God, that they may be judged mercifully and soon be welcomed into the heavenly Jerusalem

## Week 34, Saturday

*Rev 22:1-7, Ps 95, Luke 21:34-36*

For the church, the people God shepherds, the flock He guides, for her unity in faith and morals under the direction of our Holy Father

That indulgence and wordly cares may be kept in check, so that we may remain aware of those whose lives are marred by poverty, exile, and oppression, and find ways to help them for the sake of Christ

That the rivers of life-giving waters may begin to flow, healing the sick, washing clean the sinner, refreshing the weary, and removing every curse

That our Blessed Mother, who has perfumed this church year with the fragrance of her feasts and her graces, may take us under her protection as we prepare to begin a new year, and draw us close to her divine Son

That our beloved dead may be among those who look upon the face of God and bear His name on their foreheads, reigning with Him forever and ever

# PROPER OF SAINTS

**Conversion of St. Paul, January 25**
*Acts 22:3-16, Ps 117, Mark 16:15-18*

For the conversion of every Christian heart to the wishes of the Master so that all may be one flock with one Shepherd

For all who oppress and persecute their fellow men and women, that they may be brought to the moment of their own Damascus encounter with Jesus, who suffers in and along with their victims

For missionary vocations, that many young people may be inspired by the Lord's command to go out into the whole world and proclaim the Good News to all peoples

For all who have asked our prayers, for the homeless, the sick, the addicted, and the imprisoned, that they may experience by the power of grace how steadfast is the kindness of the Lord

For those who have died, that they may come face to face with their Savior in the kingdom of heaven

**Sts. Timothy and Titus, January 26**
*2 Tim 1:1-8, Ps 96, Luke 10:1-9*

For our Holy Father, our bishops and priests, that they may stir into flame the strong and loving Spirit of their holy ordination for the building up of the church

For nations which hold a long tradition of Christianity, that they may be the first to promote life, morality, justice, and peace upon the earth

For missionaries, who still carry out the work which St. Paul entrusted to Timothy and Titus, that their work may grow and prosper in the world

For those who are sowing in tears, who are sick, bereaved, abandoned, unemployed, or lonely, that through the loving intervention of the disciples of Jesus they may know joy and healing

That God, who gave us a spirit of power and love and self-control upon the earth, may now purify our loved ones who have died and give them a spirit of rejoicing and glory in heaven

## St. Thomas Aquinas, January 28

*Wis 7:7-10, 15-16, Ps 119, Matt 23:8-12*

For the teachers and theologians of the church, that prudence may be given to them, and that they may prefer wisdom to riches, health, and splendor

For those in positions of power and influence, that they may have the statutes and commands of the Lord ever in their minds and hearts

That we may be happy to be perpetual disciples of the one Master, taking our place with Him as willing servants of each other

For all who are suffering and are in need of loving intercession, that the one Father who is in heaven may comfort them with His grace and the help of their brothers and sisters

For those who have been humbled in death, that they may now be exalted in the heavenly kingdom

## Presentation of the Lord, February 2

*Mal 3:1-4, Ps 24, Heb 2:14-18, Luke 1:22-32*

For the priests of the church, that they may allow the divine High Priest to purify and refine them as precious and pleasing sacrifices in His honor

That those who are engaged in the struggle for life, for the poor, for peace and justice, may feel within themselves the eventual victory of the King of Glory, the Lord of Hosts

For all consecrated souls, all who have vowed themselves to the Lord's service, that this day dedicated to them may bring the grace of renewed fervor and joy

For the aged, that like Simeon and Anna they may experience the intimate consolation of the Holy Spirit, and the joy of beholding the face of Jesus

For all of us at this festive Eucharist, who surround the altar with our shining lights and proclaim Jesus as the Light of the World, that we may offer ourselves as He did in the temple, fully and without reservation

For our beloved departed, especially those undergoing the Lord's purification, that this Holy Sacrifice may bring them release into heaven

### St. Scholastica, February 10

*Song 8:6-7, Ps 148, Luke 10:38-42*

For the church, that she may set the Lord as a seal upon her heart, serving Him with unfailing devotion

That the princes and judges of the earth, the leaders of all people, may exalt the name of the Lord alone in their decisions and laws

For all who have chosen the better part, spending their lives listening at the feet of the Lord, that they may be respected for their hidden service in the church

For those who are anxious and worried, depressed and fearful, that they may be invited into the inner joy of the Lord in the midst of their troubles

That our dear ones who have died may find that love cannot be quenched, and may encounter the Lord in the triumph of His love for them

### Our Lady of Lourdes, February 11

*Isa 66:10-14, Jdt 13, John 2:1-11*

For the church, the Jerusalem from on high, that God will send His grace flowing toward her like a river for the refreshment of all her little ones

That Mary, the highest honor of our race, whose deed of hope for her people will never be forgotten, may help us all to hope for and work toward a culture of life and peace

That our Blessed Mother may again see our need and intercede with her divine Son, providing us with the good wine of spiritual joy

For our dear sick ones, remembered today and prayed for throughout the church, that Mary may comfort and console them, and heal them in the waters of mercy

For all our departed ones, who tried to do whatever Jesus told them, that the water of their mortal life may now be changed into the new wine of heaven's delights

## Chair of St. Peter, February 22

*1 Pet 5:1-4, Ps 23, Matt 16:13-19*

For our Holy Father, the Rock of our unity, whose faith never fails to strengthen His brethren, for all His intentions, for His health, and for the success of His ministry

That the words and deeds of Christians may be a leaven in the dough of the world, raising its ideals to those of life, justice, and morality

For our bishops and priests, that they may give God's flock a shepherd's care, living as examples for the people, winning for themselves an unfading crown of glory

That we may ponder deeply our own response to the question of Jesus: "Who do you say that I am?" and allow the Father to reveal His Son to us so that we may give Him our undivided allegiance

That the Lord may Himself shepherd those who are in the dark valley of illness, diminishment, depression, or grief, giving them courage and an anointing of hope and joy

That Jesus, who gave the power to bind and loose to Peter, may loose our dear deceased loved ones from all their sins and give them a place at the heavenly banquet

## St. Patrick, March 17

*1 Pet 4:7b-11, Ps 96, Luke 5:1-11*

For the missionaries of the church, that they may always be willing to put out into deep water and lower their nets again at the command of Jesus

That those who have received the gifts of power and influence may use them as stewards with the strength that God supplies and for the good of all

For all who have inherited the faith preached by St. Patrick, for all who honor His heritage, that in their lives God may always be glorified through Jesus Christ

That our love for one another may be intense, especially for those who are most in need of the gift of reverent compassion

For those who have brought their boats to the shore of the final passing, that they may follow the Lord into His glorious kingdom

## St. Joseph, March 19

*2 Sam 7:4-5a, 12-14a, 16, Ps 89, Rom 4:13, 16-18, 22, Matt 1:16, 18-21, 24a*

For the universal church, placed under the patronage of St. Joseph, that He will be to her a faithful provider and protector, a giver of strength and direction

That through the intercession of St. Joseph every house and kingdom and nation may stand firm before the Lord in righteousness of heart

For the grace of faith, that in the company of St. Joseph we may act upon the word of the Lord promptly and with gratitude

That those who are undergoing a season of suffering and doubt may have the grace to hope against hope, believing in God who can call into being the grace and light they need

That we may all be granted a happy death through the intercession of St. Joseph, and that those who already rest with their ancestors may be taken into the abundant life of heaven in His blessed company

## Annunciation, March 25

*Isa 7:10-14, 8-10, Ps 40, Heb 10:4-10, Luke 1:26-38*

For the church, that she may be in our age and in every age the virgin made fruitful by God's power and His gracious word, especially in the souls of those who are soon to be reborn in baptism

For the conversion of all who have turned away from the path of peace, that Mary, Queen of Peace, who built her life on God's justice, may soften our hearts and change our ways

That with Mary we may offer our consent to every initiative of the Lord, seeking to do His will in all circumstances as His humble and obedient servants

For the poor, the sick, the imprisoned, the addicted, the oppressed, and the sorrowing, that Mary, who won God's heart by her loving obedience, may now obtain from Him the special grace needed by each one

For our dear deceased brothers and sisters, consecrated to God by the offering of the Body of Jesus Christ, that they may be freed from all sin and brought rejoicing into heaven this day

### St. Mark, April 25

*1 Pet 5:5b-14, Ps 89, Mark 16:15-20*

For the apostolic preachers of our own day, that the Lord may continue to work with them and confirm the message they preach, especially through the great sign of their personal sanctity

That God, who opposes the proud but bestows favor on the humble, may prosper the work of the humble ones who stand firm for the cause of life, justice, and peace

For the gift of good missionary vocations in the church, that the Gospel may be spread into the whole world

That we may be sober and vigilant, steadfast in faith, and strong in suffering, that God may restore and confirm us in His love

For all who have asked for our prayers; for the sick and those passing through a time of anxiety and need, that they may cast their cares on God who tenderly cares for them

That Jesus, who has taken His seat at the right hand of God, may purify our departed brothers and sisters and receive them into the mansions He has prepared for them in heaven

### St. Joseph the Worker, May 1

*Col 3:14-15, 17, 23-24, Ps 90, Matt 13:54-58*

For our leaders in the church, that they may manifest the wisdom of the Lord Jesus in their words and deeds

That Christ's peace may reign in our hearts and in the hearts of all men and women

That our work may be modeled on the work of St. Joseph, done for the Lord alone and in the name of Jesus

For all who need our prayers, that our faith may bring the power of miracles to alleviate every distress

For our beloved dead, that they may come in to their promised inheritance as followers of Christ the Lord

### Sts. Philip and James, May 3

*1 Cor 15:1-8, Ps 19, John 14:6-14*

For our Holy Father, our bishops and priests, successors of the apostles, that they will continue to hand down to us what they themselves have received in faith and in practice

For the fair and just re-building of all the war- and famine-ravaged countries of the world, that through compassion and respect they may again know peace

For vocations, men and women of courage and love who will glorify the Father by their faith and the witness of their total consecration

For all the intentions we bring to this Eucharist, for our loved ones and friends, for the most forgotten little ones who suffer alone

That our dear departed loved ones may be brought purified and rejoicing into the company of the apostles in heaven

### St. Matthias, May 14

*Acts 1:15-17, 20-26, Ps 113, John 15:9-17*

For our Holy Father, our bishops and priests, chosen in a special way by Jesus to go forth and bear fruit, that they may be strong friends of Jesus whose fruit will endure

For peace, that we may be part of the divine work that lifts up the lowly and the poor to seat them with respect and dignity at the common table of God's bounty

That we may know Jesus from the inside, as one knows a friend, by making our own the motivation of self-sacrificing love that was His identity and His joy

For vocations, that in the midst of the praying community, the One who knows the secrets of hearts may continue to choose apostles as He chose Matthias, for the mission of evangelization

For all who are sorrowing: for the sick, the bereaved, those in economic hardship, those caught in the chains of addiction, that our loving prayer and service may bring them a share in the Lord's joy

That Jesus, who looks on us as His friends, may gather our faithful departed into the embrace of heaven's fellowship

## Visitation of the Blessed Virgin Mary, May 31

*Zeph 3:14-18 or Rom 12:9-16, Isa 12, Luke 1:39-56*

For our Holy Father, our bishops and priests, as they face the trials and challenges of our times, that Our Lady may share with them the profound trust for which she has been called blessed

For peace; that we may learn to have the same attitude toward all, putting away ambitious thoughts and taking our place with Mary among God's lowly ones

That Jesus may make us fervent and humble, so that we may never be sent away empty with the rich or cast down from our place with the mighty, but find joy in God who saves us

For the sick among us, the poor, the imprisoned and addicted, and all who have special need of prayer, that Mary, who sang of God's mercy to His little ones, may mediate His loving kindness in all their needs

For all who have died and are still awaiting the blessed vision of their hope, that Mary may visit them with the gift of entrance into the joy of heaven

## St. Barnabas, June 11

*Acts 11:21b-26, 13:1-3, Ps 98, Matt 5:33-37*

For our Holy Father, our bishops and priests, that they may be filled with grace and the Holy Spirit, and that through their ministry many may be added to the Lord

That the blessing of peace which Jesus instructed His apostles to offer each house they entered may come down upon our world, and that we may be deserving of it

For vocations, that many more generous young people may be set apart for the work to which the Lord will call them

For those who are suffering, who have asked our prayers in a time of anxiety or pain, that they may be faithful to the Lord in firmness of heart, and soon experience His merciful help

For our beloved dead, that through the offering of this Holy Sacrifice they may find salvation and a melodious song to bring before the Lord

### Nativity of St. John the Baptist, Vigil

*Jer 1:4-10, Ps 71, 1 Pet 1:8-12, Luke 1:5-7*

For the preaching work of the church, that Jesus Christ may be proclaimed in His suffering and in His glory by all her holy leaders

For the prophets whose role it is to root up and to tear down the culture of death, and to build and plant the culture of life, that they may have no fear before the nations

For those whom the Lord has formed in the womb to be His dedicated servants, that they may hear and follow their sacred call

For all who mourn and suffer in this life, who feel barren and sterile, that like Zachariah and Elizabeth they may be surprised by the angel of the Lord, bringing them joy and gladness again

For our dear ones who have died, that they may rejoice with inexpressible joy touched with glory over the surpassing gift of their salvation in the heavenly kingdom

### Nativity of St. John the Baptist, June 24

*Isa 49:1-6, Ps 139, Acts 13:22-26,*
*Luke 1:57-66, 80*

For the holy leaders of our church who are polished arrows and sharp swords of truth for God's glory, that they may not toil in vain but receive God's reward in the conversion of their people

For those who cry out in our own day in the wilderness of unresponsive hearts for life, for justice, and for the ways that lead to peace, for their courage and the success of their mission

For vocations: that many more young people may come to hear the promptings of the Lord who has called them from birth to possess the joy of being His servants and showing forth His glory

For all of us surrounding the table of this Eucharist with our hidden intentions and all the sufferings that have been entrusted to our prayer, that our communion with Jesus may bring an answer of divine love to all our petitions

For those who have gone before us marked with the sign of faith, that John the Baptist and all the saints may come to meet them and bring them rejoicing into heaven

## Sts. Peter and Paul, Vigil

*Acts 3:1-10, Ps 19, Gal 1:11-20,*
*John 21:15-19*

For our leaders in the church, set apart and called by God's favor to their holy ministry, that like Sts. Peter and Paul they may be zealous in proclaiming the Gospel

For world leaders, that the cry of the poor may reach them, and the rights of the unborn and the elderly may become their priority in justice and compassion

That with Peter we may be ready to give a confident response to Jesus' question: "Do you love me?", accepting the consequences of our devotion with a generous heart

For the city of Rome, graced with the martyrdom of the two greatest apostles, and that the Holy Roman Catholic Church may flourish with a new evangelization in all the corners of the world

For those who are crippled by life's trials, who are sick or poor or grieving, that they may encounter the power of Jesus Christ and find a reason to praise the mercy of the Lord

For all who have died in the faith of Jesus Christ, that the angels may now escort them to a place of light, happiness, and peace

## Sts. Peter and Paul, June 29

*Acts 12:1-11, Ps 34, 2 Tim 4:6-8, 17-18,*
*Matt 16:13-19*

For our Holy Father, successor to St. Peter, that the Lord may continue to make Him a rock on which He can build up the church in our own time

For all who work for life, for justice, and for peace, that the Lord will give them courage to finish their race and to keep their faith in His divine help for their cause

For vocations, that willing young hearts may take on the challenge of priestly ministry and the power to bind and loose in Christ's name

For missionaries, that the Lord may stand by their side and give them strength, so that through them the proclamation might be completed and all nations may hear the Good News

For all who are held bound, whether by sickness, addiction, or external oppression, that with all of us praying fervently on their behalf, God's angel may lead them to freedom and new life

For our beloved dead, whose lives have been poured out like a libation, that they may be purified to receive the crown of righteousness from the Lord, the just Judge of all

### St. Thomas, Apostle, July 3

*Eph 2:19-22, Ps 117, John 20:24-29*

For the whole church, built firmly on the faith of the first apostles, that under the guidance of our Holy Father, this temple of living stones may be built up into a worthy home for its indwelling Spirit

That Jesus may come through the doors of hearts and nations that fear or greed have locked, with the miracle of His gift of peace

For the work of evangelization wherever the church is reaching out, that many who are strangers and aliens to Christ may become fellow citizens of the saints and members of the household of God

For all who are suffering, that they may probe the wounds of Jesus with humility and faith, and read there the focus and sustained energy of His redeeming love

For the faithful departed, who in their earthly life did not see Jesus and yet believed in Him, that they may rejoice now in His living presence

### St. Benedict, Solemnity, July 11

*Prov 2:1-9, 1 Cor 1:26-31, Matt 19:27-29*

For our leaders in the church, that they may be men and women after God's own heart, wise and loving in all their ways, who follow Christ gladly and leave all else behind

For world leaders who must negotiate delicate and dangerous decisions, that they may seek God's wisdom and understanding, so that their paths may be guarded with justice

For all Benedictine monks who keep this day as a festival day in honor of their holy founder, that His blessing may make them strong and fervent in the Lord-

That God may choose and call many more generous hearts from the world's little ones to give up everything for the glory of His name

For all of us who participate in this Holy Sacrifice, that we who receive the source of wisdom in Jesus may be wise and loving in our interaction with one another

For our beloved dead, that they may be found in Christ Jesus, our redemption and our righteousness before the Father

## St. Mary Magdalene, July 22

*general intentions*

For our Holy Father, our bishops and priests, that with the whole church they may take their stance of faith in the resurrection which was first proclaimed by Mary Magdalene

That the angels who announced good news to Mary Magdalene may also bring the glad tidings of peace to our world, helping us in our work for life and justice

For vocations, especially to contemplative life, that many more generous hearts may respond to the One who seeks to be their Rabboni, their beloved Teacher and Spouse

For all who stand weeping by the tomb of their hopes and dreams, that they may hear themselves called by name and filled with good news from the Lord Jesus

For our beloved departed ones, that they may receive the living fruit of Jesus' resurrection in their own entrance into His eternal kingdom

## St. James, July 25

*2 Cor 4:7-15, Ps 126, Matt 20:20-28*

For the church in all her humanity, feeling still the rising of ambition and indignation as did the first apostles, that the Master may again inspire her with His ideal of humble service in roles of leadership

For those who speak up for the poor and oppressed little ones, the threatened unborn, the despised minorities, that God may do for them great things and make their harvest a cause for rejoicing and hope

For all who are persecuted for their faith, that they may never despair no matter how they are crushed, and have strength to speak out for what they believe

For all of us at this Eucharistic sacrifice, renewing the mystery of the dying and risen life of Jesus, that we may feel this rhythm in our own lives, and consent to let death work in us so that others may live

For the sick, the addicted and lonely, the aged and dying, those whose vessel of earth weighs heavily upon them, that they may make contact with the treasure inside and its surpassing power to save them

For our beloved departed ones, that they may be admitted to the kingdom of heaven rejoicing, carrying their sheaves

### Sts. Joachim and Anne, July 26

*Sir 44:1, 10-15, Ps 132, Matt 13:16-17*

For our Holy Father, our bishops and priests, that they might be godly men whose wisdom is retold in the assembly

For the holiness of our lay people in the church, and for holy families in which the values of life and morality are enshrined

For all of us sharing in this Eucharist, who are blest even beyond seeing the Lord and hearing His word to the point of receiving Him into our hearts, that this union may make us the saints He desires us to become

That those who suffer and grieve under a heavy cross may come in faith to see how close is their union with the Crucified One, who supports them in all their trials

For all those whose bodies are peacefully laid away, whose virtues have not been forgotten, that they may be with God

### St. Martha, July 29

*John 11:19-27 or Luke 10:38-42*

For the church, that like St. Martha she may hold fast to her belief in Jesus as the Son of God, the one who was to come into the world, the only Redeemer

That we may never allow ourselves to be anxious or worried about the direction of world events, but bring them to the feet of Jesus with perseverance and trust

That we may welcome Jesus into our homes and into our hearts as Martha did, serving Him with devotion and giving Him the joy of our faith

For those who are living through a time of great distress, especially those who, like St. Martha, are grieving the death of loved ones, that Jesus may come to them with grace and hope

That Jesus, the Resurrection and the Life, may raise up to life and glory our dear ones who have fallen asleep in the Lord

## St. Ignatius of Loyola, July 31

*1 Cor 10:31–11:1, Ps 34, Luke 14:25-33*

For the church, that it may always lay its foundation in the Lord's Word and complete the work relying on His grace

That the angel of the Lord may encamp around world leaders who give Him reverence and obedience in all their decisions and plans

For all who truly wish to follow Jesus, that they may be willing to leave behind family and all their possessions, carrying their cross in His company

For the Jesuits, that as they work for the glory of God, not seeking their own benefit but that of the many, they may in all things be imitators of Christ

For all who are lowly and despised, marginalized, poor, grieving, imprisoned, or addicted, that through our earnest prayer they may again be radiant with joy

For our departed loved ones, that through God's mercy they may have the resources to finish all that they began in this life in their efforts to follow Jesus, and find a place in His glorious kingdom

## St. Alphonsus Ligouri, August 1

*Rom 8:1-4, Ps 119, Matt 5:13-19*

For the church, called the salt of the earth by Jesus himself, that she may season all she touches with the savor of spiritual freedom and grace

For our leaders in the world, that they may be the first to obey God's commandments, upholding the dignity of every human being made in His image

That we may live according to the spirit, fulfilling all the righteousness of the law by imitating God's Son who took on our flesh to free us from sin

For the Redemptorists, that their light may shine brightly in the world, and that many new vocations may bring their good deeds into the future of the Catholic Church

For all who labor under a spirit of condemnation, who are heavily laden with illness, guilt, or grief, that God may free them from their burdens in Christ Jesus

For those who have died marked with the sign of faith, that they may glorify their heavenly Father by their joy and gratitude in His kingdom of light and peace

## St. John Mary Vianney, August 4

*Ezek 3:17-21, Ps 117, Matt 9:35–10:1*

For the watchmen of the church, that they may have the courage to speak out and warn those in danger of sinning

That as God's prophetic people we may stand up for the values we have received from Jesus, dissuading others from disastrous choices in leadership among the nations

For our priests, that their holy patron, St. John Vianney, may console and uphold them in their ministry, and that the Master of the harvest may send out more laborers to help them

For those who are troubled and abandoned in our own day, that the Good Shepherd may give His followers grace to cure and comfort them, driving out every evil spirit and disease

For our dear ones who have passed beyond the gates of death, that they may encounter the One whose kindness is steadfast and whose fidelity endures forever

## Transfiguration of the Lord, August 6

*Dan 7, Ps 97, 2 Pet 1, Mark 9:2-10*

For the successors of the apostles, that this feast of the Lord's transfiguration may flood their souls with a renewed vision of faith to give them strength for all their trials

For those who have received a portion of dominion for the good of their people, that they may share the same goals and values with the Son of Man, who by right possesses all glory and dominion

For all souls of deep prayer for whom this feast holds a great attraction, that the inner vision of which they are sometimes granted a taste may radiate in their lives of joyful surrender

For all who suffer deeply in mind, body, and spirit, that Jesus, who strengthened His apostles for His passion by the vision of His glory, may come to lighten their darkness

For our deceased loved ones, that the Father may come to greet them with the revelation of His beloved Son in heaven

## St. Dominic, August 8

*1 Cor 2:1-10a, Ps 96, Luke 9:57-62*

For the preachers of the church, that what they have left behind may not hold them back, but that they will joyfully follow Jesus wherever He goes

That the families of nations may give to the Lord the glory due His name by governing their peoples with equity and respecting the dignity of every child of God

That we may have ears to hear the wisdom of the spiritually mature, the mysterious wisdom hidden in the cross of Jesus, blossoming into glory for all who are one with Him

For all the followers of St. Dominic, that their message and proclamation may be accompanied by a demonstration of spirit and power, the fruit of a deep inner life of contemplation

For those who know nothing but Jesus crucified in their lives, whose days are hidden in suffering under the shadow of the cross, that God's glory may be revealed in them through an outbreak of grace and joy

For our departed loved ones, that they may soon come into the inheritance which no eye has seen, which God has prepared for those who love him

## St. Lawrence, August 10

*2 Cor 9:6-10, Ps 112, John 12:24-26*

For the church, that her generosity with God and humanity may increase the harvest of her righteousness

For statesmen and all who work in the world community, that they may be an upright generation deserving of God's blessing

That we may not cling to our tiny lives as grains of wheat, but be willing to fall into the earth and die in order to produce much fruit and preserve ourselves for eternal life

That the sick, the poor, and the grief stricken may find in the followers of Jesus cheerful givers who are able to make every grace abundant for them

For those who have died after a life of service to Christ, that they may be where He is, honored by the Father in heaven

## St. Clare, August 11

*Phil 3:8-14, Ps 16, Matt 19:27-29*

For our Holy Father, our bishops and priests, and all our leaders in the church, that they may attain perfect maturity in the spirit and be fully possessed by the Lord Jesus

For peace, that the judgment of the holy ones in the future age may already be operative in the world, forming it in following the Prince of Peace

For the grace of spiritual poverty, that we may cheerfully accept the loss of all things so that we may gain Christ, sharing in His sufferings so as to share in His glory

For the Poor Clare sisters on their feast day, that the Lord may be their allotted portion and cup and their promised hundredfold

For all who need our prayer, whose portion is the suffering of Christ, and for our beloved dead, that God may show them the path to life and give them fullness of joy in His presence

## Assumption of the Blessed Virgin Mary, Vigil

*Chron 15, Ps 132, 1 Cor 15, Luke 11:27-28*

For God's holy church, as Mary, the ark of His covenant, is taken up and brought into the tent that is God's dwelling place in heaven, that there may be great rejoicing among the people

That God's justice may prevail once again upon the earth, and that we may become a peace offering pleasing in His sight by our work for life and morality

That we may take our place with Mary among those who are blessed, not for physical closeness to Jesus, but for hearing and observing God's word

That Jesus, who has freed us from the law by His grace and from death by His resurrection, may help us to serve Him in grateful freedom as adopted sons and daughters of the Father

That the feast of Mary's triumph may be a blessing on all who still labor and suffer here below, especially on those who are ill or grieving

That the victory of death may be overcome in our loved ones who have left this life, and that they may be where Mary is, rejoicing in God's triumph

## Assumption of the Blessed Virgin Mary, August 15

*Rev 11:19, Ps 45, 1 Cor 15:20-26, Luke 1:39-56*

For the church, God's temple, the shrine of the ark of the covenant, that she may shine like Mary with the radiance of faith and love

That Our Lady, who sang of God's power in raising up the lowly, may stir up in all people a reverent love for the smallest of God's children

That we who celebrate Our Lady's Assumption today, may renew our hope in our own resurrection, taking our part in the struggle to destroy every sovereignty and power that opposes God's victory in our lives

That Mary, who always desires to give more than to receive, may make this feast a day of health for the sick, hope for the discouraged, and grace for all her children

For those who have gone before us marked with the sign of faith, that they may be brought to life in Christ who has destroyed death as the final enemy under His feet

## St. Bernard, August 20

*Sir 15:1-6, Ps 119, John 17:20-26*

For unity among all the disciples of Jesus, that we may all be one as He desired, so that the world may believe that Jesus was sent by the Father who is the source of all unity

That the powerful and the wealthy may come to be faultless in their ways by keeping to God's commands and treasuring His promise

That we who are the Father's gift to Jesus may be a source of joy to Him, nourished with the bread of understanding and walking always in His love

For the Cistercians and all who generously follow the contemplative way of life, that they may be embraced with wisdom and brought to perfection in the Lord Jesus

For those who have asked our prayers, and all who are undergoing privation and pain, that the Father, who loves them as He loved Jesus, may give them a share in the joy of the Lord

For our beloved dead, that where Jesus is they may also be, seeing His glory and rejoicing in His love

## Queenship of the Blessed Virgin Mary, August 22

*Isa 9:1-6, Ps 113, Luke 1:26-38*

For our ministers in the church, sons, daughters, and servants of Mary, that she may bring all her queenly power to help them in the burdens of their demanding vocations

That Mary, Queen of Peace, may bring again to our war weary world her Son, the Wonderful Counselor and Prince of Peace who can guide the nations

For all who still walk in darkness, who have no faith, that through the efforts of evangelization and the prayers of Mary, they too may see a great light and share in the joy of salvation

That the handmaid of the Lord, whose humility and obedience on earth have earned for her queenship in heaven, may help us in the self emptying that is the seed of our eternal glory

For all who need our prayers: for all who suffer in mind and body, and for our beloved dead, that the Queen of Mercy may visit them with grace, peace, and all the joys of heaven

## St. Bartholomew, August 24

*Rev 21:9-14, Ps 145, John 1:45-51*

For the church, the New Jerusalem, the Bride of the Lamb, that the remembrance of her radiant future destiny may strengthen her present correspondence with grace

That the example of the apostles, who fearlessly preached God's truth at the cost of their own lives, may help those who must stand up for the hard truths that will make God's peace possible in our world

That we may be without guile before Jesus, approved for our honesty and transparent goodness

For all the intentions we gather from the silent depths of our own hearts, that we may pray with confidence, realizing that through our Eucharistic communion, they become the intentions of the beloved Son

For all our dear departed ones, that they may see the heavens opened and the angels of God descending to carry them up to the Son of Man

## St. Augustine, August 28

*1 John 4:7-16, Ps 119, Matt 23:8-12*

For the church, that she may remain in Jesus, held fast in Him by the gift of the Holy Spirit

For the world's powerful ones, that they may learn the ways of servant leadership, seeking God's commands in their decisions and policies

That we may come truly to love one another, begotten of God and knowing God, that His love may be brought to perfection in us

For the followers of St. Augustine, brothers and sisters under one Master, the Christ, that His words may be the source of their holiness and His grace may call many to join them in their discipleship

For those most in need of love, who are suffering or grieving in any way, that our prayers may be a comfort to them and our actions show them the gentle care of the Father

For those who have gone before us, that as they remained in God by love in this life, so now they may be rejoicing in His kingdom of love forever

## Passion of St. John the Baptist, August 29

*2 Thess 3:6-10, 16-18, Ps 128, Mark 6:17-29*

For the leaders of the church, that they may be a prophetic voice speaking out in our world, calling everyone back to the law of the Lord

That world leaders may heed the voices of the prophets who cry out in the wilderness of the world's poverty and need, so that justice and peace may return to the earth

For all who are called to martyrdom in our own day, that they may be brave and steadfast in their witness

For all who are in special need at this time and for all who have asked our prayers, that healing, strength, and comfort may be theirs

For our beloved dead, that through the intercession of St. John the Baptist, they may be cleansed of their sins and come rejoicing into the Father's house

### Nativity of the Blessed Virgin Mary, September 8

*Mic 5:1-4 or Rom 8:28-30, Ps 13,
Matt 1:18-23*

For the church, called and predestined to be conformed to the image of Jesus, that our Immaculate Mother may assist this work of divine grace

For peace, that the One who is our peace may again shepherd us in the majestic name of the Lord, our God, according to His justice and compassion

For all who are tempted to divorce, that the Holy Spirit, who intervened in the life of Mary and Joseph in a completely unexpected way, may intervene for them in the name of reconciliation and understanding

For all who have asked our prayers, for the sick, the dying, the bereaved, the imprisoned, and those in desperate economic circumstances, that this feast may be a new birth of joy in their lives

That we who receive the full fruits of our redemption in this Eucharist may give thanks today for its first budding in Mary's birth, joining our thanksgiving to her exultant Magnificat

That Mary, loving mother to all the faithful, may welcome all the faithful departed into the kingdom of love and grace that is heaven

### Exaltation of the Cross, September 14

*Num 21:4b-9, Ps 78, Phil 2:6-11,
John 3:13-17*

For our leaders in the church, that they may be show forth in their personal lives and in their ministry the choice that Jesus made for the humility and obedience that saved us through His cross

That God, who sent His Son into the world not to condemn it but to save it, may inspire our world leaders with the light and strength they need to navigate these difficult times with every effort to preserve peace

That we who receive in this Holy Eucharist the one whose name is above every name, may truly acknowledge Him as Lord of our lives and allow Him to mark our lives with the saving mystery of His holy cross

For all who suffer: the sick, the elderly, those who are near death, those who suffer because of their resistance to God, that Jesus crucified may be lifted up in their lives like the serpent in the desert for their healing and new direction

For our faithful departed ones, signed with the holy cross, that the full redemption of Jesus may lead them into the joys of heaven

## Our Lady of Sorrows, September 15

*Heb 5:7-9, Ps 31, John 19:25-27*

For our Holy Father, our bishops and priests, that they may be an example to God's people of the obedience that is learned through suffering

That God in His justice may be a rock of refuge, a stronghold for all who are oppressed, making haste to deliver them through Christians brave enough to work for justice and peace

That on this memorial of her sorrows we may do all we can to console our Blessed Mother for all she suffered for our salvation, and allow her to be a loving presence in our own sorrows

That the sufferings of Jesus and the sorrows of His Virgin Mother may encourage us to accept our share of the cross in our lives as part of the redeeming work of God in the world

For all who have died and for those who grieve them, especially the mothers who share in Mary's sorrow, that the grace of resurrection may lift them up in joy

## St. Matthew, September 21

*Eph 4:1-7, 11-13, Ps 19, Matt 9:13*

For those who are given the task of ministry, to build up the Body of Christ, that we may all work together to attain unity of faith and knowledge of the Son of God

That grace may be given to those who exert power on the earth according to the measure of Christ's gift, to equip them to build a culture of life and a society of peace

For those who feel caught in a sinful life, that like St. Matthew they may experience the merciful summons of Jesus, who came to call not the righteous but sinners

That we may live with humility and patience, preserving and re-establishing the unity of the Spirit in the church, under the one God and Father of us all

For those in need of healing in body, mind, or spirit, that Jesus, who described himself as the physician who attends to all who are sick, may help and restore them

For those who have been summoned from this earthly life, that they may experience now the fruit of the hope given to them in baptism, and eternal rest in God's kingdom

### Sts. Michael, Gabriel and Raphael, Archangels, September 29

*Dan 7 or Rev 12, Ps 138, John 1:47-51*

For the whole church in her war against the powers of evil, that Michael the Archangel may continue to fight on our side, so that salvation and power and God's kingdom may prevail

That God may build up strength and discernment within those who possess power and influence in the world, so that their decisions may be wise and promote the cause of peace

For all of us receiving in this Eucharist the One whom angels and archangels adore, that our reverence may resemble theirs

That Raphael, God's remedy, and Gabriel, bearer of glad annunciations, may still be at work in the lives of all those who suffer, bringing them healing and joy

For our beloved departed ones, that they may see the heavens opened and the angels of God surrounding the Son of Man who is their Savior

### Holy Guardian Angels, October 2

*Exod 23:20-23, Ps 91, Matt 18:1-5, 10*

For our leaders in the church, that their angels may guard them in all their ways and be channels of God's wisdom and authority in them

For leaders of nations, that the angel guardians of each country may inspire them with counsels of prudent action and reverence for each human person made in the image of God

For children and all who are blessed with simple and childlike hearts, that their angelic innocence may be a pattern of life for all of us who wish to enter the kingdom of God

That this day dedicated to our angel guardians may help us to be more aware of the divine world that is hidden to our eyes but not to our souls

For all who are in need of special prayer today, that through the intercession of the holy angels they may dwell in the shelter of the Most High and find refuge beneath His wings

For our beloved dead, that the angels may have charge over them, to lead them safely through all purification into the heart of God's kingdom of love and peace

## St. Francis of Assisi, October 4

*Gal 6:14-18, Ps 16, Matt 11:25-30*

That the grace of the Lord Jesus Christ may be with the church, teaching her the sublime wisdom of His cross

For those in authority and power, that it may be the Lord who counsels them, turning their eyes to the poor and the lowly

That we may be among the childlike to whom the Father reveals His secrets and in whom Jesus finds His delight

For the followers of St. Francis, that the world may be crucified to them and they to the world, so that the Lord Himself may be their allotted portion and their cup of pure joy

For those who labor and are burdened under a load of suffering, sickness, or grief, that Jesus may give them rest and His followers may bring them relief

For our faithful departed ones, that they may find the path to life, fullness of joy in God's presence, and the delights at His right hand forever

## Our Lady of the Rosary, October 7

*general intentions*

For all those in the church who faithfully pray the rosary, that the garlands of daily meditations on the divine mysteries in Mary's company may bring her blessing into their lives

For all who work for peace, that Mary, Queen of Peace, may obtain for them the divine assistance that will make peace possible

That in this Eucharist in which we encounter, not an angel, but the incarnate Word Himself, may call forth from us the total surrender that Mary once gave Him

For all of us living out the mysteries of Jesus in our lives, and especially for those united most closely with His passion, that Mary may be there for them as she was for Jesus

For all those who have gone before us, that they may receive the reward of their kindness and faithfulness in heaven

### St. Teresa of Avila, October 15

*Rom 8:22-27, Ps 19, John 15:1-8*

For all of us, the members of the church, saved in hope, graced with the first fruits of the Spirit, yet groaning for the redemption of our bodies, that we may wait with the patience of endurance and the effort of good works

That the fear of the Lord and respect for His ordinances may become the abiding motivation of our world leaders as they direct the policies of our age

That we may glorify the Father by remaining in His Son, the true vine, bearing much fruit and becoming truly the disciples of Jesus

For all who follow St. Teresa along the Carmelite way of prayer, that the Spirit may come to the aid of their weakness, interceding for them with inexpressible groaning and obtaining all that they need from the Father of Mercy

For those undergoing the pruning of illness or distress, that our fervent prayer and this Holy Sacrifice may bring them relief and new growth

For our departed dear ones, that as they remained in Jesus during this life, so they may now be found in Him among the glories of the heavenly kingdom

### St. Luke, October 18

*2 Tim 4:9-17, Ps 145, Luke 10:1-9*

For our holy ministers in the church, that they may go before the Lord in strength and humility, and that new vocations may come to join them, so that the harvest may not be lost in our generation

That there may be in our day many more people of power and influence on whom the blessing of peace can come to rest, as they work for justice in our world

For all who minister to the sick, that St. Luke, who combined the roles of evangelist and healer, may help them bring health of body and soul to those they serve

For women in the church, for whom St. Luke had a special place of honor in His Gospel, that with patient dialogue and prudent understanding, their roles may emerge clarified and respected

For travelers, that St. Luke, who was such a faithful companion of St. Paul in His journeys, may being them safely and in good health to their destinations

For our loved ones who have died, that our prayers may be efficacious for them, bringing them God's mercy and heaven's happiness

## Sts. Simon and Jude, October 28

*Eph 2:19-22, Ps 19, Luke 6:12-16*

For our leaders in the church, that like Jesus, they may spend time in silent prayer before every major decision in their ministry

For our elected officials, that they may be true to the natural law, especially to its demands of life and justice for all, so that we may deserve the blessing of God's peace

For all of us, fellow citizens of the holy ones, that built upon the foundation of the apostles and their successors, we may become a pleasing dwelling place for God in the Spirit

For vocations to the apostolic life, that new disciples may be called to proclaim the Good News in our own day

For all those whose lives are made difficult by sickness, poverty, loneliness, or abuse, that our loving prayer for them may bring them relief

For our beloved departed ones, that through the power of this Holy Sacrifice their purification may be quickly accomplished, and they may be taken into the household of God in heaven

## All Saints, Vigil

*Rev 7:2-4, 9-14, Ps 24, 1 John 3:1-3, Matt 5:1-12a*

For the church, surrounded by its great cloud of witnesses who have gone before us and who now rejoice in heaven, that we may imitate their example of holiness and be filled with courage through their prayers

That those who have been marked with the seal of God upon earth may fight bravely in the battles now waging for the salvation of the world

That we who are God's children may take hold of the hope we have in Him, keeping ourselves poor in spirit, pure of heart, and gentle so that we may inherit His kingdom

For those who are persecuted for the sake of righteousness, who endure evil because of Jesus, that they may rejoice in anticipation of the great reward that will be theirs in heaven

For those who are mourning in a time of suffering and privation, and for all who need prayer to turn back to the ways of God, that the blood of the Lamb may purify and console them

For all our dear ones who have died, especially for those who still undergo purgation in hope of heaven, that our loving prayers may speed them on their way to God's kingdom of joy

## All Saints, November 1

*Rev 7:2-4, 9-14, Ps 24, 1 John 3:1-3, Matt 5:1-12a*

For those who approach God's altar on behalf of His church, that as they ascend the mountain of the Lord and stand in His holy place they may always come before Him with clean hands and pure hearts

That those who are in positions of power and influence in the world may be peacemakers who respect the life and dignity of all the children of God

That we may be among the poor in spirit, the gentle and merciful, the clean of heart, so that we may inherit the blessings of God's kingdom

For the grace of good vocations, especially to the priesthood, that the Gospel of life and truth may be proclaimed and the number of God's holy ones be increased

For all who are in a period of great distress, especially those who are being persecuted for their faith, that they may remain close to the Lamb who was slain, to be made strong in His victory

For all our beloved departed ones, who were children of God in this life, that they may soon see God as He is and stand before His throne with the palms of victory in their hands

## All Souls, November 2

*general intentions*

That the church may be strong in her faith in the resurrection of the dead, and diligent in prayer for those who have gone before us

That the example and leadership of our deceased leaders who honestly worked for justice, life, and peace may be rewarded before God with everlasting joy

That as we remember today all those who have died and still need the charity of our prayers for their purification and release, our intercession may be fruitful on their behalf

For all who mourn the loss of loved ones, especially the loss of children who have died or those who succumbed to natural disasters and violence, that the family's sufferings may be eased by hope in the life to come

That the power of this Holy Sacrifice, by which Jesus released us all from the bonds of everlasting death, may free the souls in purgatory who have the most need of God's mercy

## Dedication of the Lateran Basilica, November 9

*Ezek 47, Ps 46, 1 Cor 3, John 2*

For our leaders and teachers in the church, who build upon the foundation of Jesus Christ in their proclamation of His Gospel, that their work may be blessed

For those in a position of power and influence in the world, that they may take God as their refuge and their strength and do His work for life, justice, and peace

For all the members of the church, watered by the flow from God's sanctuary in her sacraments, that we may produce works of mercy and grace

That Jesus may cleanse and purify the house of God that is within each of us, making us holy and righteous in His sight

For all who need our prayers in a time of distress, sickness, or bereavement, that living waters of healing and hope may flow again in their lives

For all who have gone before us marked with the sign of faith, that as they were part of God's temple on earth, they may rejoice in His house forever in heaven

## Presentation of the Blessed Virgin Mary, November 21

*Zech 2:14-17, Matt 12:46-50*

That our Blessed Mother may live the mystery of her presence in the house of the Lord again in today's church, radiating her hidden attraction to enkindle us all in God's service

For peace; that Mary, Queen of Peace may bring into God's presence the peace offerings of prayer and penance she has harvested from her children, to turn the tide of world events back to the God of peace

That we who ponder God's word within His temple and share the fruits of this perfect sacrifice may rededicate ourselves with Mary to His service

For all who are in need of Mary's tender care in their sickness, poverty, or grief, that with her we may go forth from this holy temple to serve and love them in Jesus' name

For our dear ones who have died, that they may be brought into God's heavenly temple with gladness and joy

## St. Andrew, November 30

*Rom 10:9-18, Ps 19, Matt 4:18-22*

For the preachers of the Good News, without whom none of us would believe in Jesus, for their own needs and intentions and for their joy in the Lord

For the poor and oppressed people of the world, from the endangered unborn to the victims of war and terrorism, and for the leaders to whom their destiny has been entrusted

For vocations; that many more young men and women may hear the Lord calling them from the scene of their earthly occupations, and have the grace to abandon all to follow him

For all of us receiving this Eucharist, who confess that Jesus is Lord, that He may truly be Lord of our lives and that we may refuse Him nothing

For all who labor under a burden of suffering, that through the intercession of St. Andrew, who rejoiced at the sight of His cross, they too may be given courage and hope

For our beloved departed ones, who believed in the God who raised Jesus from the dead, that they too may be raised up and given their destined place in His kingdom

## St. Francis Xavier, December 3

*1 Cor 9:16-19, 22-23, Ps 117, Mark 16:15-20*

For the missionaries of the church, that they may be impelled by the Lord's command to proclaim the Gospel to every creature, and the Lord may work with them through acts of mighty power

That the rulers and the powerful of the world may again hear the Gospel with its demands for justice and the dignity of every human being

For the conquest of the world for Christ after the example of St. Francis Xavier, that this great preacher to the nations may inspire our evangelizing efforts at home and abroad

That the healing and consoling signs that accompany the Gospel may be worked upon the sick, the poor, the imprisoned, the lonely, those in troubled marriages, and those who need to return to the sacraments once again

For our dear departed ones, that Jesus, who has taken His seat at the right hand of God, may welcome them into His glorious kingdom through the intercession of all His saints

## Immaculate Conception, Vigil

*Gen 3:9-15, Ps 98, Eph 1:3-6, 11-12, Luke 1:26-38*

For the church, that God who chose us from the foundation of the world and destined us for adoption in Christ Jesus, may see His loving will accomplished in each baptized soul

That our heavenly Father, for whom nothing is impossible, may hear our prayers for peace, for life, and for justice, and change the hearts of the powerful from within

That we may imitate Our Blessed Mother's humble and faith-filled consent to the unfolding of the plan of God in our lives

That the Holy Spirit may overshadow all who partake of this Holy Eucharist, as we receive Jesus in our hearts, so that we may truly become God's servants and handmaids in this world

For all who have asked for our prayers in a time of sickness, grief, or financial hardship, that God's angel may come to them with good news and grace as He once came to Mary

For our dear departed ones, that the stain of Adam may be washed clean in the blood of Christ, and they may soon be admitted into the joys of heaven

## Immaculate Conception, December 8

*Gen 3:9-15, Ps 98, Eph 1:3-6, 11-12, Luke 1:26-38*

For the whole church, keeping this festival of Mary's Immaculate Conception, which is a sign of our own vocation to holiness, that we may gratefully cooperate with our grace as Mary did

That Mary, Queen of Peace, may hear the anguished prayers for peace that rise from the hearts of her suffering children, and intercede with her divine Son for the conversion of heart which alone brings true peace

For the United States, consecrated to the Immaculate Conception, that we may foster a culture of life and a civilization of strong morality before our God, as our founding fathers envisioned

For all who want to hide from God as they feel the guilt of their sin, that God may find them and continue the dialogue until truth does its cleansing work and salvation triumphs in Jesus

For all the sick and suffering who have been recommended to our prayers, that with Mary Immaculate, they may let it be done to them according to God's word, surrendering to His grace in peace

For our loved ones who have died, that God who chose them may cleanse them and make them immaculate for the praise of His glory in heaven

## Our Lady of Guadalupe, December 12

*Rev 11–12, Jud 13, Luke 1:26-38*

For the church, who like Mary is portrayed as the great sign of the woman in labor to give birth, that her travail may bear fruit in the triumph of Jesus

That the reign of God and the authority of His Anointed One may give power to every effort, no matter how humble, toward justice, morality, and peace

For all Americans, who have been given a patroness in Our Lady of Guadalupe, that her self portrait as a native of the continents may help restore the balance of respect and resources among all who call America home

For expectant mothers, who like Mary carry the future of the world within them, that no consideration may force them to cut off this gift of life, and that they may be supported and loved for their motherhood

For the sick, the lonely, the hungry, the refugees, and all who are in direct contact with their human lowliness, that Mary may visit them with her joy and comfort, as she once did with Juan Diego

For our dear ones who have died, that they may find in Mary's arms a safe haven, and she may lead them along secure paths to the heavenly kingdom

## St. Stephen, December 26

*Acts 6:8-10, 7:54-59, Ps 31, Matt 10:17-22*

For the whole church, exposed at the same time to the tenderness of the Infant Savior and the rigors of martyrdom, that Christ may be chosen at all times

That the Spirit of the Father may speak through all those who are in the vanguard of the struggle for life and for the dignity of every human being from conception to natural death

For all who are persecuted for their faith and for their moral standards, that the inner vision of the glory of Jesus may sustain them to the furthest limits of forgiving patience

For all who have asked our prayers, who are sick, lonely, or depressed during these festive days, that a spirit of grace and power may sustain them and hearts may open to love them in Christ's name

For those who have spent their last Christmas on earth, that they may now see the heavens open and the Son of Man standing at the right hand of God in glory

## St. John, December 27

*1 John 1:1-4, Ps 97, John 20:2-8*

For our leaders in the church, who continue to proclaim and bear witness to the Word of life in their preaching and in their living, that their testimony may be strong and clear

For our leaders in the world, that they may have the wisdom to exhaust every effort of patience and diplomacy before employing military might in the difficult situations that confront them

That we who have fellowship with the Father in His Son, Jesus Christ, whom we receive in this Eucharist, may radiate the joy of that communion into every human encounter today

For all who are in need, who are sick or homeless or abandoned during these festive days, that they may be heard, seen, and touched, for they are Jesus in His distressing disguise

For our faithful departed, that they may come into possession of the eternal life that became visible for love of us all

## Holy Innocents, December 28

*1 John 1:5–2:2, Ps 124, Matt 2:13-18*

For the church, that like St. Joseph she may be obedient to every command of the Lord that protects and delivers the innocent members of the Body of Jesus

For the rulers of this world, that they may not be like Herod, thinking only of preserving their own power, but use that power to uphold the dignity of every human being under their jurisdiction

For children who are at risk in our world: the abandoned, those who come into this world with defects and diseases, and those who need access to clean water and medical care, that they may be loved and helped in the name of Jesus

For mothers who have made the tragic choice of abortion and are now bewailing deep within their souls the loss of their children, that Jesus may be for them an offering for sin and the forgiveness that heals them

For all of us, that we may walk in the light, preserving fellowship with one another, and allowing the Blood of Jesus to cleanse us from all sin

For those who have died, that Jesus, our Advocate with the Father, may release them from every impediment to their entry into His glorious kingdom

# NATIONAL HOLIDAYS

*For Use in the Dioceses of the United States*

## Memorial Day

*general intentions*

That the church and her holy ministers may always proclaim and teach Jesus as the Way, the Truth, and the Life

For our nation, that as we remember our fallen heroes today, we may use wisely and well the freedom they kept alive and safe by their sacrifice

That the resurrection of the dead may be our great hope, and that our prayers and sacrifices may rise to God in union with the perfect sacrifice of Jesus, to obtain forgiveness and a splendid reward for all who have gone before us

For the safety of travelers on this holiday weekend, and that families reunited for the celebrations may experience peace and renewal in their relations with one another

That Jesus, who ascended into heaven to prepare a place for His own, may welcome into eternal mansions of joy those who have given their lives in the service of their country

## Independence Day

*general intentions*

For the whole church, especially the church that has taken root in the United States, that her members may be the gentle and the clean of heart who will lift the country toward the God of our Fathers

That we may remember God in our prosperity, and bring down His blessing on our land by our generous sharing of the riches that have been given to us

That we may use our treasured freedom to pursue the kingdom of God in our midst, upholding moral values and making our voices heard on the side of life and justice

That today's celebrations may be safe and joyful, that our patriotism may be renewed and our ideals strengthened through an outpouring of divine grace

For the poor, for those who mourn, for all who have asked our prayers, that they may be comforted and lifted up in freedom of spirit

For all who have gone before us, especially those who have given their lives to uphold our freedom, that God may bring them into the Promised Land of heaven

## Labor Day

*general intentions*

That the church may always uphold the dignity of work, integrating it into a life of holiness and a longing for the coming of the kingdom of God

For our nation as it celebrates this last summer holiday of the season, that we may remain a united nation, working together under God's direction and guidance

That we may work with freedom and wisdom of heart, setting aside all worry and dedicating ourselves to obedience, so that our hearts may remain at peace in the midst of all our labors

For the unemployed and those who long for honest work, for all who are going though a time of trial, that God Himself may work in their lives for hope, healing, and joy

For those who once worked at our side and who have now passed beyond the shadow of death, that their portion may be everlasting rest in the Father's house

## Thanksgiving Day

*general intentions*

In thanksgiving for freedom to practice our faith in the United States of America, and for our pastors and teachers in the church, who bring us Christ's sacraments and are themselves signs of His presence

In thanksgiving for our nation, so blessed by God; for our leaders and lawmakers, that we may show our gratitude by our reverence for the God who fosters our growth from the womb and fashions us according to His will

In thanksgiving for this year's harvest, and that our gratitude may overflow in generosity to those who are still hungry

For the renewing of family bonds on this day of tradition and thanksgiving together, for the healing needed by so many; for those who are sick, lonely and imprisoned on this day of family feasting and joy

For all of us offering this Eucharist, the Thanksgiving prayer of Jesus to the Father, that we may speak our praises at the feet of the Lord whom we receive in Communion and bring Him grateful hearts

In thanksgiving for our dear ones who have gone before us in death, for all the beautiful memories and gifts of love they left in our lives, and that they may be singing their own song of thanks in the courts of heaven